Language, Communication & Education

A Reader Edited by BARBARA M. MAYOR and A.K. PUGH
at the Open University

CROOM HELM
London & Sydney
in association with
The Open University

Selection and editorial matter © The Open University 1987

Croom Helm Ltd, Provident House, Burrell Row,
Beckenham, Kent BR3 1AT

Croom Helm Australia Pty Ltd, Suite 4, 6th Floor,
64-76 Kippax Street, Surry Hills, NSW 2010 Australia

British Library Cataloguing in Publication Data

Language, communication and education: a
  reader.
  1. Language and languages   2. Communication
  I. Mayor, Barbara   II. Pugh, A.K.   III. Open
  University
  400   P90

  ISBN 0-7099-3590-0

Croom Helm US, 27 South Main Street,
Wolfeboro, New Hampshire 03894-2069

Library of Congress Cataloging-in-Publication Data

Language, communication, and education.

  Includes bibliographical references.
  1. Language and languages. 2. Sociolinguistics.
3. Language and education. 4. Literacy. I. Mayor,
Barbara, 1949-   . II. Pugh, A.K. III. Open
University.
PL06.13118 1987   410   86-19320
ISBN 0-7099-3590-0

Typeset in 10pt Times Roman by Leaper & Gard Ltd, Bristol, England
Printed and bound in Great Britain by Mackays of Chatham Ltd, Kent

Language, Communication and Education

Contents

Preface

Communication, increasingly a main industry of the modern world and rapidly growing as a major area of study, is not a narrow academic discipline but benefits from a broad, multi-disciplinary approach. This breadth is reflected in the two collections of readings, of which this is one, produced for the Open University course EH 207, 'Communication and Education'. As its title suggests, the emphasis in the course is on those modes and media of communication which are most relevant to education. Thus, considerable space is devoted there to media such as television and computers although the much longer-established print media are also considered.

Media require messages, and these 'messages' have to be within conventions which are understood by participants in the communication. Despite the advent of new media, language remains the predominant mode of communication, whether in spoken or written form. The conventions of language, and of particular languages, have to be learnt, whether formally or informally. The systems of language are highly complex, as our first section indicates, but there is more to communicating through language than simply knowing the 'rules' of a language. This is confirmed by the articles included here on learning communication skills, and it is illustrated by several other articles in the volume. Language is not merely used for passing messages, but is itself an integral part of many social situations. Not only does it reflect (and so reinforce) differences between people in terms of power and perceived status; it can also often serve to define the roles of participants. It can be used to control and deprive as well as to share. Indeed language rarely involves simple one-way passing of information. Readers and listeners are also participants in communication, even if they can often only respond by their varying perceptions and constructions of what they receive.

The three main areas treated in this collection are language as a system of communication, language in society and the role of language in learning. The other volume includes articles more concerned with the communications media. This division closely parallels the shape of the course for which these books of readings were prepared, where they are used in conjunction with printed course units and other materials, audiocassettes and television programmes. Details of the availability of these other components may be obtained from Open University Educational Enterprises, 12 Cofferidge Close, Stony Stratford, Milton Keynes MK11 1BY.

A collection of readings, like a course, is a collaborative effort. We are grateful to the many colleagues who have proposed articles, offered criticisms and suggestions and in other ways helped us in this compilation. We hope that our students and others who use this book will find the articles varied, insightful and stimulating, representing important research and thinking in a field of more than academic interest.

Barbara Mayor and Tony Pugh
February, 1986

Notes on Contributors

Stuart A. Altmann, Department of Biology, University of Chicago.

Michael Argyle, Department of Psychology, University of Oxford.

Bowman K. Atkins, Department of Anthropology, Duke University, New Carolina.

Howard B. Beckman, Wayne State University School of Medicine.

Wynford Bellin, Department of Psychology, University of Reading.

Dwight Bolinger, Department of Romance Languages and Literatures, Harvard University.

Pierre Bourdieu, Centre de Sociologie Européenne, Paris.

Shirley Brice Heath, School of Education, Stanford University.

Jerome Bruner, New School for Social Research, New York.

S. Pit Corder, Department of Linguistics, University of Edinburgh.

A.D. Edwards, Department of Education, University of Manchester.

Derek Edwards, Department of Social Sciences, Loughborough University of Technology.

Susan M. Ervin-Tripp, Institute of Human Learning, University of California, Berkeley.

E.A. Fisher, Bureau of Statistics, UNESCO.

Richard M. Frankel, Wayne State University School of Medicine.

V.J. Furlong, Department of Education, University of Cambridge.

Howard Giles, Centre for the Study of Communication and Social Relations, University of Bristol.

Kenneth S. Goodman, Department of Elementary Education, University of Arizona, Tucson.

Roger Hewitt, Institute of Education, University of London.

Cheris Kramarae, Department of Speech Communication, University of Illinois at Urbana — Champaign.

Lilian Lawson, British Deaf Association, Carlisle.

Dick Leith, Department of English and Foreign Languages, City of Birmingham Polytechnic.

Kenneth Levine, Department of Sociology, University of Nottingham.

William F. Mackey, Department of Linguistics, Laval University, Quebec.

Neil Mercer, School of Education, The Open University.

Lesley Milroy, Department of Speech, University of Newcastle-upon-Tyne.

Patricia C. Nicholls, Department of English, San Jose State University.

William O'Barr, Department of Anthropology, Duke University, New Carolina.

P. David Pearson, Center for the Study of Reading, University of Illinois at Urbana — Champaign.

Terry Phillips, School of Education, University of East Anglia.

Oliver Sacks, Department of Clinical Neurology, Albert Einstein College of Medicine, New York.

Paula A. Treichler, Department of Speech Communication, University of Illinois at Urbana — Champaign.

Dorothy Stock Whitaker, Department of Social Administration and Social Work, University of York.

Bencie Woll, School of Education, University of Bristol.

Kathleen Zoppi, College of Medicine and Speech Communication, University of Illinois at Urbana — Champaign.

SECTION 1

LANGUAGE AND OTHER COMMUNICATION SYSTEMS

INTRODUCTION

Each of the articles in this introductory section explores a different aspect of human communication, only the first of which might conventionally be called 'language'. Yet each system is equally rule-governed and, like spoken language, interpretable by those who are initiated into the culture.

In 'Primate Communication' Altmann works towards a definition of human language by examining those features which distinguish it from the communications systems of other primates. He comes to the conclusion that human language is indeed outstanding in several key respects, although it is not unique in every one of them; nor is it clear *why* human beings should have developed language in the way they have. This is a field in which our knowledge is still in its infancy, despite what now amounts to a substantial body of research.

By contrast, research into the nature of human sign languages is relatively recent and expanding fast. In their article, Woll and Lawson examine the features which qualify British sign language as a fully developed communication system that can replace spoken language for all the normal communication needs of its users. In so doing, they draw many parallels with spoken languages. They are also at pains to point out the particular strengths of sign languages, such as their ability to express complex ideas economically via a number of *simultaneous* movements.

The article by Sacks, a neurologist, describes in a very vivid way the interlocking nature of verbal and non-verbal communication between human beings. It is only in cases of brain damage that it is possible to observe either of these aspects operating in isolation, and their inadequacy as separate systems becomes immediately apparent to the observer. Normally, of course, verbal and non-verbal components of communication are working together towards the same communicative end. Sacks describes what can happen when one channel is blocked out.

Bourdieu's article 'The Berber House' describes a very different kind of non-verbal communication but one which is no less syste-

3

matic. It can be hard for us to recognise the symbolic value of the various features in our own immediate environment because we and the objects co-exist in the same culture. By entering into a culture which will to most readers be unfamiliar, it becomes possible to look in a more detached manner at the way in which human beings express meaning through the design and location of the objects around them.

Barbara Mayor

1.1 Primate Communication

STUART A. ALTMANN

Let us suppose for the moment that we are in a grove of acacia trees on the savannahs of East Africa. In the trees above our heads there is a group of the common African green monkey, sometimes called the vervet. Suddenly, a martial eagle swoops down on the vervets. The first vervet that sees the approaching eagle gives an alarm bark. At the sound of this vocalization all the vervet monkeys suddenly drop from the branches of the trees to the dense undergrowth, where they are safe from the attack of the eagle.

Here is a vocalization given by one member of a social group that is heard and responded to by other members of his group. Such vocalizations are obviously used for communication. But can we call this kind of communication a "language"?

On these same savannahs of East Africa, baboons, which are large, ground-living monkeys, are fairly abundant. At night, these animals sleep either in trees or on cliff faces. The small infant baboon sleeps huddled against its mother.

As the infant becomes older, however, the mother becomes progressively more reluctant to allow the infant to sleep next to her. This rejection by the mother seems to be a traumatic situation for the infant, and in the evening, as a group of baboons approaches their sleeping trees, the repeated cooing and screeching of a rejected infant can be heard. Sometimes the infant's calling is successful and the mother allows the infant to sleep next to her.

As a final example, in the rain forest of Central and South America there is a monkey, called the howler monkey, that produces one of the loudest sounds in the animal kingdom. When two groups of howler monkeys come together, the calling of the adult males between the two groups can be heard for a great distance. The males do not wait for the appearance of another group before giving their call, however. They howl each morning at about sun-

Source: Altmann S.A. (1973) 'Primate communication' in Miller G.A. (ed.), *Communication, Language and Meaning*, New York, Basic Books, pp. 84-90.

rise and at other times of the day as well, even though no other group of howler monkeys is visible through the dense foliage. This howling vocalization seems to serve as a proclamation of an occupied territory and each group tends to avoid those areas from which the howls of other males come.

Each species of monkey or ape has a small repertoire of such socially significant vocalizations. For example, the green monkey and the howler monkey each have about twenty distinct calls in their repertoire. And each of these vocalizations generally elicits a distinct response in the other members of the social group.

Should we refer to such systems of vocalizations as languages? One's immediate response to this question is *no* — that only people have the ability to use language, to speak. But if we ask ourselves what it is that distinguishes the speech of humans from the kinds of vocalizations that we have heard in these monkeys, the answer is not a simple one. Thus, one reason for looking closely at the communication systems of other animals is that we may sharpen our ideas of what is unique about human language.

Man is a primate; that is, he belongs to the group of animals that includes the monkeys, the apes, and the prosimians. And so, for evolutionary reasons this group of animals is of particular importance for comparisons with man: we share a common heritage with the nonhuman primates and for that reason they bear many similarities to us in the chemical composition of their bodies, their anatomy, their behavior, and so forth. Perhaps they have inherited systems of social signaling that are similar to our language. Thus another reason for studying the communication of nonhuman primates is that we may learn something about the evolution of man's ability to speak.

In addition, these primate signaling systems are interesting in their own right. These animals live in complex social groups. The coordination of group activities depends upon the ability of the animals in the group to communicate with each other. We therefore have an unusual opportunity to study the relationship between the social behavior of individuals and the kind of social system that they live in.

Unfortunately for the sake of such comparisons, the study of behavior and social communication in nonhuman primates is in its infancy. More time and effort have been devoted to the study of any of a number of human languages, such as Navaho, than have been spent on all the rest of the primate species put together. Only within the last few years have there been any concerted attempts to understand the social signals of these animals. Nevertheless, from what is now known about communication in the monkeys and apes, we can make some interesting comparisons with our own language.

We have already said that many nonhuman primates are able to communicate by means of vocalizations and that these vocalizations may trigger responses in other members of their group. In addition, these animals, like man, communicate by various non-vocal signals, including visual signals such as gestures, postures, and facial expressions, by various odors emitted by scent glands, and so forth. As with human speech, most of the social communication of nonhuman primates is specialized, in that this signaling behavior serves no function other than social communication.

A classical way of distinguishing human speech from the communication of other animals is to say that man uses symbols. But exactly what does it mean to say that we use symbols? Or to put it the other way around, if there were an animal that could use symbols, how would we know it?

Unfortunately the term "symbol" is too ambiguous to be very useful here: it has come to mean too many different things to different people. But certainly, a central property of what most people mean when they talk about symbols is to say that there is some kind of fixed association between the symbol and some object or event in the real world. Such messages are called "semantic messages" and in some sense a semantic message stands for the object or event.

There are examples of semantic messages in the social signals of nonhuman primates. For example, the alarm calls of vervet monkeys are semantic, in that a vervet monkey gives essentially the same response to the sound of the alarm call as it gives to the sight of an approaching eagle: in both cases, the animal drops from the branches of the tree into the undergrowth.

For the most part, however, the social signals of monkeys and apes are not semantic: the messages do not stand for something else. They are simply social signals to which a response is given. In this they are much more like the cry of a newborn infant than they are like the speech of human adults.

A striking characteristic of human speech is that we often talk about things that are not immediately present. We may talk about events that occurred in a different place or at some remote period in time. This characteristic of human speech — that these semantic messages are often markedly displaced in time or space from whatever objects or events they stand for — is an extremely important property. It gives us the flexibility of discussing things that are not present at the moment. We can therefore readily discuss past events and use our experience with such past events to plan for the future. For example, if you want to talk about whether or not to buy a cow, you do not need to have a cow in front of you in order to use the word "cow." Similarly, the person to whom you are talking does not need to have a cow there in order to understand what you mean by that word. Nonhuman primates seem to have a much more limited capacity to displace their semantic messages in time or space from whatever the messages stand for. These animals are much more tied to their immediate sensory environment.

Perhaps the most important characteristic of human speech is that it enables us to communicate about everything, even if we must create new words or sentences to do so. We have names for all the things that are familiar to us and if we encounter something new we can make up a new name for it. In fact, hundreds of new words are introduced into our language every year. Similarly, we can make up whatever sentences we need in order to say what we mean. We are not limited to those sentences with which we are already familiar.

This ability to generate new sentences grows out of the process by which each human child learns to speak during the first few years of its life. The child does not simply memorize a number of sentences that are then used at the appropriate time or place. Rather, the child somehow acquires the ability to combine the various words in its vocabulary into meaningful sentences. Some of these sentences may never before have been used by anyone, yet they can be understood.

This remarkable ability to produce countless new words and new sentences, and to use this ability to talk about anything, is not present in the social signaling of any nonhuman primate. Of course, new vocalizations must evolve within primate societies from time to time. There is no other way to account for the present diversity in vocalizations that we find in species of monkeys and apes. But each such change probably involves a considerable change in the genetics of the population. The evolution of such primate vocalizations is therefore limited by the rate at which such genetic changes can take place.

Human language is not subject to any such restriction. Our ability to make up or learn new words and to transmit these new words to other members of our society means that human language can evolve independently of any further genetic changes. The same is true of our ability to produce countless new sentences.

Each of us was born with the ability to learn a language — not just the particular language of our parents but any language spoken by any human beings. If, for example, an Indian child were raised in a Spanish-speaking family he would grow up speaking Spanish. Thus, each human child is born with the potential for becoming a speaker and understander of any human language despite great differences in the vocabularies and the grammars of languages. But the monkey infant has no such flexibility. An infant monkey that is raised with monkeys of another and very different species still gives for the most part just those social signals that are characteristic of its own species, though it may come to understand those of the species with which it lives. This would seem to indicate that monkeys, at least, have much more flexibility at understanding foreign social signals than they do at using them. As is often the case with human behavior, recognition is easier than recall and reproduction.

We have indicated that human languages are universal, in that we can speak about anything, and that this universality depends upon our ability to coin endless new words and to generate new sentences apparently without limit, so that no matter what new situation arises we are able to talk about it. If the universality of our language depends upon language being constantly open to the introduction of new words and new sentences, and if this universality is lacking in the social signaling systems of monkeys and apes, then it might be worth looking carefully at those characteristics of man that enable him to have an open signaling system.

The ability of a child to learn a large number of words, even words that are newly introduced into the vocabulary, requires a good memory. Undoubtedly the evolution of language went hand-in-hand with the evolution of man's learning capacity. The number of words in any human's vocabulary is immensely larger than the number of vocalizations or other social signals in the repertoire of any monkey or ape. Even so, a new word can always be introduced into our vocabulary.

By what trick are we able to generate an endless string of new sentences? When we speak, we string together a number of sounds into a word and then a number of words into a sentence. The sounds that make up a word have no meaning of their own, but they are essential in enabling us to distinguish one word from another. For example, the English words "pan" and "ban" have very different meanings, yet they differ structurally only in that one begins with the sound that we represent with the letter "p" and the other begins with the sound that we represent with the letter "b." But these sounds by themselves have no meaning. We recombine a fairly small number of basic sound units, called "phonemes," into a very large number of words or word stems, which linguists call "morphemes." Similarly, we string words together in different ways to form different sentences.

Of course, not every string of words forms a meaningful statement. This is to say that our language has a certain grammatical structure or syntax to it. Even with this restriction, however, our sentences are sufficiently long that the number of meaningful word combinations that are available to us is probably so large as to be inexhaustible during our lifetime. If, in addition, we recognize that there is no upper limit to sentence length, then we can generate an indefinitely large number of meaningful sentences.

In recent years there have been attempts to see whether or not a monkey or an ape could learn a set of arbitrary signals like those of human language and could acquire the ability to recombine these in ways that were new to the primate and that were still meaningful. The chimpanzee, like many other animals, has some ability to learn arbitrary social signals. There is now some evidence that a chimpanzee can be taught to understand combinations of such social signals. Under the right conditions it may spontaneously generate new, meaningful combinations and may thereby communicate in novel ways. These are the rudiments of a form of communication that resembles human speech.

Such natural abilities of chimpanzees might have been intensified through natural selection to the point where chimpanzees would now speak. But in fact, they do not: there is no evidence from recent field studies of chimpanzees that these animals make much use of these latent abilities. This raises an interesting question about the evolution of man. What conditions were present in the evolution of early man that selected for the ability to communicate by means of the unique signaling system that we call "language"? For that question we still have no good answer.

1.2 British Sign Language

BENCIE WOLL and LILIAN LAWSON

Deaf people communicate in a language foreign to most of the population of Britain, despite the fact that they are neither an immigrant group nor living in geographical isolation from the rest of the population. They form one of the least-understood minorities in our community: about thirty thousand people in the United Kingdom, whose serious or profound hearing loss began at birth or before they developed language. [...]

Very little is known of the early history of British Sign Language (BSL), although there are references to sign languages in the middle ages; but one can assume that wherever groups of deaf people have been in contact, sign languages have been established. While it may be assumed that deaf families have always signed, the role of schools for the deaf in bringing together groups of deaf children must not be underestimated, since only five per cent of deaf children have deaf parents. Certainly, with the founding of the first schools for the deaf in Britain in the eighteenth century, BSL was firmly established among deaf children who did not have deaf parents. By the 1820s signs were being used as the communication medium in the education of the deaf throughout Western Europe and America (Hippisley Tuckfield 1839, Dickens 1865, Scott 1870, Lane 1976). [...]

But what is BSL? Is it really a language? What are its unique features? A number of myths have grown up about British Sign Language and other sign languages, and one way to shed light on the nature of sign languages is to discuss these myths.

MYTH 1. THERE IS ONE UNIVERSAL SIGN LANGUAGE

Some people have suggested that sign language is universal, easy to learn and can be used by people anywhere with ease of under-

Source: Woll B. and Lawson L. (1981) 'British sign language' in Haugen E., McClure J.D. and Thomson D. (eds), *Minority Languages Today*, Edinburgh University Press, pp. 218-34.

standing. However, this is not the case. <u>Deaf people of one country use different sign languages from deaf people of another country</u> (Battison and Jordan 1976, Jordan and Battison 1976, Moody 1979). For example, American Sign Language (ASL) and BSL differ from each other much more than American and British English, and are, in fact, mutually unintelligble. Figure 1 shows how the 'same' sign may have different meanings in ASL and BSL, and figure 2 shows how the same meaning is conveyed by different signs in each language. (Sign glosses are conventionally represented in upper-case letters.) It is really not surprising that this should be the case. Deaf people do not generally move from one country to another; many countries ban deaf people as immigrants. Those sign languages which are similar have in most cases been influenced by educationalists who have trained in other countries and brought back signs to schools in their home countries. In the case of, for example, Australian Sign Language, which is closely related to BSL, both the influence of educators and a single, large family with hereditary deafness, have been responsible. Some American and British signs appear to be cognates, but not enough is known of the history of either language to explain this adequately.

MYTH 2. SIGN LANGUAGE IS DERIVED FROM VISUAL PICTURES

While many signs seem to support this claim, other signs seem to bear little or no visual relationship to their referents. The issue of the iconicity of signs is rather complex. We have already seen that the same meaning may be expressed by different signs in different sign languages. This may occur because the signs, although iconic, represent different features or properties of the referent. While some signs may have iconic elements, such as in figure 3a, speakers of the language may not necessarily know the source of the iconicity. A child learning the sign MILK may never have seen a cow being milked by hand, and the German army no longer wears helmets with spikes. This in no way impairs or assists the learning of new vocabulary. In addition, iconic origins are often imputed to signs where none is known, or where the known origin of the sign is iconic, but different. The BSL sign WOMAN (figure 4a) is sometimes etymologised as deriving from 'a woman's cheek being soft', while others say that it derives from the bonnet strings of the

ASL SALT
BSL FATHER

Figure 1. Same form, different meanings.

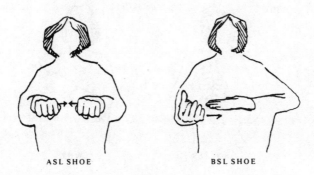

ASL SHOE   BSL SHOE

Figure 2. Different forms, same meaning.

eighteenth century. The American CRACKER is etymologised as deriving from the British sign BISCUIT (figure 4b), the origin of which is explained as deriving from the way the Scots break hard biscuits with their elbows. A large number of signs, however, do seem to represent their referents iconically. This feature of sign languages is usually held to be in contrast with the form of words in spoken languages, where there is an arbitrary relationship between symbol and referent. The words in spoken languages which are non-arbitrary, such as onomatopoeic words, or those involving sound symbolism, are regarded as peripheral. As sign languages represent iconically referents that can be described with a visual image, so spoken languages represent 'iconically' objects that can be described with a sound image. As more objects can be represented with a picture than with a sound, the contrast between spoken and sign languages may be one of degree rather than of kind.

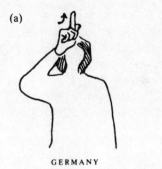 

Figure 3. (a) Iconicity of signs, (b) non-iconicity of signs.

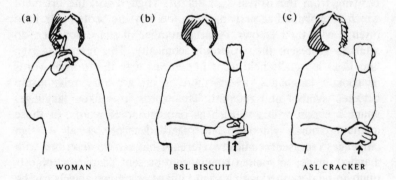

Figure 4. Etymology of signs.

MYTH 3. SIGNS ARE ONLY GESTURES

While it is recognised that spoken languages have phonologies consisting of a limited number of sounds which differ from language to language, and a limited number of combinations of these sounds, the claim has been made that sign languages consist of unlimited numbers of gestures which are infinitely variable. If this were true, sign languages would be very unlike spoken languages. Spoken languages consist of a limited number of constituent sounds, combining in a limited number of ways one after the other to form a word. Sign languages also contain a limited inventory of constituents; but these are location, handshape, movement, and orientation, and instead of occurring successively like the phonemes of a language, they occur simultaneously. Each sign, therefore, consists of a simultaneous bundle of these four elements or parameters. The number of each of these parameters is limited, just as the number of phonemes in a spoken language and the way in which they combine is limited. Additional constraints prohibit, for example, signs where the two hands move independently, constraints which do not operate in gesture or mime. Figure 5 shows pairs of BSL signs, each of which differs in one parameter from the other, and thus form minimal pairs. These small but significant contrasts enable the language to use a small number of elements to form a great many signs.

MYTH 4. SIGN LANGUAGE IS JUST PARASITIC ON ENGLISH

Many hearing people learn the manual alphabet as children — in the Boy Scouts or Girl Guides — and often think that BSL is just the fingerspelling of words from English or other spoken languages. We have seen already that signs may not be at all like English words, but a number of points should be made about the manual alphabet in its own right. First, there is more than one manual alphabet. Apart from Great Britain and countries such as Australia and New Zealand, most manual alphabets are one-handed, and there are several different one-handed alphabets, such as the Irish, American, French and Swedish. Most deaf people know and use fingerspelling, and it can serve a number of roles. Fingerspelling can be used for proper names, place names and technical vocabulary for which signs do not exist. Signs

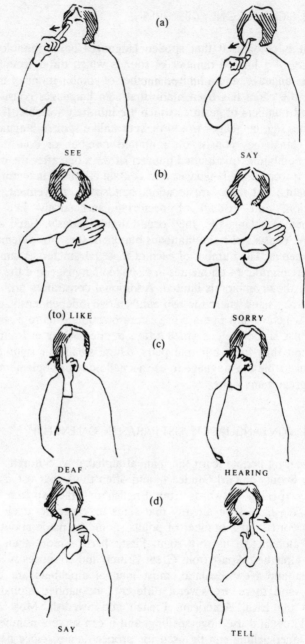

Figure 5. Minimal pairs: (a) location, (b) movement, (c) handshape, (d) orientation.

derived from fingerspelling may also be used, often so accom-
modated and modified in their borrowing that they are unrecog-
nisable as having originated in fingerspelled words. Signers may
use both fingerspelled forms and signs for the same referent,
depending upon context and audience. Most signs, however, are
neither derived from, nor are one-to-one translations of, English
words. For example, signs like SMELL-COOKING and NOT-LIKE can
only be translated by English phrases, while English words like
'believe' and 'parents' have as equivalents the compound signs
THINK-TRUE and MOTHER-FATHER respectively (figure 6).

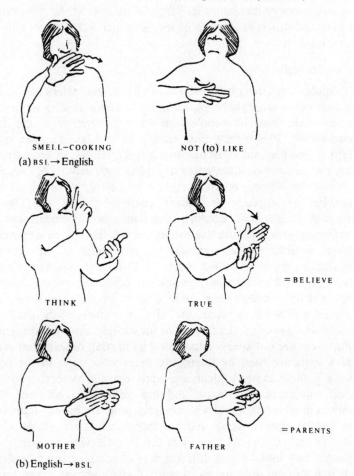

SMELL–COOKING   NOT (to) LIKE
(a) BSL → English

THINK   TRUE   = BELIEVE

MOTHER   FATHER   = PARENTS

(b) English → BSL

Figure 6. Non-equivalence of BSL–English and English–BSL translations.

MYTH 5. SIGN LANGUAGE HAS NO GRAMMAR

The notion that BSL is ungrammatical is based on two assumptions: First, the rather confused assumption that if BSL is a derivative of English, then it must be structured just like English, and therefore, where it is unlike English it has no grammar. The second assumption is that sign languages must be structured just like spoken languages, even if not like English. BSL is an independent language, however, with its own grammar, and this is the grammar of a visual-manual language, sharply different from the grammar of an auditory-articulatory language. A number of the most interesting and different features of BSL grammar will be dealt with at length below.

Complex Signs

'Complex signs' may be considered to be the equivalent of English idioms in the sense that complex signs, like English idioms, are not easily understood by people who are not members of the deaf community. It is usually not possible to translate complex signs into simple English words or glosses; it is often found necessary to use phrases or whole sentences to explain the meaning of complex signs. Like idioms, complex signs may be 'forms of expression peculiar to language or person' (definition from the *Oxford English Dictionary*). Complex signs may be also compared to 'colloquialisms', because like colloquialisms, these signs are usually found in informal settings and are not found in such formal settings as conferences and meetings. Complex signs, in the past, were (and still are by some) considered to be 'vulgar signs', 'home-made signs', 'childish signs', and 'deaf–dumb signs' by some deaf people who are very verbal, and also by teachers of the deaf and social workers of the deaf. Reasons for such opinions are that complex signs are not always understood by hearing people; that complex signs are used by fluent BSL users who were, in the past, usually dumb as well as deaf, and were regarded by teachers of the deaf (incorrectly) as 'naive and low verbal persons'; and that mouth movements found with complex signs are usually unrelated to English spoken words and are therefore not acceptable. Only since research into BSL began in the late nineteen seventies, are people now looking in a different way at complex signs, realising their important role in BSL. Figure 7 gives several examples of complex signs. These complex signs frequently incorporate other essential features of face and body movements, such as specific mouth movements, eye movements, and blowing out or sucking in of the cheeks. The mouth movements, in particular, are typically unrelated to spoken English words.

Classifiers

'Classifiers' of BSL are in many ways similar to classifiers of American Sign Language, and so it is quite appropriate here to

(a) Eyes like chapel hat pegs

(b) I can't be bothered

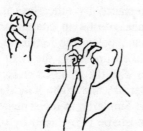

(c) Are you kidding me?

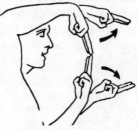

(d) I'm so amazed

(e) It should have happened but it didn't

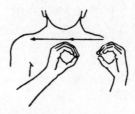

(f) Nothing for a long time

Figure 7. Complex signs and idioms.

quote Wilbur's definition of classifiers: 'Classifiers (the term attributed to Frishberg 1975) are a form of pronoun in ASL that seem to be defined primarily by the handshape. They are substituted into a sentence when potential violations of signing space occur.... They also occur in place of a noun when that noun cannot phonologically blend into the verb' (Wilbur 1979, p. 57). A partial list of BSL classifiers is given in figure 8. The occurrence of classifiers is morphophonologically governed. When these classifiers occur, they may serve as dummy pronominal elements which in certain environments can be replaced by other lexical items (Wilbur 1979, p. 58). For example, UNDER in citation form is made with the flat hand palm down, below the left hand, palm down. To indicate 'the person walked under it', the right handshape in UNDER would be replaced with the BY-LEGS classifier. In the sentence 'the car drove under it', the right handshape is replaced with the BY-CAR classifier. Similarly, in the sentence 'the ship sailed under it', the right handshape is replaced by the BY-BOAT classifier (figure 9). What has changed in these examples is the information about what noun class is under consideration. The motion and location of the classifier defines the subject and object of the verb (Kegl 1979). Classifiers thus serve to focus on certain qualities or features of their noun referents in very precise ways.

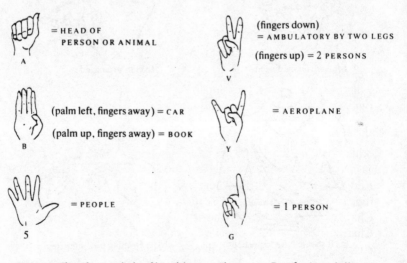

Figure 8. Classifiers, Labels of handshape such as A, B, 5, refer to notation system: see Kyle, Woll and Carter 1979 for details.

(a) UNDER

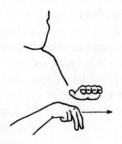

(b) A PERSON WALKED UNDER

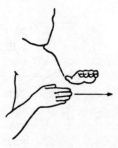

(c) A CAR DROVE UNDER

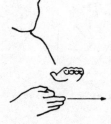

(d) A SHIP SAILED UNDER

Figure 9. Classifier incorporation.

For example, a classifier might identify a class of objects that is one-dimensional, two-dimensional, or three-dimensional, flexible or rigid, of prominent curved exterior, long or round.

Modulation

'Modulation' of signs involves inflectional changes of signs from their citation forms. Such changes include

Reduplication of a sign, where the motion of hand(s) may be repeated once or more.

Change of location during the articulation of a sign.

Change of duration of articulation of signs.

The example TRIP may help to illustrate the notion of modulation. The citation form of TRIP is made with a left bent v handshape placed behind the right bent v handshape which moves forward (away from the signer) (figure 10). COMMUTING is a modulation of TRIP: the modulated sign involves repetition of movement of the right hand several times (figure 10). TRAVEL ALL OVER THE PLACE is also a modulation of TRIP: the modulated sign involves changes of direction of articulation or movement of the right hand, which starts by moving to the left of the signing space, returns to the left hand, moves forward, and finally returns to the left hand and moves to the right of the signing space (figure 10). [...]

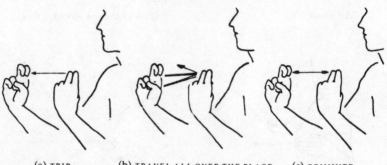

(a) TRIP   (b) TRAVEL ALL OVER THE PLACE   (c) COMMUTE

Figure 10. Base form and modulation.

ACKNOWLEDGEMENT

This research is supported by grants from the DHSS 'Sign Language Learning and Use', and from the SED 'Tense and Aspect in BSL'.

REFERENCES

Battison, R. and Jordan, I.K. (1976) Cross-Cultural Communication with Foreign Signers: Fact and Fancy, *Sign Language Studies 10*, 53-68.

Brennan, M. (1978) Communication, paper presented at the Strathclyde Regional Inservice Course on Deaf Education.

Conrad, R. (1979) *The Deaf School Child*, London: Harper & Row.

Croneberg, C. (1976) The Linguistic Community, in *A Dictionary of American Sign Language* (W.C. Stokoe, D. Casterline and C. Croneberg). Silver Spring: Linstok Press.

Deuchar, M. (1977) Sign language diglossia in a British deaf community. *Sign Language Studies 17*, 347-56.

—— (1981) Variation in British Sign Language, in *Perspectives on British Sign Language* (eds B. Woll, J.G. Kyle and M. Deuchar). London: Croom Helm.

Dickens, C. (1865) Dr. Marigold's Prescription. Reprinted in *Christmas Books, Tales and Sketches.* Garden City: Nelson Doubleday.

Fischer, S.D. (1978) Sign Language and Creoles. Chapter 13 of *Understanding Language through Sign Language Research* (ed. P. Siple). Academic Press.

Frischberg, N. (1975) Arbitrariness and iconicity: historical change in American Sign Language. *Language 51*, 696-719.

Hippisley Tuckfield, Mrs (1839) *Education for the People.* London: Taylor & Walton.

Jordan, I.K. and Battison, R. (1976) A Referential Communication Experiment with Foreign Sign Languages. *Sign Language Studies 10*, 69-78.

Kegl, J. (1979) Further Breaking Down the ASL Verb. Paper presented at the NATO Advanced Institute on Sign Language, Copenhagen.

Kyle, J.G., Woll, B. and Carter, M. (1979) *Coding British Sign Language.* University of Bristol, School of Education Research Unit.

Lane, H. (1976) *The Wild Boy of Aveyron.* Cambridge, Mass.: Harvard University Press.

Lawson, L. (in press) The Role of Sign in the Structure of the Deaf Community, in *Perspectives on British Sign Language* (eds B. Woll, J.G. Kyle and M. Deuchar). London: Croom Helm.

Llewellyn-Jones, P., Kyle, J.G. and Woll, B. (1979) Sign Language Communication. Paper presented at the International Conference on the Social Psychology of Language, Bristol.

Markowicz, H. (1979) Sign languages and the maintenance of the deaf community. Paper presented at the NATO Symposium on Sign Language Research, Copenhagen.

Moody, W. (1979) La Communication Internationale chez les Sourds. *Reéducation Orthophonique 17*, 213-23.

Scott, W.R. (1870) *The Deaf and Dumb.* London: Bell and Daldy.

Stokoe, W.C. (1969) Sign Language Diglossia. *Studies in Linguistics 21*, 27-41.

—— (1979) Diglossia Revisited and Bilingualism Related. Unpublished paper.

Trudgill, P. (1972) Sex, Covert Prestige and Linguistic Change in the Urban British English of Norwich, *Language in Society 1*, 179-96.

Wilbur, R.B. (1979) *American Sign Language and Sign Systems.* Maryland: University Park Press.

Woodward, J. (1975) How you gonna get to heaven if you can't talk with Jesus?: the Educational Establishment versus the Deaf Community. Paper presented at the Annual Meeting of the Society for Applied Anthropology, Amsterdam.

1.3 The President's Speech

OLIVER SACKS

What was going on? A roar of laughter from the aphasia ward, just as the President's speech was coming on, and they had all been so eager to hear the President speaking ...

There he was, the old Charmer, the Actor, with his practised rhetoric, his histrionisms, his emotional appeal — and all the patients were convulsed with laughter. Well, not all: some looked bewildered, some looked outraged, one or two looked apprehensive, but most looked amused. The President was, as always, moving — but he was moving them, apparently, mainly to laughter. What could they be thinking? Were they failing to understand him? Or did they, perhaps, understand him all too well?

It was often said of these patients, who though intelligent had the severest receptive or global aphasia, rendering them incapable of understanding words as such, that they none the less understood most of what was said to them. Their friends, their relatives, the nurses who knew them well, could hardly believe, sometimes, that they *were* aphasic.

This was because, when addressed naturally, they grasped some or most of the meaning. And one does speak 'naturally', naturally.

Thus to demonstrate their aphasia, one had to go to extraordinary lengths, as a neurologist, to speak and behave unnaturally, to remove all the extraverbal cues — tone of voice, intonation, suggestive emphasis or inflection, as well as all visual cues (one's expressions, one's gestures, one's entire, largely unconscious, personal repertoire and posture): one had to remove all of this (which might involve total concealment of one's person, and total depersonalisation of one's voice, even to using a computerised voice synthesiser) in order to reduce speech to pure words, speech totally devoid of what Frege called 'tone-colour' (*Klangenfarben*) or 'evocation'. With the most sensitive patients, it was only with such a grossly artificial, mechanical speech — some-

---

Source: Sacks, O. (1985) *The Man Who Mistook his Wife for a Hat*, London, Duckworth, pp. 76-80.

what like that of the computers in *Star Trek* — that one could be wholly sure of their aphasia.

Why all this? Because speech — natural speech — does *not* consist of words alone, nor (as Hughlings Jackson thought) 'propositions' alone. It consists of *utterance* — an uttering-forth of one's whole meaning with one's whole being — the understanding of which involves infinitely more than mere word-recognition. And this was the clue to aphasiacs' understanding, even when they might be wholly uncomprehending of words as such. For though the words, the verbal constructions, *per se*, might convey nothing, spoken language is normally suffused with 'tone', embedded in an expressiveness which transcends the verbal — and it is precisely this expressiveness, so deep, so various, so complex, so subtle, which is perfectly preserved in aphasia, though understanding of words be destroyed. Preserved — and often more: preternaturally enhanced ...

This too becomes clear — often in the most striking, or comic, or dramatic way — to all those who work or live closely with aphasiacs: their families or friends or nurses or doctors. At first, perhaps, we see nothing much the matter; and then we see that there has been a great change, almost an inversion, in their understanding of speech. Something has gone, has been devastated, it is true — but something has come, in its stead, has been immensely enhanced, so that — at least with emotionally-laden utterance — the meaning may be fully grasped even when every word is missed. This, in our species *Homo loquens*, seems almost an inversion of the usual order of things: an inversion, and perhaps a reversion too, to something more primitive and elemental. And this perhaps is why Hughlings Jackson compared aphasiacs to dogs (a comparison that might outrage both!) though when he did this he was chiefly thinking of their linguistic incompetences, rather than their remarkable, and almost infallible, sensitivity to 'tone' and feeling. Henry Head, more sensitive in this regard, speaks of 'feeling-tone' in his (1926) treatise on aphasia, and stresses how it is preserved, and often enhanced, in aphasiacs.[1]

Thus the feeling I sometimes have — which all of us who work closely with aphasiacs have — that one cannot lie to an aphasiac. He cannot grasp your words, and so cannot be deceived by them; but what he grasps with infallible precision, namely the *expression* that goes with the words, that total, spontaneous, involuntary expressiveness which can never be simulated or faked, as words alone can, all too easily ...

We recognise this with dogs, and often use them for this purpose — to pick up falsehood, or malice, or equivocal intentions, to
tell us who can be trusted, who is integral, who makes sense, when
we — so susceptible to words — cannot trust our own instincts.

And what dogs can do here, aphasiacs do too, and at a human
and immeasurably superior level. 'One can lie with the mouth,'
Nietzsche writes, 'but with the accompanying grimace one nevertheless tells the truth.' To such a grimace, to any falsity or
impropriety in bodily appearance or posture, aphasiacs are
preternaturally sensitive. And if they cannot see one — this is especially true of our blind aphasiacs — they have an infallible ear for
every vocal nuance, the tone, the rhythm, the cadences, the music,
the subtlest modulations, inflections, intonations, which can give —
or remove — verisimilitude to or from a man's voice.

In this, then, lies their power of understanding — understanding, without words, what is authentic or inauthentic. Thus it
was the grimaces, the histrionisms, the false gestures and, above
all, the false tones and cadences of the voice, which rang false for
these wordless but immensely sensitive patients. It was to these (for
them) most glaring, even grotesque, incongruities and impro-
prieties that my aphasic patients responded, undeceived and
undeceivable by words.

This is why they laughed at the President's speech.

If one cannot lie to an aphasiac, in view of his special sensitivity
to expression and 'tone', how is it, we might ask, with patients — if
there are such — who *lack* any sense of expression and 'tone',
while preserving, unchanged, their comprehension for words:
patients of an exactly opposite kind? We have a number of such
patients, also on the aphasia ward, although, technically, they do
not have aphasia, but, instead, a form of *agnosia*, in particular a
so-called 'tonal' agnosia. For such patients, typically, the
expressive qualities of voices disappear — their tone, their timbre,
their feeling, their entire character — while words (and grammatical constructions) are perfectly understood. Such tonal
agnosias (or 'atonias') are associated with disorders of the *right*
temporal lobe of the brain, whereas the aphasias go with disorders
of the *left* temporal lobe.

Among the patients with tonal agnosia on our aphasia ward
who also listened to the President's speech was Emily D., with a
glioma in her right temporal lobe. A former English teacher, and

poetess of some repute, with an exceptional feeling for language, and strong powers of analysis and expression, Emily D. was able to articulate the opposite situation — how the President's speech sounded to someone with tonal agnosia. Emily D. could no longer tell if a voice was angry, cheerful, sad — whatever. Since voices now lacked expression, she had to look at people's faces, their postures and movements when they talked, and found herself doing so with a care, an intensity, she had never shown before. But this, it so happened, was also limited, because she had a malignant glaucoma, and was rapidly losing her sight too.

What she then found she had to do was to pay extreme attention to exactness of words and word use, and to insist that those around her did just the same. She could less and less follow loose speech or slang — speech of an allusive or emotional kind — and more and more required of her interlocutors that they speak *prose* — 'proper words in proper places'. Prose, she found, might compensate, in some degree, for lack of perceived tone or feeling.

In this way she was able to preserve, even enhance, the use of 'expressive' speech — in which the meaning was wholly given by the apt choice and reference of words — despite being more and more lost with 'evocative' speech (where meaning is wholly given in the use and sense of tone).

Emily D. also listened, stony-faced, to the President's speech, bringing to it a strange mixture of enhanced and defective perceptions — precisely the opposite mixture to those of our aphasiacs. It did not move her — no speech now moved her — and all that was evocative, genuine or false completely passed her by. Deprived of emotional reaction, was she then (like the rest of us) transported or taken in? By no means. 'He is not cogent,' she said. 'He does not speak good prose. His word-use is improper. Either he is brain-damaged, or he has something to conceal.' Thus the President's speech did not work for Emily D. either, due to her enhanced sense of formal language use, propriety as prose, any more than it worked for our aphasiacs, with their word-deafness but enhanced sense of tone.

Here then was the paradox of the President's speech. We normals — aided, doubtless, by our wish to be fooled, were indeed well and truly fooled ('*Populus vult decipi, ergo decipiatur*'). And so cunningly was deceptive word-use combined with deceptive tone, that only the brain-damaged remained intact, undeceived.

NOTE

1. 'Feeling-tone' is a favourite term of Head's, which he uses in regard not only to aphasia but to the affective quality of sensation, as it may be altered by thalmic or peripheral disorders. Our impression, indeed, is that Head is continually half-unconsciously drawn towards the exploration of 'feeling-tone' — towards, so to speak, a neurology of feeling-tone, in contrast or complementary to a classical neurology of proposition and process. It is, incidentally, a common term in USA, at least among blacks in the South: a common, earthy and indispensable term. 'You see, there's such a thing as a feeling tone ... And if you don't have this, baby, you've had it' (cited by Studs Terkel as epigraph to his 1967 oral history *Division Street: America*).

1.4 The Berber House

PIERRE BOURDIEU

The interior of the Kabyle house is rectangular in shape and is divided into two parts at a point one third of the way along its length by a small lattice-work wall half as high as the house. Of these two parts, the larger is approximately 50 centimeters higher than the other and is covered over by a layer of black clay and cow dung which the women polish with a stone; this part is reserved for human use. The smaller part is paved with flagstones and is occupied by the animals. A door with two wings provides entrance

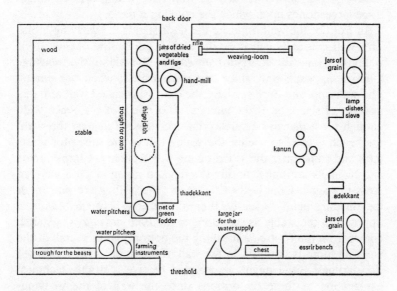

Figure 1. Plan of the house.

Source: Bourdieu P. (1973) 'The Berber House' in Douglas, M. (ed.), *Rules and Meanings: the Anthropology of Everyday Knowledge*, Harmondsworth, Penguin Education, pp. 98-110. (Original source: Excerpts from P. Bourdieu, 'The Berber house or the world reversed', *Echanges et communications: Mélanges offerts à Claude Lévi-Strauss à l'occasion de son 60ᵉ anniversaire*, Mouton, 1971, pp. 151-61 and 165-9.)

to both rooms. Upon the dividing wall are kept, at one end, the small clay jars or esparto-grass baskets in which provisions awaiting immediate consumption, such as figs, flour and leguminous plants, are conserved; at the other end, near the door, the water-jars. Above the stable there is a loft where, next to all kinds of tools and implements, quantities of straw and hay to be used as animal-fodder are piled up; it is here that the women and children usually sleep, particularly in winter. Against the gable wall, known as the wall (or, more exactly, the 'side') of the upper part or of the *kanun*, there is set a brick-work construction in the recesses and holes of which are kept the kitchen utensils (ladle, cooking-pot, dish used to cook the bannock, and other earthenware objects blackened by the fire) and at each end of which are placed large jars filled with grain. In front of this construction is to be found the fireplace; this consists of a circular hollow, two or three centimeters deep at its centre, around which are arranged in a triangle three large stones upon which the cooking is done.[1]

In front of the wall opposite the door stands the weaving-loom. This wall is usually called by the same name as the outside front wall giving onto the courtyard (*tasga*), or else wall of the weaving-loom or opposite wall, since one is opposite it when one enters. The wall opposite to this, where the door is, is called wall of darkness, or of sleep, or of the maiden, or of the tomb; a bench wide enough for a mat to be spread out over it is set against this wall; the bench is used to shelter the young calf or the sheep for feast-days and sometimes the wood or the water-pitcher. Clothes, mats and blankets are hung, during the day, on a peg or on a wooden cross-bar against the wall of darkness or else they are put under the dividing bench. Clearly, therefore, the wall of the *kanun* is opposed to the stable as the top is to the bottom (*adaynin*, stable, comes from the root *ada*, meaning the bottom) and the wall of the weaving-loom is opposed to the wall of the door as the light is to the darkness. One might be tempted to give a strictly technical explanation to these oppositions since the wall of the weaving-loom, placed opposite the door, which is itself turned towards the east, receives the most light and the stable is, in fact, situated at a lower level than the rest; the reason for this latter is that the house is most often built perpendicularly with contour lines in order to facilitate the flow of liquid manure and dirty water. A number of signs suggest, however, that these oppositions are the centre of a whole cluster of parallel oppositions, the necessity of which is never completely due to technical imperatives or functional requirements.

The dark and nocturnal, lower part of the house, place of objects that are moist, green or raw — jars of water placed on benches in various parts of the entrance to the stable or against the wall of darkness, wood and green fodder — natural place also of beings — oxen and cows, donkeys and mules — and place of natural activities — sleep, the sexual act, giving birth — and the place also of death, is opposed, as nature is to culture, to the light-filled, noble, upper part of the house: this is the place of human beings and, in particular, of the guest; it is the place of fire and of objects created by fire — lamp, kitchen utensils, rifle — the symbol of the male point of honour (*ennif*) and the protector of female honour (*horma*) — and it is the place of the weaving-loom — the symbol of all protection; and it is also the place of the two specifically cultural activities that are carried out in the space of the house: cooking and weaving. These relationships of opposition are expressed through a whole set of convergent signs which establish the relationships at the same time as receiving their meaning from them. Whenever there is a guest to be honoured (the verb, *qabel*, 'to honour' also means to face and to face the east), he is made to sit in front of the weaving-loom. When a person has been badly received, it is customary for him to say: 'He made me sit before his wall of darkness as in a grave', or: 'His wall of darkness is as dark as a grave.' The wall of darkness is also called wall of the invalid and the expression 'to keep to the wall' means to be ill and, by extension, to be idle: the bed of the sick person is, in fact, placed next to this wall, particularly in winter. The link between the dark part of the house and death is also shown in the fact that the washing of the dead takes place at the entrance to the stable. It is customary to say that the loft, which is entirely made of wood, is carried by the stable as the corpse is by the bearers, and the word *tha'richth* refers to both the loft and to the stretcher which is used to transport the dead. It is therefore obvious that one cannot, without causing offence, invite a guest to sleep in the loft which is opposed to the wall of the weaving-loom like the wall of the tomb.

In front of the wall of the weaving-loom, opposite the door, in the light, is also seated or rather, shown off, like the decorated plates which are hung there, the young bride on her wedding-day. When one knows that the umbilical cord of the girl is buried behind the weaving-loom and that, in order to protect the virginity of the maiden, she is made to pass through the warp, going from the door towards the weaving-loom, then the magic protection attributed to the weaving-loom becomes evident. In fact, from the point of view of the male members of her family, all of the girl's life is, as it were, summed up in the successive positions that she symbolically occupies in relation to the weaving-loom which is the symbol of male protection: before marriage she is placed behind the weaving-loom, in its shadow, under its protection, as she is placed under the protection of her father and her brothers; on her wedding-day she is seated in front of the weaving-loom with her back to it, with the light upon her, and finally she will sit weaving with her back to the wall of light, behind the loom. 'Shame,' it is said, 'is the maiden', and the son-in-law is called 'the veil of shames' since man's point of honour is the protective 'barrier' of female honour.

The low and dark part of the house is also opposed to the high part as the feminine is to the masculine: besides the fact that the division of work between the sexes, which is based upon the same principle of division as the organization of space, entrusts to the woman the responsibility of most objects which belong to the dark part of the house — water-transport, and the carrying of wood and manure, for instance — the opposition between the upper part and the lower part reproduces within the space of the house the opposition set up between the inside and the outside. This is the opposition between female space and male space, between the house and its garden, the place *par excellence* of the *haram*, i.e. of all which is sacred and forbidden, and a closed and secret space, well-protected and sheltered from intrusions and the gaze of others, and the place of assembly (*thajma'th*), the mosque, the café, the fields or the market: on the one hand, the privacy of all that is intimate, on the other, the open space of social relations; on the one hand, the life of the senses and of the feelings, on the other, the life of relations between man and man, the life of dialogue and exchange. The lower part of the house is the place of the most intimate privacy within the very world of intimacy, that is to say, it is the place of all that pertains to sexuality and procreation. More or less empty during the day, when all activity — which is, of course, exclusively feminine — is based around the fireplace, the dark part is full at night, full of human beings but also full of animals since, unlike the mules and the donkeys, the oxen and the cows never spend the night out of doors; and it is never quite so full as it is during the damp season when the men sleep inside and oxen and the cows are fed in the stable. It is possible here to establish more directly the relationship which links the fertility of men and of the field to the dark part of the house and which is a particular instance of the relationship of equivalence between fertility and that which is dark, full (or swollen) or damp, vouched for by the whole mythico-ritual system: whilst the grain meant for consumption is, as we have seen, stored in large earthenware jars next to the wall of the upper part, on either side of the fireplace, the grain which is intended for sowing is placed in the dark part of the house, either in sheep-skins or in chests placed at the foot of the wall of darkness; or sometimes under the conjugal bed, or in wooden chests placed under the bench which is set against the dividing wall where the wife, who normally sleeps at a lower level, beside the entrance to the stable, rejoins her husband. Once we are aware that birth is always rebirth of the ancestor, since the life circle (which should be called the *cycle of generation*) turns upon itself every third generation (a proposition which cannot be demonstrated here), it becomes obvious that the dark part of the house may be at the same time and without any contradiction the place of death and of procreation, or of birth as resurrection. [...]

Thus, the house is organized according to a set of homologous oppositions: fire: water; cooked: raw; high: low; light: shadow; day: night; male: female; *nif*: *horma*; fertilizing: able to be fertilized; culture: nature. But in fact the same oppositions exist between the house as a whole and the rest of the universe. Considered in its relationship with the external world, which is a specifically masculine world of public life and agricultural work, the house, which is the universe of women and the world of intimacy and privacy, is *haram*, that is to say, at once sacred and illicit for every man who does not form part of it. [...]

One is not justified in saying that the woman is locked up in the house unless one also observes that the man is kept out of it, at least during the day.[2] As soon as the sun has risen he must, during the summer, be in the fields or at the assembly house; in the winter, if he is not in the field, he has to be at the place of assembly or upon the benches set in the shelter of the pent-roof over the entrance door to the courtyard. Even at night, at least during the dry season, the men and the boys, as soon as they have been circumcised, sleep outside the house, either near the haystacks upon the threshing-floor, beside the donkey and the shackled mule, or upon the fig-dryer, or in the open field, or else, more rarely, in the *thajma'th*. The man who stays too long in the house during the day is either suspect or ridiculous: he is 'the man of the home', as one says of the importunate man who stays amongst the women and who 'broods at home like a hen in the henhouse'. A man who has respect for himself should let himself be seen, should continuously place himself under the gaze of others and face them (*qabel*). He is a man amongst men (*argaz yer irgazen*). [...] In opposition to man's work which is performed outside, it is the nature of woman's work to remain hidden ('God conceals it'): 'Inside the house, woman is always on the move, she flounders like a fly in whey: outside the house, nothing of her work is seen.' Two very similar sayings define woman's condition as being that of one who cannot know of any other sojourn than that tomb above the earth which is the house and that subterranean house which is the tomb: 'Your house is your tomb'; 'Woman has only two dwellings, the house and the tomb.'

Thus, the opposition between the house and the assembly of men, between the fields and the market, between private life and public life, or, if one prefers, between the full light of the day and the secrecy of the night, overlaps very exactly with the opposition between the dark and nocturnal, lower part of the house and the noble and brightly-lit, upper part. The opposition which is set up between the external world and the house only takes on its full meaning therefore if one of the terms of this relation, that is to say, the house, is itself seen as being divided according to the same principles which oppose it to the other term. It is therefore both true and false to say that the external world is opposed to the house as male is to female, or day to night, or fire to water, etc., since the second term of these oppositions divides up each time into itself and its opposite.[3] [...]

As a microcosm organized according to the same oppositions which govern all the universe, the house maintains a relation with the rest of the universe which is that of a homology: but from another point of view, the world of the house taken as a whole is in a relation with the rest of the world which is one of opposition, and the principles of which are none other than those which govern the organization of the internal space of the house as much as they do the rest of the world and, more generally, all the areas of existence. Thus, the opposition between the world of female life and the world of the city of men is based upon the same principles as the two systems of oppositions that it opposes. It follows from this that the application to opposed areas of the same *principium divisionis,* which in fact forms their very opposition, provides, at the least cost, a surplus of consistency and does not, in return, result in any confusion between these areas. The structure of the type a: b; b_1: b_2 is doubtless one of the simplest and most powerful that may be employed by a mythico-ritual system since it cannot oppose without simultaneously uniting (and inversely), while all the time being capable of integrating in a set order an infinite number of data, by the simple application of the same principle of division indefinitely repeated. [...]

But one or the other of the two systems of oppositions which define the house, either in its internal organization or in its relationship with the outside world, will take prime importance according to whether the house is considered from the male point of view or the female point of view: whereas, for the man, the house is less a place one goes into than a place from which one goes out, the woman can only confer upon these two movements and the different definitions of the house which form an integral part with them, an inverse importance and meaning, since movement towards the outside consists above all for her of acts of expulsion and it is her specific role to be responsible for all movement towards the inside, that is to say, from the threshold towards the fireplace. The significance of the movement towards the outside is never quite so apparent as in the rite performed by the mother, on the seventh day after a birth, 'in order that her son be courageous': striding across the threshold, she sets her right foot upon the carding comb and simulates a fight with the first boy she meets. The sallying forth is a specifically male movement which leads towards other men and also towards dangers and trials which it is important to *confront* like a man [...]

The two symmetrical and inverse spaces are not interchangeable but hierarchized, the internal space being nothing but the inverted image or the mirror-reflection of the male space. It is not by chance that only the direction which the door faces is explicitly prescribed whereas the interior organization of space is never consciously perceived and is even less desired to be so organized by the inhabitants. The orientation of the house is fundamentally defined from the outside, from the point of view of men and, if one may say so, by men and for men, as the place from which men come out. The house is an empire within an empire, but one which always remains subordinate because, even though it presents all the properties and all the relations which define the archetypal world, it remains a reversed world, an inverted reflection. 'Man is the lamp of the outside and woman the lamp of the inside.'

NOTES

1. All the descriptions of the Berber house, even the most exact and methodical ones (such as R. Maunier, 1930a and b), or those that are most rich in detail concerning the interior organization of space (such as those made by E. Laoust, 1912, 1920, or by H. Genevois, 1955) contain, in their extreme meticulousness, regular omissions, particularly when it is a question of precisely situating things and activities. The reason for this is that these descriptions never consider objects and actions as part of a symbolic system. The postulate that each of the observed phenomena derives its necessity and its meaning from its relation with all the others was the only way of proceeding to a systematic observation and examination capable of bringing out facts which escape any unsystematic observation and which the observers are incapable of yielding since they appear self-evident to them. This postulate is rendered valid by the very results of the research-programme which it establishes: the particular position of the house within the system of magical representations and ritual practices justifies the initial abstraction by means of which the house is taken out of the context of this larger system in order to treat it as a system itself.

2. In order to hint at how much the men are ignorant of what happens in the house, the women say: 'O man, poor unfortunate, all day in the field like a mule at pasture.'

3. This structure is also to be found in other areas of the mythico—ritual system: thus, the day is divided into night and day, but the day itself is divided into a diurnal—diurnal part (the morning) and a diurnal—nocturnal part (the evening); the year is divided into a dry season and a wet season, and the dry season is comprised of a dry—dry part and a dry—wet part. There should also be an examination of the relation between this structure and the structure which governs the political order and which is expression in the saying: 'My brother is my enemy, my brother's enemy is my enemy.'

REFERENCES

Genevois, H. (1955), *L'Habitation Kabyle*, Fort-National.
Laoust, E. (1912), *Etude sur la Dialecte Berbère du Cherona*, Levoux.
Laoust, E. (1920), *Mots et Choses Berbères*, Maisonneuve Larose.
Maunier, R. (1930*a*), 'Le culte domestique en Kabylie', in *Mélanges de sociologie Nord-Africaine*, Alcan.
Maunier, R. (1930*b*), 'Les rites de la construction en Kabylie', in *Mélanges de sociologie Nord-Africaine*, Alcan.

SECTION 2
STANDARDISATION AND DIVERSITY IN LANGUAGE

INTRODUCTION

We are often encouraged to think of a language as if it were a homogenous entity. This impression is confirmed by the strong pressures, notably nowadays from the educational system, towards conformity to national norms or standards, especially in written language. However, linguists observe that languages which are still spoken are always in a state of change. To some extent this is because of various pressures to speak in certain ways. The language of a national high-status group is not the only one which enjoys prestige in a country. There are other allegiances to be demonstrated and confirmed through language. Most speakers are able to vary their accent and even within one person the consistency implied by standardisation will be very hard to find. The readings in this section clarify these issues. They also examine the factors of a social or political nature which contribute to the adoption of certain forms or varieties of language.

In the first article in this section, Leith traces the development of standard English in four stages which he suggests are applicable to the growth of other standard languages. The final stage, codification, involves an attempt to eliminate the variation which exists within a language and to stem change. Leith considers that standardisation is as complete as it is ever likely to be in English, yet there remains considerable diversity in pronunciation and still some variation in grammar and in written forms.

Variation in pronunciation is the subject of an influential article by Giles which is our second reading here. In a series of studies, Giles examined the factors which cause us to value certain accents under certain conditions. This included research into whether one moves more towards or away from the accent of the person one is speaking to. We may, for example, move nearer to received pronunciation (RP) in certain circumstances and more towards a local or regional accent in others. Giles was particularly interested in how our judgements on people's qualities are affected by our perception of their accent. He found that the status of received pronunciation is not so unambiguously high as might be assumed

39

and that while some favourable qualities are attributed to speakers of RP, other positive qualities are perceived in speakers who use other accents.

The article by Milroy reports a study of the social factors which contribute to the maintenance of a particular variety of language. In her study of three areas of Belfast, she correlated the particular accent features with the speakers' ratings on an index which assessed their personal network structure, i.e. the strength of their ties to their community. She suggests that strong local ties are associated with the maintenance of vernacular norms.

Adoption of a particular language variety, with low prestige in society, is not restricted to members of the kind of very closeknit community which Milroy studied. Some features of a particular language variety may be adopted by those who are outside the group who usually speak it. Thus, as Hewitt shows, creoles such as London Jamaican are not only used to maintain the group identity and solidarity of their speakers; the children of other minority groups and white working-class adolescents can also learn to use creole in an attempt to further their friendships with its speakers and because of its high prestige in their particular subculture. This adoption of creole features is not always appreciated by established creole speakers.

Motives and pressures for adopting particular varieties of language are also examined in the article by Nichols, which is concerned with women's language in three widely dispersed and very different communities. She shows that in some communities women may be more receptive to newer styles and varieties, although in other circumstances they may exert a more conservative influence. Women do speak differently from men she concludes, but the differences are due to different occupational, educational and other experiences as well as the fact they are women.

Attempts to standardise the language of a nation state are not facilitated by the existence of groups within the nation speaking a quite different language. Hence the unfavourable treatment, historically, of Welsh by the English which Bellin discusses. However, a suppressed language may also serve to unite a minority, although ironically it is likely to be of benefit to that suppressed language if it, too, is standardised. The survival of Welsh has been in the balance for a long time; although its use in education and administration (both standardising influences) has helped allay the fears that it was dying, and its cultural vitality is widely acknowledged, Bellin nevertheless sees the need for commitment and vigilance on the part of the speakers of Welsh if their language is not to become moribund.

Tony Pugh

2.1 Standardisation in English

DICK LEITH

During the last 600 years the standard variety of English has been established as the superordinate one. Today, at least within Britain, the process of standardisation is probably as complete as it ever will be. Here we shall trace this long and complex process. [...] We shall see how standardisation proceeded in four inter-linked and often overlapping stages. First, we see the _selection_ of the east midland dialect as the dominant variety; then we discuss the conditions of its _acceptance_ by the powerful and educated classes, and the implications this has for speakers of other dialects. Third, we chart the _elaboration_ of the functions of the standard, as it developed in the domains previously associated with French and Latin. Fourth, we describe the stage of _codification,_ the attempts to 'fix' the standard variety in dictionaries and grammars, a process most clearly associated with the eighteenth century. Finally, we shall see how codification can be regarded as the expression of class attitudes to language.

The stages we have outlined above are applicable to the growth of standard varieties everywhere. Throughout the world, moreover, the process can be characterised by an important feature: it involves somewhere along the line an element of engineering, a conscious attempt to cultivate a variety that can be used for all purposes. [...] Coupled with this trend is the desire to have it recorded and regularised, to eliminate variations and, if possible, change. While the latter may be unattainable, the aims of standardisation remain inviolate. They have been described as maximal variation in function, and minimal variation in form.

The consequences of the process are far-reaching. [...] A standardised language gives its speakers a sense of historicity. Indeed, identification with the prestigious aura of the standard may be so strong that for many people the standard variety is the language itself. And an unfortunate corollary of this is that many have been

Source: Edited version of Chapter 2 of Leith, D. (1983) *A Social History of English*, London, Routledge & Kegan Paul, pp. 32-57.

43

convinced that they themselves do not speak their own language, or at least do not speak it 'properly', because they do not speak the standard. Yet while we defer to the notion of the standard, there is evidence that many have only an imperfect knowledge of its forms and structures. As we shall see, one of the effects of the codification process is that we have a much better knowledge of what to avoid saying than what we are taught it is correct to say. Despite exposure to print, and spoken manifestations of the standard in the mass media, knowledge of it is often more passive than active. This is a fact often overlooked by educationalists, and indeed linguists. The process of standardisation cannot be seen as merely a matter of communal choice, an innocent attempt on the part of society as a whole to choose a variety that can be used for official purposes and, in addition, as a lingua franca among speakers of divergent dialects. It involves from the first the cultivation, by an elite, of a variety that can be regarded as exclusive. The embryonic standard is not seen as the most useful, or the most widely-used variety, but as the best. Moreover, all sorts of arbitrary and at times spurious arguments are found to justify its forms and structures. In short, the process means the creation of a class dialect, that is imposed on an often resentful, and sometimes bewildered, populace.

It is not surprising, therefore, that there should be some widespread misunderstandings about standard English. One of these is that it is restricted only to formal kinds of utterance. This idea has gained acceptance, presumably, from its association in people's minds with contexts and situations where power is exercised — the classroom, the courtroom, the institutions of government. But like any linguistic variety, the standard has its dimensions of variation, including that of informality-formality, since for many people it must function as the medium of everyday conversation. Unlike other varieties, though, it is peculiarly subject to debate and analysis — about what usage is permissible and what is held to be correct. As we shall see, this preoccupation with fixity has often acted as a kind of brake on the natural tendency towards variation and change.

The standard is less fixed and monolithic than many suppose, partly because today it has a widely used spoken form (used, moreover, by many people without their realising it!). Since speech, by its very nature, is less amenable to being fixed than writing, the concept of standard English makes most sense when we are referring to the written word. When we are taught to write, it is standard English that we are taught. Moreover, this is largely true wherever English is learned in school; and the written standard is much the same in every part of the world where English is known and used.

Writing, then, is an indispensable component of standardisation. Indeed, it is difficult to conceive of a standard variety without a written form. At the same time, the existence of a writing system does not presuppose the existence of a standard. For instance, West Saxon was used as a written standard in English in the tenth century when no spoken one existed. But once a standard variety has been selected, writing is a powerful agent for its dissemination especially as literacy spreads and printing makes written materials more readily available. As the written forms acquire prestige, and are considered to be 'correct', they increasingly exert a pressure on speech. The written standard acts as a norm, a yardstick, and a guide [...]

SELECTION OF THE STANDARD VARIETY

The origins of the standard variety of English lie with the merchant class based in London. The dialect they spoke was the east midland one — associated at first with Norfolk, later with Northamptonshire, Leicestershire, Bedfordshire — and already by the fourteenth century this was a class dialect within London. The lower class spoke another dialect, a south-eastern one, the antecedent of Cockney. The dialects were similar in many respects but there were some regular differences; for instance, the merchant would say *mill*, with the short *i* of *pin*, but the tradesman said *mell*, with the *e* of *pen*. Vestiges of this pattern have been found in Cockney speech today. It is important to stress this linguistic stratification in London, since the subsequent history of the standard variety has much to do with its relationship to the speech of the Londoner in the street.

By the end of the fourteenth century, East Midland was an embryonic written standard. Within the dialect, however, there were variations, often associated with the birthplaces of bourgeois immigrants into London; so at first we see in use a number of different written standards. After about 1430, however, one of these variants became increasingly dominant, its use in government and official documents aided by the newly-established secular scriptoria. By the end of that century, the fixing of the selected variety was greatly strengthened, and accelerated, by the printing press.

We cannot yet assume the existence of a standard that is spoken. It is one thing for a minority of literate people to adopt a different written form; quite another for them to change their speech-habits overnight. As we shall see, it took some time for the east midland speech of the London merchants to acquire prestige. But there is another reason why East Midland, or variants of it, may have been quite widely adopted during the later Middle Ages. Students from all over England mixed in the two universities of Oxford and Cambridge, both only about sixty miles from London. In the triangle formed by these three centres, a great deal of east midland speech would have been heard, and possibly used as a kind of lingua franca among a mobile social group. If such a popular standard existed, it would have helped to spread East Midland, not because of its prestige value, or because it was imposed by the most powerful group, but because of its usefulness in communicating with people who spoke another dialect. One of these uses, among lower-class people, was as a medium for popular culture: in particular, the tradition of folk-song, which flourished in the age of standardisation. From the broadsheets of the sixteenth century to the song-collection of contemporary singers, the linguistic medium for folk-song is one that does not, on the whole, reflect regional differences. We do not know whether this is to be attributed to the people themselves, or to the commercial presses: but it seems clear that while ordinary people spoke in their local dialect, they did not sing in it.

So far, we have identified both regional and socio-economic factors in the selection of the standard variety. There is a political dimension as well. A standard tends to emerge when ideas about nationhood and political autonomy are gaining currency: and we find that in other European kingdoms where a degree of centralisation had occurred early, standard varieties were emerging at this time. But they were not always associated with the same power base in society. In both France and Spain, it was the usage of Court and monasteries in the areas of political power — the regions of Paris and Castile respectively — that determined the selection of the standard. In countries where political autonomy was achieved relatively recently, standardisation took a different course. Thus, while Tuscan developed as a literary standard during the later

Middle Ages in Italy, it did not have a political dimension until the unification of the country in the 1860s. By that time, the municipal standards of Italian in the old, independent city-states had become regional standards; and not only do these persist today, but they are tolerated to an extent unknown in France and England. Norway today has two competing standards: one a Danish-influenced legacy of Danish rule, the other a standard consciously engineered after independence from Denmark in 1814, and based on the Norwegian dialects of the west. These examples show the inextricability of language standardisation and social, political, and economic processes.

ACCEPTANCE OF THE STANDARD

By about the middle of the fifteenth century, the east midland dialect had been accepted as a written standard by those who wrote official documents. But its acceptance was tacit rather than explicit, a matter of convention rather than *diktat*. For when Caxton — who had spent much of his life on the continent — came to set up his press, he did not realise that the variety he was print-ing was a written standard. Instead, he complained about the dif-ficulty of choosing a dialect that all could understand, and also — like a good many people since — about how English had changed since he was young.

By the sixteenth century, the standard variety was well-established in the domain of literature. If we contrast the literary output of the Elizabethans with the great flowering of literature in the fourteenth century, we find a striking difference in language. For the dialect of Chaucer was not the dialect of Langland, who wrote *Piers Plowman*; *Gawain and the Green Knight*. The student of fourteenth-century English literature must come to terms with a range of regional vocabularies, grammars, and spelling-systems that seem bewildering in their diversity. Thus, while Chaucer wrote in the east midland dialect as it was spoken in London, he was not yet writing in a *national* literary standard, since his contemporaries had their own, local standards. By Shakespeare's time this regional variation in the language of printed literature had all but disappeared.

The establishment of a national literary standard had crucial repercussions, not only for literature, but for fixing the sense of a linguistic norm. In medieval England, there could be no sense of a norm for English usage, for reasons already explained above. Once a norm has been established, at least in the written language, it becomes possible to break it for stylistic purposes — in particular, for representing the speech of people from regions far away or belonging to social groups whose language is supposed to have certain clearly identifiable characteristics. In the later Middle Ages, regional differences in speech were as familiar to some people as they were to Caxton in the fifteenth century — and, in the writing of the Cornishman Trevisa, subject for some caustic descriptions — but it was hardly possible for a medieval writer to try to represent dialects other than his own, if the scribes copying the manuscript in other parts of the country were going to change it into their own dialect. A famous example of this in fourteenth-century literature is Chaucer's depiction of northern speech in *The Reeve's Tale*. When the manuscript was copied in the north midlands, the language was changed to such an extent that the linguistic differences between the speech of the north country students and the rest of the poem were ironed out. Chaucer's norm was not the norm elsewhere, so his copyists could not appreciate his attempt at deviation.

In the course of the sixteenth century, the growing sense of a literary norm can be seen by the numerous attempts to represent the speech of foreigners, the linguistic characteristics of Welsh, Scottish, and Irish people, and the speakers of other dialects of English. It is now that we begin to see the social stereotyping of such speakers. Increasingly, they play the role of buffoon or boor. Non-standard speech is equated with simplicity or roughness; and in order to depict those qualities in literature, some form of *marking* for non-standard features is adopted. A tradition is established which has lasted until the present day, and which has been translated into cinema and television soap-opera: deviation from the norm implies social comment in the minds of author and audience alike. [...]

In the absence of other guides or models, a spoken standard has to be anchored to a particular social group. It was a phonetician, Hart, who did this most clearly. In three works (1551, 1569, 1570) he mentions the 'learned' and 'literate' elements, and this theme is renewed during the following century by Price (1665) and Coles (1674). What these people were ultimately doing was describing their own usage — a tendency not uncommon among linguists of the twentieth century. Other observers are more specific about locale. The standard is set in London, particularly at Court; and a famous observer, Puttenham, writing in 1589, may be referring to the London-Oxford-Cambridge triangle mentioned earlier when he states that the best speech can also be heard within a radius of sixty miles round London.

It is highly significant that early attempts to define a spoken standard involve an element of evaluation. From the first, the issue of standardisation is bound up with notions about what constitutes the 'best', or 'truest', or 'most courtly' speech. The educated speech of the Court in London was now prestigious, and people like Hart and Puttenham were concerned with the speech-habits of aristocratic and wealthy people living in other regions. For now that urban speech in London was also *urbane*, speech in the country-side was 'barbarous', as Edmund Coote described it in 1597. It was incumbent on the provincial gentry to adapt to the standards culti-vated in the capital.

A crucial question to be asked about this stage of the standard-isation process is, acceptance by whom? Acceptance by govern-ment functionaries and small groups of literati is not the same as acceptance by the aristocracy of the shires; still less is it acceptance by the vast majority of ordinary people who worked in the fields. But by the end of the sixteenth century, we have an accepted written standard, and some prestigious speech forms, that were being promoted consciously and unconsciously by a tiny elite. We do not know, however, the extent to which we can speak of a standard of pronunciation at this time, or how widespread that pronunciation was among the aristocracy in general. What we can be sure of is that the prestige of one dialect triggers the disparage-ment of the others. Kentish is only the first to be stigmatised. In the course of the following centuries, the dialects of other parts of England are labelled variously as 'offensive', 'disgusting', 'barb-arous', and 'cant', and by the beginning of the twentieth century, the mud-slinging has come back to its source. Disparagement is directed this time towards an urban dialect, that of London itself; but it is the working-class dialect, Cockney, that is singled out in a School Board report as speech unworthy of citizens living in the capital city of an Empire. By then, of course, standard English is a subject taught in schools: and 'acceptance' is backed up with the teacher's rod.

ELABORATION OF FUNCTION

The dialects lost status for another reason. As we have seen, they lost their writing systems as the standard was developed; and so they were no longer used for either literary or devotional writing. In short, their range of functions was restricted as those of the standard were elaborated. They became *patois*, unwritten vehicles for informal, everyday conversation among equals. The process of standardisation may be said, therefore, to have involved an accompanying process of patoisation.

The new standard had to function in those domains previously associated, either fully or in part, with the use of Latin and French: law, government, literature, religion, scholarship, and education. Progress for English against the incumbent languages in these domains was often rather uneven, slow, and at times controversial, and the circumstances of its adoption were often different in each case. Inertia, the jealous guarding of ancient privileges, or feelings about the inadequacy of English delayed the advance of the standard. Occasionally even Acts of Parliament were required to support its implementation.

The stage we are describing points towards one of the two major goals of standardisation: maximal variation in function. And since the standard has to be omnifunctional, it will develop new structures and new meanings, appropriate to its use in different domains. Each group of specialists — lawyers, the writers of religious texts, administrators, and later, journalists and advertisers — cultivate their own varieties within the standard; and each new recruit to these professions must learn to write it, and often to speak it too. Thus the standard cannot be as monolithic as people like to imagine: it has to develop variations to suit its wide range of functions.

The linguistic consequences of this process were profound. The major source of variation was no longer regional, as different styles (some linguists call them *fields of discourse*) developed their own particularities. Often these were influenced by Latin and French usage, as though the early practitioners were trying to match the dignity of those languages by distancing their use of English from the everyday. Extreme cases of this are the English of religion and the English of law, whose special qualities today derive from the fact that they were in process of formulation during the sixteenth and seventeenth centuries. In all styles, words developed additional technical meanings as they came to be used in certain contexts, and these technical meanings often influenced casual spoken usage. In sum, English vocabulary became differentiated to an extent previously unknown, in that words can be identified as 'literary', or 'legal', or 'technical' in one sphere or another.

We have already seen the importance of the fourteenth century in the development of the standard. In 1362, for example, English was used for the first time in the domains of both government and law. But in the first of these, the use of French in written documents persisted for about a century after this date; and in law, it was used in some circumstances until the eighteenth century. An Act was passed in 1731 to limit its use in this domain once and for all, along with Latin (which was also occasionally used for keeping records). Today, legal English still employs Law French and Law Latin phraseology, such as *fee simple* and *habeas corpus.*

That English could function as a literary medium was apparent to all by the end of the sixteenth century; but acceptance of its potential in this respect was won only after a great deal of controversy. For many writers and scholars had a crisis of confidence about the suitability of English for great works of literature; they felt it could never match the heights achieved by the writers of ancient Rome and Greece. What is important here is not that English was in any way actually impoverished as a language, but that some people felt that it was. At one extreme, English was felt to be so 'dull', 'cankered', and 'barbarous' that it was irredeemable. At the other, some thought that there was nothing worth saying that could not be said in English. A compromise view held that English could attain the *eloquence* of the classical languages if two courses of action were taken. The first was to produce handbooks of composition, based on the classical manuals of rhetoric, to guide writers of English. The second was to inject thousands of Latin loan-words into the language. Some advocates of this second course — contemptuously known as *inkhorns* — went overboard in larding their speech with Latinisms, and became figures of fun in Elizabethan drama. In *Love's Labour's Lost,* the pedantic Holofernes spends a great deal of time exercising his ability to translate backwards and forwards between Latin and English.

By about the 1580s, the air had cleared. The middle view had prevailed, and English was declared to have achieved a state of eloquence. A balance had been achieved between native usage and

foreign importation, and the patterns of rhetoric had been successfully applied to literature in English. Moreover, some poets like
Spenser and Sydney had written works that many felt were a
match for any literature. And with this new-found self-confidence
came a self-*conscious* delight in the flamboyant manipulation of
stylistic levels. We can see this in the way Shakespeare sets off the
native English idiom against the polysyllabic Latin one, by asso-
ciating them with different kinds of character, or different moods.
Also, he dramatises such differences of vocabulary, either by juxta-
posing them within the same speech, or by intensifying a dramatic
moment with the most simple language. In *Measure for Measure*,
the returning Duke pretends to honour his self-righteous but
corrupt deputy, Angelo, by saying his record in office deserves 'A
forted residence 'gainst the tooth of time/And razure of oblivion'
(V. i. 12-13). 'Tooth of time' is native; 'razure of oblivion',
latinate. But when it is Mariana's turn to plead for Angelo's life, a
key moment in the play, every word is from the Anglo-Saxon: 'O
my dear lord,/I crave no other, nor no better man' (V. i. 428-9).
[...]
    It has been suggested that the crucial stage in functional elab-
oration is the development of a medium for serious, expository
prose. Inspired by the example of the Authorised Version, writers
began to cultivate prose to such an extent that the seventeenth century has been called the century of prose: and a significant aspect
of that trend was the increased use of English in writing of a
scientific and scholarly nature. Although the tradition of prose in
English stretches back as far as King Alfred, and persisted during
the Middle Ages for religious texts of a didactic or devotional
nature — written, it has been suggested, for women, who were not
allowed to learn Latin — that tradition had been weakened in contact with French and Latin. This was particularly so where scholarship is concerned. The tradition of scholarly writing in Latin was so
long, its audience so wide, that as late as 1687 Newton chose to
write his *Principia* in that language. But this choice of Newton's
stands at the end of a tradition. Fed by a developing interest in
science and philosophy, people wrote political pamphlets, journals,
essays, and the first newspapers, in English. By the end of the
seventeenth century, the range of possibilities for expression in
prose had expanded to cover imaginative, fictional writing. Such a
wide functional range engendered further self-consciousness
among writers of English, and enhanced the status of the language.

The displacement of Latin as the automatic language of scholarship was part of a wider process, the extension of English in education. In considering the roles of language in education, we need to distinguish between languages that are taught, and those that function as media of learning. In the Middle Ages, Latin had been both a taught language and the medium of instruction in the universities. But in schools the latter role had been filled by French. Both languages were being challenged in the education system by English as far back as the fourteenth century. A contemporary observer, Trevisa, records that in grammar schools throughout England, French was being abandoned as the medium of instruction; and in the University of Oxford an edict of 1340 forbidding the use of English among students suggests that the latter had made their preferences clear. Two trends underlie these changes: the general reaction against French, and the gradual loosening of the Church's hold on institutions of learning and literacy.

Formal education was extended throughout the fifteenth and sixteenth centuries. Grammar schools were founded, often for the children of merchants; and some of these deliberately excluded clergy from teaching positions. The growth of secular education increased the demand for learning in English: and this was met after the introduction of printing. Books in English sold more widely than those in Latin. And when the Protestant Reformation had promoted the English language as a medium for religious instruction, the identification of Latin with learning was undermined still further.

A major goal of education still remained, however: the learning of Latin, and the cultivation of a good written style in that language. During the literary and cultural Renaissance of the sixteenth century, Greek was added to the syllabus; and Latin, ironically enough, was the object of renewed interest and enthusiasm. But it was the classical Latin of writers like Cicero, rather than the medieval variety of the Church, that was studied and analysed. Latin had received a fresh boost, but as a taught language rather than as a medium of learning. Paradoxically, enthusiasm for Latin ultimately furthered the cause of English. It promoted the debate about the suitability of English discussed earlier, and it led to massive translation into English, which in turn directed people's minds to the forms and structures of the vernacular. One outcome of this was the beginnings of interest in the history of English itself.

During the Renaissance, education seems to have lost some of its exclusiveness. We must remember, moreover, that in this period, like any other, education was not synonymous with schooling. There is evidence of extensive elementary literacy during the Tudor and early Stuart periods: in Shakespeare's London, perhaps half the population could read. The broadside presses printed ballads in their hundreds of thousands; and by familiarising people with written English, the Authorised Version provided the basis for the teaching of reading and writing in the many different kinds of schools that were established for ordinary people until education was made compulsory after 1870. Latin remained important to the education of elites: it was still a requirement for certain university courses, and hence for certain occupations until well into the present century. But education for most people, if, when, and where it was available, had been vernacularised; and it was the standard variety that had become the medium of teaching. In time, however, it was also to become the form of English taught not only to foreign and second-language learners, but to the English themselves.

CODIFICATION

We said above that a standard variety is one that can be taught. A taught language inevitably becomes increasingly subject to attention and scrutiny, aimed at describing its forms and structures. But as we have seen, one of the two goals of standardisation is the attainment of minimal variation of form. In practice, this means trying to eliminate variation within the standard, and stemming the process of linguistic change. Both these interrelated aims — which run counter to the natural development of language — constitute the stage in the standardisation process that has been called codification.

Codification is undertaken by a small elite of scholars. Its method has less to do with description of linguistic forms, however, than with *prescription*: the evaluation of variants as 'correct', and the stigmatisation of variants which, for one reason or another, are felt to be undesirable. As we shall see, the arguments for justifying one variant in preference to another are often arbitrary, irrational, and inconsistent. This is because variants are associated, inevitably, with particular social groups; and certain social groups are felt to be more worthy of emulation than others. Unfortunately for the codifiers, the speech of London in the early years of standardisation was extremely mixed. There was still considerable variation in the usage of upper-class society, particularly in pronunciation; what is more, such usage was constantly being pulled hither and thither by aristocratic fashion, educated pedantry, and the unmonitored speech of ordinary Londoners. But by the early nineteenth century, the recommendations of the codifiers could be embraced by those social classes who felt the need to mark their speech off from that of the class below.

In the codification of English, the example set by other languages is of paramount importance. The codifiers looked back at classical Latin, and envied the illusion of fixity and order lent by the Latin grammarians, and the matching usage of the great writers like Cicero. But they also had other models to go on. Both Italy (in 1582) and France (in 1635) had developed Academies — bodies of learned men, who could make pronouncements on particular variants and changes. For a time, the idea of an English Academy was mooted. But by the middle of the eighteenth century, support for such an institution had fallen away. The Académie française, it seemed, had failed to fix the unfixable, just as it is failing today. Perhaps also, the English codifiers wanted to retain the freedom to make, and break, the rules as they chose. Thus codification in France has always been a more centralised and formalised affair than in England, where it has tended to be more *ad hoc*. Either way, the effects are much the same. It seems the higher the premium on codification is set, the less tolerant and the more rigid is the attitude to linguistic variation and change.

Recommended usage in England, therefore, is identified not with the decisions of a committee, but with particular books, written or compiled by established scholars and literary men. The most famous of these is undoubtedly the *Dictionary* of Dr Samuel Johnson. We have already mentioned this in connection with spelling; but it is even more important for the codification of words and meanings. When we think of dictionaries today, we have in mind what Johnson achieved — an alphabetical list of all the words in the standard language, with their meanings. Before Johnson, what dictionaries were available were not of this type. They were either dictionaries of hard words, or bilingual ones. The first was a list of those words which were felt to be difficult to understand because they were largely unassimilated into the mainstream of usage: they were often polysyllabic, Latinate words. The time for such dictionaries, not surprisingly, was the early seventeenth century; the 'inkhorn controversy' might have been resolved, but people needed to know about those foreign loan-words which made English 'eloquent'. The second type of dictionary corresponded largely with our idea of a 'French-English' one — an aid to translation, rather than a statement of the vocabulary of the standard variety. What Johnson did was altogether different. He listed the *range* of meanings for each word, including the commonest; and he illustrated each strand of meaning with quotations from writers. But in addition to this, Johnson saw lexicography as a contribution to the study of a language. Not only does he catalogue words and meanings, but he also has something to say about the nature of language, its history, and also its grammar.

The prestige enjoyed by the *Dictionary* during the late eighteenth and early nineteenth centuries was enormous. This was partly because it answered a need frequently felt by educated and literary people, and voiced as early as two centuries before by the scholar Mulcaster. But it was also because Johnson was regarded as a great man, with an established literary reputation. A dominant element in our cultural tradition has been the cultivation of the idea of the great mind, whether literary, philosophical, or whatever; and just as classical scholars needed their Cicero, so the English literati of the late eighteenth century saw Johnson as the source of knowledge and wisdom about the English language. His *Dictionary* could even be viewed as constituting the language itself.

The individuality of Johnson can be seen on almost every page of his *Dictionary*. He can be as frivolous, prejudiced, and wrong, as he can be erudite: but one thing we never lose sight of is his personality. Since Johnson, unfortunately, we have tended to forget the fact that dictionaries are compiled by people. Instead, we tend to revere them as the products of some mysterious, superhuman omniscience. [...]

The second half of the eighteenth century was also the high water mark for the codification of grammar. It is with regard to this aspect of linguistic structure that the prescriptive nature of codification can be seen most clearly. Certain grammatical forms and structures were judged as 'correct', while others were stigmatised as 'vulgar'. The legacy of these pronouncements is still strong today: many people are extremely nervous about being incorrect in speaking and writing. And certain of the stigmatised usages have become embedded in our present-day consciousness, as pitfalls to avoid. In general, people have a much clearer idea about what they are supposed to *avoid* saying, than what the codifiers recommend for them.

The grammarians sought to justify one usage at the expense of another by applying certain principles. The most important of these is probably the example of Latin. Grammars of Latin had been available for centuries, and all scholars knew and used them; hence, the grammatical categories established by the Latin scholars were applied, ready-made, to the grammar of English. The fact that by the eighteenth century Latin was usually encountered only in its written form gave rise to the idea that it was a fixed, regulated, and invariant language. English, by comparison, seemed untidy: it was therefore felt to be appropriate to promote grammatical variants which corresponded, in one way or another, to equivalents in Latin. Thus, the English pattern *it's me*, which had been common for centuries and still is, was deemed incorrect since the Latin construction *ego sum* made use of the subject form of the pronoun, *ego*, rather than the object form *me*: English people should therefore say *it's I*. The pervasiveness of such reasoning can be judged by the fact that people still write about this shibboleth in letters to the press.

Knowledge of Latin presupposed a knowledge of etymology, the origins of words. As well as disliking variation, the grammarians also hated change: hence, correctness was associated with what used to be the case, and the further back you could go, the better. Such arguments were very common where the meanings of words are concerned, but the 'etymological fallacy' was also applied to justify certain constructions. *Different from* was preferable to *different to*, or *different than*, because the *di* part of the word originally indicated 'division' or 'separateness'; and therefore *from* suits the etymological argument better. Similarly, the construction *averse to* and *under the circumstances* were considered incorrect, since the meanings of the *a* in *averse* and the *circum* in *circumstance* are respectively 'from' and 'around', and these meanings were not felt to be congruent with those of *to* and *under*. The grammarians failed to see that the use of such prepositions as *to* and *from* is in any language highly idiomatic.

A final principle involved the application of a kind of algebraic logic to stigmatise some constructions and promote others. Perhaps the most notorious example concerns the pattern of negation in English. In common with many languages today, English had since Anglo-Saxon times signalled negation by the cumulative use of negative particles. Hence, *I don't know nothing* was a traditional English pattern. By the end of the eighteenth century this had been condemned as illogical, by applying the principle that 'two negatives make a positive'. That great writers like Shakespeare used the traditional construction was a source of some embarrassment to the grammarians.

As in the case of dictionaries, we tend to forget today that grammars are written by people, who are not only individuals, but who also may reflect the interests of certain social groups. Grammar also has its great mind, to some extent, in that many people today look to Fowler and his *Modern English Usage* as an arbiter of usage. In Fowler, too, we find a personality, who is able moreover to temper the tradition of prescriptivism with a liberalism that acknowledges linguistic variation and change. The strength of that tradition should not be underestimated today. [...]

Pronunciation is the most difficult aspect of language to codify. As we have seen, our spelling is a most imperfect and inappropriate model for the sounds we make; yet people have felt bound by it for more than 400 years. Already in the sixteenth century some scholars interested in the codification of pronunciation had begun to consider the relationship between sounds and spellings: their arguments in effect are a rehearsal of those discussed above. Hart, a phonetician, argued that spelling should be reformed so as to draw it into line with pronunciation. Mulcaster, a headmaster, rejected this plea for a phonemic model, arguing that people pronounced differently. But others were already proposing the inversion of this priority. Sir Thomas Elyot, author of the immensely influential *Governor* of 1531, wrote that noblemen's sons should omit no letter in their pronunciation, a view echoed by the pronouncing dictionaries of 300 years later, and heard ever since.

Attempts to base pronunciation on spelling were not helped by developments in the writing system in the early phase of standardisation. The early printers introduced spellings that had nothing to do with sounds, like the *ue* of *tongue*. Other spellings were remodelled by scholars themselves, to show their origins: the nativised spelling *dette* had a *b* inserted to show that it came from Latin *debitum*. In cases like *debt* and *island* (where the scholars got the etymology wrong: they put an *s* into *iland*, thinking it to be from Latin *insula*) pronunciation has remained unaffected, and we are left with a spelling difficulty; but in other cases, as in *perfect*, the etymological spelling gives us the basis for modern pronunciation, displacing *parfit*. Such pedantry was not the only complicating factor. As we said before, the early standard was a very mixed variety, mingling not only the pronunciations of different areas, but also to some extent their traditional spelling systems. The spelling of *busy*, for instance, may reflect the old Winchester standard, whereas its pronunciation is an east midland one. Some pronunciations themselves appear to have a south-western origin. The glide consonant /w/ in *one* can be heard at the onset of other words, such as *oak* (*wuk*), in that area today. (Other dialects, for example those in Northumberland, have a different glide, the initial sound of *yet*; hence, *one* is *yan*.) Finally, some pronunciations seem to have had an East Anglian source. The famous example of spelling irregularity in *bough, though, rough, cough*, and *tough* shows how spelling can create the illusion of relationship among words that are either of different origin (the vowels of some of these words are historically unrelated) or whose pronunciations have diverged. We find that in the first two words, the final consonant, represented by *gh*, is no longer sounded, but the last three have the eastern /f/.

We do not know the circumstances governing the adoption of some pronunciations rather than others. It has been suggested that in some cases choice was motivated by a desire to maintain or even establish distinctions among pronunciations that were either not made in other dialects, or were being lost in them. Thus, the adoption of a south-western pronunciation of *one* could create a useful distinction between that word and *own*. Though this may be true in some instances, it is wrong in any event to conclude that 'standard' pronunciation (or grammar and vocabulary for that matter) is richer in distinctions than other dialects or varieties. Traditional distinctions may be preserved by teaching them as correct, but adherence to tradition may deprive us of a variety of useful innovations.

In the early years of standardisation, the precepts of the codifiers had to compete with the push and pull of fashion. Some pronunciations were undoubtedly adopted because, for one reason or another, they were considered prestigious. But by the end of the eighteenth century, codification of the other levels of structure led to the production of the pronouncing dictionary, a book in which the pronunciation of words in the standard variety could be looked up. In these works, there is both an appeal to spelling as a guide, but also an appeal to tradition.

Johnson's *Dictionary* had codified not only words but their spellings also; and now that spelling was virtually fixed, it was a good deal easier to recommend pronunciations based on them. Moreover, Johnson himself had written that the best pronunciations were those that accorded with the spelling. This precept was put into effect by John Walker, the writer of *A Critical Pronouncing Dictionary* (1791). If there was an *h* in the spelling, then *h* should be sounded. The verbal ending *-ing*, as in *going*, should not be pronounced *-in'*, for the same reason. The pronunciation of whole words, like *forehead, often,* and *waistcoat,* should moreover be reformed in accordance with spelling, to replace *forrid, offen,* and *weskit.* Certain pronunciations, however, were too firmly entrenched in upper-class society to be changed. Admitting that the new pronunciation of *cucumber* suited the spelling better than the old *cowcumber,* Walker felt reluctant to recommend it. But the spelling-pronunciation won out in the standard variety, and *cowcumber* is now only heard in dialect.

There is another crucial dimension to Walker's approach. Notions of correct pronunciation are formulated against a background of what to avoid; and it becomes increasingly clear that it is lower-class pronunciations that must be avoided. And the most barbarous kind of pronunciation was that associated with the Cockney speech of London. Cockneys, said Walker, should know better, since they did not have the excuse of living miles away from the centre of power, culture, and fashion. Thus, the differences that existed between their speech and that of so-called polite society were 'a thousand times more offensive and disgusting' than differences which occurred elsewhere.

By the early nineteenth century, then, correct pronunciation was an issue of class. And the identification of the 'best' pronunciation with a particular social class is given institutional expression by the development of the fee-paying public school system. In these schools, a pronunciation that may be described as codified grew up, or was cultivated and taught. The desiderata of the scholars could at last be put into practice in controlled conditions. But the recipients of this privilege have always been only a tiny minority, a minority drawn primarily from the wealthy and powerful groups in English society. In no other country in the world are pronunciation and social class so closely and clearly linked.

In the public schools, the predominantly east midland basis of the upper-class London pronunciation gradually lost its regional colour. It became a purely class accent, and was accordingly evaluated in ways which reflect the attitudes of the most powerful social group. Known today to linguists as Received Pronunciation — a term in which the adjective 'received' has the now obsolete sense of 'socially acceptable in the best circles' — this accent is still widely claimed to be the best form of pronunciation (although linguists themselves usually attest their neutrality on this matter). Received Pronunciation (RP) is often described, not in terms of the class that uses it, but as the most beautiful and euphonious of accents. Most strikingly, its status as an accent has even been denied: if you speak RP, you speak English 'without an accent'.

It need hardly be said that this view was often accepted and even fostered by ordinary people wherever English was spoken. Persuaded that their own regional accents were ugly or slovenly, people have often accepted the view that RP offers a prestigious norm. Many of our popular designations of RP — 'Queen's English', 'Oxford English', 'BBC English' — reflect its association with power, learning, and influence. And RP has been a powerful agent in the re-structuring of regional pronunciations which originally had quite different sound-systems. Yet while RP exerts prestige at the overt level, there has been no widespread, wholesale adoption of the accent. For the vast majority of the population, RP may be all the things we have listed above, but it is also the speech of a social class that they have no ambition to emulate.

CODIFICATION AND SOCIAL CLASS

We have seen that from the first the standard variety is associated with power in society. Throughout the period of standardisation, an increasingly dominant source of power has been the ownership of capital. By the nineteenth century, the factory system was producing enough wealth for its owners to acquire positions in society. But ownership of a fortune does not guarantee refined behaviour or courtly manners. The new entrepreneurs needed to be 'socially acceptable in the best circles'. What more accessible way of doing this than to embrace the standards of correctness in speech, now that these had been codified and made widely available?

Recent research in both England and the USA shows that the class most anxious about linguistic usage is the lower middle class. Insecurity about social status is reflected in nervousness about being incorrect in linguistic behaviour. In the early nineteenth century, it was the industrialists who felt insecure about status, and who therefore provided the need for a 'superior' kind of English. The adoption of the codified standard would mean that your speech could be sharply different from that of the working class, who, as a consequence of the process of industrialisation, were flooding into the cities in their hundreds of thousands. It was in *their* speech, appropriately enough, that the stigmatised pronunciations and grammatical items could be found.

Codification could be said to have become a weapon of class. What the codifiers had done, ultimately, was to propose and cultivate a code of linguistic forms which were in some degree different from those in use among the vast majority of the population. By analysing 'correct' usage in terms that only a tiny minority of educated people could command, the codifiers ensured that correctness remained the preserve of an elite. The usage of most people was wrong, precisely because it was the usage of the majority. The worst aspects of the codification process were institutionalised in the compulsory state education system introduced after 1870. The doctrine of correctness was preached with mechanical inflexibility: attention to linguistic form overrode considerations of linguistic function. Not surprisingly, millions of people left school convinced that not only were they ignorant of their own language, but they were stupid as well.

It would, however, be mistaken to suggest that the codifiers were a tightly-knit group of conspirators extending across several generations, intent on laying traps for the unwary. In fact, they did not by any means represent a homogeneous body of opinion; they often argued amongst themselves, and some laid the foundations for the serious study of language and of linguistic history. But the codifiers did pave the way, however unwittingly, for the mystification that has often characterised discussion about language. Many people today, when they examine the work of the eighteenth-century grammarians, are struck by the triviality of the examples cited, and by the tortuousness of the arguments. And if the judgments are arbitrary, and the result of special pleading, it may well be because the codifiers themselves were not unaffected by allegiances of class and background.

Codification of the standard was not based on an informed and systematic analysis of language. It is not surprising, therefore, that there is little consensus today about what items upset us or gladden our hearts. A recent survey among employers, examiners, and teachers shows that while some people make a fuss about *it's me*, others like to wax haughty on *different to/than/from*. We all have a linguistic *bête noire*. But one of the most depressing results of codification is that as well as encouraging this prescriptive stance, it has tended to elevate personal taste into a norm, a characteristic particularly apparent in the pages of Johnson, Walker, and Fowler. In view of the social history of the past two centuries, this was perhaps unavoidable: but we should remember today that individual preference and informed understanding are not necessarily the same thing.

NOTES

The four stages of standardization are proposed by Haugen (1966). A great deal of the data in this reading is from Dobson (1955). Williams (1961) offers a clear social and political perspective.

For sixteenth-century attitudes to English see Jones (1953). A very good introduction to Shakespeare's language is by Quirk (1974). On prose, see Gordon (1966). For contemporary attitudes to usage, Mittins *et al.* (1970) is excellent; it discusses the history of certain shibboleths. On the middle-class 'market' for correctness, see Wyld (1936) and Labov (1972).

REFERENCES

Dobson, E.J. (1955) 'Early modern standard English', *Transactions of the Philological Society*, pp. 25-54. Reprinted in Lass, R. (1969), *Approaches to English Historical Linguistics*, New York, Holt, Rinehart & Winston.

Gordon, I.A. (1966) *The Movement of English Prose*, London, Longman.

Haugen, E. (1966) 'Dialect, language, nation', *American Anthropologist*, 68, 922-35. Reprinted in Pride, J. and Holmes, J. (1972) *Sociolinguistics: Selected Readings*, Harmondsworth, Penguin.

Jones, R.F. (1953) *The Triumph of the English Language*, Oxford University Press.

Labov, W. (1972) *Sociolinguistic Patterns*, University of Pennsylvania Press, Oxford, Blackwell.

Mittins, W. *et al.* (1970) *Attitudes to English Usage*, Oxford University Press.

Quirk, R. (1974) 'Shakespeare and the English Language', *The Linguist and the English Language*, London, Arnold pp. 46-64.

Williams, R. (1961) 'Standard English', *The Long Revolution*, Harmondsworth, Penguin.

Wyld, H.C. (1936) *A History of Modern Colloquial English*, Oxford University Press.

2.2 Our Reactions to Accent

HOWARD GILES

An English schoolboy would only ask his friend: 'Wassa time, then?' To his teacher he would be much more likely to speak in a more standardized accent and ask: 'Excuse me, sir, may I have the correct time please?' People are generally aware that the phrases and expressions they use are different from those of earlier generations; but they concede less that their own behaviour also varies according to the situation in which they find themselves. People have characteristic ways of talking which are relatively stable across varying situations. Nevertheless, distinct contexts, and different listeners, demand different patterns of speech from one and the same speaker.

Not only this, but, in many cases, the way someone speaks affects the response of the person to whom he is speaking in such a way that 'modelling' is seen to occur. This is what Michael Argyle has called 'response matching.' Several studies have shown that the more one reveals about oneself in ordinary conversation, and the more intimate these details are, the more personal 'secrets' the other person will divulge.

Response matching has, in fact, been noted between two speakers in a number of ways, including how long someone speaks, the length of pauses, speech rate and voice loudness. The correspondence between the length of reporters' questions when interviewing President Kennedy, and the length of his replies, has been shown to have increased over the duration of his 1961-63 news conferences. Argyle says this process may be one of 'imitation.' Two American researchers, Jaffe and Feldstein, prefer to think of it as the speaker's need for equilibrium. Neither of these explanations seems particularly convincing. It may be that response matching can be more profitably considered as an unconscious reflection of speakers' needs for social integration with one another.

Source: Giles, H. (1971) 'Our reactions to accent', *New Society*, 14 October 1971.

This process of modelling the other person's speech in a conversation could also be termed speech convergence. It may only be one aspect of a much wider speech change. In other situations, speech divergence may occur when certain factors encourage a person to modify his speech away from the individual he is dealing with. For example, a retired brigadier's wife, renowned for her incessant snobbishness, may return her vehicle to the local garage because of inadequate servicing, voicing her complaint in elaborately phrased, yet mechanically unsophisticated language, with a high soft-pitched voice. These superior airs and graces may simply make the mechanic reply with a flourish of almost incomprehensible technicalities, and in a louder, more deeply-pitched voice than he would have used with a less irritating customer.

We don't know enough yet about all aspects of speech, but I have been experimenting with response matching in the use of accents, and have attempted to apply the ideas of speech convergence-divergence to cope with the phenomenon of accent change.

To begin with, it is necessary to abstract a speaker's accent repertoire. This is schematically represented in Fig. 1. Obviously, accent response matching is not of such a power as to occur between people regardless of their regional colourings. We do not order curry (or sausage and chips, for that matter) in an Indian restaurant with a Peter Sellers brogue. Response matching at this level operates with pronunciation patterns in which the speaker has had some extended experience. In its full range, the repertoire comprises a continuum of accent usage — standard variant, to the broadest local regional variant (whatever it may be). This standard accent in Britain has been called 'received pronunciation' (RP) by linguists. It is conventionally envisaged as the accent of a BBC newscaster.

Now, the way most people's accents change are along this single continuum, from BBC to regional — but there are exceptions. It is likely that, if an individual lives in an area with two dialects (such as Cardiff, which has its own accent besides the more common south Wales lilt), then there would be at least one other regional 'branch' (as is shown in Figure 1).

There is also the possibility of another 'branch' in the opposing direction, that is towards affected RP, more popularly thought of as the accent of the upper classes. Though most people can both standardize and broaden their most usual way of speaking (i.e.

affected
pronunciation

received
pronunciation

idiolect

broad
regional "B"
(eg South Wales)

broad
regional "A"
(eg Cardiff)

Figure 1.

their *idiolect*) at least slightly, it is also true that some people are practically immobile in this respect due to the limitation of their early vocal environments (for example, ghetto children; but, perhaps even more so, public school children).

Accent change in conversation may take either one of two directions, depending on whether the speaker wishes to be accepted by his listener — when his accent will converge — or whether he wishes to emphasize differences — in which case his accent may grow more dissimilar.

Accents can converge in two ways. To appreciate the distinction between the two, it is necessary to assume that the way that pronunciation varies in a speaker's repertoire also reflects prestige. This being the case, 'standard' patterns of pronunciation will have the highest status while the broadest regional varieties will have the lowest. So if a speaker thinks that his listener's way of speaking is higher than his is in terms of accent prestige (ie. it is more 'standard'), then, provided he wants to be accepted by the listener, he will modify his accent and *upward* accent convergence will occur. The only other direction of accent convergence is 'down', and implies that a speaker thinks his listener's pronunciation puts him in a lower prestige bracket — in other words, it's broader.

Since accent prestige often reflects social status, a move like this on the part of the speaker may be adopted so as to reduce embarrassment, due to social differences, and to prepare a common basis for the communication of ideas and feelings. This assumes, of course, that 'downward' convergence is more conscious than 'upward'.

Naturally enough, accent divergence can take on two directions also (see below). Think of a woman who has bought some expensive clothing in an exclusive store which neither changes articles, nor refunds the cash after they have been bought. When the woman returns home she discovers a glaring flaw in the dress and returns it to the shop assistant demanding a replacement. The assistant has her instructions and soon finds a rather persistent customer on her hands. Of course, the floor manager is summoned to a situation he is all too familiar with and he assumes his usual authoritative and unrelenting approach, polishing his accent to a fine gilt edge (*upward* divergence). His aloof manner and his immediate dismissal of the whole affair arouses the woman's indignation and she storms off, voicing disgust in an unrefined manner (*downward* divergence).

I have been looking at just one direction of accent response matching, but, nevertheless, an important social one in Britain — 'upward convergence'.

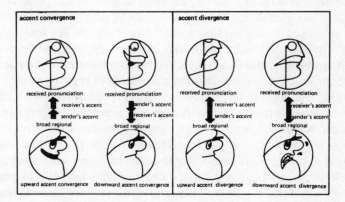

Figure 2.

It's unlikely that most people, when talking, achieve enough flexibility in pronunciation to be considered *similar* by their listeners — unless the gap in the prestige between their accents is very small. From the work of Wallace Lambert, and his colleagues at McGill University in Canada, on the way people evaluate various spoken languages and dialects, we know that there may be three 'rewards' for the speaker who upgrades his accent one or two notches towards his partner. These are: (i) an increase in perceived status; (ii) an increase in perceived favourability of personality; and (iii) an increase in the perceived quality and persuasiveness of the content of the message. So, if a person wishes to ingratiate himself with a person whom he is talking to, and whose accent has more prestige, it would seem reasonable for the speaker to show himself (and what he says) in the most favourable light.

Before proceeding to show that 'upward accent convergence' actually occurs in social interaction, I thought that it would be ideal at first to try to show that the range of accents does, in fact, reflect social prestige, with RP being superior in this respect. Second, I have tried to test whether or not these three potential 'rewards' work.

In order to find out whether RP really did have more prestige than regional varieties, I used the 'matched-guise' technique. This consisted of playing tape recordings of speakers with different accents, reading the same emotional-neutral passage of prose, to listeners who we asked to rate these voices on certain dimensions, including status. Actually, all the voices were produced quite realistically (after laborious practice) by the same male speaker, so that all accents were matched for timbre, speech rate, personality and so on. This procedure was necessary to stop listeners reacting to aspects of these voices other than that of accent. We found that RP and affected RP had by far the most prestige, while even certain foreign accents (French, German and northern American accents) had more social standing than our own regional ones.

Other interesting findings also emerged. For instance, we found that twelve-year-olds relied heavily on aesthetic judgments of accent when allocating prestige, unlike their more objective 17-year-old counterparts. As expected, subjects rated their own regional variety more favourably than listeners who were not from their region, although this bias did decrease with age and was more pronounced with working class and male people. Nevertheless, subjects appeared to 'repress' recognition of their own accent by rating the attitude item, 'an accent identical to your own' more favourably than the voice or name label representing their own region.

In another study, listeners had played to them the matched-guises of mild and broad variants of northern Irish, south Welsh and Birmingham accents. Listeners could easily detect these differences in accent broadness and rated the mild variants consistently superior in prestige and pleasantness, to the broader variants. Interestingly enough, 21-year-old listeners heard a greater difference between the variants than 12-year-olds, who, on the other hand, thought there was more difference in prestige between the variants than did the maturer group. Welsh listeners also tended to think there was less of a physical difference between the mild and broad Welsh voices than the Somerset listeners.

It would seem safe to conclude from these studies, therefore, that pronunciation differences between accents, and also within the same accent, are associated with prestige. This then enables the speaker at least one 'reward' for standardization, in that the milder his accent, the greater status he has.

We also investigated the second reward (concerned with personality gains and accent) by using the 'matched-guise' technique. A two minute tape-recorded prose passage was read in three accents (RP, mild south Welsh and Somerset) by two male speakers, and this was played to listeners who were asked to evaluate the voices on 18 adjective traits (for example, generous-mean, intelligent-dull). The notion of 'accent' was never introduced and listeners were told that their immediate impressions from the voice was all that we wanted. Besides certain interesting age, regional and personality differences, a distinct pattern of values emerged. We found that RP speakers were seen more favourably in terms of their competence (their ambition, intelligence, self-confidence, determination and industriousness) but less favourably in terms of personal integrity and social attractiveness (their seriousness, talkativeness, good-naturedness and sense of humour) than the regional speakers. The same was true for RP versus northern English and Scottish speakers. Although this finding was somewhat surprising it does explain, in part, the vitality of regional accents.

The third 'reward' (concerned with the importance of content and accent) we looked at, first of all, by finding out whether 17-year-olds' attitudes towards capital punishment were stable over a period of seven days. As this fact was substantiated in a pilot study, the experiment proper was designed. More than 500 sixth formers' attitudes towards capital punishment were obtained, so that five groups of 50 subjects might be formed, each matched for sex, and attitude scores. Seven days after these attitudes were given, each group was provided with the same information against capital punishment, but in a different way — in typescript, or in one of the four recorded male matched-guises of RP, south Welsh, Somerset and Birmingham (that is, in decreasing order of accent prestige). After the passage had been given them, each group was asked for its attitude on the topic as it then stood, together with a rating of the quality of the argument.

Even though the argument was exactly the same, irrespective of its mode of presentation, the quality ratings, as expected, were related to the prestige of the accent. Rather surprising, however, was the finding that only the regional guises were effective in producing a significant change in attitudes; the typescript and RP guise were not. It may be that the integrity associated with regional speech (as I mentioned earlier) is a more pervasive force in persuading people, than what they see as the expertise of the argument or the speaker. Alternatively, it may have been that listeners were surprised more by the stand taken by the regional than the RP speaker, as this view is perhaps seemingly uncharacteristic of the group a regional voice is thought to represent. In this case, listeners may have afforded the regional guises great integrity despite the quality of their arguments and hence their greater effectiveness. Although more research needs to be done on this, the speaker, by means of 'upward convergence,' would seem to attract a third 'reward' by what is seen as the increased quality of his message. 'Upward convergence' is rewarding then — but how exactly does it occur? We tested this by having nine sixth formers with Bristol accents interviewed individually by someone their own age, but with a strong Bristol accent like themselves; and separately by someone of higher social status with an RP accent.

The similar-status interviewer was a sixth former that we got from a different school. He was trained in the art of interviewing over a number of pilot trials and until he and the other interviewer achieved equivalent styles of informality; the use of slang was to be avoided wherever possible. The interviews themselves were tape recorded, unknown to the interviewees, by means of concealed microphones; and they did not know the true purpose of the study.

They were, in fact, told that their personalities were being assessed in each interview (thereby assuring their cooperation), and that the hypothesis we were testing was that someone of equal station in life would be more accurate in their assessments (when compared to a more objective pencil-and-paper test of personality) than someone of a higher status, who would probably have a totally different value system. The interviewees were also told that the results of the study would be used for recommendations to industry on personnel selection and to colleges for student selection. Each interview lasted about 20 minutes and after the first 15 of these, the interviewees were posed a standard question on their attitudes towards capital punishment.

The first minute's speech, in response to the capital punishment question in each situation, was recorded into a third 'analysis' tape but edited such that the interviewer's voice did not intrude. A group of Welsh students and a matching group of Bristol students were asked to listen to each of these nine pairs of voices and, having heard them, determine whether they could detect a difference in accent and a difference in how formal the grammar was. If they could detect differences between members of a pair, they were asked to say which accent was the broader, and which was grammatically the less formal; they then had to rate how wide these differences were. It was emphasized that there were no right or wrong answers and it was up to them to determine when modifications had occurred, if at all.

The listeners claimed to see differences within all nine pairs. But, more important, the differences they saw, in accent *and* grammatical change, were in the direction we predicted. In other words, listeners (without knowledge of how these voices were obtained) identified the nine voices spoken in the presence of the RP interviewer as less broad, and also grammatically more formal, than the voices produced by the *same* speaker with the regional interviewer.

However, we found interesting differences between the two groups of listeners in their reactions to these speech changes. For instance, the Bristol listeners made significantly more 'errors' in identifying accent (but not grammatical) change than the Welsh 'aliens.' It may be that people become saturated with their own local accent so that they are less efficient at detecting variations in it. Furthermore, from the Welsh listeners' ratings, there was no relationship between the extent of a speaker's accent shift and the extent of his grammatical shift. This seems to indicate that listeners can successfully analyse speech changes in two independent ways. But, when we look at the Bristol listeners' ratings, we see that they saw a *strong* relationship between the extent that a speaker changed his accent and the extent that he changed his grammar. Because both groups rated a speaker's change of accent very similarly, it looks as though the Bristol listeners were relying more than the Welsh on grammatical cues when weighing up how much a speaker's accent had changed.

It would appear that grammatical changes were important aspects of the speakers' accent convergence, since I thought the interviewers were similar in how formal their grammar was — and they were, of course, trained to be so.

Until recently, speech was rarely seen as a dynamic, flexible process. Even now, we lack an adequate theory of what speech changes a particular person or situation will provoke in all ways — like accent and grammar. But with our attempts to produce at least a temporary framework for the study of one variable (the listener's accent) on one aspect (the speaker's accent), perhaps a more comprehensive picture will eventually emerge.

REFERENCES

Howard Giles, 'Evaluative reaction to accents' (*Educational Review*, vol. 23, 211-227, 1970); 'Patterns of evaluation in reactions to RP, south Welsh and Somerset accented speech' (*British Journal of Social and Clinical Psychology*, 1971).

W. Labov, 'Phonological correlates of social stratification' (*American Anthropologist*, vol. 66, No. 6 (2), pp. 164-176, 1964).

J.D. Matarazzo, A.N. Wiens, R.G. Matarazzo and G. Sascow, 'Speech and silence behaviour in clinical psychotherapy and its laboratory correlates,' in J.M. Schlein, H.F. Hunt, J.D. Matarazzo and C. Savage (eds), *Research in Psychotherapy*, vol. 3 (Washington DC, American Psychological Association, 1968).

J.T. Webb, 'Subject speech rates as a function of interviewer behaviour' (*Language and Speech*, vol. 12, pp. 54-67).

2.3 Social Network and Language Maintenance

LESLEY MILROY

INTRODUCTION

Many of those recent urban sociolinguistic studies which follow the general model provided by Labov (1966) have tried to account for patterns of variability in language and have frequently looked for evidence of ongoing linguistic change. Although the study of urban language described here makes use of a number of Labov's concepts and analytic techniques, the emphasis is not on *change* and *variability*, but rather on *stability* and *focusing*. In this respect I share with Le Page (1979) an interest in the question of how a stable set of linguistic norms emerges and maintains itself in a relatively focused form. Although this question is seen by Le Page, a creolist, to be of fundamental importance to sociolinguistic theory, it is not one which is often asked by scholars working in the urban dialectological tradition of Labov.

The kind of linguistic norm still most commonly referred to in the literature is the publicly legitimized *prestige* norm. All fully standardized languages appear to be characterized by norms of this kind, which are codified in the form of grammars, dictionaries and elocution handbooks. The manner in which these norms emerge diachronically and are maintained in a relatively focused form by mechanisms such as a writing system and public educational and broadcasting systems has been carefully analysed by Haugen (1972). A model of sociolinguistic structure such as that proposed by Labov depends fundamentally on the investigator's ability to identify a single set of prestige norms of this kind. Moreover, analytic procedures which link language variability to hierarchically stratified social groupings tacitly assume the speech community's awareness of a set of prestige norms which underlies

Source: Milroy, L. (1980) 'Social network and language maintenance' in Pugh, A.K., Lee, V. and Swann, J. (eds), *Language and Language Use*, London, Heinemann Educational, pp. 35-45.

regular and consistent sociolinguistic stratifications. These prestige norms may be seen as symbolizing publicly recognized values of a status-oriented kind.

However, scholars have long been aware of the existence of other, sometimes opposing, sets of norms which also have a powerful capacity to influence linguistic behaviour; these may be described as vernacular norms. Characteristically, vernacular norms are perceived as symbolizing values of solidarity and reciprocity rather than status, and are not publicly codified or recognised. Black English Vernacular is one famous example of a set of highly focused vernacular norms; most industrial cities have associated with them low status varieties which also are overtly stigmatized.

Many bidialectal and bilingual communities maintain, in a parallel way, low status dialects or languages in their repertoires which have the capacity to persist, often over centuries, in the face of powerful pressures from a legitimized norm. Social psychologists have concluded that it is the capacity of these low status varieties to symbolize solidarity and group identity, values important to their users, which accounts for their persistence (Ryan 1979). From their systematic studies of patterns of code-shifting, linguists have arrived at a similar conclusion. For example, Blom and Gumperz (1972) suggest that two sets of norms, the standard and the dialectal, exist side by side in the Norwegian town of Hemnesberget because of their capacity to symbolize opposing sets of values — those of solidarity and local loyalty as opposed to the status-oriented and cosmopolitan. In many ways, Gal's recent study of a bilingual community in Austria provides a corollary to Blom and Gumperz's conclusions in showing how one of the two codes may disappear when the values it symbolizes cease to be important to its users (Gal 1978).

We therefore know in a general way *why* low status varieties persist, but are not yet in a position to answer the question posed by Labov (1972) with regard to Black English Vernacular, of *how* it manages to maintain itself in a consistent form over long periods of time. Although it is clear that low status norms are not codified and maintained by institutional means, the social mechanisms which *do* maintain them are not at all apparent.

In a recent study of the phonology of the low status urban vernacular of Belfast, this problem was considered (see Milroy, L. 1980 for a fuller account of the investigation).

The aim of the research was to produce an account, in as much detail as seemed reasonable, of patterns of variation within a single social class in three different communities in inner city Belfast. The fieldwork was carried out (during 1975-6) by means of a modified participant observation technique, and attention was focused on pre-existing social groups in each of the three areas. The data presented here are derived from extensive analyses of the language of forty-six working-class speakers. Both sexes are represented in this sample, and two age groups (18-25; 40-55) are considered.

Before describing procedures and presenting results, it is necessary to give a brief account of the general social characteristics and informal social organisation of the three communities. This is because one of the main analytic procedures discussed here depends on the notion of the individual's *personal network* structure — that is, the character of his informal social ties with those around him.

THE COMMUNITIES

The social structure of Belfast differs from that of many British and North American cities in that the possibilities of upward social mobility are very much more limited. The same group of people — the migrants, mostly Catholic, who came to the city in search of work during the late nineteenth and early twentieth centuries — has occupied the lowest status position for very many years, and has not been displaced by subsequent waves of immigrants. In this respect, Belfast is quite unlike most British industrial cities. Many investigators relate the persistent and notorious problems of ethnic conflict in the city to this immobility (see Boal 1978 for an influential and lucid account of the stability and persistence of patterns of segregation and conflict). It was therefore the language of pre-existing social groups in three *stable* poor working-class communities which was studied — Ballymacarrett (Protestant), the Clonard (Catholic) and the Hammer (Protestant). Ballymacarrett, arguably due to its location in the shipyard area at the centre of a heavy industrial complex, differed from the others in suffering very little from male unemployment. The Clonard (Catholic), and the Hammer (Protestant) suffered male unemployment rates of around 35 per cent. This distribution of male unemployment had a considerable effect on informal social relationships in the areas, as

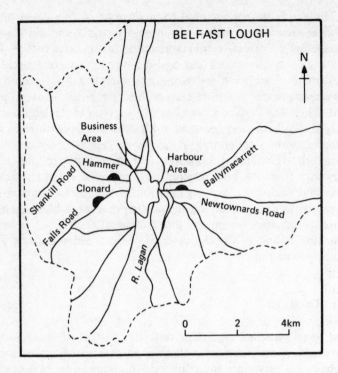

Ballymacarrett men tended to work locally and find their entertainment in local pubs and clubs, often interacting almost exclusively within narrow territorial boundaries. Women were much
more inclined to look for work outside the locality, and men's and
women's activities were sharply polarized. Although the same
patterns of social organization could be found in the Clonard and
the Hammer at a time when the traditional Ulster linen industry
provided local employment, this declining industry has for some
time been almost non-existent in the inner areas of Belfast. During
the research period, men from the Clonard and the Hammer were
travelling to different parts of the city in search of employment,
often shared domestic and child-care duties, and contrasted less
markedly than their Ballymacarrett counterparts with women in
their socialization habits. Despite these local differences, the
informal social structure of all three communities corresponded to
the dense, multiplex, often kin-based network patterns described
by many investigators as characteristic of stable working-class

communities, and particularly characteristic of areas like Ballymacarrett where men work together at a homogeneous and traditional form of employment (Young and Wilmott 1962; Fried 1973; Dennis, Henriques and Slaughter 1957). The communicative pattern which recurs in these accounts is one of people interacting mostly within a clearly defined territory, tending to know each others' social contacts (i.e. having relatively *dense* personal networks) and tending to be linked to each other by *multiplex* ties. This means that they are linked to each other in several capacities simultaneously — for example, as kin, neighbours and co-employees. Following Bott's arguments (Bott 1971), social anthropologists now generally agree that a social network of this dense multiplex type, which in effect constitutes a bounded group, has the capacity to impose general normative consensus on its members. This point is of general relevance to the reasoning used here. For the moment, it is worth recalling Labov's remarks on the capacity of closeknit peer groups to impose consensus on specifically *linguistic* norms upon their members (Labov 1972: 257).

Although this relatively dense, multiplex network structure could be found in all three Belfast working-class communities, in very sharp contrast to middle-class neighbourhoods, the extent to which *individuals* were linked to local networks varied considerably. Some people for example worked outside the area and had no local kin and no local ties of voluntary association, while others were linked to local networks in all these capacities. These differences in personal network structure, which appeared to be the result of many complex social and psychological factors, cut across categories of age, sex and locality. Predictably, much *individual* variation in language use could not be accounted for by grouping speakers into these categories, although they are certainly relevant to any account of sociolinguistic structure. The strongest vernacular speakers appeared however rather consistently to be those whose local network ties were strongest. This observation was treated as a hypothesis, and tested in the manner described in the following section.

LANGUAGE/NETWORK CORRELATIONS

An individual network score on a scale of 0-5 was calculated for each of the forty-six informants. This scale took account of the character of the individual's network ties in the sectors of work, kin, neighbourhood and voluntary association (see Cubitt 1973 for a discussion of the general importance of these particular network sectors). The score assigned to each individual provided a means of reflecting differences in multiplexity and density of personal networks without using corporate group constructs based on, for example, *status* as a means of differentiating individual speakers.

An informant's network score was calculated by assigning him one point for each of the following conditions he fulfilled:

1. Membership of a high density, territorially based cluster (i.e. any identifiable bounded group).
2. Having substantial ties of kinship in the neighbourhood. (More than one household, in addition to his own nuclear family.)
3. Working at the same place as at least *two* others from the same area.
4. The same place of work as at least two others of the same sex from the area.
5. Voluntary association with workmates in leisure hours. This applies in practice only when conditions three and four are satisfied.

Condition one is designed as an indicator of density, and reflects Cubitt's (1973) insistence on the importance of taking account of the density of specific clusters in considering networks (as we are here), as norm enforcement mechanisms. (A cluster is defined as a portion of a personal network where relationships are denser internally than externally.) The Jets, Cobras and T-Birds described by Labov (1972) form clusters; many of the young men in the Belfast communities belong to similar clusters; some of the middle-aged women belong to clusters of six or seven individuals who meet frequently to drink tea, play cards and chat. Some individuals on the other hand avoid association with any group of this kind.

Conditions two, three, four and five are all indicators of multiplexity; if they are all satisfied, the proportion of the individual's interactions which are with members of the local community is very high. Three and four are intended to reflect the particular capacity of an area of homogeneous employment to encourage the development of dense, multiplex networks; four also reflects the fact that polarization of the sexes usually occurs when there is a large number of solidary relationships in a specific neighbourhood.

It may appear at first sight that multiplex ties of the kind reflected in conditions three, four and five are usually contracted by men, and that men would, therefore, automatically score higher on the network strength scale. In fact, since both the Hammer and the Clonard are areas of high *male* unemployment, individual women frequently score as high as or higher than men.

The scale is capable of differentiating individuals quite sharply. Scores range from zero for someone who fulfils none of the conditions, (although a zero score is rare) to five for several informants who fulfil them all. Such individuals must be considered extremely closely integrated into the community in the sense that their kin, work and friendship ties are all contracted within it; additionally, they have formed particularly close ties with a corporate group (such as a football fans' club) or a less formal group based in the area. The defined territorial base associated with the kind of network structure which interests us here is reflected in conditions one and two. This is very important, for geographical mobility appears to have the capacity to destroy the structure of long established networks (Turner 1967; Young and Wilmott 1962).

It is important to emphasise that the network strength scale is designed fundamentally as a tool for measuring differences in an individual's level of integration into the local community. It is not claimed that this scale is the *only* means of doing so; for example attitudinal factors are likely also to be good indicators. However, the major advantage of the scale adopted here is that the indicators are based on an explicit set of procedures for analysing social relationships. Further, they can be observed directly and are subject to checking and verification (see Boissevain 1974 for a full account of network theory and Milroy L. 1980 for a discussion of its relevance to sociolinguistic method and theory).

Scores for each individual speaker on eight separate phonological variables were calculated (using the methods developed by Labov 1966) and a large number of rank order correlation tests carried out as a means of testing the hypothesis that network patterns were related to patterns of language use. When all subjects were considered together, significant results were obtained for five of the eight variables. This result appears to confirm the hypothesis that the strongest vernacular speakers are those whose network ties are strongest. Of those eight variables, only the five significant ones are considered here.

Before proceeding further, it is necessary to explain the relevant phonological features associated with these variables. This account is necessarily brief and partial; a fuller description of the complexities of this urban vernacular phonology can be found in Milroy J. (1981) and to a more limited extent in Milroy L. (1980) and Hughes and Trudgill (1979).

1. (a) Index scores are used, measuring degrees of retraction and back-raising in items of the /a/ class (e.g. *hat, man, grass*). A five point scale is used, ranging from one for tokens with [æ] to five for tokens with [ɔə]. Scores are based on 60-80 tokens per speaker.

2. (th) Percentage scores measure deletion of intervocalic [ð] in a small lexical set (e.g. *mother, brother*). Since the lexical distribution of this variable is limited, scores are based on only 856 tokens for all speakers — approximately 16-20 tokens per speaker.

3. (ʌ) Percentage scores measure frequency of the [ʌ] variant in a small lexical set which alternates between the /ʌ/ and /ʉ/ word-classes: e.g. *pull, shook, foot*. Altogether, 1500 tokens are considered. An account of this word class and its importance for theories of lexical diffusion and linguistic change can be found in J. Milroy (1980).

4. (ε¹) Percentage scores measure frequency of a low vowel [æ] (as opposed to a mid-vowel [εə] in items of the /ε/ class (*peck, bet, went, health*). This analysis is restricted to monosyllables closed by a voiceless stop, or by a voiceless obstruent preceded by a liquid or nasal.

5. (ε²) Percentage scores measure frequency of the same low vowel in di- and polysyllables.

The correlations between individual scores for these variables and individual network scores are presented in Table 1. This significant relationship between network structure and language use was further explored by dividing the informants into subgroups based on sex, age and area and again correlating linguistic scores with network scores. It is the results which emerged when the subgroups were divided according to age which are considered here.

Since N = 16 (maximum) in this second set of tests, significant results were less easily obtained than when N = 46, as previously.

Table 1. Correlations between network scores, and linguistic variable scores for all subjects. N refers to the number of subjects tested for a given variable

Variable	r	t	N	level of significance
(a)	0.529	3.692	37	$p < .01$
(th)	0.485	3.591	44	$p < .01$
(Λ)	0.317	2.142	43	$p < .05$
(ε^1)	0.255	1.709	44	$p < .05$
(ε^2)	0.321	2.200	44	$p < .05$

Where the N is so relatively small, therefore, significant results are likely to indicate a rather close relationship between network and linguistic variables.

In fact, it is only in Ballymacarrett that many phonological variables correlate significantly with personal network structure. Four of the eight give statistically significant results in Ballymacarrett, one in the Hammer and none in the Clonard (see Table 2 and footnote).

To interpret these results, it is necessary to refer back to the variant network patterns in the three communities. In Ballymacarrett *male* networks seemed more closeknit largely as a result of local employment and contrasted sharply with the relatively looseknit *female* network pattern. This contrast between the sexes was not apparent in other areas. A series of analysis of variance tests were carried out to check on significant differences in the distribution of *network* scores by age, sex and area (see Milroy L. 1980 for details). Although many significant differences and interactions emerged, the important result for our purposes here is that *only in Ballymacarrett* are male and female network scores significantly different (means = 3.9583: 1.3333). These may be compared with the Hammer (2.125: 1.875) and the Clonard (2.750: 2.875). Considered overall, network scores did not vary significantly simply according to area.

CONCLUSION

Pulling the threads of the argument together, we may infer from the overall correlations that personal network structure is of great

Table 2*. Correlations between network scores and linguistic variable scores calculated separately for three areas. B = Ballymacarrett, H = Hammer, C = Clonard

Variable		r	t	N	level of significance
(a)	B	0.930	8.360	13	p < .01
	C	0.345	2.287	15	p > .05
	H	−0.344	2.286	9	p > .05
(th)	B	0.816	4.679	13	p < .01
	C	0.011	0.039	15	p > .05
	H	0.346	1.379	16	p > .05
(ʌ)	B	0.426	1.560	13	p > .05
	C	−0.042	0.151	15	p > .05
	H	0.247	0.920	15	p > .05
(ε^1)	B	0.771	4.016	13	p < .01
	C	−0.118	−0.429	15	p > .05
	H	0.053	−0.199	16	p > .05
(ε^2	B	0.719	3.433	13	p < .01
	C	0.027	0.098	15	p > .05
	H	0.096	0.361	16	p > .05

*One further variable (I), showed a significant relationship to network scores only in the Hammer:
r = 0.528, t = 2.327, N = 16, p < .05.

importance in any attempt to describe patterns of language use. When a speaker belongs to a stable, low status community, a dense, multiplex personal network structure predicts relative closeness to vernacular norms. However, the *constraints* on the capacity of network structure to influence language use are equally important, for the relationship between language and network is not absolute. It exists in its most consistent form in the community where traditional differences between the socialization patterns of the sexes are maintained, with men contracting more closeknit localized ties than women. Thus, with regard to the social mechanisms which impel some speakers to use higher levels of the vernacular than others, we must conclude that the variables of sex and network structure work together in a complicated way. Any explanation of why there is a higher correlation between language and network in Ballymacarrett than in the other areas must take into account the network structures of both sexes as well as overall areal differences in network structure.

I would interpret these results from the perspective of socio-

linguistic theory by referring first to the widely accepted anthropological view that a closeknit network has the capacity to function
as a norm enforcement mechanism; there is no reason to suppose
that linguistic norms are exempted from this process. Moreover, a
closeknit network structure appears to be very common — some
would claim universal — in low status communities (Lomnitz
1977). This link between social status and personal network
structure, taken together with the correlations between language
and network reported here, begins to explain the complicated
social mechanisms which enable low status varieties to persist over
long periods of time despite counter-pressures of various kinds.
The closeknit network may be seen as an important social
mechanism of vernacular maintenance, capable of operating
effectively in opposition to a publicly endorsed and status-oriented
set of legitimized linguistic norms.

NOTE

This paper draws its data from research projects, HR3771 and HR5777, supported
by Social Science Research Council grants. The help of SSRC is gratefully
acknowledged here as is that of James Milroy, Rose Maclaran, Domini O'Kane and
Sue Margrain, who have worked on the Belfast projects.

REFERENCES

Blom, J.P. and J. Gumperz (1972) 'Social meaning in linguistic structures:
    codeswitching in Norway' in Gumperz and Hymes (eds.), 407-434.
Boal, F.W. (1978) 'Territoriality on the Shankhill-Falls divide, Belfast: the
    perspective from 1976', in Lanegran and Palm (eds.), 58-77.
Boissevain, J. (1974) *Friends of Friends: Networks, Manipulators and Coalitions*,
    Oxford, Blackwell.
Boissevain, J. and Mitchell, J.C. (eds.) (1973), *Network Analysis: Studies in Human
    Interaction*, The Hague, Mouton.
Bott, E. (1971) *Family and Social Network* (Rev. ed.), London, Tavistock.
Cubitt, T. (1973) 'Network density among urban families', in Boissevain and
    Mitchell (eds.), 67-82.
Dennis, N., Henriques, F.M. and Slaughter, C. (1957) *Coal is our Life*, London,
    Eyre and Spottiswood.
Fried, M. (1973) *The World of the Urban Working Class*, Cambridge Mass, Harvard
    University Press.
Gal, S. (1978) 'Variation and change in patterns of speaking: Language shift in
    Austria', in Sankoff (ed.), 227-238.
Giles, H. and St. Clair, R. (eds.) *Language and Social Psychology*, Oxford,
    Blackwell.

Gumperz, J. and Hymes, D. (1972) *Directions in Sociolinguistics*, New York, Holt Rinehart & Winston.

Haugen, E. (1972) *The Ecology of Language*, Stanford, Stanford University Press.

Hughes, A. and Trudgill, P. (1979) *English Accents and Dialects*, London, Arnold.

Labov, W. (1966) *The Social Stratification of English in New York City*, Washington, DC, Center for Applied Linguistics.

Labov, W. (1972) *Language in the Inner City*, Philadelphia, Penn. University Press.

Lanegran, D.A. and Palm, R. (eds.) (1978) *An Invitation to Geography*, (2nd ed.), New York, McGraw Hill.

Le Page, R.B. (1979) Review of Dell Hymes' *Foundations of Sociolinguistics* and Norbert Dittmar's *Sociolinguistics*, *Journal of Linguistics* 15, 168-179

Lomnitz, L.A. (1977) *Networks and Marginality*, New York, Academic Press.

Milroy, J. (1980) 'Lexical alternation and the history of English' in E. Traugott *et al* (eds.).

Milroy, J. (1981) *Regional Accents of English: Belfast*, Belfast, Blackstaff.

Milroy, L. (1980) *Language and Social Networks*, Oxford, Blackwell.

Ryan, E.B. (1979) 'Why do low prestige language varieties persist?' in Giles and St. Clair (eds.), 145-157.

Sankoff, D. (ed.) (1978) *Linguistic Variation: Models and Methods*, New York, Academic Press.

Traugott, E. *et al.* (eds.), *Papers from the 4th International Conference in Historical Linguistics*, Amsterdam, Benjamins.

Turner, C. (1967) 'Conjugal roles and social networks', *Human Relations*, 20, 121-130.

Young, M. and Wilmott, F. (1962) *Family and Kinship in East London*, Harmondsworth, Penguin.

2.4 White Adolescent Creole Users and the Politics of Friendship

ROGER HEWITT

There are two apparently contradictory assertions which are frequently made with regard to black British adolescents of Caribbean origin and creole language. One is that creole suffers from *low prestige* both within 'white British society' and also amongst black people themselves. Rosen and Burgess (1980) write: 'Dialect culture is almost entirely an oral culture and its status in the eyes of its users is rarely high'. This is also a major theme of Viv Edwards' (1979) book, *The West Indian Language Issue in British Schools*. The other assertion is that amongst black adolescents creole is employed as an 'instrument of identity'. Edwards notes that one 'possible explanation' of why creole forms persist in the language of West Indian children 'is a semi-conscious decision to preserve their separate identity.' The Select Committee on Race Relations and Immigration (1976) also reported in their 'Enquiry on the West Indian Community' that:

'It is often pointed out to us that sometime during their early teens at secondary school many West Indian pupils who up till then have used the language of the neighbourhood, begin to use creole dialect... Its use is a deliberate social and psychological protest, an assertion of identity.'

The second of these observations is often suppressed when ideas concerning multicultural provision are discussed. Hence the argument for a dialect component in multicultural education runs smoothly from noting the low prestige of creole to arguing for the use of creole dialect materials in schools to enhance the self-respect of pupils. A wider social usefulness is also sometimes claimed for creole in primary and secondary education:

Source: Hewitt, R. (1982) 'White adolescent creole users and the politics of friendship', *Journal of Multilingual and Multicultural Development*, 3 (3), pp. 217-32.

'... the using of linguistic diversity within the classroom ...
allows for the modifying of attitudes to language and to dialects
in ways which could be central to combat racism and prejudice
generally.' (Rosen and Burgess, 1980: 126).

Thus there are said to be two potential consequences for affording
to creole a place in educational institutional contexts:

(a) improving the prestige of creole amongst children,
    especially black children.
(b) combating racism.

Both of these motivations have been attacked from a radical perspective. Maureen Stone (1981), applying Bourdieu's cultural
analysis to the British situation, writes:

'In this analysis the personality characteristics and lifestyles
which are associated with cultural disadvantage or deprivation
would be defined as forms of "heretical culture" against which
the legitimate culture (through the schools) must defend itself.
One of the possible ways of defence may be to "legitimize" certain aspects of the heretical culture — thus, for example, the
incorporation of creole dialect into the curriculum might serve
this purpose.'

while in her suggestive unpublished paper, 'Multicultural Fictions',
Hazel Carby claims that —

'to assume that increased familiarity with dialect forms, by white
teachers, educationalists, and I include white authors of children's fiction, will change racist attitudes and consequently
racist social relationships is naive.'

She then makes the following quotation from a paper by Bruce
Boone:

'... it has become historically evident that a new linguistic-
cultural problematic is shaped when oppressed groups find
themselves under the necessity of speaking not only (or only
partly) their own language but the language of another
dominating group.'

I wish, for the time being, to step to one side of this debate and
to examine the second assertion which I mentioned at the outset,
that *unintegrated* observation to the effect that for many black
adolescents creole is a resource of identity and its use an assertion
of cultural difference.

The broad picture of creole use by children of Caribbean paren-
tage in this country is described in the Rampton Report (1981) in
the following terms:

> 'West Indian children in this country speak in a variety of ways.
> Some are able to speak creole, and use it on certain occasions;
> many, regardless of their island of origin, are developing what
> has been described as "Black British" or "British Jamaican".
> Other children speak mainly in standard English. Children orig-
> inating from St. Lucia and Dominica are sometimes able to
> understand French creole. A few are able to use several forms.
> Very few, apart from new arrivals, speak exclusively in creole.'

In London the most widely used creole form employed by children
born here is 'British Jamaican', more commonly called 'London
Jamaican', and it is the development of this dialect, within the context of a black youth culture, that is particularly relevant to the
question of the 'assertion of identity'. An understanding of the
wider development of black youth culture is important in assessing
the meanings of creole language used by the second and subsequent generations.

BLACK BRITISH YOUTH CULTURE

Black adolescents show a highly differentiated set of orientations
both towards the dominant white cultures and towards West
Indian/black British youth culture. Differences in age, gender,
social class, neighbourhood and parents' provenance all exert an
influence on the construction of black adolescent social identities
and in many cases the role of visible youth cultures is minimal. It is
clear, nevertheless, that the location of social identity can be a
complex matter for many young black people, and black culture,
its music, styles of dress and ambivalent relationship to the Rastafarian religion, provides one kind of support within a structure of
often contradictory elements. Many therefore position themselves

in some kind of relation to it.

Unsurprisingly this ethnic youth culture is undergoing constant change as influences from the West Indies, black America, and indigenous black British cultural products, are combined into the definition. A corollary of this is that its social and political meaning is not as uniform as is sometimes suggested. As a set of practices and symbolisms it displays a number of contrary perceptions of the relations 'black youth' have to other social groups. The culture is an amalgam of sometimes conflicting ideological strands obscured beneath an ambivalent imagery. One such strand — and a key concept in the development of black youth culture — was the concept of 'dread' which was derived from the Rastafarian religion where it is a term of esteem. Amongst Rastafarians it continues to have this meaning but amongst many young people it came to be used with cultural rather than religious overtones. To be truly 'dread', in this cultural sense, was to be especially worthy of respect as an initiate of an essential black Jamaican cultural mystery, the indicators of which were a commitment to reggae music rather than American 'soul' music, the use of creole as a primary mode of discourse, and an assiduously maintained separation from intercourse with white people. In this form it represented a strong statement of cultural separatism and a deliberate avoidance of contamination by white values. This 'ideal' definition was in practice hedged in and transected by other strands in the developing culture but it was, and to some extent continues to be, influential.

Close involvement with white society contradicts the ideal definition of 'dread'. For many the balance between success in a society where the conditions of economic life are governed by white people, and the need — in peer group contexts — to maintain an identity related to the concept of 'dread' is an uneasy one. The concept has become much less central since the end of the 1970s and the word now often carries a more general meaning that may simply be equated with 'good'. It thus remains for generations growing into the culture an ideological resource but one submerged beneath the surface of cultural life and open to distortions. It is significant for this discussion, however, that during the 1970s, the developing creole of black youth came to be referred to as 'dread talk' and the same ambiguity that applies to maintaining an identity constructed in relation to the concept of 'dread' can also be seen in expressions of attitude to creole use.

While wishing to speak creole, adolescents understand the

reasons why their parents often discourage their use of it. They understand the arguments that too habitual a use of creole might affect their written English and that this in turn might affect employment prospects. It is also frequently observed that those black adolescents who are regularly in trouble with the police speak creole almost exclusively when they are together:

C.A.:
(male, 16 years old)

I think my mum, in a way, thinks I shouldn't be speaking it because she thinks it's a bad influence on me. But as I get older, I go my own way; I meet a lot of black kids and start speaking it to them. And I come home sometimes and just have a little thing with my dad and she thinks I might go my own different way, end up in bad company. 'Cos a lot of black boys, when they're in trouble, all you hear them talk is dread. Nothing else, and you can here them say, "De Babylon come", an' all that, and, you know, their whole attitude change towards the whites.... And my mum thinks it might be bad for me, that I might pack up my lessons and turn bad. That's why she thinks I shouldn't speak it so much.

R.H.: What do *you* think?

C.A.: Well, I think if I can ... if I don't let it go to my head it's all right. If it starts to involve my school work and I fall behind, then I'll think again.

However, there is a social and cultural demand by black youth that influences adolescents towards creole use:

R.H.: But you enjoy talking creole?

C.A.: Yes. 'Cos I feel ... sounds funny ... I feel black and I'm proud of it, to speak like that. That's why, when I talk it, I feel better than when I'm talking like now. You know what I mean? ... When I speak more dread I feel more lively and more aware. In a way I feel I'm more happier.

| R.H.: | Do you reckon you speak it more now than you used to? |
| C.A.: | Yes. *Much* more. 'Cos, sounds funny but, I just kind of feel that as a black I should speak it and I feel that now if I'm ... say I'm walking the street and a black man goes to me, "Dread, d'you have the time", if I turn round and say. "No. Sorry, I haven't got the time." I'm gonna sound funny. So I go, "No, man, mi na got de time. Sorry Dread." That's the way it is. And sometimes you just look at someone and you know you've got to speak it. You'd feel a right idiot if you went up to a Rasta and said, "Excuse me have you got the time?" He's gonna think, "No man, you na black." That's it. So you have to speak (their? your?) own language. |

This informant, like many others, has to balance his own pleasure at speaking creole and the group expectation that as a young black he *should* speak it, with his mother's representations of the economic and social demands of white society. Mothers rather than fathers frequently feature in reports of parental pressure on this issue. This does not always mean that fathers are not concerned, however. It represents the role of the mother as the parent most involved with the children's upbringing. Fathers do nevertheless, often permit sons to use creole to them as here with 'I just have a little thing with my dad'. The same licence does not usually extend to daughters.

The equation made here between 'dread talk' and conflict with the police and with educational aims as expressed in school life — the hard and soft faces of state authority — suggests that *one* of the uses of 'London Jamaican' is as a language of opposition, the dialect in which the registers of resistance may be most properly employed. The parental view of this dimension, refracted here through the boy's perception, indicates something of the concern many black parents feel about the terms in which 'success' is posed for their children and the fact that black adolescents have re-invested creole with an oppositional meaning. However, a 'generation gap' is, itself, part of the new dialect. 'London Jamaican' lacks many of the Jamaican parent forms. Rural idioms are shed and new items are generated exclusively with a metropolitan urban context. There is a high turn-over of new words and expressions and a high level of innovation. (These observations are not the result of any systematic study of the speech of black adolescents but are based on my own casual observations in the field, interviews with adolescents and conversations with teachers and youth workers.) Much of this linguistic growth is independent of the speech of parents and, despite parental reservations concerning its low prestige in the wider community, it has established itself amongst young people as a prestigious symbol of group solidarity, even where personal skill with it is limited.

Thus the situation with 'London Jamaican' is similar to that described by Labov (1972) in his accounts of the Black English Vernacular of pre-adolescents in New York, to Ramirez' (1974) comments with regard to the use of Chicano dialect of Spanish by adolescents, Ryan's (1979) evidence concerning Mexican American non-standard English, and other cases. It is certainly consistent with Lesley Milroy's (1980) view that:

'instead of positing a sociolinguistic continuum with a local vernacular at the bottom and a prestige dialect at the top, with linguistic movement of individuals in a generally upward direction, we may view the vernacular as a positive force; it may be in direct conflict with standardised norms, utilized as a symbol by speakers to carry powerful social meanings and so resistent to external pressures.'

In this sense, therefore, many black adolescents have made their own 'provision' for improving their prestige and that of their dialect within the contexts that are most meaningful for them and in relation to the power structures in which they see themselves embedded. Indeed such is the prestige and 'street credibility' of this dialect that in recent years it has even attracted children of other ethnic groups. Cases of Turkish and Greek children using creole forms are not uncommon and Asian boys have been known to adopt the blazonry of black youth culture in dress, employing 'London Jamaican' in speech. However, the most notable trend has been the acquisition of creole by white British working-class children, as an additional linguistic skill, and it is in the context of this that some of the most significant social meanings of creole language use by black adolescents are disclosed. (In order to forestall any misuses of this research I wish to make it clear that in no way does the use of creole by white adolescents constitute a misdirection of language skills. These skills are developed *in addition to* normal speaking and writing skills.)

WHITE ADOLESCENT CREOLE USERS

An increasing number of white adolescents experiment with the creole they hear spoken by their black friends. This experimentation varies from the acquisition of a few words and phrases to a usage at least as fluent as that of their black peers. Through the use of creole forms by white working-class children an attempt is made to mediate cultural difference, and there is evidence that the processes of social adjustment involved in negotiating contexts of black/white creole use are themselves instrumental in shaping friendship.

Along the borderline of ethnicity the use of creole by white adolescents and its points of success and failure are particularly illuminating when viewed in synchronisation with the cultural strategies of black adolescents. The interface of these mutual experiments provides a social laboratory within which the play of personal and social elements can be observed in the minutiae of everyday speech. In engaging in this linguistic exchange, however tentatively, adolescents are involving themselves in a semiotic which is intelligible only by reference to relations between social groups.

It is unnecessary for the purposes of this paper to describe white creole use in detail. However, a brief sketch may be useful before considering the interactive aspects.

White creole users can be divided into those who employ creole 'seriously' as part of normal conversation with their black peers, and those who use it 'jokingly', 'just mucking about', in playful ways — as indeed do some black youngsters. (This distinction has been made by numerous informants. It is clearly unsuitable for analytical purposes but is, I believe, useful to an initial description of this kind.) Those who use it 'jokingly' are unable or unwilling, for a number of reasons, to use it as part of serious discourse. Those who use it 'seriously' have, in most cases I have so far investigated, been those who learned some creole at primary school age. Most, but not all, come from areas of fairly dense immigrant settlement and all have a high proportion of close black friends within and without school. Those who only speak it 'jokingly' tend to have come to use creole at secondary school age, although some maintain that they were aware of it being spoken by black children at primary school. This 'joking' use of creole is sometimes limited to a few words and phrases, sometimes extended to full sentences. Despite the lexical limitations of those whose creole use is restricted to play, the problems which these limitations give rise to and reflect are frequently more socially illuminating than the successes of the most fluent white creole speakers.

The most fluent white creole speakers have often started to speak creole in a way similar to those who can only use it in play; they did so, however, at a much earlier age and their acquisition seems to have been almost involuntary. In several interviews informants describe the surprise they experienced when they first uttered creole words. 'It just came out,' they say. Such involuntary use can be nurtured at an early age in numerous 'street' contexts and, as the children grow older, these skills are added to, paralleling the increasing creole use of their black peers over the same period. Thus by the time they are about fourteen to fifteen years old they may be making matter-of-fact statements to their black friends like, 'Mi a go blango' (*I am going for a smoke*) with no suggestion of humour or of using the language self-consciously as an external entity that is part of playful interaction. Their use is 'serious', part of normal conversation, and not done for display purposes.

The jocular use of creole is a primary linguistic and social means through which black and white cultural differences are mediated in friendship across all levels of skill. This use includes uttering creole in the classroom and other contexts where teachers or other third parties are excluded; using creole abuse terms to the uninitiated thereby taking up an identification with black friends to share an 'us versus them' feeling; talk about members of the opposite sex, and formalised abuse. Any use of creole *can* signify acceptance of black friends and the desire to be accepted. In jocular uses the language is often treated as something external to the natural discourse of both parties, almost as a toy might be used, except that in this case the toy is constituted by a social relation and held at a distance for safety. Where the content is free from social connotations the social dimension may not be immediately in evidence:

White boy: Oh, Royston, ya goin' football on Saturday?
Black boy: Mi na go football! Who for?
White boy: Check some gyal later.
Black boy: Na. Mi na wan check gyal now.
White boy: Rassclaht! Fink ya bent.

Both boys here were using strong Jamaican pronunciation and the white boy was almost indistinguishable from the black boy, except for the substitution of the cockney 'f' for the creole 't' in 'fink ya bent'.

Less easy to quote out of context are the phatic and scatological utterances which also pepper exchanges between black and white adolescents in competitive contexts such as sport or in classroom banter. The following are all exchanges between close friends.

Black boy (to white boy):   Come, come fe a kickin na ya bloodclaht!
White girl (to black girl):   Wa'appen to you chile? Cat bit you?
White girl (to black girl):   Go piss off, ya bahty!
White boy (to black boy):   Check me some o' ya fag, bahtyman!
White boy (to black boy):   Shut ya bambaclaht!

As in all such banter the abuse rests on a solid foundation of pre-established friendship and the extremity of the abuse is often in inverse proportion to the closeness of the friendship — indeed, paradoxically, it can even serve to deepen friendship.

Those who use creole forms seriously with their black friends may only use the odd word incorporated within standard cockney syntax or may converse naturally and at length in creole. Their use of creole may constitute a friendly 'chipping in' in conformity with the linguistic norms of adolescent neighbourhood life or they may use the dialect strategically to gain acceptance by a group or an individual.

In the following instance a thirteen-year-old white girl is playing a Space Invaders machine in a south London youth club. She has discovered that the machine is faulty and will allow her to play endlessly without her having to put money in. A group of black boys of about her own age crowd round the machine and attempt to make deals with her as to when they can have a turn. They com-

plain that she has been too long at the machine. One boy begins
the sentence —

    'By the time half-past nine come ...'   (i.e. 'comes')

The girl quickly interrupts —

    'Half past nine *come*!'   (i.e. 'has come')

She continues to play and the boys settle down subdued by her
determination. With eyes fixed on the screen as she plays, she asks
the boy who had spoken:

    'Have you heard the school band? I'm in it. I play drums and I
    toast!'

'Toasting' is the name given to the improvised singing and talking
which black 'sound system' operators do over 'dub' reggae records.
It is only done in creole and good toasters are well respected. The
girl is, therefore, making a large claim about her familiarity with
creole and with black youth culture. The boy, already feeling badly
disposed towards her, replies:

    'The only thing you could toast is bread.'

The girl makes no comment but, as she continues to play, registers
each set-back and loss in the game by using creole expletives:

    'Ratid!'
    'Bambaclaht!'
    'Rass!'

She also fights off one attempt to usurp her position at the machine
with,

    'Try it, bwai!'

Throughout this exchange the girl was obviously eager to establish
her credentials as an initiate of black culture. She did not know the
boy well and her first attempt was in the *content* of what she said
— her claim to be able to toast. She spoke, however, in standard
English. When her claim was derided she continued her attempt

linguistically by adopting creole forms. These were not used with direct communicative intent — which could have provoked a rebuttal — but were exclamations for display purposes and were guaranteed in context by her obvious exasperation at the game.

Her apparent confidence in this strategy was related to the fact that she had a number of close black friends with whom she intermittently used creole forms and was a well-accepted follower of black youth culture within her primary (mainly black) peer group. None of her close friends was present during this exchange, however, and the situation was further complicated by the factor of gender. In the first instance she had refused to relinquish the game and was determinedly playing in the face of strong, albeit plaintive, opposition. She then assumed that the boys' continued attendance represented an acceptance of her control and an interest in the game *she* was playing. At this point she made her attempt to establish herself as an initiate of black culture. Her claim to toast was probably elaborated from some limited experience in school. Made in this context her boast was obviously misjudged and provoked not admiration but a derisive rejection — 'the only thing you could toast is bread'. Her difficulty arose partly because she was attempting *two* socially provocative manoeuvres, and it became evident that both the position of control of the machine which she sought to maintain, and the cultural identity she hoped to establish, could not be achieved across cultural *and* sexual borders. She therefore forsook her gender role and adopted an essentially *male stance* in order to underwrite both manoeuvres simultaneously. This she did by her use of swear words, not directed at the group of boys but plainly employed for their audition. The strategy went beyond any customary female role — even the 'facety' (cheeky) stance sometimes adopted by black girls in their dealing with boys. By adopting the language and posture of an older black boy she combined two strategies, one on behalf of her gender in defence of her control of the game, the other on behalf of the cultural identity she wished to establish. The defiant, 'Try it, bwai', displayed a contempt written into the role itself, which pre-empted both the position of 'young male' and that of 'young black' that might have been marshalled against her by any of the boys. It proved a powerful combination. Her 'bluff' was not called and she continued to play. Such self-conscious and strategic use of creole is in contrast to her totally spontaneous use of 'come' in 'Half past nine come!' at the outset. Here her use of the creole form was clearly without ulterior purpose and, judging by her language in other contexts, may well have become natural to her regardless of her interlocutor.

This encounter displays four important elements in the social practice of white creole use: (1) the linguistic norms of neighbourhood culture; (2) the attempt to extend white creole use beyond the friendship base; (3) the employment of language as an interactive strategy; and (4) the defence of black culture from outside incursions. The last of these is vital in situating the other three. It is to this, therefore, that I now turn.

REACTIONS

The use of creole by black adolescents is arguably the strongest single marker of black youth culture and it is consistently present throughout the different forms assumed by that culture. As such its use by whites is a potentially sensitive practice. The acquisition and use of creole by white adolescents requires the participation and encouragement of their black peers and yet the most commonly expressed attitude of black youngsters to the idea of white creole speakers is one of hostility. The following statements are very typical of black attitudes to white creole use:

'They should stick to their own culture and not try to impersonate no one else.' (Black boy, 15 years old)

'I think they're taking the mickey.' (Black boy, 16 years old)

'It seems they are stealing our language.' (Black boy, 15 years old)

'The Rastas round our way say it's our identity. They identify their speech with their colour and their actual cult. And they say that somebody is trying to intervene if they copy their ways.' (Black girl, 16 years old)

'When I hear white girls talking like that it's poison to my ears.' (Black girl, 17 years old)

Such statements represent a very specific kind of 'boundary maintenance' that is a materially situated expression of the social and economic relationships between the black sector of the subordinate class and the white community. They also form part of a collective ideology that is born out of past and present struggles over meaning. Throughout expressions of this kind two major themes are readily discernible: one in which creole use by whites is taken as *derisive parody* and hence an assertion of *white superiority*: the other in which it is interpreted as a further white appropriation of one of the sources of *power* — 'it seems they are stealing our language.'

Suspicions concerning these meanings are inscribed within the hostility which creole use by whites often produces. The first suspicion relates to the consequences of an unbroken history of exploitation and its legitimations articulated in numerous forms throughout the dominant ideology; the second relates to white responses to black aimed at claiming an area of cultural space in which oppositional stances may be adopted. Both are to be found amongst the multiple strands of black youth culture and are activated within specific social contexts.

Given these elements within black group ideology, how is it possible that white adolescents manage to acquire the creole language skills which can only be developed interactively? Quite simply there is often a discontinuity between collective ideology and individual practice. The same children who verbally condemn creole use by whites may themselves have close white friends whom they tolerate or even encourage in its use. Notably in group discussions, white creole speech will be roundly criticised even by those who permit it in interactive contexts. While group consciousness dictates the exclusion of whites from this key area of ethnic identification, in the privacy of close friendship it is both accepted and engaged in as a badge of closeness and an instrument of friendship.

That this particular means of friendship promotion is chosen is not accidental. It is precisely because creole is the linguistic expression of a structural relationship between social groups that it can be employed, within carefully annexed areas, to 'stand for' the community whose language it is, and for the meaning system engendered by the structural relationship. Thus between close black and white friends, the use of creole by the white friend is treated as a kind of 'dumb show' or pre-figuring of intended relations between that individual and the wider black collectivity: it is the substitution of a relation to language for the more complex

relation to the black community. By temporarily freeing themselves from the constraints of their respective groups, the friends
can achieve in language a *fictive social relation over and above
their relation of friendship.* The cultural context of the friendship is
established through a mutual 'willing suspension' of belief in the
ethnic boundaries which are treated as external to the friendship.

Whilst it is inevitably rare to find informants able to reflect on
this dimension of inter-ethnic friendship formation, the following
extracts from an interview with a seventeen-year-old white boy,
Steve, who had ceased to use creole, may be illustrative. The
informant is looking back on the period during which he employed
creole. From the age of eight he had had a close black friend called
Johnny. When he first entered secondary school the number of his
black friends increased and this initiated an identification with
black culture:

> 'I started going round with black kids when I was eleven and
> then I got this thing in me about being black in a white person's
> body. Then all me friends used to speak patois and I just kind of
> picked it up.'

His primary source of information with regard to the dialect was
Johnny. He explained that they would go to black parties together
and Johnny would answer his questions about the language that he
heard:

> 'When you're a young kid you ask your parents, "What does
> that mean? What does that mean?" Well, I was asking Johnny.'

> 'My friend Johnny, he really used to like to tell me about these
> things, about what they all mean ...'

At this time, he explained, he also fabricated for himself false ethnic credentials:

> 'I went around saying I was born in Jamaica, my grandmother
> was a half-caste woman and all things like that'.

Indeed he did his best to assume the position of a young black
male:

'I used to suck my teeth but I wouldn't dream of doing that now.'

By seventeen he had come to regard this period of his life as an immature 'stage' of his early adolescence, conducted with Johnny's complicity because Johnny too was 'going through a phase':

'At this time we was both young — we were exactly the same age — so we were both going through the same thing. Probably thought it was cool for me to speak it ... but we both got older.'

He explained the end of this period in the following way:

'See, at that time I was about the only white boy on that particular scene. Then, when I got to the age of about fifteen, sixteen, more white boys started coming round with us and Johnny used to say to me, "When you hear them speak, you never hear them speak patois". He used to say, "They're cool. They don't try and copy." And then I decided maybe it was stupid, you know? That's when I started coming out this stage. It was when he kind of turned the tables and said, "Well, you sound stupid, a white person speaking patois."'

Most dyadic friendships of this kind do not involve such a radical reconstruction as to include a fictitious ancestry, but the element of private conspiracy from which wider creole use is generated is very common. Where the friendship base of creole speech extends firmly beyond a dyad, the edifice of social identity may be both constructed by a slightly different process and dismantled — where it is — in more complex ways. Nevertheless what is true here for dyadic friendships is also often true for whites within constellations of black friends which have gradually become part of such 'conspiracies'. There is, in such cases, a *core group* which functions as does the single close black friend in dyadic relationships. Such an extension of the dyad is inevitably more flexible but the underlying principle of a conspiracy — free from wider group pressure — within which fictive social relationships are achieved through the use of creole, remains the same.

The structural social positions assumed within this strategy are essentially *stances within the value system* and can effect a resistence to the racism pervasive in white culture. The constructed social identity fails to provide a site on which racist ideology is reproduced, and instead the 'fictive social relation' recasts the relation to racist practice:

Steve: 'I think if you've known a black person, I don't know what it is but you just get into it. And they talk about their problems, things like National Front, things like that, and you feel that it's wrong as well, so you start calling them all the things that they call them. So you class yourself ... When you see a National Front march and people calling black people "niggers" and things like that, it hurts you as well, 'cos they're hurting your friends.'

Such articulations are not uncommon for white creole speakers. In another interview, a fifteen-year-old creole-speaking white boy states clearly a view of the press coverage of race issues which displays a keen perception of the ideological structuring of media presentation, albeit in starkly simple terms:

'When a black person mugs someone the papers give more publicity to that. If a white person mugs someone they think, "Oh, he's a white person, he's mugged someone, don't worry about that." Where's if a black person mugs someone, they think, "We'll put that in the paper. Make white people hate blacks more."'

Here the same social subjectivity for which creole is the appropriate dialect becomes simultaneously the site of a critical penetration of the racist ideology of the dominant culture. The survival of these positions is not, however, a simple matter.

Paradoxically the social identities constructed by whites from the oppositional ideology of the black community, are themselves subjected to the limitations imposed by black group closure, as well as by responses from other whites, so that, in order to survive, they are in constant process of re-assessment, refinement and modification. The borderline of close friendship and wider group acceptance is re-encountered incessantly in the contexts of friendship interaction. Creole use is frequently the subject of reassessments but the semiotic of language use may be equally replaced by that of clothing, as the following interview exchange displays. The interview is with two close friends, a white girl (fifteen years old) and a black girl (also fifteen).

White girl: Some black girls do reject me. When they see me in all nice clothes, reggae clothes, and they haven't got them they say, "What is she wearing them clothes for?"

Her black friend explained: There are lots of white girls round our way with black friends but that's recently. They've only recently come into the black thing and got more into it. But *she's* grown up with it and people can't seem to see that.

This complex, formed by the interplay between the parturition of social identity within friendship and black group closure, provides the ground on which the rules of wider creole use by whites are formed. The contexts in which white adolescents can use creole are limited by these informal rules.

White adolescents may speak creole freely with their close black friends but where they are in the company of black adolescents who they do not know they will not speak it until the friendship is established to such a point that they can feel confident about not provoking hostility by using it. Failure to be sensitive to the issues which inform this hostility can lead to serious consequences for the white speaker; fighting has been reported to me as one consequence of this failure of judgement.

Where a white speaker is with black friends and they are joined by one or more black friends who are unknown to the white speaker, the informal rule is that the white speaker will refrain from using creole. "I would know not to use it," as one informant expressed it. The contexts of friendship and trust need to be created prior to the use of creole, or at least gradually, stage by stage. Each extension of context has to be earned. Creole use cannot automatically signal friendliness, and the only cases that have been reported to me of white adolescents using creole to unknown black adolescents — even where such use was intended in a friendly way — have resulted in the provocation of hostility. Knowing the rules, and being sensitive to the possible interpretations that may be placed by black adolescents on white creole use, is clearly part of learning the language. Herein lies an implicit recognition that creole use is a social act with social meanings.

The shifting surfaces of individual and group interaction reflected in these contextual rules tend to filter social attitudes and sensitivity to the issues affecting black people rather than any cultural or linguistic facility. Those children who are most competent at handling the rules are likely to be those who from an early age have successfully avoided the racism inherent in the dominant culture. Their success is not a result of their ability in dialect but their ability is a mark of their avoidance of racism. Conversely those who fail to observe the rules correctly may do so because they have not sufficiently understood the full social dimension of their situation. Their failure with the rules signals a failure of their understanding of racism and its implications for personal interaction.

There is, of course, no 'final stage' for the white creole user, no point at which his/her use of creole is no longer a matter for reassessment — although beyond a certain point of integration it is called into question less frequently. Creole use may signal certain positions but it cannot represent a faultless *guarantee*:

> As I see it, if a person's willing to pick up black people's language and speak it out with us we wouldn't think they're racist, but we don't know. Outward approach we'd think, no, they're not, but it depends. You don't *know*. I've known quite a few incidents with people we'd thought were friends, so you don't know by that. You can't tell by that. (Black girl, 15 years old)

Despite the interactive complexities, it is clear that between friends the use of a relation to creole as a fictive social relation can assist friendships to process the political and ideological discontinuities between the groups to which they belong. This, furthermore, provides such white working-class adolescents with a critical instrument for the construction of social identities in which racist ideology fails to reproduce itself. Thus at 'street level' within the racially mixed community both dominant ideology and dominant linguistic norms may be together neutralised in small social pockets and under notably sensitive conditions. Given the interactive delicacy in which such results are achieved, the class positions of those who engage in these linguistic and social manoeuvres, and the oppositional content of the creole whose prestige is therein established, the educational multiculturalist's aims with which we began would seem to be, at best, optimistic.

The multiculturalist's expectations regarding the results of using dialect materials in school can only be maintained in isolation from the facts of creole use by adolescents in real situations. As Hazel Carby (n.d.) points out:

'Much work on non-indigenous dialect usage by racial and ethnic groups has followed that of William Labov in attempting to establish the credentials of dialect: to insist upon its effectivity for communication and to counter accusations of 'poor speech' reflective of 'poor ability'. This emphasis, necessary to counter linguistic fallacies, has had an unfortunate consequence in the concentration upon language as a system separate from its social activity and the construction of meanings.'

Given the fact that creole is *in practice* treated as a prestigious dialect by many black adolescents and one within which are encoded intuitions regarding their need for maintaining a value system alternative to that provided by official, and predominantly white, authorities, its use in schools, regardless of 'good intentions', runs the risk of being taken as an attempt to neutralise a linguistic and cultural challenge. Even with respect to those black adolescents who do not articulate to themselves the oppositional meaning of creole dialect, to suggest that initiatives by the school can achieve any significant improvement in the prestige of dialect in relation to standard *within the dominant value system* with which children deal in school, could be construed as cruelly misleading while the social relations which are described by the stratification of language remain. As Halliday (1978) puts it:

'social dialects ... are both a direct manifestation of social hierarchy and also a symbolic expression of it, maintaining and reinforcing it in a variety of ways: for example, the association of dialect with register — the fact that certain registers conventionally call for certain dialectal modes — expresses the relation between social classes and the division of labour.'

With regard to that other putative object of creole dialect use within schools — the combating of racism — I believe it is clear from the materials presented in this paper that this, no less than language use, is a structural matter concerning ideological positions. The fragile successes in overcoming racism through complex, community based, cultural interactions are sadly ghettoised by the inevitable relationships between social groups with antagonistic objectives, caught in a long history of exploitation. Beore looking to simplistic solutions, schools should first examine *their* roles within this process.

None of this is to argue, however, that teachers should not be equipped with the best means to help children achieve their academic goals. Clearly teachers should have sufficient knowledge of the creole forms relevant to any 'interference' displayed in children's attempts at writing standard English. It may also be the case that, as part of oral English work, dialect materials of all sorts might be employed with sensitivity as a means of encouraging some feel for a variety of registers and a relish for the effective use of language. Children should be exposed to 'good talkers' as much as to 'good writers', but the object of these activities can only be to allow children to advance in those language skills which it is the business of the school to teach and for which they and their parents have every right to hope. To pretend to go beyond this is to attempt a misplaced version of that 'fictive social relationship' which some children so tentatively build.

NOTE

This paper draws on research which I am conducting within the Sociological Research Unit, University of London Institute of Education. I began work in this area in 1979 whilst employed as an English teacher in an Inner London secondary school. To gain access to other contexts of creole use by white adolescents I then also worked in a number of racially mixed South London youth clubs. From these bases I was both able to observe interactions and to gain further contacts for the purpose of interviewing and making recordings of spontaneous speech. The research is now funded by the Nuffield Foundation.

REFERENCES

Carby, Hazel V. (n.d.) 'Multicultural Fictions', Centre for Contemporary Cultural Studies, Birmingham, Stencilled Occasional Paper No. 58.
Edwards, V.K. (1979) *The West Indian Language Issue in British Schools, Challenges and Responses*, Routledge and Kegan Paul, London, 66.
Halliday, M.A.K. (1978) *Language as Social Semiotic*, Edward Arnold, London, 113-14
Labov, William (1972) *Language in the Inner City; Studies in Black English*

Vernacular, University of Pennsylvania Press, Philadelphia.

Milroy, Lesley (1980) *Language and Social Networks*, Basil Blackwell, Oxford 1.

Ramirez, K.G. (1974) 'Socio-cultural aspects of the Chicano dialect', in G.D. Bills (ed) *Southwest Areal Linguistics*, Institute for Cultural Pluralism, California.

Rampton Report (1981) *West Indian Children in Our Schools. Interim Report of the Committee of Inquiry into the Education of Children from Ethnic Minority Groups*, June 1981, HMSO, 22.

Rosen, Harold and Burgess, Tony (1980) *Languages and Dialects of London School Children*, Ward Lock Educational, London, 108.

Ryan, E.B. (1979) 'Why do low-prestige language varieties persist?' in Howard Giles and Robert St. Clair (eds) *Language and Social Psychology*, Basil Blackwell, Oxford.

Select Committee on Race Relations and Immigration (1976) *Evidence on Education from the Community Relations Commission*, November 1976, 5.

Stone, Maureen (1981) *The Education of the Black Child in Britain, The Myth of Multiracial Education*, Fontana Paperbacks, 33.

2.5 Women in Their Speech Communities

PATRICIA C. NICHOLS

Many words have been spent on the subject of "women's speech." Perhaps because women are so readily identifiable as a group it is assumed that women speak as a group. Women's experiences have much in common throughout the world, to be sure. And it is possible that we may identify certain common patterns in women's lives and in women's speech. But women are members first and foremost of their own small speech communities, and it is in the daily context of their lives, as speaking members of a larger group that their language must be examined. Without this contextual grounding, we are doomed to repeat the stereotypic nonsense of past generations about the language use of women.

What is a *speech community*? It is not necessarily the same as a political entity or an ethnic grouping. It is defined by the shared communicative process of a group, whose members may or may not have frequent face-to-face contact with each other. One definition which has been offered is: "a community sharing rules for the conduct and interpretation of speech, and rules for the interpretation of at least one linguistic variety."[1] It is not enough to speak the same language or dialect; the rules of use must be shared also. Two English speakers may utter the same string of words; one may mean the string to be interpreted as a command, while the other may understand it as a simple statement of fact. On the other hand, speakers may share rules for use, but speak entirely different languages. Certain countries of eastern Europe, for example, are said to share norms for greetings, topics of conversations, and the conduct of conversations, although different languages are spoken. In the working definition of *speech community* used here, both the language variety and the norms for its use must be shared by all members of the community, though it is

Source: Nichols, P.C. 'Women in their speech communities', Chapter 9 in McConnell-Ginet, S., Borker, R. and Furman, N. (eds), *Women and Language in Literature and Society*, New York, Praeger, pp. 140-9.

not necessary that they all speak the same in similar speech situations.

A major new approach to the study of language and sex has recently developed within the discipline of linguistics. Variously called *sociolinguistics* or the *sociology of language*, this paradigm recognizes language variability as playing an essential role in language change. An early conference defined the task of the sociolinguist thus: "to show the systematic covariance of linguistic structure and social structure — and perhaps even to show a causal relationship in one direction or the other."[2] The sociolinguistic tradition has from the beginning taken linguistic diversity to be a subject worthy of study, in and of itself. Variable language use is taken to be a potential source of insight about processes of language change, rather than in need of "regularizing" or simply a matter of "performance" and thereby unworthy of study. Using data from spoken language, often recorded by electronic means, contemporary sociolinguists study the language varieties used by several social groups within a larger speech community. Often the variable language use of a single speaker in different speech situations or styles is studied as well.

The growing body of studies on the language use of women in a variety of settings and cultural groups provides convincing evidence that differences will exist in the speech of men and women in every social group.[3] From other perspectives, sociologists and anthropologists have observed that men and women have different roles and life experiences within their social groups all over the world, though these experiences and roles may differ from society to society. Dell Hymes, from his long-standing concern with language in use, has pointed out that differences in the social situations which are available to some speakers, and not to others, lead inevitably to inequality among speakers.[4] Simply to document that men and women speak differently in every known society, while an important starting point, is not enough, however. We need now to formulate hypotheses about the connection between the kinds of life experiences available to women and the kinds of language use they will exhibit.

Sociolinguistic respect for and interest in variation in linguistic structures as they are used by different segments of a social group must be combined with an ethnographic concern with language as it is used in specific contexts within the speech community. Ethnography is "any rigorous attempt to account for people's behavior in terms of their relations with those around them in differing situations."[5] An ethnographic approach to language use sees it as behavior occurring within social and cultural contexts that are systematically linked to one another. It grounds the analysis of language use in the realities of the lives of individuals within particular social-cultural systems and requires that language use be understood in terms of speakers' positions within those systems.

While sociolinguistic studies select representative speakers from a variety of social classes and ethnic groups and elicit speech from the same speakers using a variety of styles, what such studies often fail to note are the parameters of the particular speech community and the life experiences available to members of that community which might influence language use. Part of this failure stems from the discipline of sociology, since the sociolinguists have relied on measures of social classification developed within sociology for describing the speech community. There is increasing evidence that these measures are not adequate for sociology itself, and they are patently inadequate for use in studies of language variation. First and foremost, the family unit is arbitrarily taken to be the primary social unit in all systems of social stratification used within sociology. Second, the occupation of the head of this family unit is used as the major index of social class, and all members of a family unit are assigned to the same social class. As early as 1964, Walter Watson and Ernest Barth discussed the inaccurate classifications of women which result within sociology from such practices. More recently, Marie R. Haug has shown that in many marital pairs where both partners work, wives' occupational and educational levels exceed that of their husbands, especially at the lower end of the occupational scale.[6] In Haug's analysis, the use of one of the major indexes of social position had led to misclassification of about one-third of all families. Haug proposes a measure of social class which would take the highest level attained by either spouse as that of the entire family. This proposal, however, does not address the larger question of whether or not the family unit is the social unit of primary importance to linguists. In particular, it does not address the question of how to classify women who live outside family units for all or part of their lives. Is women's language use related to familial position on the social scale or more fundamentally to their life experiences — at school and on the job, as well as within the family unit?

I suggest that the conflicting findings of many sociolinguistic studies about language and sex roles are related, at least in part, to this failure to consider women's life experiences as members of their speech community. By relating women's language use only to their membership in family units, linguists have missed important facets of their interaction with the wider community. Particularly in the industrialized societies where most of the sociolinguistic studies have been conducted, these interactions can be rich and varied, over time and geographic space.

THREE STUDIES OF WOMEN IN THEIR COMMUNITIES

Three recent studies have combined the sociolinguistic respect for variability with the ethnographic appreciation of contextual factors which may affect language use. They are described here as examples of the direction in which we must move for adequate descriptions of the ways in which sex role can interact with language use.

Elinor Keenan discusses the speech of men and women in a small village in contemporary Madagascar in terms of "norm-makers" and "norm-breakers."[7] Indirectness is considered to be the community norm in speaking, and men are skilled in the avoidance of confrontation. Women, on the other hand, are more straightforward, especially in the expression of anger or criticism. Other wives openly express critical feelings which their husbands hold toward another party but cannot appropriately express in public. Criticism or anger voiced by a woman is not considered as shocking as it would be if it came from a man. The majority of bargaining encounters in the markets are conducted by women, with men selling items which typically have a more or less fixed price. The directness characteristic of women's speech among these Malagasy people is more in tune with the speech use of Europeans than is the indirectness of men's speech. As European languages and customs are introduced in urban contexts and in the schools, the language use of the entire community is changing to some extent toward that previously characteristic only of the women. This change is particularly noticeable in commercial settings. In other settings the older norms are still honored, particularly in public social situations within the community itself.

Susan Gal has studied a community in Austria which is bilingual in Hungarian and German.[8] In this community, the economic base is gradually changing from one based on a farming economy to one based on industrial jobs held in urban centers outside the community. Hungarian is the language used to conduct the daily affairs of the community; German is associated with the wider world in which industrial jobs are to be found. Women are consistently choosing to speak German in this setting, as they choose both jobs and mates in industrial centers outside their peasant village. In contrast, men who choose to remain in the village and engage in a farming life maintain Hungarian as their primary language. In terms of community speech norms, women are displaying innovative linguistic behavior.

My own study of a small speech community in rural South Carolina indicates something of the complex role which sex-related choice can play in linguistic change as a community moves from a pre-industrial to an industrial economy.[9] On a river island in an area which was heavily populated in the 1700s by West African slaves, the language now spoken comprises a continuum ranging from an English-related creole known as Gullah at one extreme to a regional variety of standard English at the other. In between these extremes a dialect of English known as Black English Vernacular is found. This dialect shares features with dialects spoken by blacks in other parts of the United States, as described by William Labov and colleagues, and by Walt Wolfram and Ralph Fasold.[10] Within this coastal South Carolina speech community of some two hundred members, all of whom are black, the transition from a creole to a dialect of English can be observed in the speech of members of the same family. The speech of the entire community is changing in the direction of a standard variety of English.

A quantitative study of three morphosyntactic features in the speech of men and women in three different age groups indicates that young and middle-aged women are changing most rapidly toward a variety of standard English.* In the oldest age group in

---

*These morphosyntactic features were the pre-infinitival complementizer fE $[f\partial]$, *the third person singular pronouns ee* [i] and *Em* [∂m], and the static-locative preposition *to* [tu], as illustrated in the following sentences:
(1)   I come fE get my coat.
       'I came to get my coat.'
(2)   And *ee* was foggy, and they couldn't see.
       'And it was foggy, and they couldn't see.'
(3)   Can we stay *to* the table?
       'Can we stay at the table?'

this community, men and women speak much the same, using more of the older creole features than any other group except the youngest group of men. Young men between the ages of 15 and 25 use more creole features in their speech than any other group of adults in this community.

While these facts are interesting in and of themselves, they tell us little about the meaning of these differences unless we know something of the experiences available to members of the community. Residents of the community all belong to the three or four major families which have owned land on the island since it became possible for blacks to buy land there in the late 1800s; though there are now some differences in income level, there are no major divisions in social status. Originally, the major economic base of the island was the communal growing of rice, supplemented by individual gardens, hunting, and fishing. The tasks involved in the rice crop were divided according to both sex and age. Because transportation to the mainland was a long and tedious trip by rowboat over several miles of river, the community was largely self-contained and had little interaction with the mainland population on a daily basis. A few male members took jobs off the island for extended periods of time, returning to help with the rice harvest at a certain time of the year. With the increasing availability of motorized transportation after World War II, jobs could be taken closer to home by commuting daily via motor boat and automobile. Both men and women now work off the island at some time in their lives. Island children have been transported daily to mainland schools for the past decade. All of the islanders now have contact with some portion of the mainland population on a regular basis, but the nature of this contact is different for men and women. The jobs held by men are usually in the construction industry, often in situations where several islanders work together. No special spoken or written language skills are required in these jobs. Up until the past ten years, most island women held jobs as domestic workers, either in private households or in motels which operate during the summer in a nearby resort town. Recently women have been obtaining jobs as sales clerks, an occupation requiring use of a fairly standard variety of spoken English as well as some writing skills. One woman has worked as mail carrier on the mainland, and a few have left the island entirely to work as school teachers in mainland schools. Young men can make more money within the construction industry than they can

as school teachers, and none of the men attend college except to
obtain some technical training from the two-year vocational
colleges in the region. Several of the women in the youngest age
group have attended either college or secretarial school.

On the island itself, men and women participate in speech situations according to patterns which have long existed in the community. Generally, men are the primary public speakers. The
Sunday church service is the major weekly social event on the
island and is attended by most of the residents. Women teach the
two children's Bible-study classes, while the adult class is taught
either by a (male) deacon or by the oldest and most respected
woman in the community. The women attending seldom comment
during this class, although they are present and free to speak if
they wish. In the church service itself, the head deacon typically
opens the service and conducts the rituals prior to the sermon,
which is given by an ordained minister from the mainland once a
month. Women participate primarily through the musical portion
of the service; they conduct and comprise most of the choir.
General observations to be made about the language characteristic
of this major community social event are that it ranges across the
entire linguistic continuum found in the community, but that men
are the primary speakers throughout.

In homes men are also the primary speakers in mixed company,
unless a woman is the oldest living member of a given household.
Women typically talk freely among themselves, but an older
woman will limit her participation in the conversation when her
husband enters the room. Age seems to be at least as important a
factor as sex in determining who will occupy the most conversational space in a given interchange. In homes where an older
woman is the senior member of the household, her opinions are
deferred to when family decisions are made, and she generally
speaks more than other family members in mixed groups. In
homes where both a male and a female of approximately the same
age reside, the male speaks more than the female in mixed
company. Children are typically quiet in the presence of adults and
often spend hours listening to adult conversations without inter-
rupting. The oral tradition valued by the entire community is
handed down by the older inhabitants of the island, often in the
form of stories told to these children.

In school the picture of language use is complex. School-age
children interact with each other daily on their boat rides to the

mainland and in after-school games on the island. Boys and girls play together until about the age of ten. After ten the activities of the boys and girls become segregated by sex, with girls helping with the inside chores and boys with the outside. The language of island girls and boys begins to show differences, with the boys continuing to use many creole features and the girls moving rapidly toward a variety of standard English. Island girls typically do well in school and are often at the top of their class. Island boys usually experience some difficulty with academic subjects, though they are good athletes and generally well liked by their mainland peers. Most boys are excellent story tellers and excel in activities requiring oral language skills — provided a standard variety of English is not required. Island girls perform better than their male peers in activities requiring writing and reading skills in standard English, though they are inexperienced story tellers and must be coaxed into telling a story in front of a group.

Comparative data were obtained on the speech of older men and women in a nearby mainland community and are summarized in Table 1. In a group where few older adults had an opportunity to attend school and most were consequently illiterate, the occupational opportunities were far more limited for all adults than for those in the island community. The differences in life experiences and communication networks are reflected in the greater use of standard English features by men in this less-educated mainland group. Women here worked as domestic laborers and as seasonal farm workers on large plantations in the area. Men held laboring jobs on these plantations or unskilled factory jobs in nearby towns. In this group older men typically had traveled more than the women they lived with, and consequently had a wider communication network. Older mainland men used about the same number of creole features in their speech as the older island group described above, while the mainland women in ther age group used more creole features than any other speakers in either community. In the contexts of these two adjacent social groups, women are more innovative than men in the island group and more conservative than men in the mainland group. In both of these groups, the differences in speech are related to differences in available occupational and educational experiences for each sex and the communication networks associated with these life experiences.

In three widely dispersed speech communities — a village off the east coast of Africa, a village in central Europe, and a rural

Table 1. Percentage of Creole and Nonstandard Varients[a] Used by Sex and Age Groups

	Speaker	Preposition		Pronouns		Complementizer		Overall c/ns	Sex groups c/ns	
		%	N	%	N	%	N	%		%
MAINLAND old	1f	100	(7)	39	(87)	66	(12)	68	f	73
	2f	90	(20)	79	(101)	65	(26)	78	-----	
	3m	70	(10)	15	(103)	20	(5)	35	m	34
	4m	50	(4)	47	(15)	0	(3)	32		
	old adults							53%		
ISLAND old	5f	57	(7)	14	(50)	43	(7)	38	f	31
	6f	67	(6)	3	(68)	0	(7)	23	-----	
	7m	70	(10)	23	(96)	11	(28)	35	m	37
	8m	70	(10)	39	(66)	6	(30)	39		
	old adults							34%		
ISLAND middle	9f	0	(1)	0	(19)	0	(7)	0	f	4
	10f	25	(4)	0	(48)	0	(7)	8	-----	
	11m	30	(10)	14	(125)	0	(24)	15	m	23
	12m	86	(7)	6	(49)	0	(11)	31		
	middle adults							8%		
young	13f	100	(2)	0	(5)	0	(3)	33	f	17
	14f	0	(15)	0	(114)	0	(36)	0	-----	
	15m	100	(4)	40	(5)	17	(12)	52	m	47
	16m	100	(1)	8	(66)	17	(12)	42		
	young adults							32%		

[a]N = number of possible occurrences. f = female speaker. m = male speaker.

This table of data will also appear in two other articles discussing different aspects of my research: "Variation among Gullah Speakers in Rural South Carolina: Implications for Education," in *Proceedings of the Fifth Annual Conference of New Ways of Analyzing Variation in English* (Washington, D.C.: Georgetown University Press, forthcoming) and "Linguistic Options and Choices for Black Women in the Rural South," in *Language and Sex II* ed. Nancy Henley, Barrie Thorne, and Cheris Kramarae (Rowley, Mass.: Newbury House, forthcoming).

community in the southern United States — women exhibit a wide range of linguistic behavior in terms of the norms of their communities. In the Malagasy community on Madagascar, women maintain their directness of speech as outside European influences reinforce that portion of the speech community's repertoire. In terms of this context, women here exhibit conservative linguistic behavior. In the Austrian community, women are adopting German as their primary language as they choose an urban-oriented, rather than peasant, life. Men, who remain in the village in greater numbers than women, retain the older farm-associated Hungarian language. In this context, women exhibit innovative linguistic behavior. In rural South Carolina, women in two black communities are exhibiting both innovative and conservative behavior. In one community, as educational and occupational opportunities expand to include situations requiring the use of a standard variety of English, young and middle-aged women are abandoning creole forms more rapidly than men. In another community, where both education and job choices are severely limited, older women maintain the creole forms characteristic of the speech community to a greater extent than any other group of speakers. In all three studies, women are found to speak differently than men in their communities in ways that are significant for the groups as a whole. These differences interact with ongoing language, but women's role in language change is unique for each group.

That men and women will speak differently in at least some portion of the linguistic repertoire of a speech community has been well documented in a variety of geographic and cultural settings. Where the life experiences of men and women are more nearly similar, will their respective linguistic behaviors also be more similar? This question is the kind that studies of language and women's lives must address in the immediate future if we are to make any sense of the linguistic differences we are describing.[11]

Language can operate as a door — one which either opens to new experiences or which closes off a wide range of human interaction. What kind of door language is for women will depend upon the unique experiences available to them within particular speech communities.

ACKNOWLEDGMENT

This paper has benefited greatly from discussions with Barrie Thorne and Pamela Tiedt.

NOTES

1. Dell Hymes, "Models of the Interaction of Language and Social Life," in *Directions in Sociolinguistics*, ed. John Gumperz and Dell Hymes (New York: Holt, Rinehart and Winston), p. 54.
2. William Bright, ed., *Sociolinguistics: Proceedings of the UCLA Sociolinguistics Conference, 1964* (The Hague: Mouton, 1971), p. 11.
3. See especially the discussion in Mary Ritchie Key, *Male/Female Language* (Metuchen, N.J.: Scarecrow Press, 1975); the annotated bibliography and original

studies in Barrie Thorne and Nancy Henley, eds., *Language and Sex: Difference and Dominance* (Rowley, Mass.: Newbury House, 1975); and the summaries of unpublished research in Pamela Tiedt and Sharon Veach, eds., *Women and Language News (Stanford, Cal.: Stanford University Department of Linguistics, 1977).*

4. Dell Hymes, "On the Origins and Foundations of Inequality Among Speakers," *Daedalus* 102.3 (1973): 59-86.

5. R.P. McDermott, "Social Relations as Contexts for Learning in School," *Harvard Educational Review* 47 (1977), p. 200.

6. Walter Watson and Ernest Barth, "Questionable Assumptions in the Theory of Social Stratification," *Pacific Sociological Review* 7 (1964): 10-16; Marie R. Haug, "Social Class Measurement and Women's Occupational Roles," *Social Forces* 52 (1973): 86-98.

7. Elinor Keenan, "Norm-Makers, Norm-Breakers: Uses of Speech by Men and Women in a Malagasy Community," in Richard Bauman and Josel Sherzer, eds., *Explorations in the Ethnography of Speaking* (Cambridge: Cambridge University Press, 1974) pp. 125-43.

8. Susan Gal, "Peasant Men Can't Get Wives: Language Change and Sex Roles in a Bilingual Community," *Language in Society* 7 (1978): 1-16.

9. Patricia Nichols, "Black Women in the Rural South: Conservative and Innovative," in Betty Lou Dubois and Isabel Crouch, eds., *The Sociology of the Languages of American Women: Papers in Southwest English IV* (San Antonio: Trinity University, 1976) pp. 103-14.; Patricia Nichols, "Linguistic Change in Gullah: Sex, Age and Mobility" (Ph.D. diss., Stanford University, 1976).

10. William Labov, Malcah Yaeger, and Richard Steiner, *A Quantitative Study of Sound Change in Progress* (Philadelphia: U.S. Regional Survey, 1972); Walt Wolfram and Ralph Fasold, *The Study of Social Dialects in American English* (Englewood Cliffs, N.J.: Prentice-Hall, 1974).

11. See Susan Ervin-Tripp, "What Do Women Sociolinguists Want?: Prospects for a Research Field," in Dubois and Crouch, eds., *Sociology of the Languages of American Women, op. cit.,* pp. 3-16.

2.6 Welsh and English in Wales

WYNFORD BELLIN

WELSH: DEATH OR NEW VITALITY?

The prophecy in the dark ages was that Wales would lose everything but its language and religion. In a Saunders Lewis poem, a mysterious mentor disappears when asked:

'Eu hiaith a gadwant a oes coel ar frud?'
'Their language they will keep': is there credibility in the prophecy?

Today, terms like 'Welsh-speaking' refer to a bilingual situation. Even the terminology 'Welsh as a first language' refers to simultaneous acquisition of both languages (see Bellin, 1984). During the 1960s it became a widespread assumption that confining Welsh to particular domains of usage and to particular locales would lead to the disappearance of the language. Hence dramatic campaigns by Cymdeithas yr Iaith Gymraeg (The Welsh Language Society) and intensive lobbying, which led in turn to changes in the status of Welsh. The Welsh Language Act of 1967 in particular (see Cyngor yr Iaith Gymraeg/Council for the Welsh Language, 1978) gave equal validity to Welsh in law and administration. However, equal validity is not equal status (see Davies, 1973), and bilinguals who make extensive use of Welsh receive constant reminders of the ease with which rapid language shift can take place. Mass media in English, moreover, seem increasingly to intrude on the hitherto most stable domain of usage, the home. The campaign for a television channel on which Welsh language programmes could be concentrated and given a share of prime time remains to be chronicled.

Also during the 1960s, popular awareness of the dramatic

Source: Edited version of Bellin, W. (1984) 'Welsh and English in Wales', Chapter 27 in Trudgill, P. (ed.), *Language in the British Isles*, Cambridge: Cambridge University Press, pp. 449-79.

decline in the proportion of Welsh speakers in Wales over the century sharpened. In popular parlance, Welsh was 'dying' and English was too strong for it. However, at the same time, and in spite of the prevalence of the death metaphor, a new cultural vitality came to be acknowledged (see Jones, 1973). Social analyses substantiate this popular awareness and indicate a tension between the possibility of the death of Welsh on the one hand, and the viability of the language on the other. Successive Censuses document the decline of Welsh, while various surveys point to the emerging cultural vitality of the language.

Table 1. Landmarks in British constitutional history directly affecting Wales

1284	Wales conquered. English law established (Statute of Rhuddlan). Legal use of Welsh retained.
1485	Battle of Bosworth. Welsh nobles follow Tudor monarchs to London.
1536 and 1542	Statue of Wales (Acts of Union) unites Wales and England, excluding Welsh language from officialdom.
1746	Wales and Berwick Act. England deemed to include Wales.
1886	Foundation of Cymru Fydd (Wales of the future) with home rule aims.
1914	Welsh Disestablishment Act. Anglican church disendowed in Wales.
1925	Plaid Genedlaethol Cymru/Welsh National Party, later Plaid Cymru, founded.
1963	First direct action by Cymdeithas yr Iaith Gymraeg/Welsh language Society.
1964	James Griffiths appointed first Secretary of State for Wales.
1966	Gwynfor Evans, leader of Plaid Cymru, first elected to the Westminster parliament.
1967	Welsh Language Act. Equal validity for the Welsh language in Wales. Wales no longer deemed to be part of England.

Williams (1980) describes two kinds of factor that always underlie a language shift: aggregate structural factors, like in-migration of non-Welsh-speaking population; and behavioural-evaluative factors, like the perceived utility of the language. The tension in the Welsh language situation can be seen as a result of the tension between and within these two kinds of factors.

HISTORICAL BACKGROUND

Modern Welsh is the descendant of what was the original language of most of Britain. Outside Wales, the British language survived the Anglo-Saxon conquest longest in Cornwall, Devon, the Lake District and south-western Scotland, but by late medieval times, the only strongly surviving descendants were Cornish and Welsh. For the last 200 years, Welsh in Wales has been the only survivor, and even there it is spoken by a minority of the population (although there are also communities of native speakers in Argentina).

In the history of Wales, after English rule was established in 1284, both political and cultural events have influenced the status of the Welsh language. Table 1 shows some landmarks in British constitutional history which have had direct effects on Wales. Most events before the late nineteenth century served to submerge Welsh identity on a political level, but in the late nineteenth century Wales began to assume more of a distinctive identity.

Morgan (1981) discusses why nationalist feeling subsided as soon as the Anglican church was disestablished in Wales in 1914. The unifying influences of the two world wars militated against separatist tendencies and expanded widening spheres of influence for central government. The reason for listing the beginning of direct action campaigns in the language cause in table 1 is because Rees (1973) and Jones (1973) emphasize the break between the language movement and movements with separatist aims. Morgan (1981) and previous commentators agree on the importance of the way in which Cymdeithas yr Iaith Gymraeg (The Welsh Language Society) went its own way after its foundation in 1962, even to the extent of damaging the electoral prospects of Plaid Cymru candidates (see also Williams, 1977). After the break, political pressures were exerted on elected representatives and existing institutions without waiting for major political change, and language issues were addressed more directly. [...] When the possibility of a measure of devolution of government was put to a referendum in Wales in 1977, only 11 per cent of the electorate (one-fifth of the votes cast) were in favour; there was a majority against devolution even in areas with high proportions of Welsh speakers (in Scotland a majority voted for devolution).

Table 2 lists some recent cultural and educational events which have had consequences for the Welsh language. [...]

Education movements till the middle of the nineteenth century (see table 2) favoured Welsh, but then came the reports of government commissioners (the 'blue books') notorious for general anti-

Table 2. *Some events in the history of culture and education in Wales*

[...]	
1937	New constitution for the National Eisteddfod with Welsh as the official language (Machynlleth).
1939	First primary school to teach through the medium of Welsh founded (privately) in Aberystwyth.
1950	National Eisteddfod adopts the all-Welsh rule (Caerffili).
1956	First secondary school to teach through the medium of Welsh founded (Glan Clwyd, Rhyl).
1967	Gittins report (DES, 1967) gives a new place to the Welsh language in education.
1971	Mudiad yr Ysgolion Meithrin (Welsh preschool education movement) founded.
1974-79	Cyngor yr Iaith Gymraeg/Council for the Welsh Language set up to advise the Secretary of State on matters concerning the language.
1980	Government averts a fast to the death by Gwynfor Evans, leader of Plaid Cymru, by honouring election pledges on a fourth television channel.
1982	Welsh language programmes concentrated on a fourth television channel.

Welsh prejudice, as well as educational recommendations (see Coupland, 1954; Jones, 1966; Le Calvez, 1970; Evans, 1975; Khleif, 1980). 1870 saw the first act of parliament concerning elementary education placed on the statute book, and from the end of the nineteenth century a very anglo-centric education system worked against the Welsh identity, which had been forged by affection for the language, nonconformist religion and a distinctive brand of radicalism.

The influence of the education system took some time to take effect. But other factors working against the language took effect rapidly. The biggest percentage drops in the Welsh-speaking population were between 1911 and 1921, and 1931 and 1951. Nevertheless, as Morgan (1981) suggests, there was considerable complacency in 1921, because the overall number of Welsh speakers was the highest ever, and the Welsh language seemed secure around the hearth, in religious institutions and voluntary cultural activities like the *eisteddfodau*.

The periods of biggest decline coincided with massive population disruptions, as economic depression and war led to rural-urban migration, international migration and a selective loss of young and well-educated people. However, the list of events in table 2 reflects the activity of a variety of groups and individuals in continually extending the domains where the Welsh language could be used. Such activity did not always take a spectacular form. Le Calvez (1970) documents the struggles for an education policy within local authorities by people who understood what could be achieved with existing institutions.

A particular view of the historical background to the linguistic situation in Wales, which accounts for both the 'colonialist' kind of event which submerged the status of Welsh, and the concessions towards Welsh which have been recently wrested from the initially unsympathetic authorities, is put forward by Aull (1978) in a 'state bureaucracy' model. As the state bureaucracy expanded its political and administrative apparatus, there was increasing encroachment on local concerns and organizations in Wales. Thus the eagerness in the nineteenth century to have all of Wales as an English-speaking area was more a matter of bureaucratic convenience than colonialist intervention; the death metaphor never seems to shade into a murder metaphor. However, there comes a point in any area of centralist concern where it is simpler to hand the problem down, and at such a point the role of people like directors of education in local authorities, or influential figures in broadcasting takes on a new importance. Hence the current situation where, after a number of concessions have been secured, the cultural vitality of the Welsh language is acknowledged in spite of the pervasiveness of the 'death' metaphor.

DEMOGRAPHIC CHARACTERISTICS

Bowen and Carter (1974, 1975) provide invaluable maps showing the percentage of Welsh speakers in wards and parishes as at 1971, and the relative percentage change since 1961, given the overall reduction for the whole of Wales. They speak of anglicization spreading from towns and coastal areas along the valleys, breaking up and splintering territories in Dyfed, Powys and Gwynedd, where Welsh had been spoken by the large majority of inhabitants. Williams (1981) claims a continuity between the 1971 Census and previous ones, with anglicization as an 'innovation' spreading through a hierarchy of urban centres. Over successive censuses, progressively fewer urban centres remain in the category of having a high proportion of Welsh speakers.

Map 1, the map provided by Bowen and Carter, suggests a

division of Wales into three kinds of area: (i) Welsh-speaking areas
(y Fro Gymraeg) with a high proportion of speakers of the
language, (ii) mixed language areas (without a clear majority either
way) and (iii) anglicized areas. Advances have been made in
characterizing social areas on the basis of census data [...]
    Changes in population between censuses have a notable effect
on Welsh speaking areas. The 1961 Census showed effects of rural
depopulation, and the 1971 Census showed suburbanization
robbing these areas of population still further. A study of
migration (Y Swyddfa Gymreig/Welsh Office, 1979) showed a net
immigration into Dyfed, Powys and Gwynedd of the oldest and
youngest age groups. By 1971, rural Wales was established as a
resort and retirement area, with considerable numbers of second
homes owned mainly by permanent residents in England. Map 2
shows the proportions of second homes in 1980 in the districts
within the administrative counties.
    As an echo of a wider secular trend (the rural-urban turn-round
in other countries) rural Wales showed small net increases in
population in the 1970s. The continuation of trends apparent in
the 1979 migration study meant that Gwynedd and Clwyd drew
population from the north-west of England, and Dyfed drew
people from the south-west of England. Given that rural Wales
was sparsely populated anyway, small net changes in population
can have a considerable impact on the language situation.
    Bowen and Carter (1975) and Carter and Williams (1978) see
great significance in the shrinkage of an integral *bro Gymraeg* and
its probable split-up in the 1981 Census. Their account of negative
symbolic values becoming prevalent as the proportion of bilinguals
diminishes can be linked with studies of the importance of social
networks for language shift. Boissevain (1974) describes certain
key figures in small communities as 'brokers'. Change of ownership in a garage or tavern makes an impact on a village in providing a new pivot for social networks. Gal (1979) describes how
bilingualism, when associated with a vanishing way of life, can
decline as social networks loosen and migration removes community members who might have held them together. Population
increases in Welsh-speaking areas can have a dramatic effect when
large by comparison with the 2.2 per cent for the whole of Wales.
[...]

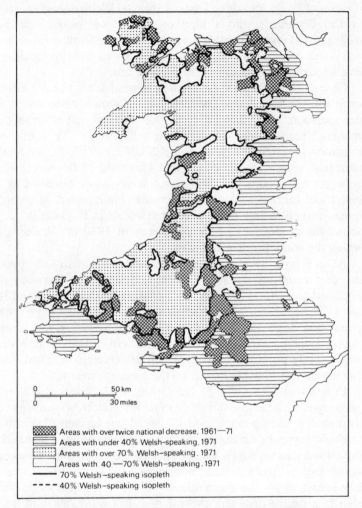

Map 1. The relation between Welsh-speaking areas 1971 and the decrease in Welsh speakers 1961-71 (with permission of Professor H. Carter and the Royal Geographical Society)

WELSH AND ENGLISH IN EDUCATION

The most radical changes in the status of the Welsh language have taken place in education (see Jones, 1966; Le Calvez, 1970; Centre for Information on Language Teaching, 1976; Khleif,

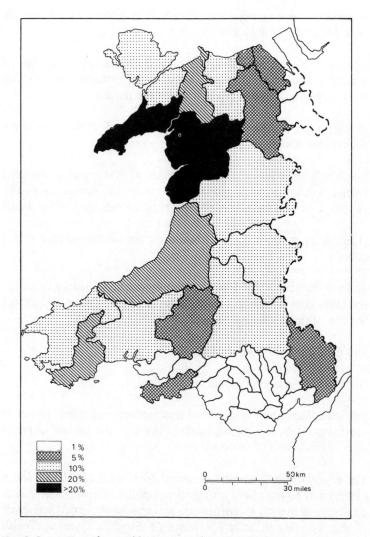

Map 2. Proportion of second homes in Wales in 1980 (drawn using figures collated by Cymdeithas yr Iaith Gymraeg/the Welsh Language Society)

1980). The contrast with the past can be appreciated by comparing selected statements from the nineteenth century concerning the Welsh language and institutions (set out below) with the various official statements of the 1980s. First consider these extracts from the (1847) Report of the Commissioners, the 'Blue Books' (similar sentiments were expressed in an article published by the weekly *New Statesman* in July 1981):

a peculiar language isolating the mass from the upper portions of society ... the Welsh element is never found at the top of the social scale ... his language keeps him under the hatches

(living) in an underworld ... and the march of society goes completely over his head

the Welsh language is a vast drawback to Wales and a manifold barrier to the moral progress and commercial prosperity of the people ... it bars the access of improving knowledge to their minds

(English is) in the process of becoming the mother-tongue of the country

no book on geography, history, chemistry, natural history or any of the useful arts or sciences owes its origins to an Eisteddfod except for two or three treatises on agriculture

and the London *Times* of 1866:

the Welsh language is the curse of Wales

an eisteddfod is one of the most mischievous and selfish pieces of sentimentalism ... a foolish interference with the natural progress of civilization and prosperity

The story of the Commission is told by Coupland (1954), Jones (1966) and Evans (1975). Consider now the following statements on Welsh in the school curriculum and in schools, issued on behalf of the Secretary of State for Wales (Y Swyddfa Gymreig/Welsh Office, 1980, 1981):

issues relating to the Welsh language generate strong and conflicting feelings

most authorities in Wales have already formulated Welsh language policies for their schools it is no longer possible to count on vigorous Welsh-speaking communities alone to safeguard pupils' ability to speak Welsh whatever the medium of their education

for effective bilingual education the Welsh language should be accorded an appropriate place in the community life and not be confined to the classroom

Welsh is now used as a medium in a number of schools over most areas of the curriculum, including mathematics and science

fortunately the once common practice of offering a straight choice between Welsh and French in secondary schools has largely been discontinued

the encouragement given to the Welsh language provision by successive governments has had a significant impact in schools in recent years

studies undertaken of schools which follow bilingual policies have shown that children's general education does not suffer as a result

a number of studies suggest that learning through the medium of a second language enhances achievement in the mother tongue and may assist in the understanding of concepts

The statements about bilingual education are made in the light of figures such as those in table 3, and large-scale research projects such as that undertaken by the Schools Council (1978). As Le Calvez (1970) records, none of the educational changes were achieved without assiduous defence of policies by education authorities as well as more dramatic campaigns.

The results of education policies are important for challenging the claim that the decline of Welsh is somehow inevitable. The local authority with the most consistent education policy is Gwynedd. The declared aim is bilingual education in spite of the in-migration of the 1970s and 1980s. In the mid-1970s a report by the inspectorate gave cause for alarm to supporters of such policies (Swyddfa Addysg Cymru/Welsh Education Office, 1977). The percentage of bilingual children in the primary school age-range was sinking fast. The inspectorate used teachers' assessments with

Table 3. *Changes in education in Wales over years*

(a)   Primary school pupils fluent in Welsh (headteachers' assessment) expressed as a percentage for the whole of Wales

1975	1976	1977	1978	1979
10.6	10.6	12.8	13.5	13.7

(b)   Designated bilingual schools or departments in English-speaking areas (Ysgolion Cymraeg)

	1950	1960	1970	1977	1978	1979	1980	1981
Primary	7	28	46	52	52	53	53	53
Secondary	0	1	4	8	8	11	11	13

(c)   Numbers of pupils in bilingual schools or departments in English-speaking areas

	1970	1980
Primary	6253	9550
Secondary	2017	7860

(d)   Numbers of Welsh medium entries in examinations for the 16+ and 18+ age groups

	1974	1980
Advanced Level GCE		
Entries	102	319
Subjects	6	19
Ordinary Level GCE		
Entries	829	2861
Subjects	14	30
CSE		
Entries	786	2047
Subjects	17	33

Source: Welsh Office, *Statistics of Education in Wales* vols. 1-5.

a five-fold classification. Children were categorized as 'initially Welsh-speaking', 'initially English-speaking now considered fluent in Welsh', 'initially English-speaking with a developing command of Welsh', 'initially English-speaking with a very restricted command of Welsh' and there was a category for no knowledge of Welsh. Oral fluency was considered for infants, and written work entered into the classification for juniors.

Monitoring teachers' assessments using these categories satisfied the inspectorate that they were adequate for purposes such as judging suitability for receiving bilingual secondary education — a resource which was by then in demand. A number of educational innovations were aimed at increasing the proportion of bilingual primary school children. To improve provision for Welsh as a second language, *athrawon bro* (area teachers) were appointed to look after more than one school without being attached to any particular school. Besides mobility, the possibility of co-ordinating provision was catered for. Table 4 gives data from Gwynedd which was the basis for evaluating the success of *athrawon bro* in four parts of the county.

Table 4(a) shows percentages of children who were 'initially Welsh-speaking' in the primary schools of four areas. In spite of a drop in enrolment, percentages stay the same between 1979 and 1980 after rounding. So there was a relative increase in the proportion of children in that category. For the whole county the overall percentage of children speaking Welsh on entering school rose from 44.6 per cent to 44.9 per cent between 1979 and 1980. Table 4(b) shows pupils for whom Welsh was a second language. A rise in the percentage in the 'now fluent' category and a fall in the 'restricted command' category was the basis for attributing success to the educational innovation. But the question for the sceptic is whether the changes in the percentages merely reflect proximity to high percentages of Welsh-speaking children, rather than any achievement attributable to educational methods.

The classification of children for whom Welsh is a second language is an ordered scale. The districts can be ranked according to the percentage of children initially speaking Welsh, so scores can be assigned to rows and columns of the original tables of frequencies for each year (recoverable from the 1979 and 1980 columns in table 4). It is possible to calculate what the percentages would be in each year, if there was a simple linear trend on the percentage of first-language children in a district. (See Fienberg, 1977 and references in Singer, 1979, section L1.)

Table 5 shows how the actual percentages differ from those expected according to a linear trend on the percentage of first-language children. The table indicates that Meirionydd did worse than would be predicted from the number of first-language children in 1979, while East Gwynedd did better than would be predicted. The 1980 differences in table 5 show that *athrawon bro* succeeded in improving the situation in Meirionydd and Anglesey, while exploiting the advantages of West Gwynedd more fully. The table shows how they raised the percentage of fluent children overall.

Changes in language provision since 1975 succeeded in raising the percentage of fluent children in primary schools for all Wales from 10.6 per cent in 1975 to 13.7 per cent in 1979. But educational changes have been made hand in hand with changes in parental aspirations. According to surveys conducted for the

Table 4. *Primary school pupils in four parts of Gwynedd*

(a)   Percentage of pupils with Welsh as a first language, over two years

	Total pupils	1979 Welsh as L1 (%)	Total pupils	1980 Welsh as L1 (%)
West Gwynedd	6225	75	6151	75
Meirionydd	3371	52	3218	52
Anglesey	8201	39	7807	39
East Gwynedd	7675	24	7365	24

Note: Since the totals decrease, stable percentages represent a relative increase.

(b)   Pupils with Welsh as a second language in primary schools in four areas of Gwynedd, over two years

	Now fluent %	Developing command %	Restricted command %	Little knowledge %
1979				
West Gwynedd (1558)	43	31	14	12
Meirionydd (1627)	28	34	28	10
Anglesey (5034)	13	51	23	12
East Gwynedd (5855)	14	41	32	13
1980				
West Gwynedd (1558)	47	32	13	8
Meirionydd (1555)	30	38	24	8
Anglesey (4792)	15	50	25	10
East Gwynedd (5618)	16	42	31	11
Change				
West Gwynedd	+4	+1	−1	−4
Meirionydd	+2	+4	−4	−2
Anglesey	+2	−1	+2	−2
East Gwynedd	+2	+1	−1	+2

Note: Numbers in brackets are percentage bases.

Source: Reports of Gwynedd Local Authority.

Gittins report (Department of Education and Science, 1967; Le Calvez, 1970), there was demand for bilingual primary education but not secondary education. In the survey for Cyngor yr Iaith Gymraeg/Council for the Welsh Language (see Harrison *et al.*, 1981), conducted ten years later and after increased provision of bilingual primary education, 70 per cent of mothers whose children could not speak Welsh nevertheless wanted bilingual secondary education for their children. (The figure for those with bilingual children was 90 per cent.)

It must not be thought that the mothers' aspirations were necessarily realistic, since the overall situation in schools is very variegated. It is still possible to come from a Welsh-speaking home

Table 5. *Differences between observed percentages (O) of second-language children and percentages expected (E) if there were merely a linear trend on the percentage of L1 children in each district (Gwynedd)*

	Second-language category			
	Now fluent (O-E)	Developing command (O-E)	Restricted command (O-E)	Little knowledge (O-E)
1979				
West Gwynedd	4	−3	−3	2
Meirionydd	−2	−4	8	−2
Anglesey	−3	7	−4	−1
East Gwynedd	2	−4	2	0
1980				
West Gwynedd	6	−3	−2	1
Meirionydd	−4	−1	5	0
Anglesey	−4	6	−2	0
East Gwynedd	2	−4	1	1

Note: Although percentages and percentage differences are used to summarize, statistics for significance testing were calculated with the frequencies in original contingency tables.

and attend a school where the language has very little place, or where it is confined to use in religious instruction. It is also possible to come from such a home and be educated partly through the medium of Welsh and partly through the medium of English (with English implicitly associated with science and technology). The fully bilingual education pattern is much scarcer than might be expected from the success attributed to it. Then there are children from monolingual (English only) homes in all the varied patterns of school practice, and large numbers for whom Welsh is a lesson once or twice a week.

What has been shown in the changed education systems in Wales is that there is no inevitability about the decline of the language. If school and community could exert a combined influence, further language decline could be arrested if not reversed.

SOCIAL STRUCTURE AND THE TRANSMISSION OF WELSH

A crucial question for the future of a language is whether older people will speak it with children. In this respect, demographic changes which are out of the control of speakers seem to influence

Table 6. *Ceredigion, Dyfed: percentages of children in primary schools with only English as their first language, and for whom Welsh was a second language, according to parental linguistic status* (Percentage bases in brackets)

	1949 survey %
Parents:	
Both Welsh-speaking (3463)	5
One Welsh-speaking (709)	58
Neither Welsh-speaking (598)	89

	1961 survey %
Parents:	
Both Welsh-speaking (2612)	8
One Welsh-speaking (771)	81
Neither Welsh-speaking (1037)	97

	1967 survey %
Parents:	
Both Welsh-speaking (2641)	10
One Welsh-speaking (989)	85
Neither Welsh-speaking (1147)	99

	1973 survey %
Parents:	
Both Welsh-speaking (2633)	10
One Welsh-speaking (997)	82
Neither Welsh-speaking (1864)	100

Source: Reports of Dyfed Local Authority.

factors within the control of speakers in the way that Bowen and Carter (1975) and others, notably Lewis (1971, 1973) suggest. Table 6 comes from surveys of schools in Ceredigion, a district of Dyfed. In 1949, it seemed possible to acquire Welsh before school in spite of having parents who could not speak the language, even though only 11 per cent of children did so. By 1961, the community could not provide conditions for acquisition. A child from a non-homogeneous marriage (linguistically speaking) was very unlikely to acquire Welsh. The size of the percentage for that category means that many mothers who spoke Welsh were not transmitting the language, even though they lived in an area with a high percentage of speakers. There is some slowing in the trend which may have been due to the changes in the status of the language in the 1960s. But choice of language with children is something that is within the control of bilingual mothers. A survey of such mothers was commissioned by Cyngor yr Iaith Gymraeg/ Council for the Welsh Language, and conducted in ten towns where over 60 per cent of the population spoke Welsh, according to the 1971 Census (see Cyngor yr Iaith Gymraeg/Council for the Welsh Language, 1978; Harrison *et al.*, 1981). The sampling was purposive, in that bilingual mothers not transmitting Welsh were sought out for comparison with those that had bilingual children. However, the questionnaire was presented as a general inquiry into the role of mothers in upbringing.

One of the main findings was that geographical location was much less important than socioeconomic status. The highest status mothers showed greater language loyalty in terms of transmission than any other group.

Two questions can be answered from the results: 'Are elites turning round and giving a lead back to language loyalty?' 'Does a fall in the proportion of speakers in the community inevitably break up social networks?'

The possibility of elites giving a lead in language loyalty would have repercussions for the claim by Khleif (1980) that loyalty to minority languages poses a dilemma for social mobility. The survey used the Registrar General's classification of occupations (as used in the Census), and mothers with experience of class 4 or 5 occupations were nearly as likely to transmit Welsh as those with experience of professional occupations. The mothers who were least likely to have bilingual children were those with experience of class 3 occupations. Given the likelihood of transmission at either end of the social scale, it would be an oversimplification to claim that elites were setting a countervailing trend to that followed by the most numerical occupational group (see Harrison *et al.*, 1981: 32-8).

The associations between socioeconomic status and transmitting Welsh confirmed the observation that speaking Welsh cuts right across social-class differences. Roberts and Williams (1980) summarize by describing bilinguals in Wales as members of a 'status group' in the Weberian sense — a social movement which cuts across other social differences. Boissevain (1974) would want to pit analysis in terms of social networks against analysis in terms of social stratification, but stratification was relevant to the way social networks seemed to operate.

Mothers were asked about how many Welsh speakers they

would be likely to encounter in various locales, and what were their language preferences with peers. Those with bilingual children gave higher estimates of the number of Welsh speakers they might encounter. Differences in language preferences with peers were complicated by fluctuations according to social status. Most of the mothers had received an amount of education consistent with a class 3 occupation and a potential for social mobility upwards. Among that most numerous group, a shift to preferring English with peers seemed to precede bringing children up to speak only English. That association would be predicted by social network analysts, but in the same social category mothers with bilingual children tended to have an absence of a preference for Welsh or English with peers, rather than a preference either way. Nevertheless, lower on the social scale a preference for Welsh was associated significantly with having bilingual children, as if there were low status social networks sustaining language with peers and in transmission. The high status mothers followed the low status pattern, but associations were much weaker, as if they were less dependent on social support (see Harrison *et al.*, 1981: 39-42).

Such a kaleidoscope of social influences cannot be reconciled with a view of the language situation as an inevitable historical process moving in the direction of anglicization, whether the analysis is in terms of the spread of innovation, social structuring, or social networks. There is sufficient lack of determinacy, and enough countervailing tendencies, to require room for language stabilization as well as shift.

MASS MEDIA

Even when the language situation in Wales was very stable, ambivalence could be detected. The poet Gwenallt complained 'Dy iaith ar ein hysgwyddau megis pwn' ('Your language on our shoulders like a burden'). And language loyalty certainly also went together with conserving old ways and values. However, changes in domains of use for Welsh in the 1960s led to a wide variety of forms of cultural expression. Besides the volumes edited by Jones (1972) and Stephens (1973) there are also descriptions of lively youth subcultures like that described by Emmett (1978), in which Welsh is an ingroup language even though trends from outside Wales are being adopted.

The response to changes in technology for communication is also indicative of a new situation. There has never been a daily paper in Welsh, but there have always been weeklies. The 1970s saw a new printing technology (web-offset production), and Betts (1976) describes how seven monthly publications in Welsh were launched between 1974 and 1975. These were popular presentations of local news — *papurau bro* (lit. 'local newspapers'). By July of 1981, the National Library of Wales could list 46 such publications. The numbers of *papurau bro* for each county, and for Liverpool and Cardiff are as follows (taken from the National Library of Wales list, July 1981):

17	Gwynedd
14	Dyfed
5	Clwyd
4	Powys
2	West Glamorgan
1	South Glamorgan
1	Cardiff
1	Liverpool

Changes in broadcasting in the 1970s also allowed radio programmes in Welsh to be moved from the medium wave-band to the VHF wave-band. News and current affairs could then be broadcast in Welsh, with a much fuller service than when Welsh and English might compete from being on the same wave-band. From the mid-1970s Welsh speakers, even when a minority, could hear international news in Welsh and read about local events without any great expense. Cultural participation with consistent use of Welsh was made available on a new scale. (See Betts, 1976, for problems encountered when social or cultural usage aims at including both languages.) Audience research shows the extent of participation with mass media. Table 7 gives results from research commissioned by BBC and the IBA. The survey, conducted in 1980, used a quota sample intended to represent Welsh speakers from all over Wales. At the time of the survey, there were several constraints on the timing of television programmes in Welsh, so the figures for viewing Welsh programmes are impressive.

Table 7. *Figures from self-estimates of listening and viewing behaviour, made by 891 Welsh speakers (BBC/IBA survey)*

Activity	%
Hearing	
a radio programme in Welsh at least once a day	45
a play in Welsh, competing with Sunday prime viewing time, once a month or more	14
Watching in either language	
a TV programme five or six days of the week	96
a TV programme every day of the week	90
Watching TV programmes in Welsh	
five or six days of the week or more	64
at least once a day	55
a BBC programme in Welsh every day of the week	53
an ITV programme in Welsh every day of the week	48

CHANGING SYMBOLIC VALUES

What does ability to speak Welsh mean to the bilingual person? The changes in the status of the language, and educational changes, mean that the answer will depend on whether the person comes from one of the areas of limited economic potential, whether Welsh is a second language acquired at school, whether there are plenty of other speakers around — and a host of other complicating factors. (A controversial caricature of social life in Cardiff by Jones, 1978, includes people with all these different characteristics along with monolinguals who are at various stages of learning Welsh, portrayed in terms of their ability to join in a social situation where Welsh is being used.) Sharp *et al.*, (1973) report on a large-scale survey of attitudes in children learning Welsh at school. They found that favourable attitudes to Welsh declined sharply between the ages of 11 and 15. Roberts and Williams (1980) criticize the level of aggregation in the study, and suggest that factors like the level of institutional support need to be taken into account, but their own surveys suggest that reliance on any one kind of institution for maintenance (whether school, family or religious institutions), leads to less use of Welsh and less favourable attitudes than when a number of institutions give mutual encouragement. Harrison *et al.*, (1981) also face the fact that attitudes in the mothers they interviewed were inconsistent.

Table 8. *Reasons for learning Welsh in Further Education classes: reasons ticked by 182 evening-class students in Clwyd, 1980*

Number ticking	Reason given
122	because I have come to live in Wales
111	to understand and communicate with neighbours
109	to get involved/integrate into social life
107	to ensure survival of the language
101	to understand radio/TV programmes
71	to learn a new language
64	because I am Welsh/Welsh descent
63	because I am interested in languages
50	to help my children
22	because my spouse speaks Welsh
20	to improve my job prospects

Note: Multiple answers were allowed.

Gal (1979) regards symbolic values as of secondary importance to forms of association, since they alone did not explain language shift in the community she studied. However, they are important for the relations between Welsh and English in Wales in the monolingual majority. Why should a monolingual want to learn Welsh? Giles and Powesland (1975) comment on the remarkable movement for learning Welsh in adults which began in the early 1970s. They link the movement with a rise in ethnic feeling. However, this does not seem necessarily to be the case, especially as monolinguals (English speakers) moving into Wales often show considerable enthusiasm for learning Welsh. Table 8 gives results from surveys among adults learning Welsh in Clwyd. What is striking is the sheer 'integrative motivation' (cf. Harrison, 1980) even though Clwyd has few areas with very high percentages of Welsh speakers: there is no real need of the language for plain communication with neighbours. However, if these answers are linked with the acknowledged cultural vitality of modern Wales, the motivation may well be a desire to participate in what is going on. If speaking Welsh is in fact associated with cultural vitality rather than economic failure, then clearly symbolic values have changed over the period between the last two censuses. Favourability to the Welsh language cuts across social differences and even across origins, inside or out of Wales.

TRENDS INDICATED BY CENSUSES AND SURVEYS

This chapter claims, as far as the Welsh language situation is concerned, that a tension exists in popular awareness between adherence to the 'death' metaphor and acknowledgement of cultural vitality. [...]

However, all the survey evidence quoted in this chapter can be interpreted as evidence against a consistent and uniform process leading to the decline of the Welsh language. [...] The figures from the 1981 Census were therefore awaited with great tension. Could the dispersion of speakers and the dissolution of communities be offset to any extent by mass media communication and benefits of bilingual education? Could improvement in the status of the language affect language choices with the next generation, as well as producing appreciable numbers of second-language speakers? Had imprisonment and protests been in vain? The level of public awareness and the evidence from surveys with intermediate categories of linguistic ability meant that the census figures for bilinguals would have to be taken seriously.

The first information from the 1981 Census concerned the population changes and indicated very negative influences from aggregate-structural factors. Nevertheless, Bellin (1982) gave 17 per cent as the most optimistic prediction for the overall percentage of Welsh speakers, and 14.5 per cent as an extrapolation from previous censuses. In the event, the overall percentage turned out to be 19 per cent, which must be a vindication of the endeavours made to save the language in the 1960s and 1970s.

The prediction that can be uncovered in the 'death' metaphor is that of a uniform continuous process. Both the ten-year census and survey evidence can be used to show that there was something distinctive about 1971 and even optimistic about 1981. The sting in the 'death' metaphor is the suggestion of inevitability. If Welsh speakers maintain their commitment, and the monolingual majority gain enthusiasm for measures taken to draw that sting, then Wales may become a stomping ground for students of language stability instead of students of language shift.

APPENDIX: GOVERNMENT REPORTS AND OTHER DOCUMENTS QUOTED

WHITE PAPER
Our changing democracy: devolution to Wales and Scotland. Cmnd 6348, 1975.
CENSUS REPORTS
Census 1971: Report on the Welsh language in Wales. Office of Population Censuses and Surveys, 1973.
Census 1981: preliminary report: England and Wales. Office of Population Censuses and Surveys, 1982.

Figures were also taken from reports of previous censuses (1911-61).

OTHER REPORTS
Primary Education in Wales. Department of Education and Science: Central Advisory Council for Education (Wales), 1967.
Welsh in the primary schools of Gwynedd, Powys and Dyfed/Y Gymraeg yn yr ysgolion cynradd Gwynedd, Powys a Dyfed. Welsh Education Office/Swyddfa Addysg Cymru. Survey no. 5/Arolwg Rhif 5, 1977.
A Future for the Welsh Language/Dyfodol i'r iaith Gymraeg. Council for the Welsh Language/Cyngor yr Iaith Gymraeg, 1978.
Migration into, out of and within Wales in the 1966-71 period/Mudo i Gymru, o Gymru ac oddimewn i Gymru yn ystod y cyfnod 1966-1971. Welsh Office Occasional Paper no. 4/Papur achlysurol rhif 4 y Swyddfa Gymreig, 1979.

CONSULTATIVE DOCUMENTS
Welsh in the school curriculum: proposal for consultation by the Secretary of State for Wales/Y Gymraeg yng nghwrs addysg yr ysgolion:cynigion ymgynghorol gan Ysgrifennydd Gwladol Cymru. 1980.
Welsh in the schools/Y Gymraeg yn yr ysgolion. 1981.

REFERENCES

Note: References to official publications (HMSO, Office of Population Censuses and Surveys, Welsh Office and the Department of Education and Science) are given in the Appendix.
Aull, C.H. 1978. Ethnic nationalism in Wales: an analysis of the factors governing the politicization of ethnic identity. Ph.D. dissertation, Duke University, Durham, North Carolina, USA.
Bellin, W. 1982. The application of loglinear models to figures from the Welsh language question in the Census. Paper given at the Sheffield Sociolinguistic Conference.
—— 1984. Welsh phonology in acquisition. In Ball, M. and Jones, G. (eds.) *Readings in Welsh Phonology.* Cardiff: University of Wales Press.
Betts, C. 1976. *Culture in Crisis: the Future of the Welsh Language.* Upton, Merseyside: The Ffynnon Press.
Boissevain, J. 1974. *Friends of Friends: Networks, Manipulators and Coalitions.* Oxford: Blackwell.
Bowen, E.G. and Carter, H. 1974. Preliminary observations on the distribution of the Welsh language at the 1971 census. *Geographical Journal* 140: 432-40.

—— 1975. The distribution of the Welsh language in 1971: an analysis. *Geography* 60: 1-15.
British Broadcasting Corporation and Independent Broadcasting Authority, 1981. *Listening and viewing among Welsh speaking people in Wales.* Broadcasting Research Department report LR/81/1.
Carter, H. and Williams, S.W. 1978. *Aggregate Studies of Language and Cultural Change in Contemporary Wales.* London: Routledge and Kegan Paul.
Centre for Information on Language Teaching. 1976. *Bilingualism and British Education: the Dimensions of Diversity.* CILT Reports and Papers 14. London: Centre for Information on Language Teaching.
Coupland, R. 1954. *Welsh and Scottish Nationalism: a Study.* London: Collins.
Davies, C. 1973. Cymdeithas yr Iaith Gymraeg. In Stephens, M. (1973).
Emmett, I. 1978. Blaenau boys in the mid-1960s. In Williams, G. (1978).
Evans, G. 1975. *Land of my Fathers: Two Thousand Years of Welsh History.* Swansea: John Penry.
Fienberg, S.E. 1977. *The Analysis of Cross-classified Categorical Data.* Cambridge, Mass.: MIT Press.
Gal, S. 1979. *Language Shift: Social Determinants of Linguistic Change in Bilingual Austria.* New York: Academic Press.
Giles, H. and Powesland, P.F. 1975. *Speech Style and Social Evaluation.* London and New York: Academic Press.
Harrison, G.H. 1980. Social motives in the transmission of a minority language: a Welsh study. In Giles, H. *et al.* (1980).
Harrison, G.H., Bellin, W. and Piette, A.B. 1981. *Bilingual Mothers in Wales and the Language of Their Children.* Cardiff: University of Wales Press.
Jones, D.G. 1973. The Welsh language movement. In Stephens, M. (1973).
Jones, G. 1978. *Dyddiadur dyn dŵad.* Caernarfon: Cyhoeddiadau Mei.
Jones, R.B. 1972. *Anatomy of Wales.* Peterson Super Ely, Glamorgan: Gwerin publications.
Jones, W.R. 1966. *Bilingualism in Welsh Education.* Cardiff: University of Wales Press.
Khleif, B.B. 1980. *Language, Ethnicity and Education in Wales.* The Hague: Mouton.
Le Calvez, A. 1970. *Un cas de bilinguisme, le pays de Galles. Histoire, littérature, enseignement.* Lannion: Skol.
Lewis, E.G. 1971. Migration and language in the USSR. *International Migration Review* 5: 147-79.
—— 1973. Language contact in the USSR and Wales. *Planet* 20: 53-64.
Morgan, K.O. 1981. *Rebirth of a Nation: Wales 1880-1980.* London/Cardiff: Oxford University Press/University of Wales Press.
Rees, C. 1973. The Welsh language in politics. In Stephens, M. (1973).
Roberts, C. and Williams, G. 1980. Attitudes and ideological bases of support for Welsh as a minority language. In Giles, H. *et al.* (1980).
Schools Council Committee for Wales. 1978. *Bilingual Education in Wales 5-11: Report by Eurwen Price with an Independent Evaluation by C.J. Dodson.* London: Evans/Methuen Educational.
Sharp, D., Thomas, B., Price, E., Francis, G. and Davies, I. 1973. *Attitudes to Welsh and English in the Schools of Wales.* London and Cardiff: Macmillan/University of Wales Press.
Singer, B.R. 1979. *Distribution-free Methods for Nonparametric Problems: a Classified and Selected Bibliography.* Leicester: British Psychological Society.
Stephens, M. (ed.) 1973. *The Welsh Language Today.* Llandysul, Dyfed: Gomer Press.
Stephens, M. 1976. *Linguistic Minorities in Western Europe* Llandysul, Dyfed: Gomer Press.

Williams, C.H. 1977. Non-violence and the development of the Welsh language
society *Welsh History Review* 8: 426-55.
—— 1980. Language contact and language change in Wales, 1901-1971: a study in
historical geolinguistics. *Welsh History Review* 10: 207-38.
Williams, S.W. 1981. The urban hierarchy, diffusion and the Welsh language: a
preliminary analysis 1901-1971. *Cambria: a Welsh Geographical Review* 8:
35-50.

SECTION 3

LANGUAGE, POWER AND CONTROL

INTRODUCTION

The first two articles in this section focus on the linguistic *system*, which is the property of a community, and describe the social processes whereby gradual change in that system is brought about. Language, and in particular vocabulary, changes in line with social norms, and these in turn embody the values which are dominant in society. It is therefore often argued that language is disproportionately influenced by those who have social power. As Leith puts it 'language has a vital part to play in the exercise and consolidation of power. ... the connotations that become criterial originate with the socially powerful' (pp. 147 and 149). However, this still begs the question of whether language determines or simply reflects the prevalent definitions of reality. This is not just an abstract question but one which affects our daily approach to the language we use. Both Leith and Bolinger recognise that language is a powerful tool which has its own part to play in the process of social change. As Bolinger argues 'Sexism in language will grow less as women are accepted more in the roles that men have traditionally occupied. ... but it will come about by applying pressures, of which awareness of the (linguistic) stereotypes and protest against them is one,' (p. 164).

The article by Ervin Tripp on the address system of her own particular variety of American English looks in detail at one way in which power is exercised in *interaction*. In this she illustrates a general point, that speakers may negotiate the balance of power afresh in each interaction but this is only possible if both parties are referring to the same underlying rules: 'Only because they shared (the same) norms could the ... act have its unequivocal impact' (p. 172).

The last three articles in the section focus on language in three *specific contexts* where there is an inherent imbalance of power: doctors' surgeries, courtrooms and classrooms. Each of them illustrates the fact that power is not necessarily exercised in the *amount* of talk or even of silence, but rather in the management and style of talk. In particular, power may be exercised through asking questions, which not only pre-determines the topic and the direction of the conversation but also ensures the speaker the right to the next-but-one turn. In the case of teachers and doctors, this power regularly extends even further to an interpretation and evaluation of the response. As Edwards puts it 'What pupils "can mean" is located within the teacher's frame of reference.' (p. 220.) Such imbalance of power frequently leads to communication failure because the weaker partner in the interaction is unable to get his or her point of view recognised, let alone establish the topic of conversation. In the words of Treichler *et al.*, there is no 'shared orientation' (p. 190) between the participants.

O'Barr and Atkins point out that 'a powerful position (in an interaction) may derive from either social standing in the larger society and/or status accorded by the (context)' (p. 215). In many instances, of course, these two elements of general social status and specific role will work *together* in placing the individual at a relative advantage or disadvantage. However, it is as well to keep the two aspects distinct in our minds. Indeed, O'Barr and Atkins quote cases, such as that of a policeman testifying in court, where higher status is indeed accorded by the context.

Finally, we need to remember that the specific language features characteristic of the socially powerless may actually feed back into the situation to reinforce their subordinate status. In Edwards' words, 'social identities and social relationships are signalled and reproduced in the act of speaking.' (p. 220). O'Barr and Atkins went on (in experimental work which is not reproduced here) to study how powerless language might affect those situations in which it is found and reported that speakers tended to be judged 'less convincing, less truthful, less competent, less intelligent and less trustworthy'. They concluded, that powerless language may be a reflection of a powerless social situation but it also would seem to reinforce such inferior status' (O'Barr and Atkins, 1980, p. 110).

Barbara Mayor

REFERENCES

O'Barr, W.M. and Atkins, B.K. (1980) '"Women's language" or "powerless language"?', in McConnell-Ginet, S., Barker, R. and Furman, N. (eds) *Women and Language in Literature and Society*, New York, Praeger, pp. 93-110.

3.1 The Vocabulary of Power, Rank and Status

DICK LEITH

Groups who occupy a subordinate or oppressed position in society invariably suffer from linguistic disparagement. Homosexuality is regarded as deviant behaviour, and is often referred to in abusive terms (like *bent* and *queer*), just as women and Black people find themselves at the receiving end of a rich vocabulary range, at best patronising, at worst offensive. Sometimes these words are wielded innocently, in that some people are genuinely unaware of their pejorative meaning; but more often than not they are used as conscious symbols of an attitude. And, just as politically-conscious Black people have struggled to promote words like *Black* at the expense of *nigger* or *coon*, so *gay* has become instrumental in the cause of homosexual equality; moreover, people who support such causes are expected to use these terms, since the use of the traditional terms is an index of a social stance. Thus, on a range of sensitive social and political issues we have to choose our vocabulary with care, and cultivate a conscious, highly self-critical attitude to the issue of words and meanings.

The heightened awareness of language exhibited by such groups as gays and feminists is the intelligent response of the exploited or the powerless. It stems above all from the recognition that language has a vital part to play in the exercise and consolidation of power. Not unnaturally, the powerful in society have long recognised this. It is a matter of everyday experience that in political discourse meanings are manipulated and words chosen to load the dice in favour of one point of view. Evaluative connotations of words like *democratic* are cultivated at the expense of their conceptual meaning, so that a word denoting particular kinds of political organisation becomes what we might call a 'purr' word, used merely to win approval for a particular position. The word *moderate*, connotatively favourable but referentially vague when

Source: Leith D. (1983) *A Social History of English*, London, RKP, pp. 77-86.
© Dick Leith.

applied to politics, has been widely used to enlist support for people whose political views are often fundamentally conservative. [...]

SEMANTIC CHANGE IN WORDS DENOTING RANK AND STATUS

The proposition that different social groups may use words differently extends to the words used for the social groups themselves. As we have said, such words are particularly sensitive to the development of pejorative or affective meanings. It is therefore instructive to explore some aspects of the vocabulary of rank and status: how reference is made to the social hierarchy, and how people of different status address each other. We shall discuss the major trends in the history of the words chosen. First, terms originally denotative of rank often become evaluative and, second, those denoting the more powerful groups are most likely to retain their status as rank-terms.

While the relationship among these status and rank terms, being based on a hierarchy of power in society, are clear, they are more fluid than those of more highly structured hierarchies, such as the army. The army has evolved a *set* of mutually exclusive terms, the individual meaning of which depends entirely on an understanding of the meaning of the others: thus, we can only know what *captain* means if we understand its relation to *major, lieutenant,* and *corporal,* and so on. Social relations are in general, however, less static, so the meanings of their terminology are more susceptible to change; but we must beware of assuming that any change in meaning automatically accompanies, or signals, a change in social structure. The relationships between the words and the things they signify are more complex than that, as we shall see.

The Anglo-Saxon system of rank-terms was largely restructured after the Norman Conquest. *Cyning* and *cwen* (king and queen), *half-weard* and *hlaefdige* (lord and lady — the former being a warden of loaves, the latter a kneader of them) survive, in senses known to the Anglo-Saxons; but other terms were pushed into new meanings by the introduction from French of *duke, prince, squire, villain,* etc. The Anglo-Saxons used *aldormann* to denote a man responsible to the king for administrating a large territory, *þegn* (modern 'thane' or 'thegn'), a lesser landowner, and *ceorl* (churl) to denote the lowest rank of freeman. Another word was *eorl*, which denoted high status in general, and which, like *þegn*, was used in poetic texts in the sense of 'warrior'. In the period of Viking power, the meaning of *eorl* was influenced by the related Scandinavian word *jarl*, which had a similar meaning to *aldormann*; and the word has survived the Norman Conquest in this later sense. *Aldormann* has become specialised, in terms of municipal power and status, while *þegn* has been superseded by the French *baron*, and interestingly enough by the Anglo-Saxon term *cniht*. Originally *cniht* was not a rank term, but denoted a boy or lad; inferiority in age gave way to inferiority of status, and the word came to mean a servant. But there are different kinds of servant: a king's servant had to be of noble blood, and the word was specialised to the kinds of meaning hitherto represented by *þegn*.

The meanings of words denoting low social status seem to have been affected by further borrowings from French. One of these, *gentle*, had already acquired an evaluation of approval by the time it was borrowed into English in the thirteenth century. Originally it had meant 'high-born', but its meaning widened to include those characteristics felt by the high-born to be appropriate to their social position. If *gentle* — something of a key-word in the history of English — denoted good breeding and gracious behaviour, then words like *churl* could be associated with coarseness. By about 1300, *churl* had lost its technical sense as a term of rank, and indicated low breeding in general; from that point, connotations of 'rudeness' gradually became criterial. Interestingly enough, the French borrowing *villein* dropped even further. By 1300 again, its primary meaning was 'base'; from there it is only a short step to the present wholly pejorative meaning of 'villain'. While both these words have become pejorised, a later borrowing, *peasant*, has retained its early meaning, 'one who works the land', as well as a later pejorative one. By the end of the sixteenth century we find it used affectively — almost as a 'snarl' word — in Elizabethan drama, notably in Marlowe's *Edward II*.

In the examples cited, the criteria relating word to referent have shifted from the functional to the evaluative. It is difficult not to interpret this development as the projection of attitudes that are upper-class on to the words. To put it another way, the connotations that become criterial originate with the socially powerful: the dominant class imposes the dominant connotations. We see this process at work among words that were not associated with rank, like *vulgar, common, illiterate,* and *lewd.* The last two examples show the high social value that has come to be placed on literacy and learning. *Illiterate* is now a rough synonym for 'stupid', and the meaning of *lewd* has changed dramatically over the last thousand years. Originally meaning 'lay' at a time when learning and the Church were virtually synonymous, it could also mean 'unlearned'. By the seventeenth century it was applied to those of low social status, implying that by that time learning was associated with class. By about 1700 it meant 'worthless' of objects, 'unprincipled' of people; and from the latter meaning, a special kind of unprincipledness became criterial, that relating to sexual conduct. Hence the meaning 'lecherous'. [...]

THE SEMANTIC DISPARAGEMENT OF WOMEN

Power relationships do not of course necessarily involve social stratification. Adults have generally exercised power over minors, and women have been controlled by men, in ways that cut across class boundaries. Male power, and male attitudes, therefore, are reflected in the ways in which women are talked about. Men have developed a rich vocabulary of affective words which denigrate women who do not conform to a male ideal; and there has been a constant tendency to develop new meanings denoting the availability of women as sex objects. It has been estimated that there are over 1000 words which in their history have denoted women and have also meant 'whore'.

Words which classify women by age tend to reflect the male predilection for the younger, sexually attractive female. Unfortunately, many of these words are not recorded in early varieties of English, so that it is often difficult to trace their history. *Hag* is rare before the sixteenth century, but is probably related to an Anglo-Saxon word for witch; from the fourteenth century, it meant a repulsive old woman, and this pejorative sense survives. *Crone* may derive from a Norman-French word for a cantankerous woman (from the fourteenth century it has meant 'withered old woman', and suchlike), but it could also come from a Germanic word for an old ewe — a sense in which it is used between the sixteenth and nineteenth centuries. Either way, women are hardly flattered. If old age is unforgivable in a woman, ugliness or slovenliness invites further ridicule. *Drab,* a possible loan from Irish

Gaelic, is recorded in the sense 'ugly woman' in 1515, and *slut*, deriving perhaps from Scandinavian, means a dirty one from the fifteenth century. Some words denoting young women had at first no sexual connotations, but they were not slow to develop them. *Doll*, originally a pet name for Dorothy, was used in the sixteenth century as a generic pet name for a mistress; and *mynx*, deriving perhaps from *minickin*, a word for a pet, came to mean a young girl, and later a wanton one.

A great many of these words developed the meaning of 'whore' at some stage in their history. The same is true of many other endearment terms, such as *sweetmeat* and *Kitty*, occupational terms like *nun, spinster*, even *laundress*; and kinship terms, such as *aunt* and *cousin*. But this process of semantic 'disparagement' does not necessarily mean that men have always regarded women of all kinds as little more than objects to be bought for self-gratification. Sexual relations among men and women have often depended on the brothel. Although even the most powerful in the land might indulge in it, whoring was socially taboo; and like all taboo subjects it generated a proliferation of terms, many of them euphemistic. In the covert patronage of prostitutes, it was necessary to keep the flow of terms going; hence even words like *nun* and *laundress* found themselves used in this sense.

NOTES

A good general history of English vocabulary is by Sheard (1954). The categories of meaning I refer to are those of Leech (1974), who has a good chapter called 'Semantics and Society'. For other examples and insights see Waldron (1967); for detailed studies of individual words, see Lewis (1968) and Tucker (1967, 1972).

Status terms are discussed in Barber (1976), and Schulz (1975) which provided the basis for the discussion on words denoting women.

REFERENCES

Barber, C.L. (1976) *Early Modern English*, London, Deutsch.
Leech, G.N. (1974) *Semantics*, Harmondsworth, Penguin.
Lewis, C.S. (1968) *Studies in Words*, Cambridge University Press.
Schulz, M.R. (1975) 'The semantic derogation of women' in B. Thorne and N. Henley (eds), *Language and Sex: Difference and Dominance*, Rowley, Mass., Newbury House pp. 64-75.
Sheard, J.A. (1954) *The Words we Use*, London, Deutsch.

Tucker, S. (1967) *Protean Shape: A Study in Eighteenth Century Vocabulary and Usage,* London, Athlone.
—— (1972) *Enthusiasm: A Study in Semantic Change,* Cambridge University Press.
Waldron, R.A. (1967) *Sense and Sense Development,* London, Deutsch.

3.2 Bias in Language: the Case of Sexism

DWIGHT BOLINGER

Those who were children before the 1920s — and many later than that, no doubt, in some localities — remember the innocent merriment of racial slurs:

> Eenie-meenie-miney-mo,
> Catch a nigger by the toe.
> If he hollers, let him go.
> Eenie-meenie-miney-mo.

> Smarty, Smarty had a party;
> Nobody came but a big fat darkie.

'For a black writer in this country to be born into the English language,' says James Baldwin, 'is to realize that the assumptions on which the language operates are his enemy. ... I was forced to reconsider similes: as black as sin, as black as night, blackhearted.'[1]

What breeds contempt is misfortune and weakness; familiarity perpetuates it. The language that white children heard taught them to despise their former slaves as surely as parades and band music taught them to respect the flag. The attitudes were implicit in the symbols. It was enough for the words and phrases to be THERE.

When Moses said to the children of Israel, among other injunctions to righteousness, 'Thou shalt not curse the deaf, nor put a stumblingblock before the blind' (Leviticus 19,14), he was countering what seems to be a universal flaw in human nature: to build self-esteem by looking down on those less fortunate. The misfortune may take any form; there is always an abundance of derogatory terms attached to it. People who are ill 'HAVE diseases' — the expression conjures visions of possession by evil spirits — that are generally viewed as loathsome, and unpleasant

---

Source: Bolinger D. (1980) 'A case in point: sexism' in *Language: the loaded weapon*, London, Longman, pp. 89-104, (Chapter 9). © Longman Group Ltd.

adjectives are attached to the afflicted themselves: *scurvy, pock-marked, consumptive, parasitic, leprous, rickety, anemic, gangrenous, syphilitic, rheumatic, scrofulous, mangy, scabby* — some of which have become free-floating synonyms of *disgusting*. The reaction of disgust no doubt arose naturally as a help to avoiding contagion; but it was just as surely a hindrance to early understanding and prevention, and its extension to the persons of the sufferers was of a kind with taunting cripples and ridiculing the feeble-minded. While the fears of some diseases have been allayed, others are as virulent as ever. In our time cancer has the leading place, and terms consecrated to it aggravate the dread: *terminal growth, metastasize*; even the word *cancer* itself carries a kind of taboo.[2]

The humble and the poor come in for their share of contempt. Just the names for farmers are a spectrum of disparagement: *hick, hayseed, yokel, clod, bumpkin, countryjake, rube* — and older terms that have been generalized such as *clown, churl, boor.* Some were applied in contempt to begin with; others were relatively neutral terms which by association with the despised class have become derogatory. The same is true of servants, whether bound or free: *villain, knave, varlet, caitiff, scullion, lackey, henchman, flunky, potwalloper, underling, errand boy.*

Extreme youth comes in for equal parts of disparagement and endearment. With their dependency, children share some of the traits of PROPERTY; like domestic animals, they are apt to be cherished when they keep their place and disciplined when they do not. Terms for 'young' are easily degraded. The apparently neutral *child* yields *childish*, biased when applied to an adult (to call a grown man *childish* is insulting; to call a boy *mannish* is merely inappropriate, and *manly* is a compliment). To find unfavourable terms for children we go a step lower on the social scale, into the animal kingdom: *cub, whelp, puppy, fledgling, kid. Callow* covers more than hair and feathers, and the cries and tears of infants give adjectives for 'weak, spiritless': *whimpering, puling, mewling, blubbering, sniveling, weepy. Brat* may originally have referred to a ragged garment.

Disease and infancy can be outlived. Race cannot. Neither can sex — which will be our showpiece, because thanks to the feminism of the past decade, more is known about sexual bias than about any other kind. The views in this article bring together ideas from a number of linguists who are also feminists. They are views from

inside, and convey a sense of the oppressiveness that women themselves — those most sensitive to language problems — believe
exists in our linguistic heritage. Male readers may find some degree
of zealous overstatement, but this should be weighed against equal
degrees of male complacency in society at large — along with a
lingering of sentiment expressed by the courtly white Southerner
confronting charges of racism: 'Why, we LOVE our Nigras!'[...]
    First, how do WORDS for women differ from words for men? As
with other relatively powerless classes, there is a heavy representation of unfavorable epithets and similar terms, more than for
men. One would think that untidiness was not preeminently a
female quality, yet most of the words for 'untidy person' listed in
Roget's *Thesaurus* are words for women — *slut, slattern, frump,
drab, dowdy, draggletail, trollop, bitch.* Not one of those currently
in use is marked as masculine. Similarly learning and scholarship
would seem to be asexual, yet while Roget lists a number of terms
in ordinary use that are mainly or exclusively masculine, only two
are feminine, and they have to do with PRETENSIONS to knowledge: *pedantess* and *bluestocking.* Many loaded terms, particularly those referring to women as sex objects, reflect women's
status as property, kept or rented for sexual services: Roget's
Thesaurus lists roughly twice as many female terms as male under
libertine. Furthermore, all the female terms are fully disparaging,
whereas a number of the male terms imply a boys-will-be-boys
tolerance: *rake, skirt-chaser, old goat, gay dog, gay deceiver, Don
Juan.* When we think of *gay dog* we mentally punctuate it with a
snicker or a jab in the ribs. As for the adjectives, the very heading
of the section in Roget has sexual overtones: *purity.* This is a term
that is rarely used for sexual inexperience in males; and as for the
entries that are directly associated with one sex or the other, hardly
any are like *satyrish, goatish* in applying primarily to males.
Female terms abound: *of easy virtue, fallen, whorish, on the streets,
unchaste, wanton.* Though *loose* looks to be an impartial modifier,
loose woman is readily understood as 'immoral woman', but *loose
man* would probably be taken as a fugitive. The simple word
woman itself is listed as a synonym of *prostitute.* Most indicative of
the attitude toward women as sex objects is the history of terms
that started out as relatively unbiased or even favorable and were
gradually degraded. Barrie Thorne and Nancy Henley quote
Duncan McDougald on the word *tart*, originally meaning a small
piece of pastry. It 'was first applied to a young woman as a term of

endearment, next to women who were sexually desirable, then to women who were careless in their morals, and finally — more recently — to women of the street'.[3] '*Queen, madam, mistress,* and *dame* have all acquired degraded meanings, whereas *prince, king, lord,* and *father* are exalted and applied to God.'[4] In separate studies, Julia Stanley and Muriel Schulz found 320 terms in English for 'sexually promiscuous woman'.[5]

Being old puts one in another class of the powerless. Being old AND female puts one on the verge of being an outcast. There are no male terms to match the contempt embodied in the words *hag, crone, witch, warhorse, biddy,* and *beldam.* There are sexual connotations here too: 'old and unattractive', 'old and sexually useless'.

Not all semantic areas put women on the down side, but the ones that favor them still have the tinge of male appreciation — what is good is what men admire in women as women, not as persons. (A stock joke in movie comedy is to have a Marilyn Monroe type say 'He loves me for my mind'.) Among the 'terms of endearment' listed by Roget are many that are applied exclusively to women or children (*sweetheart, jewel, sweetkins, babe,* etc), none that are applied exclusively to men. The skin-deep phenomenon of physical beauty is overwhelmingly feminine, but the same proportions — though the numbers are fewer — are found in the words for 'ugly person': Roget lists one for males (*satyr*) and four for females (*hag, harridan, strumpet,* and *witch*). Women carry the burden of opposite stereotypes. They are angels, because they are beautiful — and also long suffering and uncomplaining in their subordinate role. And they are devils, when they scheme to win by guile what they cannot take openly. Deception is seen as a feminine trait, but it is a recourse of the weak. Angel or devil, on pedestal or in pit, women in Western society have had the greatest trouble simply being accepted as human, and the language records all their manifestations as the 'sex with a difference'.

Epithets are the tip of the women-as-property iceberg. The language is mined with expressions that reflect women's status as a commodity, despite the disappearance long since of prearranged marriages and the obsolescence of promises to love, honor, and *obey.* A radio ad for 'home owner' loans carries the sentence *We married off our last daughter.*[6] The phrase *marry off* would never be used of male offspring except as a joke; it smacks of *auction off* and *sell off.* The word *wife* itself, though it has escaped signifying 'property' in a direct sense, is often encountered in statements like the following: *The brave pioneers crossed the plains with their wives, their children, and their cattle.*[7] Similarly *women*, as in this from the television series 'Star Trek': *Our people are the best gamblers in the galaxy. We compete for power, fame, women.*[8][...]

Commodity status is not the only form of depreciation. Terms for females — even apparently objective and neutral ones — are subtly devalued. If a woman driver makes a bad maneuver, a man may be heard to say *What does that woman think she's doing!* with *woman* lengthened and pronounced with a rise-fall-rise intonation — which makes it an expression of disregard. A similar use of *man* would be taken as an emphatic way of expressing the emotion of the whole sentence, not as a reflection on the man's sex. ... When a woman is at fault, it is often because she is a woman; when a man is at fault, it is more often because he is cruel, or dishonest, or cowardly, or ambitious.

In most forms of literature, devaluation through words related to sex takes a more subtle form which can be exposed only by collecting and counting. From the time they begin to read, children are submerged in stories and textbooks that emphasize sex roles, that use male terms preponderantly, and that present males as dominant: 'when adults write for one another, they refer to young people as *children*, almost as often as they call them *boys* and *girls*. When writing books and stories for children, however, adults use the gender words *boy* and *girl* twice as often as the neutral words *child* and *children* ... Overall, the ratio in schoolbooks of *he* to *she, him* to *her*, and *his* to *hers* was almost four to one.'[9] The same heavy weighting of male terms is found in the 200 million achievement test forms used annually in the United States.[10] Even the terms that are not explicitly male are interpreted that way if their referents in the past have been predominantly male. An item in *Our Sunday Visitor* reads as follows:

> The Catholic Theological Union in Chicago showed an increase in students from 168 to 189. But don't cheer. Among the students are twenty-two women, subtract them and the total showed a loss.[11]

From words that reflect the status of the sexes we cross the thin boundary to grammar that does the same. Gender-marking in

English syntax is limited to the pronoun system, and it is there — with the use of *he, she, him, her,* and *his* — that sex usages have raised the greatest controversy. Modern English has no pronouns in the singular that can refer indifferently to male or female — *X prides Xself on X's good sense.* The practice has been to insert the masculine. Its use has even been made official. An Act of Parliament in 1850 decreed that *he* should be used for both sexes in all parliamentary language.[12] The Associated Press Stylebook published in 1977 does the same: 'Use the pronoun *his* when an indefinite antecedent may be male or female: A reporter attempts to protect his sources.' The masculine goes for indefinite nouns as well, so that *man* occurs widely with the presumed sense of 'person, human being' — *Every man (every person) has his self-esteem: he prides himself on his good sense.* The hearer or reader is supposed to interpret this 'common gender' use of the masculine as 'he or she', 'his or her', etc.

But it is doubtful that very many do, at least consistently. Expressions like the one above from 'Star Trek', or like the ad for a hotel offering *Anything any businessman or his wife would want,*[13] show all too clearly that women are on the sidelines and that the mental picture we get when *he, him,* or *his* is used is male. Given the approved interpretation it should be just as easy to assume 'she' as 'he', but the fact is that we tend to assume 'he' unless it is LIKELY that the individual referred to is female. This explains the oddity of a sentence like *The nurse put on his hat.*[14].

It was natural for feminists to pick the 'common gender' as one of their main targets. Distrust of it dates back many years. Helena Maria Swanwick wrote in 1913,

the common pronoun is non-existent and I have not used the neuter [*it*], lest it should alarm nervous persons. Perhaps when we have got over the panic fear of unsexing ourselves, we may find it safe to speak of a human, just as we do of a baby, as 'it'.[15]

Some publishers and public bodies have tried to remove the bias. The United States Department of Labor in 1977 revised about 3,000 of its approximately 30,000 titles for occupations. Terms such as *bus boy, foreman, salesman, boom man,* and *bobbin man* were replaced with *dining room attendant, supervisor, salesperson, log-sorter,* and *bobbin winder tender.* (But nothing was done to the title of the bureau in charge of these changes: the *Manpower*

Administration.)[16] Publishers urge authors to paraphrase, and, if necessary, to repeat the combinations *he or she, his or her.* etc.

The problem was not discovered by the feminists. It is an old one in the language, and has one popular solution: the use of a plural when the antecedent is indefinite. Instead of *Everybody will choose his partner* we have *Everybody will choose their partner.* Sinclair Lewis described Doremus and Emma as having *each their own bedroom,* and Sir Walter Scott complained of being *shut up in a nasty Scotch jail, where one cannot even get the dirt brushed off their clothes.* Most speakers are unconscious of any inconsistency in a sentence like *Nobody is blaming you, are they?* where a singular *is* is repeated by a plural *are.* But the more definite the person referred to, the less acceptable the plural form becomes. The following go from normal to impossible:

If anybody wants their phone number changed. ...
If a person wants their phone number changed. ...
?If a man or woman wants their phone number changed. ...
*If a subscriber wants their phone number changed. ...

The clash is worse when a singular verb collides with a doubly plural *themselves: When a person can't think what to do with themselves,* with its *can't,* which may be either singular or plural, is not as bad as * *When a person doesn't know what to do with themselves.* For some obscure reason, the more logical *themself* is less used.[17]

The last example can of course be made passable with *When a person doesn't know what to do with himself or herself,* and this solution too is an old one. Jespersen quotes a line from Henry Fielding: *The reader's heart (if he or she have any).*[18] But Jespersen called the double pronoun a makeshift, and H.L. Mencken condemned it as 'intolerably clumsy'.[19] Another possible recourse would be to use the grammatically neuter form *it,* as Swanwick recommended. But besides wrenching our lifelong habit of restricting *it* to things, animals, and occasionally infants, this collides with two other ingrained habits. One is that of extending *it* to grown persons only as a sign of contempt. (On being jeered at by a passing motorist, you catch up with him and say, with a lofty stare, *From a distance I could have sworn it was human.*) The other is that of NOT using *it* even with animals when the wish is to personify. You observe the antics of a squirrel working on its nest and remark, *I saw him climb the tree with his mouth full of building materials.* You have not determined the sex of the squirrel so you personify with the masculine. To use the double pronoun would be absurd by today's standards: **I saw him or her climb the tree with his or her mouth full of building materials.* And to substitute *it* and *its* for *him* and *his* would destroy the personification.

The real difficulty with the double pronoun must be looked at in the light of what is meant by 'clumsy'. Anything that speakers are not used to is 'clumsy', and it might be argued that all we need to do is keep saying it and eventually it will sound all right. But this overlooks one of the two main functions of the pronouns in English. The first, of no interest here, is the distinction of a particular individual, male or female. The other is anaphoric: the function of standing for and pointing to an antecedent. English syntax requires that all finite verbs have explicit subjects and that most verbs have complements. We can manage this by repeating the noun: *When I saw Mary, Mary was getting Mary's self ready to go visit Mary's cousin, and I asked to go along with Mary.* (Even this would require the effacement of another habit, that of taking repeated *Mary's* to refer to different persons with the same name: *Mary [Jones] met Mary [Smith].*) To avoid the repetition we use the corresponding pronouns: *When I saw Mary, she was getting herself ready to go visit her cousin, and I asked to go along with her.* The pronoun adds no information; we could as well substitute a mathematical symbol. Such virtually empty words behave as empty words normally do: they are de-accented, to attract as little attention as possible. The grammars of some languages allow one or more of them to be omitted altogether — in Spanish no word for 'she' would need to be expressed at all. English downplays the *h* pronouns by dropping the *h* when it is not directly after a pause: *she was getting 'erself ready to go visit 'er cousin, and I asked to go along with 'er.* It would be unnatural to pronounce the *h* here.

But the double pronoun compels full accent and full-blown *h*'s; we cannot say **If you see the manager, call imorer,* for *call him or her.* The 'clumsiness' of the double pronoun is not only that we are unaccustomed to it but that it refuses to take the back seat that all languages reserve for pure anaphora.

There has been no lack of quixotic inventions as substitutes for the double pronoun. A few writers (including males), though nowhere in the popular press, have adopted *she* as common gender, presumably to even the score. The dialectal pronoun *thon* was once proposed, as was the French *on.* The latest at this writing is *e*, for research on whose feasibility a professor at the University of California has received a grant.[20] This appears to merit the Proxmire Golden Fleece Award, because *he* is already pronounced *e*, and hearers would simply infer that the speaker intends *he*.

So no solution is in sight. The writer or speaker has to choose between perpetuating sexist language and making a mess of the grammar. The kind of expedient that might work is the one proposed by a feminist of another era, Ella Flagg Young. She suggested dropping the *or* and combining: *himer, hiser* (and, supposedly, *heshe*). These could be played down as pronouns normally are, including dropping the *h*. It is enough to make a barely distinguishable noise in the proper slot. The problem is the same as with any other direct intervention in language: first agreeing on the expedient, then getting used to it.

What people are not used to is generally good for a laugh, and the feminists have been showered with barbs from female as well as male humorists looking for an easy joke. Even those sympathetic to the cause are sometimes intolerant of any reforms that might cause temporary discomfort. The former managing editor of the Washington *Post*, Alfred Friendly, offers the feminists a lesson in historical grammar: 'The suffix-*person* is a needless bastard born of ignorant parents. For several millennia, back to the Sanskrit word *manu, -man, man-* and the word *man* standing alone meant "person, one, human being of either sex". They still do. That *man* has the additional meaning, when used in a different context, of an adult human male is beside the point.'[21] Unfortunately, etymologies are irrelevant, and *man* suggests its own contexts.

The sexist use of the pronouns goes beyond straightforward male-female reference. It also extends to the personification of inanimate things. Ships are often called *she*. The imagery is fairly obvious: sea captains, sailors, and shipping clerks are traditionally men, and the ship is pictured as something alive that works for them and towards which they feel a certain affection. The feminine can be used for any fairly elaborate workhorse contrivance: *Look at my new power mower: ain't she a beaut?* As the linguist Uriel Weinreich points out, this usage is particularly common among male speakers to refer to objects 'lovingly handled'.[22] But if the workhorse is pictured as having a rudimentary intelligence, then the pronoun switches to masculine. Here is a conversation about a game-playing computer:

'I usually win,' the teacher continued. 'But he can play quite
well some times.'

'He?'

'Yes, that's odd, but most people call computers "he" and ships
"she".'[23]

The bestowing of feminine names on objects such as airplanes and
car trailers follows the same tendency, which also doubtless
explains why meteorologists have given us such things as
Hurricane Edith but not *Hurricane Elmer* — it takes a meteor-
ologist to view something as destructive as a hurricane with
affection — HIS property, of course. But the winds are changing: in
1978 the weathermen (*weatherpersons) agreed that male and
female names would henceforth be balanced.

A similar personification is found with abstractions, especially
the names of political entities. But rather than the 'faithful slave'
metaphor, this is probably connected with the notion of 'mother
country': *China and her millions.* Sometimes the neuter *it* works
well enough instead, but in the following, where the writer was
obviously trying to avoid *her*, it does not:

As one American Embassy counselor says, '90 per cent of our
problems would disappear if we could convince Japan that our
policy was not aimed especially at it.'[24]

This ignores two rules of English: *convince* requires an object with
something resembling a mind, and *it* is usually avoided where it
would occur in the position of the main sentence accent.

Superficially, the use of *man* in the names of occupations seems
as biased as the 'common gender' *he*, and some feminists have
attacked it just as vigorously. But there is an important grammatical difference: *he* belongs to syntax, *man* to morphology or
wordforms. *He* has to be coordinated with some other reference in
the sentence or nearby — an antecedent — and this brings it to
more or less conscious attention. *Man*, used as a kind of suffix, is
affected as such elements usually are: it tends to be swallowed up
in the larger word. *He*, too, in its normal anaphoric use, tends to
fade, but it always CAN be pronounced with its consonant and
vowel unabated. But a word such as *workman* would sound
strange with *man* not reduced to *m'n*. Newer forms do have the
full *man* — *garbage man, meter man, ice cream man*; but the

commoner ones lose the vowel: *doorman, lineman, postman, workman, chairman, trainman, chapman, fisherman.* With this less obvious suggestion of 'man', it would appear that the masculinity of the term is more a function of the word as a whole than the suffix. If *She is the chairman* sounds odd, it is for the same reason that *She is the commissioner* sounds odd — both words refer to posts once held almost exclusively by men. So it might have been better to leave most of the *man* words alone, trusting to the future feminine occupants of the positions to feminize or neutralize them. Some feminists agree that *person* was a dubious choice to replace *man.* As one feminist who is also a linguist says, 'Terms like *chairperson* seem to be specializing to women, while *chairman* is reserved for men. All that has been accomplished is the self-conscious avoidance of *chairwoman.* Meanwhile, we are subjected to a rich assortment of jokes about *Freshpersons, person-hole covers, postpersons,* and *person-eating sharks.*'[25] A local woman official in California declared that she and another female official 'both hate the term *chairperson*'.[26] [...]

[Language will, then reflect any cultural bias, but one important question remains to be asked:] Does the mere EXISTENCE of a linguistic form produce a special effect, when speakers are free to use it or not? Most feminists are convinced that sexist language is a form of enslavement. 'Our speech not only reflects our place in society,' says Sally McConnell-Ginet, 'but also helps to create that place.'[27] Julia Stanley adds, 'At its most "trivial" level, the vocabulary provided by our culture limits severely the kinds of experience we can express for ourselves.'[28] And this from Thorne and Henley: 'Language helps enact and transmit every type of inequality, including that between the sexes; it is part of the "micropolitical structure" ... that helps maintain the larger political-economic structure.'[29] Though a consensus does not make a fact, the evidence is pretty conclusive. [...]

Women are the 'marked', the 'different', sex — woman's language is described against man's as a standard, not the reverse. And this is not just a whim of linguists when they analyse — it inheres in the language. Being a Miss or a Mrs is more exceptional than being a simple Mr. The usual pronoun is *he*, not *she*, when sex is unknown. Women are 'objects' rather than 'subjects' in almost all metaphorical discourse — the property rather than the possessor, the moved rather than the mover (the Prime Mover is endowed with the pronoun *He* and pictured with a beard — a child's letter reads, 'Dear God, is it really true that boys are better than girls? I know you are one, but try to be fair. Love Sylvia.')[30] The human race is *man* and *mankind.* In the Creation, woman came second. [...]

The word *pioneer* is used of a group if any males at all are present, but if only women are involved, they are *pioneer women.*[31] The same was true till recently of many professions: *woman doctor, woman lawyer* — including marked feminines like *aviatrix, authoress, poetess, seamstress* (where sex is relevant, these persist: *actress, majorette, madam*). Linguistic asymmetry is everywhere.

Whether it can be done away with is an economic question as much as a linguistic one. Many families now require more than one wage earner, which has forced more and more women into the marketplace, in competition with men — inflation is the current equivalent of the wars that put minorities in uniform and gave them a power they had never had before. Sexism in language will grow less as women are accepted more, in the roles that men have traditionally occupied. This is a safe historical prediction — but it will come about by applying pressures, of which awareness of the stereotypes and protest against them is one. In the long run, reducing asymmetry will probably take the form of women laying equal claim to masculine characteristics in language, rather than the deliberate neutering of sex markers. Male forms are esteemed by BOTH sexes as better for the self-respect that goes with independence; the 'feminine whine' is not for today's professional women. The language is intricate, cumbersome, and strongly resistant to interference; it changes its values more easily than it changes its forms.

As for the sore points, attempts to remove the more obvious indicators of sex have been mostly cosmetic. We have seen the problems of trying to change the 'common gender' *he.* Even as simple an expedient as using *Ms* to avoid the distinction of *Miss* and *Mrs* has run into trouble. Ann Holmquist points out that *Ms* seems to have backfired — it has come to be associated with 'divorcees, widows, businesswomen, feminists and others who may be supposed to have sexual experience and to be either available or militantly liberationalist'[32] — in other words, the attempt to get an unmarked term has simply resulted in a new and different form of markedness. Robin Lakoff feels that some of the sexist aspects of language 'are too common, too thoroughly mixed throughout the language, for the speaker to be aware each time he uses them'[33] —

and correspondingly difficult to root out. But Julia Stanley says that people had better be MADE aware of them. As Holmquist says of *his* or *her*, it is admittedly cumbersome and 'grates on editors' nerves'; but it is still a 'necessary, if temporary, expedient — for raising consciousness'.[34]

The inertial mass of language is like the inertial mass of society. Women inherit their place as speakers inherit their words. We drag a vast obsolescence behind us even as we have rejected much of it intellectually, and it slows us down. [...] The rehabilitation of names of things and of creatures comes in part automatically as the things and creatures are rehabilitated, but it is a factor too in their rehabilitation — no amount of enlightened animal husbandry can erase overnight the associations of *swine, pig, hog, sow*. The gun of sex-biased language may be rusty, but it is there, and the greatest danger is unawareness that it is a gun, and is loaded.

NOTES

1. 'On Language, Race and the Black Writer', Los Angeles *Times*, 29 April 1979, Part V *p* 1.

2. See Susan Sontag, 'Illness as Metaphor', *New York Review of Books*, 26 January 1978, *pp* 10-16.

3. Barrie Thorne and Nancy Henley (eds.), *Language and Sex: Difference and Dominance*. Rowley, Mass: Newbury House, 1975, *p* 67.

4. *Ibid, p* 61.

5. Julia P. Stanley, 'Paradigmatic Woman: The Prostitute', in David L. Shores and Carole P. Hines (eds), *Papers on Language Variation*. Birmingham, Alabama: University of Alabama Press, 1977, *pp* 303-21. Muriel Schulz, 'The Semantic Derogation of Woman', in Thorne and Henley, *op cit, pp* 64-75.

6. San Francisco radio KGO, 13 March 1978, 7.30 am.

7. From an elementary school textbook, cited by Professor Ann Holmquist in an interview with Michael Fallon, Sacramento, California *Union*, 26 March 1978, *p* A4.

8. Cited by Julia P. Stanley, 'The Sexist Tradition: Words and Meaning', *Iowa English Bulletin* 27 (1978) 2.5-10, *p* 9.

9. Alma Graham, 'The Making of a Nonsexist Dictionary', in Thorne and Henley, *op cit*, 57-63, *p* 58.

10. C.E. Tittle, 'Women and Educational Testing', *Phi Delta Kappan* 55 (1973) 2.118-19.

11. Cited in *The Progressive*, January 1977, *p* 11.

12. Stanley, 'The Sexist Tradition' (note 8 above), *p* 6.

13. Hyatt Hotel advertisement, San Francisco radio KCBS, 22 April 1978, 7.08 am.

14. See Maija S. Blaubergs, 'On "The Nurse Was a Doctor"', in Reza Ordoubadian and Walburga von Raffler-Engel (eds), *Views on Language*. Murfreesboro, Tennessee: Inter-University Publishing, 1975, 87-95.

15. *The Future of the Women's Movement*. London: Bell, 1913, *p* vii.

16. Sydney J. Harris, 'Labour Department's Unisex Dictionary', San Francisco *Examiner and Chronicle*, 1 June 1975, *p* B3.

17. M. Stanley Whitley calls *himself* 'far more stigmatized'. See his 'Person and Number in the Use of *We, You*, and *They*', *American Speech* 53 (1978) 18-39, *p* 35. Among his examples is one from the Boston, Massachusetts chief of police: *And pretty soon, the law-abiding citizen, who won't own handguns, won't be able to defend themself. (p* 30).

18. *Essentials of English Grammar*. London: Allen and Unwin, 1933, *p* 193.

19. *The American Language*. New York: Knopf, 1955, *p* 460.

20. Sacramento, California *Union*, 27 March 1978, *p* C10.

21. Los Angeles *Times*, 12 May 1978, *p* 7.

22. In Danny Steinberg and Leon A. Jakobovits, *Semantics*. London: Cambridge University Press, 1971, 308-28, *pp* 316-17.

23. Hilary Abramson, 'The Games Computers Play', Sacramento, California *Union*, 14 April 1978, *p* C2.

24. *The Progressive*, February 1978. *p* 36.

25. Fallon-Holmquist interview (note 7 above).

26. Palo Alto, California *Times*, 9 November 1977, *p* 12.

27. McConnell-Ginet, *op cit, p* 542.

28. Stanley, 'The Sexist Tradition' (note 8 above), *p* 8.

29. *Op cit, p* 15.

30. Cited in Fallon-Holmquist interview (note 7 above).

31. Blaubergs, *op cit, p* 90.

32. Fallon-Holmquist (note 7 above).

33. Cited by Julia Stanley, 'Prescribed Passivity, the Language of Sexism', in Ordoubadian and von Raffler-Engel (note 14 above), 96-108, *p* 99.

34. Fallon-Holmquist (note 7 above).

3.3 Sociolinguistic Rules of Address

SUSAN M. ERVIN-TRIPP

A scene on a public street in contemporary U.S.:
    'What's your name boy?' the policeman asked ...
    'Dr. Poussaint. I'm a physician. ...'
    'What's your first name, boy? ...'
    'Alvin.'

Poussaint (1967; 53)

Anybody familiar with American address rules[1] can tell us the feelings reported by Dr. Poussaint: 'As my heart palpitated, I muttered in profound humiliation. ... For the moment, my manhood had been ripped from me. ... No amount of self-love could have salvaged my pride or preserved my integrity ... [I felt] self-hate.' It is possible to specify quite precisely the rule employed by the policeman. Dr. Poussaint's overt, though coerced, acquiescence in a public insult through widely recognized rules of address is the source of his extreme emotion.

Brown and Ford (Hymes 1964) have done pioneering and ingenious research on forms of address in American English, using as corpora American plays, observed usage in a Boston business firm, and reported usage of business executives. They found primarily first name (FN) reciprocation or title plus last name (TLN) reciprocation. However, asymmetrical exchanges were found where there was age difference or occupational rank difference. Intimacy was related to the use of multiple names.

Expanding their analysis from my own rules of address, I have found the structure expressed in the diagram in Fig. 1. The advantage of formal diagraming is that it offers precision greater than that of discursive description (Hymes 1967). The type of diagram presented here, following Geoghegan (1971), is to be read like a computer flow chart. The entrance point is on the left,

Source: Ervin-Tripp, S.M. (1969) 'Sociolinguistics', in L. Berkowitz (ed.) *Advances in Experimental Social Psychology*, Academic Press, New York, vol. 4, pp. 93-107. (This article is an extract taken from the original.)

and from left to right there is a series of selectors, usually binary. Each path through the diagram leads to a possible outcome, that is, one of the possible alternative forms of address.

Note that the set of paths, or the rule, is like a formal grammar in that it is a way of representing a logical model. The diagram is not intended as a model of a process of the actual decision sequence by which a speaker chooses a form of address or a listener interprets one. The two structures may or may not correspond. In any case, the task of determining the structure implicit in people's knowledge of what forms of address are possible and appropriate is clearly distinct from the task of studying how people, in real situations and in real time, make choices. The criteria and methods of the two kinds of study are quite different. Just as two individuals who share the same grammar might not share the same performance rules, so two individuals might have different decision or interpretation procedures for socio-linguistic alternatives, but still might have an identical logical structure to their behaviour.

The person whose knowledge of address is represented in Fig 1 is assumed to be a competent adult member of a Western American academic community. The address forms which are the 'outcomes' to be accounted for might fit in frames like 'Look, — — — —, it's time to leave.' The outcomes themselves are formal sets, with alternative realizations. For example, first names may alternate with nicknames, as will be indicated in a later section. One possible outcome is no-naming, indicated in Fig. 1 by the linguistic symbol for zero [Ø].

The diamonds indicate selectors. They are points where the social categories allow different paths. At first glance, some selectors look like simple external features, but the social determinants vary according to the system, and the specific nature of the categories must be discovered by ethnographic means. For example, 'older' implies knowledge of the range of age defined as contemporary. In some southeast Asian systems, even one day makes a person socially older.

The first selector checks whether the addressee is a child or not. In face-to-face address, if the addressee is a child, all of the other distinctions can be ignored. What is the dividing line between adult and child? In my own system, it seems to be school-leaving age, at around 18. An employed 16-year-old might be classified as an adult.

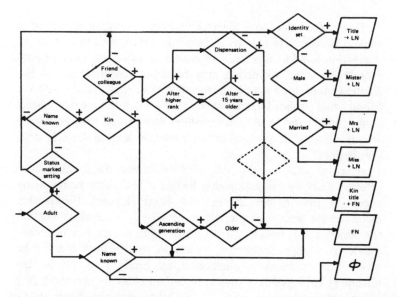

Figure 1. An American address system.

Status-marked situations are settings such as the courtroom, the large faculty meeting, or Congress, where status is clearly specified, speech style is rigidly prescribed, and the form of address of each person is derived from his social identity, for example, 'Your honour,' 'Mr Chairman.' The test for establishing the list of such settings is whether personal friendships are apparent in the address forms or whether they are neutralized (or masked) by the formal requirements of the setting. There are, of course, other channels by which personal relations might be revealed, but here we are concerned only with address alternations, not with tone of voice, connotations of lexicon, and so on.

Among nonkin, the dominant selector of first-naming is whether alter is classified as having the status of a colleague or social acquaintance. When introducing social acquaintances or new work colleagues, it is necessary to employ first names so that the new acquaintances can first-name each other immediately. Familiarity is not a factor within dyads of the same age and rank, and there are no options. For an American assistant professor to call a new colleague of the same rank and age 'Professor Watkins' or 'Mr Watkins' would be considered strange, at least on the West Coast.

Rank here refers to a hierarchy within a working group, or to ranked statuses like teacher — pupil. In the American system, no distinction in address is made to equals or subordinates since both receive FN. The distinction may be made elsewhere in the linguistic system, for example, in the style of requests used. We have found that subordinates outside the family receive direct commands in the form of imperatives more often than equals, to whom requests are phrased in other ways at least in some settings (see below).

A senior alter has the option of dispensing the speaker from offering TLN by suggesting that he use a first name or by tacitly accepting first name. Brown and Ford (Hymes 1964) have discussed the ambiguity that arises because it is not clear whether the superior, for instance, a professor addressing a doctoral candidate or younger instructor, wishes to receive back the FN he gives. This problem is mentioned by Emily Post: 'It is also effrontery for a younger person to call an older by her or his first name, without being asked to do so. Only a very underbred, thick-skinned person would attempt it' (Post 1922: 54). In the American system described in Fig. 1, age difference is not significant until it is nearly the size of a generation, which suggests its origin in the family. The presence of options, or dispensation, creates a locus for the expression of individual and situational nuances. The form of address can reveal dispensation, and therefore be a matter for display or concealment of third parties. No-naming or Ø is an outcome of uncertainty among these options.[2]

The *identity* set refers to a list of occupational titles or courtesy titles accorded people in certain statuses. Examples are Judge, Doctor, and Professor. A priest, physician, dentist, or judge may be addressed by title alone, but a plain citizen or an academic person may not. In the latter cases, if the name is unknown, there is no address form (or zero, Ø) available and we simply no-name the addressee. The parentheses below refer to optional elements, the bracketed elements to social selection categories.

[Cardinal]:	Your excellency
[U.S. President]:	Mr President
[Priest]:	Father (+ LN)
[Nun]	Sister (+ religious name)
[Physician]:	Doctor (+ LN)
[Ph.D., Ed.D.], etc.:	(Doctor + LN)

[Professor]:   (Professor + LN)
[Adult], etc.;   (Mister + LN)
(Mrs + LN)
(Miss + LN)

Wherever the parenthetical items cannot be fully realized, as when last name (LN) is unknown, and there is no lone title, the addressee is no-named by a set of rules of the form as follows: Father + Ø → Father, Professor + Ø → Ø Mister + Ø → Ø, etc. An older male addressee may be called 'sir' if deference is intended, as an optional extra marking.

These are my rules, and seem to apply fairly narrowly within the academic circle I know. Nonacademic university personnel can be heard saying 'Professor' or 'Doctor' without LN, as can school teachers. These delicate differences in sociolinguistic rules are sensitive indicators of the communication net.

The zero forms imply that often no address form is available to follow routines like 'yes', 'no', 'pardon me,' and 'thank you.' Speakers of languages or dialects where all such routines must contain an address form are likely in English either to use full names or to adopt forms like 'sir' and 'ma'am,' which are either not used or used only to elderly addressees in this system.

One might expect to be able to collapse the rule system by treating kin terms as a form of title, but it appears that the selectors are not identical for kin and nonkin. A rule which specifies that *ascending generation* only receives title implies that a first cousin would not be called 'cousin' but merely, FN, whereas an aunt of the same age would receive a kin title, as would a parent's cousin. If a title is normally used in direct address and there are several members of the kin category, a first name may also be given (e.g., Aunt Louise). Frequently there are additional features marked within a given family such as patrilineal vs. matrilineal, and near vs. distant. Whenever the address forms for an individual person's relatives are studied, this proves to be the case, in my experience.

Presumably, the individual set of rules or the regional dialect of a reader of this article may differ in some details from that reported in Fig 1. Perhaps sociolinguists will begin to use a favourite frame of linguists: 'In my dialect we say ...' to illustrate such differences in sociolinguistic rules. For example, I have been told that in some American communities there may be a specific status for familiarity beyond first-naming, where a variant of the middle name is optional among intimates. This form then becomes the normal or unmarked address form to the addressee.

'What's your name, boy?'
'Dr. Poussaint. I'm a physician.'
'What's your first name, boy?'
'Alvin.'

The policeman insulted Dr Poussaint three times. First, he employed a social selector for race in addressing him as 'boy,' which neutralizes identity set, rank, and even adult status. If addressed to a white, 'boy' presumably would be used only for a child, youth, or menial regarded as a nonperson.

Dr Poussaint's reply supplied only TLN and its justification. He made clear that he wanted the officer to suppress the race selector, yielding a rule like that in Fig. 1. This is clearly a nondeferential reply, since it does not contain the FN required by the policemen's address rule. The officer next treated TLN as failure to answer his demand, as a non-name, and demanded FN; third, he repeated the term 'boy' which would be appropriate to unknown addresses.

According to Fig. 1, under no circumstances should a stranger address a physician by his first name. Indeed, the prestige of physicians even exempts them from first-naming (but not from 'Doc') by used-car salesmen, and physicians' wives can be heard so identifying themselves in public in order to claim more deference than 'Mrs.' brings. Thus the policeman's message is quite precise: 'Blacks are wrong to claim adult status or occupational rank. You are children.' Dr Poussaint was stripped of all deference due his age and rank.

Communication has been perfect in this interchange. Both were familiar with an address system which contained a selector for race available to both black and white for insult, condescension, or deference, as needed. Only because they shared these norms could the policeman's act have its unequivocal impact.

NOTES

1. 'Rules' in this article are not prescriptive but descriptive. They may not be in conscious awareness. Unlike habits, they may include complex structures inferred from the occurrence of interpretable and appropriate novel behaviour.

2. In this system Fig. 1, it is possible to create asymmetrical address by using FN

to a familiar addressee who cannot reciprocate because of rank or age difference, and his unwillingness or lack of dispensation, e.g., a domestic servant. E. Hughes has noted a shift from TLN to FN by physicians whose patients move from private fees to Medicare. This usage does not fit into the rule in Fig. 1.

REFERENCES

Geoghegan, W. (1971), 'Information processing systems in culture', in P. Kay (ed), *Explorations in Mathematical Anthropology*, MIT Press.

Hymes, D. (ed.) (1964), *Language in Culture and Society*, Harper & Row.

Hymes, D. (1967), 'Models of the interaction of language and social setting', *Journal of Social Issues*, vol. 23 no. 2 pp. 8-28.

Post, E. (1922), *Etiquette*, Funk and Wagnalls.

Poussaint, A.F. (1967), 'A Negro psychiatrist explains the Negro psyche', *New York Times Magazine*, August 20, p. 52.

3.4 Problems and *Problems*: Power Relationships in a Medical Encounter[1]

PAULA A. TREICHLER, RICHARD M. FRANKEL, CHERIS
KRAMARAE, KATHLEEN ZOPPI,
AND HOWARD B. BECKMAN

Physician: What are you feelin' down a*bout*?
Patient: Stomach problems, back problems, *side* problems
Physician: *Prob*lems problems
Patient: Problems and *prob*lems

This chapter reports a collaborative effort by the authors to analyze a videotape of a routine clinic visit between a patient and a medical resident. Our overall purpose is to illuminate dimensions of power in this particular encounter and in medical settings generally. At one level, we define our scholarly task as learning more about the real-time organization of power as manifested in observable interactions on the videotape. At another level, we are interested in better understanding some of the formal and informal practices that accompany our individual and collective efforts as researchers. Finally, as citizens and consumers concerned with the distribution of health care resources, we are interested in connecting the results of our research to more broadly based questions about power in medical encounters. This chapter, then, is an analysis of a medical encounter that we present as a model of collaborative, interdisciplinary research on power in medical settings.

POWER IN MEDICAL INTERACTIONS

There are many reasons to examine power in medical interactions.

Source: Treichler P.A. *et al.* (1984) 'Problems and *prob*lems: power relations in a medical encounter' in Kramarae C., Schulz M, and O'Barr W.M. *Language and Power*, New York, Sage, pp. 62-88.

As patients we sometimes feel excluded from knowledge and decision making that affect our health and well-being. As consumers we may feel ineffectual or neglected in our attempts to affect the organization and delivery of health care services. As health care professionals, we sometimes feel frustrated by patients' seeming unwillingness to adhere to our therapeutic programs, and by the difficulties of delivering high-quality care under stringent time constraints. As researchers we observe that practitioners routinely take the lead in regulating the conversational exchanges through which patient problems and needs are identified; in consequence, patients' concerns are sometimes assessed on the basis of incomplete or narrowly defined knowledge. All these difficulties may be said to involve issues of power.

Though power is often taken for granted as a component of medical encounters, its conceptualization and discussion remain problematic and elusive (see Foucault, 1975; Heath, 1979; Giles, Scherer, and Taylor, 1979; Starr, 1983). This is true in part because there is no clear-cut consensus among researchers on what power means, how it functions in clinical practice, or what individual, community, and societal consequences flow from its exercise. Further, there is no independent, uncompromised stance from which studies of power can be viewed and interpreted.

But the major difficulty arises from the prevailing view that power in medical settings is a social fact, established a priori by the differential position of individuals or groups within the social structure (e.g., patients and physicians). Much like actors who have memorized and rehearsed their lines before a performance, participants are seen as bringing power with them to the health care encounter: differences in rights, duties, and obligations are known in advance. Any change in the script — for example, a physician's attempt to be primarily a listener or a patient's attempt to ask many questions — is viewed as exceptional and deviant. Thus, power is seen as a static property emanating from one individual (usually from the practitioner) or as a force applied by one individual to another.

We examine power in a different way: we view power relations as negotiated within the context of face-to-face interaction. Though we acknowledge that such "preconditions" as status, gender, and race influence participants' attitudes and expectations, we suggest that it is also important to examine the *interactive behavior* of the participant. Power as a dynamic concept emerges within patterns of communication over time and space, and cannot be located as a property of the individual. Rather, power becomes the negotiated product of a mutually constituted and mutually administered interaction system. From this standpoint, any assessment of power must take the details of interaction — for example, sequential and other complex relationships among utterances — into account.

If we think of power as a process, as bound to a relationship, then patient-physician interaction becomes not just evidence that opportunities and resources are differentially distributed, but the site where they are established and negotiated. An ongoing locus for such relations, for example, is in the exchange of information in the medical encounter. Patients generally know little of their physicians' training, career expectations, or personal life; they generally know little of what the physician remembers about them nor what is contained in their medical records. Yet they bring to the medical interaction considerable knowledge about their own physical symptoms, medical histories, and potential cause of illness; based on their lifetime experience as patients, they also bring knowledge about the nature of medical encounters. Physicians, bringing specialized knowledge and training to the encounter, nonetheless are dependent upon patients for information that will yield accurate diagnosis and treatment. The medical encounter involves a sequence of complex interactional structures in and through which knowledge and expertise are actualized.

Our view of power, then, focuses on mutual, but asymmetrical influence, and recognizes the control physician and patient exert on each other's actions. In the analysis that follows, we attempt to identify and explore the creation of power relations among the participants in a medical encounter — a physician, a patient, and a medical student. We also attempt to position ourselves as researchers in relationship to the analytic process.

METHOD OF STUDY

The encounter we report is a routine follow-up visit between Dr. David Toffer, a white second-year medical resident in a Primary Care Internal Medicine Training Program, and Mr. Joseph Stittler, a 38-year-old Black man. A third participant in the encounter is Allan, a white second-year medical student who joins the resident as part of his medical school's Introduction to Clinical Medicine curriculum and talks with the patient at the conclusion of the resident's formal interview. (All participants' names have been changed to protect their privacy.)

The data were gathered through a research and training program developed at Wayne State University School of Medicine by two of the authors — Richard Frankel, a conversational analyst trained in sociology, and Howard Beckman, an internist. Medical interviews in their program are routinely videotaped; some are transcribed and analyzed in detail for research and teaching purposes. In some cases (including this one), the physician and patient are invited independently to review and comment upon the videotaped interview; their comments, audiorecorded and then superimposed upon the original tape at relevant points, make the tape an important source of information about participants' points of view (Frankel and Beckman, 1982). A further analytic procedure was used in the current study: three researchers in addition to Frankel and Beckman, trained in different fields (linguistics, sociolinguistics, and health education), analyzed the videotape from the perspectives of their respective disciplines. This approach to communicational analysis (Pittinger, Hockett, and Danehy, 1960) yields a layered, multidisciplinary exploration of medical interaction.

THE PATIENT AND THE PHYSICIAN

This is the fifth visit between Dr. Toffer and Mr. Stittler. Prior to a follow-up visit of this kind, the physician reviews the patient's record and develops an agenda for the visit based on previously identified problems and treatment plans. Mr. Stittler's previously identified problems include hypertension, nausea and vomiting, chronic fatigue, liver enlargement, low white blood count, bronchitis, and ulcer disease. The medical record from the immediately preceeding visit noted abdominal pain associated with vomiting and cough. The patient is being treated with antibiotics and antacids. The physician thus confronts a patient with multiple problems; he must determine their current status as well as assess the results of two treatment regimens. From his point of view, this is not a visit designed to uncover new problems but rather to review old problems and continue testing to refine the diagnosis.

The patient, since his last visit, has stopped receiving social security disability payments.

The Encounter

The patient, the resident, and the medical student enter the examination room. The resident opens the interaction; addressing the patient as "Mr. Stittler," he shows him where he can put his jacket and where to sit, and explains the presence of the medical student ("Allan"). The patient talks briefly with the student, and then the resident begins the interview. (A guide to the system of transcription used to present the verbal data appears in the Appendix.)

> Physician: Great. So *how* you doing today Joseph.
> Patient: Not too good doct//or
> Physician: Not too good. I see you kinda hangin' your head low there.
> Patient: Yeah.
> Physician: Must be somethin' up (·) or down I should say. Are you feelin' down?
> Patient: Yeah
> Physician: What are you feelin' down a*bout* (0.7)
> Patient: Stomach problems, back problems, *side* problems.
> Physician: *Prob*lems problems
> Patient: Problems and *prob*lems
> Physician: Hum. What's:: we- whats goin' on   with your stomach. Are you still uh-havin' pains in your stomach?

The patient initially makes eye contact with the physician and student. But as the physician gets to the official agenda — "So how you doing today" — the patient drops his head. For most of the interview he sits slumped in the chair, head down. He seldom introduces topics, usually agrees with the resident or expands his comments slightly, and speaks at an unusually slow pace. Information is gathered by the resident without comment, although at one point the resident suggests that a problem of holding down food cannot be too severe since the records show the patient hasn't lost much weight over recent months. The physician offers the following summaries of the patient's information, and the patient confirms them: He is still throwing up food; the nausea has been worse since December; it is bad most of the time; he is having fever; he feels he's getting a cold; he feels nauseated during the day; there is pain in his lower back; he has only an occasional beer and nothing stronger. He contributes little other information except short statements of his problems. The resident moves from general questions to more specific questions about the patient's physical problems, a commonly used "funnel" approach. The topics and the preferred range of answers introduced by the questions are supplied primarily by the physician (see the sequence marked B in the Appendix). Eight minutes into the interview, the resident shifts his approach:

> Physician: (O:kay) (3.2) What do you think is uh — is goin' on here. Wadda you — wha' do you think has been happenin' with ya. Any ideas?
> Patient: Lots a' worriation
> Physician: Lots a' what?
> Patient: Worriation
>   (0.2)
> Physician: Worriation? Lotta worryin' y' mean? =
> Patient: = Yes
> Physician: What've you been worried about.
> Patient: Well I don't have no income anymore.

In response to the resident's direct query, the patient offers his explanation of the problem. In the dialogue that follows (see the sequence marked C on the transcript in the Appendix), the patient explains that his social security checks have been discontinued; as he talks, he initiates sustained eye contact with the physician for the first time since the beginning of the interview. As the doctor asks questions and provides encouraging feedback ("um hum"), the patient's answers become longer than in the preceding "funneling" section of the interview. He explains that his continuing problems began with a blow to his head 13 years earlier.

The physician then asks, "just out of curiosity," how this blow to the head occurred. (This initiates the sequence marked D on the transcript.) The patient tells the story of how he was paralyzed on his left side "for life" when he was hit from behind with a tire iron. Based on this injury and the diagnosis of a lifetime disability the patient stopped work and began to receive social security compensation. He knows this story well and, once encouraged to speak by the physician's questions and comments, tells it with animation.

Although the physical problems including pain and paralysis are still present, the social security checks supporting him for years have recently stopped coming, and he has suddenly been told that he must find work. He believes he is unable to work. The doctor listens to this recitation, asks several clarifying questions; and then shifts the topic of the discussion back to the present set of problems:

> Physician: O:kay well (more) to your cu:rrent problem right now. What you (·) you know are descri:bin' sounds like a *flu*-like kind of syndrome.

The resident returns the interview to his domain of expertise — analysis and treatment of the patient's biomedical problems. He does so by sharing his evaluation of the information as a summary statement about flu. He does not comment on or assess the problem identified by the patient (loss of income), nor does he at this point or at any other point in the discussion offer a remedy. The question thus raised is one of the negotiation and status of patient problems and the selective attention paid by the provider to the biomedical dimensions of care. An additional question is the patient's unwillingness or inability to pursue his concern over the loss of income from what he understood was a long-term disability.

For the remainder of the interview the resident concentrates on the analysis and treatment of the patient's biomedical problems. He carries out a physical examination. He spends time describing the nature of vitamin B-12 deficiency and the test the patient will undergo to rule this out as a cause of the patient's medical problems. In closing the interview, he acknowledges that the patient is "down," and expresses the hope that the test results will provide a basis for timely and efficient treatment.

Use of Questions

Several specific features of the interview are noteworthy. One is the use of questions. A general sequential property of questions is that they limit the domain of what will count as a conversationally appropriate next action (Sacks, 1966). Frankel (forthcoming) and West (1983) found that physicians routinely (99% and 91%, respectively) ask questions, and patients routinely   provide responses. In a speech exchange system in which one party chronically occupies the initiating position and the other party occupies the responding position, it follows that the initiating speaker exerts a form of organizational control over the respondent.

In the particular interaction we have been describing the physician may feel it necessary to ask so many questions (and suggest responses) because the patient is slow in offering information that can be used to construct the record of care and to make a diagnosis. For example, in one section of the transcript (see sequence marked A in the Appendix), six utterances are initiated by the physician; four of these contain questions. (One of those four contains two questions, which may raise a problem for the patient; see Shuy [1976]).

In contrast, all six of the patient's utterances are responses. Interestingly, one response — "Nervous tensions (·) can't sleep" — contains information that was not specifically solicited by the physician's previous question. More will be said about this utterance momentarily, but it is worth noting that the physician's response to the information is minimal. He acknowledges with the token, "I see." It is notable that with the exception of "*Prob*lems problems," the physician gives only minimal responses; mostly, he produces token acknowledgements: "Hum," "Hmh," and "I see." The significance of this pattern lies in the contrast between clinical problem-solving talk, in which the professional assembles a data base and tests hypotheses in an attempt to "solve" the client's problem, and casual conversation, in which a trouble or complaint is responded to much more immediately with assessments like "That's too bad" or "I'm sorry to hear that" before a solution is offered or searched for. The lack of such responses is a general characteristic of physician-patient discourse and is often attributed to the desire or goal to remain clinically detached or neutral during the data-gathering phase of an encounter (Frankel, forthcoming). Discourse strategies that yield neutral responses to highly emotional or charged information offered by a client have not been examined in the context of patient satisfaction or outcome; the physician's lack of effective response may be, in this context, an important dimension of power and control.

The Written Record

The physician's written record of care that accompanies each encounter is an important feature of the medical encounter. Like many other institutional files, the clinic's written records on patients are a "bureaucratic collection of details" (Heath, 1982) that routinely function as "factual" accounts of the patients' consultation with doctors. Since we are interested in various dimensions of influence on the communication situation itself, those record-keeping practices that occur as the encounter is ongoing provide another significant dimension in which control may be examined. At a very gross level, we can say that the decision to take notes during the encounter itself represents an influence on the physician-patient relationship. From the point of view of interaction structure, the act of writing while discourse is ongoing creates multiple sites of attention. It is well known (for example, see Kendon, 1967) that coparticipants routinely look at one another from time-to-time during face-to-face interactions. Since note-taking almost invariably draws the physician's gaze away from the patient and to the record, interpersonal attention to the patient has effectively been "cut-off." Another way of stating this proposition is to say that the act of writing affects the very interaction for which the text stands as a representative.

Using the transcript in conjunction with the videotape of the encounter Frankel has recently developed a technique for mapping the location of each episode of writing to its location relative to the discussion of the patient and physician. In this way the relationship of talk to the written record can be studied. The segment of transcript already examined (the sequence marked A in the Appendix) contains two writing episodes and is presented below. The numbers and brackets above the utterances indicate the onset and offset point for each episode in terms of elapsed time in seconds since the beginning of the visit. The left-hand margin of the transcript shows the entries made by the physician during each of the writing episodes. Quotation marks enclose each text entry.

	Physician:	What are you feelin' down a*bout* (0.7)
	Patient:	Stomach problems, back problems, *side* problems.
		[086
	Physician:	*Prob*lems problems
"2/9/82"	Patient:	Problems and *problems*
		090]
	Physician:	Hum. What's::we- whats goin' on with

		your stomach. Are you still uh- havin' pains in your stomach?
	Patient:	Yeah it's- can't hold no *food* water
	Physician:	How 'bout uh- ::are you- y' still throwin up?
	Patient:	Oh yes.
	Physician:	Hmh
		(2.0)
		[105
	Patient:	Nervous tensions (·) can't sleep.
		111]
"Still	Patient:	hhh
N&V"	Physician:	I see. An::d so this has be::en since December you've been havin' this (0.2) nausea =
	Patient:	= Oh. yeah =

It is clear even from this small sample of discourse that what is said and what is recorded do not necessarily stand in a one-to-one relationship. For example, at an elapsed time of 86 seconds into the encounter, the resident begins to write. At this point he records not the list of ailments mentioned by the patient, but the date. Parenthetically, this is also the point at which he has just completed the possibly ironic "*Prob*lems problems." The resident's "cut-off" almost immediately after this remark suggests its potentially hostile nature. The physician's writing continues across the patient's reply "Problems and *prob*lems," and into the beginning of the physician's next utterance. Given the timing of the writing episode that coincides with the patient's response to a request for a presenting complaint, the patient might conclude that the content of the physician's record is somehow tied to the information he has been giving. This possibility has particular relevance since the patient does not have visual access to the content of the entry, knowing only that writing occurs as he completes his statement of concerns.

In fact, the physician's entry has no tie whatsoever with the ongoing discourse; it is simply the recording of the date of the visit. There is, then, an ambiguity that exists between writing and its relationship to the ongoing discourse — an ambiguity whose structural features amount to a form of control regardless of content.

The second writing episode, like the first, begins after an affirmative response by the patient to a question by the physician. After minimally acknowledging the response with "Hmh," the physician pauses for two seconds and then begins to write. The content of this entry is directly tied to the previous sequence; "Are you — y' still throwin' up?" followed by, "Oh yes," produces the entry "Still N & V" (nausea and vomiting). Thus we see the physician exercising options about how and when to record pertinent information and how such options may limit the patient's participation or representation in the clinical picture that the record documents.

"Worriation" and the loss of income, the topic that was the patient's basic concern and took the most time to complete, was never entered into the record: it thus becomes a topic with no "official" status even though it may be pursued informally from visit to visit. It is also worth noting the fate of the patient's unsolicited offer of the complaint "Nervous tensions (·) can't sleep," since this concern also occurs while the physician was making an entry into the record. While the physician does provide a token acknowledgement "I see" at the conclusion of the writing episode, the information voiced by the patient is otherwise ignored for the duration of the visit. The fact that this concern was not recorded or addressed suggests that it may have been lost during the resident's record-keeping activities. This is perhaps another way in which the decision to take notes during the encounter influences the clinical picture.

PROBLEMS AND PROBLEMS

We have spent some time on the sequence in which the phrase "problems and *pro*blems" occurs (the sequence marked A in the Appendix). The resident here acknowledges, in his question, that the patient is depressed — "feelin' down." At this early point in the interview, the patient responds by listing general *medical* complaints, yet his litany seems to point the way to a problem not contained within the list; in other words, the list may signal the patient's sense of being overwhelmed with problems, yet without moving explicitly into the more troubling realm of "feelin' down." The intonation of the patient's utterance mirrors that of the physician's, with the major stress falling at its conclusion. At this point the physician *might* have pursued his opening question about "feelin" down," taking the patient's response *as* a response. Instead, however, he focuses on the first item in the patient's list, "stomach problems," and indicates that it is a known continuing condition that is being followed since he offers "are you — y' still throwing up?" This transition signals a shift out of the identification of current problems and concerns, including his own observation of the patient's depressed condition, and into an assessment of previously identified problems. Thus, at a point in the visit reserved for new problem identification and negotiation of an agenda for the day's visit, the resident has opted to concentrate on a previously established problem.

In playing back the tape, the resident commented about the patient's medical and psychosocial problems. Yet in the interaction itself, his "*Prob*lems problems" comes off as an ironic commentary on the patient's list. His emphasis on the first syllable suggests that any noun can fill the slot — that the patient's problems are multiple and ongoing and, in some sense, not interesting at all. The irony, then, is in the acknowledgement that the patient's list is "more of the same old thing" and is not a real response to why he is depressed. Yet it is also a dismissive comment, for it now makes the patient's entrance into the realm of depression even more difficult.

The patient's counterresponse captures the ironic dismissal: "Problems and *prob*lems," with the stress at the end of the utterance, highlights the physician's actual language, virtually parodying it. Literally the patient's phrase suggests that there are, indeed, two categories of problems; yet he is acquiescent when the physician, in the next utterance, singles out his stomach problems as the complaint to be taken up.

It is commonplace for sociomedical researchers to assert the dominance of the biomedical model in medicine and its preeminence over other forms of inquiry (see, for example, Engel, 1977; Kleinman, 1983; Todd, 1983). In this sequence we can perhaps see some of the complexities of this model in practice, and some of the consequences it can have for actual care. It is worth remembering that this physician is in a training program for residents, which attempts to integrate psychosocial information within a biomedical framework. In this particular interview, however, he finds this difficult to do.

Indeed, this seems to be an interview with "problems and

problems." There is a sense in which what did not get said is more striking than what did. In the next section we see a medical student addressing these problems somewhat differently.

THE MEDICAL STUDENT

Following the physical examination and concluding phase of the interaction, the resident closes the chart to signal the close of the official interview; he then asks the patient to participate in a more informal interview with the medical student who has been sitting in on the session:

> Physician: Well, I'm gonna go order some tests for you here and if you don't mind Allan would like to maybe talk with you for a couple of minutes before you split, okay, so we'll maybe try to get all your paperwork all done so you don't have to wait too long.

In several ways the resident marks the different status of the medical student's interview: "if you don't mind" suggests (at least theoretically) that the patient can refuse to be interviewed; similarly, "Allan would like" makes this a personal and rather minor favor to Allan rather than a clinical or institutional goal or requirement. The use of the student's first name as well as the qualifiers "maybe" and "a couple of minutes" further downplay significance, as does the departure from technical language in "before you split" and the suggestion that the patient has to wait anyhow for the paperwork to be done.

The medical student takes the resident's seat at the desk and opens his interview with low-key diffidence, in keeping with its unofficial status:

> Medical   I'm just kinda curious um about the pain you're
> student: having now. Has it been um progressively getting
>   worse?

The language is simple and clear; the mildly technical term "progressively" is deflated by "um." But the key word in this opening sequence is "curious." For this is a curious word in a medical interview. The request to be educated expresses a rather open-ended interest in the patient in a way we do not routinely expect to hear from physicians. Curiosity, in other words, is not what drives the typical medical interview. Indeed, the resident qualified a question about the patient's head injury with the phrase "just out of curiosity" and bracketed the lengthy response it elicited as irrelevant to the "current problem" (sequence marked D in the Appendix). For the medical student, in contrast, an expression of curiosity and what it elicits are central to his concerns at this stage in his training. Perhaps as important, the medical student's curiosity is linked to a critical interpersonal behavior: the ability to remain silent.

Into these silences the patient begins to tell his story. Unlike the resident, the student allows pauses to occur and shows a willingness to wait while the patient finds his own words. We have noted how the resident's "*Prob*lems problems" seemed rhetorically to trivialize the patient's concerns. The medical student refers to problems quite differently:

> Medical   You said you had lots of sad problems. Is [the loss of
> student: social security payments] the major one? Is there
>   anything else?

He waits three seconds. When the patient then mentions confusion, he says, "Tell me a little more about your confusion." He waits seven seconds. The patient mentions anger. The medical student says "yeah," encouraging him. The following exchange then occurs:

> Patient: I have killed before and I could do it again — easy.
> Student: Uh huh.
> Patient: And I know that the court won't hold this against me
>   cause I got a mental case — brain damage [moving
>   hands; slumps].
> Student: I see. So that was since you — since 1968?
> Patient: Yes.
> Student: Um hmmm. I see.

The medical student handles this new and rather startling

information with considerable *sangfroid* (see Part II of the transcript in the Appendix). For the rest of the interview, the medical student continues to encourage the patient to talk, eliciting new and sometimes surprising information he cannot have anticipated from the resident's interview. He learns that the patient sees a psychiatrist regularly, he has gone through an alcoholic detoxification and rehabilitation program, and he regularly takes Thorazine, a powerful antipsychotic medication that the patient feels may have a direct bearing on his stomach problems.

These are significant pieces of information, medically as well as psycho-socially. Particularly the information about Thorazine is of immediate relevance to the medical diagnosis and treatment of the patient's chief complaint. Yet none of these items appeared on the patient's official record, nor was there any provision for the medical student's interview to be incorporated into the ongoing care being provided. It appears that the medical student's role in this encounter was to practice his skills with a real patient; it was not assumed that the information obtained might have clinical relevance.

The medical student, then, though encompassed by the profession, does not yet fully embody it; his actions are minimized in terms of his impact on the actual delivery of care. Perhaps precisely because medical students often have little apparent "real" impact, most studies of medical professionalization focus on residents or mature physicians; certainly as far as the scholarly literature on language goes, we know more about such subcultures as pickpockets than we do about medical students (though the nonscholarly literature, notably fictionalized and autobiographical accounts of medical training, is rich in linguistic detail).

Yet it is as medical students that physicians first acquire the basic grammar and vocabulary of the profession, learn the techniques for eliciting and evaluating information, are required to begin integrating technical and nontechnical language, and encounter the central and unique intellectual project of the art and science of medicine: that of translating a language of flesh into a language of words, of building an intricate multidisciplinary verbal model of the human body. Along with these linguistic changes during medical school come changes in students' relationships to power and authority and in the way the human body is perceived, interpreted, described, and controlled.[2]

THE RESEARCH PROCESS

In describing and interpreting this medical encounter, we have treated power and control as the negotiated product of face-to-face interaction, derivable through formal analysis. Our findings in this way speak on behalf of the participants, implicity subsuming their views and their voices as though they were homologous with each other and with the outcomes of our analytic strategies. Such an assumption may not be warranted.

We can supplement and refine our analysis by asking the participants themselves to comment on the encounter, drawing upon their own knowledge and expertise and comparing their responses with our own conclusions. In this case, the resident and the patient independently viewed the videotape of their interaction, stopping the tape to identify and comment upon problems and concerns. Dr. Toffer, the resident, stopped the tape ten times. Twice he commented on the patient's depressed affect; the rest of his comments dealt exclusively with his hypotheses about the patient's biomedical problems (e.g., possible B-12 deficiency, upper gastric tenderness, neurologic problems secondary to trauma to the head). It is interesting that his first comment about depression occurred at a point we have discussed at length (the asterisk marks the point where the tape was stopped):

Physician: What are you feelin' down a*bout*
Patient: Stomach prob[*]lems, back problems, *side* problems
Physician: *Prob*lems problems
Patient: Problems and *prob*lems

The physician:

It's obvious when he came in, he just looked like a dishrag — just limp lying there. It's obvious he had fairly depressed affect. I don't think I've seen anybody that dramatic come into the office like that.

Thus, at least insofar as the professionals were concerned, there was agreement that the problem existed at the beginning of the encounter.

Mr. Stittler, the patient, stopped the tape four times, focusing on the stresses caused by his loss of income after 13 years of disability payments; he talked about his family problems, the test to determine disability he has been required to undergo, and his seeking psychiatric care. He was asked whether he was satisfied everything bothering him at the time of the interview had been addressed. "Not exactly everything," he responded. "I was depressed and my nerves was shot." By incorporating the patient's point-of-view, important information that could only be speculated at or proposed on the patient's behalf appeared in the same process of review. The result is a naturally controlled environment for studying the responses of the participants in their own words and under the same viewing conditions. In this way some of the problems in traditional analyses of power and control are minimized.

Frankel and Beckman (1982) report initial results from this playback technique that suggest that physicians and patients often (more than 60% of the time) independently stop the tape at identical points and comment on the same problems. Though their interpretations may vary, this high degree of concordance seems to indicate a shared orientation to the problems and concerns that unfold in the course of medical interactions. In the visit we report, in contrast, none of the commentaries occurred at the same points nor, with the exception of the physician's two comments about depression, did their topics converge. This structural evidence, tallying with the results of formal analysis, points away from a shared orientation between the patient and physician. It is perhaps significant that the patient did not return for the follow-up visit scheduled after the visit we have described.

A final perspective is provided by the medical student. In keeping with the status of his interview as informal, that portion of the videotape was not routinely transcribed for research and was in fact discovered only in the process of reviewing the "real" interview between the patient and the resident. Contacted some months later, the medical student nevertheless remembered the encounter clearly and in particular remembered that he had not discussed his findings with Dr. Toffer. Like the other participants in the encounter, he evidently also judged his interaction with the patient as unofficial and placed a different, perhaps lesser, value on the information he elicited.

The other participants involved in the study of this encounter are the researchers, who, collectively, make up the "we" of this published account. Our participation involves goals different from those of the original participants; likewise, we bring different perspectives and resources to the tasks of analysis and interpretation. While our interests, training, and analytic strategies as researchers overlap, we nevertheless acknowledge differences. A major challenge of collaborating on this project has been to achieve language and logic that all five of us, trained in different fields, find appropriate and illuminating. (The title of this chapter should only in part, however, be read as a commentary on the collaborative research process.)

CONCLUSION

In summary, both formal analysis and participants' commentaries suggest that the physician and patient in this encounter had very different concerns, only some of which were addressed during the visit. In particular, the physician's emphasis on biomedical aspects of the case, together with his style of interviewing and method of recording data, hindered a full expression of the patient's concerns and the development of a mutually agreed-upon agenda for the visit. Paradoxically, concerns expressed more readily to the medical student remained, in the absence of a mechanism that would incorporate them into the medical record, officially unspoken.

We believe that this method of analysis, which layers formal elements with the perspectives of individual participants and of researchers, enables us to look at some of the dynamic aspects of power in the medical encounter. We believe, further, that this process of acknowledging and codifying different perspectives holds promise for developing programs of intervention that are useful to all participants in medical encounters. It is important, as well, to examine our own relationship, as researchers, to our training, to our colleagues, to our audience, and to the "subjects" we are analyzing: If we want our work to have genuine impact, we need to be self-consciously reflective about our own power as researchers — power that is also not a static property but constructed in the course of our relationship with others.

APPENDIX: TRANSCRIPTS

Transcribing Conventions

The transcription method we used was developed by Gail Jefferson, at the University of California, Irvine, in the course of collaborative research with Harvey Sacks. The transcription system is intended to act as a guide to speech production activities as they occur on a micromomentary scale. The mapping of text entries from the medical record onto the discourse was developed by Richard M. Frankel.

Physician: [Right

Patient: And] if there's anything

Patient: No (0.3) an' nothing
⎡⎡since]
⎣⎣Not at all]

The onset of simultaneous speech is indicated with either a double or single left-hand bracket depending on where it occurs. Double brackets are used to indicate simultaneous turn beginnings; single brackets indicate interruption or overlap of ongoing speech. Single right-hand brackets indicate resolution points for simultaneous speech.

Patient: Something I wanna//
do]
Physician:
That's the whole-]

An alternate method of indicating overlap is the use of double oblique lines at the point of overlap or interruption.

(1.3)

Numbers in parentheses indicate pauses or breaks in speech production and are indicated in tenths of seconds. Pauses are marked both within and between speaking turns.

.?,?   Punctuation marks are used to indicate intonation and not grammar. A period indicates a sharply falling intonation; the question mark a sharply rising intonation. Commas and question commas (?̦) indicate intonation blends. , = slightly rising or slightly falling intonation. ?̦ = moderately rising intonation. Stressed syllables are italicized.

Patient: hh U:hm the: uh: (0.5)   Colons indicate a sound
            the back   stretch or prolongation of an immediately prior syllable. Each colon represents one-tenth of a second.

Physician: That's the whole-   A hyphen indicates that the immediately prior syllable has been cut off.

Physician: Y' put half a' pound on   Equals signs are used to
            this time. =   indicate that no discern-
Patient: ible time has elapsed
            = I don't know what tuh   between the completion of one speaker's utterance and the beginning of another.

hh hh   Breathing patterns are signified using hh's. A period followed by "hh's" marks an inhal-

ation; "hh's" alone stand
for exhalation.

"Feels   Dr: Don't have one. You   Brackets to the left of
warm last   just feel warm?   speaker   designations
week"   [259   indicate points in the
              Pt: Ye:s   (3.0).   Nose   interaction during which
                  bleeds.   writing   occurred.   A
              Dr: I see   single left-hand bracket
                      265]   and number indicating
              Pt: Y'r nose bleeds?   elapsed time in tenths of
                                             seconds shows the onset
                                             of writing; a single right-
                                             hand   bracket   and
                                             number shows its com-
                                             pletion. Quoted text in
                                             the left margin shows
                                             what was entered into
                                             the medical record dur-
                                             ing the writing episode.

I.
Dr. Toffer [Dr] and Mr. Stittler [Pt]; Allan is the medical student
[MS].

Dr: Havea seat there Mister Stittler (Right) over
       here you can put (·) jacket right behind
       there. (Right) over here there you go:. (0.5)
       An = ' have a se:at (0.7) (Hum) (0.7) Uh
       toda::y we're having medical students sit in
       with us if you don't mind this is Allan //
       (Mister) Stittler
Pt: (Hi how you doin')
MS: = Fine thank you
Pt: I have seen you *some*where before
MS: Oh really?
Pt: Yeah (   )
MS: ((laughs))
Dr: Maybe he:s been wandering around the
       medical centre here//(
Pt: ((laughs)) (oh yeah everywhere)

MS: ((laughs))
Dr.:   Great. So *how* you doing today Joseph
Pt: Not too good doct//or
Dr: Not too good. I see you kinda hangin' your head low there.
Pt: Yeah.
Dr: Must be somethin' up (·) or down I should say. Are you feelin' down?
Pt: Yeah

"2/9/82"

A

Dr: What are you feelin' down *about* (0.7)
Pt: Stomach problems, back problems, *side* problems.
[086
Dr: *Prob*lems problems
Pt: Problems and *prob*lems
090]
Dr: Hum. What's:: we- whats goin' on with your stomach. Are you still uh- havin' pains in your stomach?
Pt: Yeah it's- can't hold no *food* water
Dr: How 'bout uh-:: are you- y' still throwin' up?
Pt: Oh yes.
Dr: Hmh
(2.0)
[105
Pt: Nervous tensions (·) can't sleep.
111]

"Still N & V"

Pt: · hhh
Dr: I see. An::d so this has be::en since December you've been havin' this (0.2) this nausea =
Pt: = Oh. yeah =
Dr: = and stuff. (1.3) Has it gotten any *bet*ter, worse or-
Pt: Worse
Dr: Worse? Have you been able to *hold* down any *food*?
Pt: Well certain things
Dr: Certain kinds of food. Since Let's see well sinc:e (·) Oc*to*ber ((shuffling paper)) Let

me see where your weigh- oh here =
Dr: = We are we start over (again) one eighty-
six (1.0) probably if you're one seventy-
eight now so you maybe have lost about (·)
five pounds since - since October twenty-
seventh which isn't a whole lot (·) which
suggests that you must be holdin' down at
least a little bit.
Pt: Yeah just a little
Dr: what kind of things do you seem to be able
to hold *down.*
Pt: We:ll (like) fruits
Dr: Fruits?
       [170
Pt: like lemons

"No Prob w/   Dr: Mmh hmh
Fruits"   Pt   Grapes, oranges, apples
                                180]
Dr: Uh huh (·) what kind a'things aren't
y-seem t' be able tuh holding down. (0.3)
What things come up pretty *ea*sily =
Pt: = Well (0.8) (like) heavy food like
               (0.5)
Dr: Heavy food?
Pt: Yeah
Dr: What would you call heavy food, *maple*
syrup or mashed potatoes or
Pt: Yes. *beans pea:s*
               (0.7)
       [200
Dr: *Veg*etables kinda in general?

"Vegetables   Pt: Oh ye:s
bother   (1.2)
stomach"   206]
Dr: How bout uh::- (0.5) *meat.* Have you been
able to eat any kinda meat 'at all? (1.0)
chicken or hamburgers or (1.0) fish or anything? fish or anything like tha- has that
been able to stay down?
Pt: No::
Dr: That's been comin' up, *All* the time er j'st

some time.

Pt: In general *most* of the time.

Dr: Most of the time. (1.3) I see. (0.7)
       Uh::m(·)hmh: Have you been havin' any
       fever or chills at all?

Pt: Ye:s fever.

"Fever"

[237   242]

Dr: Been havin' a fever? How long have you-
       have you been havin' fevers.

Pt: Oh (4.7) (for-) (2.1) over a *week* now.

Dr: About a week?

Dr: ⌈⌈Have you taken your
Pt: ⌊⌊Ye:s

Dr: temperature with a thermometer?

Pt: I don't have none.

Dr: Don't have one. You just feel warm?

[259

"Feels warm   Pt: Ye:s (3.0)⌈⌈Nose blee:ds
last week"   Dr: ⌊⌊I see:

                      265]

Dr: Y'r nose bleeds?

Pt: Yes

B   (1.2)

Dr: That's just somethin' recently? (1.0) Just
       recently *start*ed

Pt: Yeah.

Dr: Does it start by itself or is it like after you
       blow your nose or pick your nose or
       somethin like that =

Pt: = A *cough* or (·) *sneeze* somethin' like *that*

Dr: Mmh hmh how many t:imes does this
       actually happen to you that your nose starts
       bleeding

[256

Seq: Pt: Two sometimes three times a day
"Nosebleed   Dr: Two uh three times a day
2-X a day"   Pt: Yeah.

                      297]

Dr: Am:' when did you first *start* noticin' that
       you were gettin nose bleeds.

[A portion of the transcript is omitted here.]

		[380 389]
"Claims	Dr:	(O:kay) (3.2) What do you think is uh — is
no ETOH"		goin' on here. Wadda you — wha'do you
		think has been happenin' with ya. Any
		ideas?

```
                        [380                                    389]
"Claims    Dr:  (O:kay) (3.2) What do you think is uh — is
no ETOH"        goin' on here. Wadda you — wha'do you
                think has been happenin' with ya. Any
                ideas?
                    (4.0)
           Pt:  Lots a' worriation
           Dr:  Lots a what?
           Pt:  Worriation
                    (0.2)
           Dr:  Worriation? Lotta worryin' y' mean? =
 C         Pt:  = Yes

           Dr:  What've you been worried about.

           Pt:  Well I don' have no income anymore.
           Dr:  You don't (1.0) Because you're not workin'
           Pt:  No de:y (0.7) stopped my checks last
                month.
                    (0.3)
           Dr:  What your::uh
           Pt:  Social Security =
           Dr:  = Social Security isn't payin' any more?
           Pt:  No
           Dr:  Hmh (1.0) How come- why did they do that
                (1.0) Any idea? =
           Pt:  Back in November I took a: (5.0) a
                determination us tes//They-
           Dr:  Um hum
           Pt:  = said I was able to work.
           Dr:  Mmh hmh
           Pt:  My lawyer say ( · ) y' got a good case cuz
                uh- he has no more complaints from the
                Jefferson clinic. ( · )//(((loudspeaker in
                background)) =
           Dr:  Um hum
           Pt:  That's all they did
           Dr:  All they did was ask you ques//stions
           Pt:  Told me to raise my hand (and) walk back-
```

	wards ask me a a few questions
Dr:	Um hum
Pt:	I'm able to work.
Dr:	Oh that was your evaluation for social// security.
Pt:	Yes yes
Dr:	I: see. Do you think you're able to work?
Pt:	No.
Dr:	Wadda you feel would be keepin' you from workin' right now.
Pt:	Uh- I *can't* use my left side.
Dr:	You *whole* left side?
Pt:	Yes — my a:rm my le:g
Dr:	It feel- it feels weak on that side
Pt:	Yes I can't hardly (walks and move)
	(0.3)
Dr:	You had mentioned that a *while* before um : (0.3) how *long* (0.5) has this been botherin' you this weakness on your (0.3) left side.

"L side weakness"

Pt:	Well (4.2) (first sta:rt to) on social security (0.8) back in November of sixty-nine.
Dr:	Um hum
Pt:	The doctors told me say — this'll your (life/ /(·)) ((loudspeaker in background)) (·) be paralyzed for left- =
Dr:	(Right right)
Pt:	= for life on your left side =
Dr:	= did they tell you why: you were paralyzed for life d//n you left side?
Pt:	(Somethin' wrong with the limbs)
	[539
Dr:	Did they say what the problem was at the time?

"(Since 1969)"

	543]
	(3.0) Did they//say what ca:used the weakness.
Pt:	Yes
Pt:	Yes it was a blow to the *head*
Dr:	A *blow* to the head.

"2° blow to head"

Pt:	Yes.
	550]

Dr: So you've had this problem ever since (·) that blow to your head.

[555

Pt: Yeah that happened back in April the *twel*fth nineteen sixty-eight.

(0.8)

"1968"   Dr: Um hum

Pt: Philadelphia Pennsylvania.

(0.3)

560]

Dr: How di- how did you get hit in the head just out of curiosity.

(0.5)

Pt: I was workin' at Temple University Hospital

Dr: Um hum

Pt: And this was on a Wednesday

Dr: Um hum

Pt: Pay day // used to be paid every two weeks.

Dr: Um hum

Dr: Um hum.

Pt: I (had) *caught* the *sub*way home — I was stayin' in *North* Philadelphia

Dr: Um hum

Pt: I got off uh- was goin' home I passed a Lo:dge

Dr: Um hum

Pt: About six or seven people out there (bunch) of prostitutes asked me if I wanna turn a trick you know.

Dr: Heh

(0.3)

Pt: Said I got enough problems at *home*

Dr: Yeah

Pt: One of these jokers jumped out on me and I — I start puttin' it on 'm I was doin pretty *good* too

Dr: Um hum

Pt: Somebody was behind (I heard this *trunk*) (·) car trunk slam?

Dr: Um hum

Pt: He has a ti:re iron

D {

Dr:	Um
Pt:	Cut me across the head.//I =
Dr:	Hum
Pt:	= wind up in the sa:me hospital I was workin' in
Dr:	O:h no::
Pt:	Stayed in a coma three r' four days.

[629

Dr:	In a *coma* three or four days?
Pt:	They was looking- wasn't lookin' for me to live.
Dr:	*Hum* well you certainly did.

"Was in Coma 3-4 days"

636]   [638

Pt:	I was in a wheel:l chair for (0.6) three t' four months.

(0.7)

Dr:	Hmh:
Pt:	= couldn't *walk*.

"Was in Wheelchair"

(1.0)

Dr:	What was it that kept you from walkin:
Pt:	Paralyzation.

(1.0)

Dr:	What- was it just on your left side or//both sides
Pt:	Yes

(1.0)

"w/paralyzed L side?"

Dr:	Did you have a skull fracture or anything like that at // the time =
Pt:	Yes. They had t' put a *plate* in my head.

663]

Dr:	I: see. So this has really been (·) since the a:ccident. =
Pt:	= Oh yes.

}

Dr:	You've had this weakness. O:kay well (more) to your cu:rrent problem right now. What you (·) you know are descri:bin' sounds like a *flu*-like kind of syndrome. Although u::h you do have some other problems that we're working on u:m: one thing was we had talked about you had this B-12 deficiency.

Pt: Oh yeah.

The transcript of the rest of the interview is omitted.]

II.
Allan [medical student: MS] and Mr. Stittler [patient: Pt].
Brackets enclose nonvocal behaviors and pauses. (U) = unintelligible vocalization.

MS: I'm just kinda curious um about the pain [looks at pt] you're having now. Um has it been um progressively getting worse?

Pt: Oh yes [looks up, slumps, plays with left shirt cuff)

MS: Uh huh. I see. Does it seem to be worse in the morning? Or at night?
       [2 sec]

Pt: Yes — morning

MS: Usually in the morning?

Pt: Umm [yawns]

MS: Uh. Does your left leg and arm bother you a lot?

Pt: Oh yes — there's pain.

MS: Does it tingle a lot sometimes like little needle pricks, or —

Pt: -(U) [points to upper left arm] Right here in the muscle. [slumps]

MS: Um Hmm. That's been since 1968 or so, right?

Pt: Yes

MS: Um hmm. And so you've been getting social security until just a month ago then?

Pt: Yes

MS: Um hmm. That really is a disturbing thing then when that went away. [Pt. picks at left shirt cuff] [pause] Is there anything else that's troubling you that way? You said you had lots of sad problems. Is that the major one? Is there anything else?
       [3 sec]

Pt: Umm. Get confused easy.

MS: Uh huh. Confusion. [looks at pt] Tell me a little more about your confusion. [7 sec]

Pt: Get angry. (U) [vocalizes, moves right hand] (U) violent intentions. (?)

MS: Yeah

Pt: [looks at MS] I have killed before and I could do it again — easy.

MS: Uh huh.

Pt: And I know that the court won't hold this against me cause I got a mental case — brain damage [moving hands — slumps]

MS: I see. So that was since you — since 1968?

Pt: Yes

MS: Um hmm. I see.

NOTES

1. The authors would especially like to thank the individuals who agreed to let them videotape, analyze, and publish the results of this investigation. Partial funding for this research was provided by a grant from the National Council of Teachers of English to Paula A. Treichler, a grant from the Ruth Mott Foundation to Howard B. Beckman and Richard M. Frankel, and a Program Development Grant for Residency Training in Primary Care Internal Medicine, NIH PE 15226-02.

2. General discussions of medical professionalization include Becker *et al.* (1961), Bosk (1979), Bucher and Stelling (1977), Freidson (1970), and Larson (1977). For a discussion of medical students and linguistic change that touches on the changing relationship of the physician-in-training to power and authority, see Treichler and Zoppi (1983). Increasingly, postgraduate programs such as Frankel and Beckman's are emphasizing communication as an element of primary care practice; such instruction occurs relatively late in the trainee's educational career, however, and seems different from the initial acquisition of a medical repertoire.

REFERENCES

Engel, George L. (1977) The need for a new medical model: A challenge for bio-medicine. *Science* (April 8) 129-36.

Foucault, Michel (1975) *The Birth of the Clinic: An Archaeology of Medical Perception.* New York: Vintage.

Frankel, Richard M (Forthcoming) Talking in interviews: a dispreference for patient-initiated questions in physician-patient encounters. In George Psathas and Richard Frankel, eds. *International Competence.* New York: Irvington.

Frankel, Richard M. and Howard B. Beckman (1982) IMPACT: An interaction-based method for preserving and analyzing clinical transactions. In

Lloyd Pettegrew *et al.*, eds. (pp. 71-85) *Straight Talk: Explorations in Provider and Patient Interactions.* Nashville: Humana, Inc., in conjunction with the International Communication Association.

Giles, Howard, Klaus R. Scherer, and D.M. Taylor (1979) Speech markers in social interaction. In K.R. Scherer and Howard Giles, eds. *Social Markers in Speech.* Cambridge: Cambridge University Press.

Heath, Christian (1982) Preserving the consultation: Medical record cards and professional conduct. *Sociology of Health and Illness* 4(1), 56-74.

Heath, Shirley Brice (19798) The context of professional languages: An historical overview. In J. Alatis and R. Tucker, eds. (pp. 102-18) *Language and Public Life.* Washington, DC: Georgetown University Press.

Kendon, Adam (1967) Some functions of gaze direction in social interaction., *Acta Psychologica.* 26, 1-47.

Kleinman, Arthur (1983) The cultural meanings and social uses of illness. *Journal of Family Practice.* 16, 539-45.

Pittinger, Robert E., Charles F. Hockett and John J. Danehy (1960) *The First Five Minutes.* Ithaca, NY: Paul Martineau.

Sacks, Harvey (1966) Unpublished lectures, University of California at Los Angeles.

Shuy, Roger (1976) The medical interview: Problems in communication. *Primary Care* 3(3), 365-86.

Starr, Paul (1983) *The Social Transformation of American Medicine.* New York: Basic Books.

Todd, Alexandra Dundas (1983) A diagnosis of doctor-patient discourse in the prescription of contraception. In S. Fisher and A. Todd, eds. *The Social Organization of Doctor-Patient Communication.* Washington, DC: Center for Applied Linguistics.

West, Candace (1983) "Ask me no questions . . .': an analysis of queries and replies in physician-patient dialogues. In S. Fisher and A. Todd, eds (pp. 75-106). *The Social Organization of Doctor-Patient Communication.* Washington DC: Center for Applied Linguistics.

3.5 "Women's Language" or "Powerless Language"?

WILLIAM M. O'BARR AND BOWMAN K. ATKINS

INTRODUCTION

The understanding of language and sex in American culture has progressed far beyond Robin Lakoff's influential and provocative essays on "women's language" written only a few years ago.[1] The rapid development of knowledge in what had been so significantly an ignored and overlooked area owes much to both the development of sociolinguist interest in general and to the woman's movement in particular. But as a recent review of anthropological studies about women pointed out, this interest has grown so quickly and studies proliferated so fast that there is frequently little or no cross-referencing of mutually supportive studies and equally little attempt to reconcile conflicting interpretations of women's roles.[2] A similar critique of the literature on language and sex would no doubt reveal many of the same problems. But in one sense, these are not problems — they are marks of a rapidly developing field of inquiry, of vitality, and of saliency of the topic.

Our interest in language and sex was sharpened by Lakoff's essays. Indeed, her work was for us — as it was for many others — a jumping off point. But unlike some other studies, ours was not primarily an attempt to understand language and sex differences. Rather, the major goal of our recent research has been the study of language variation in a specific institutional context — the American trial courtroom — and sex-related differences were one of the kinds of variations which current sociolinguistic issues led us to consider. Our interest was further kindled by the discovery that trial practice manuals (how-to-do-it books by successful trial lawyers and law professors) often had special sections on how female

Source: O'Barr W.M. and Atkins, B.K. (1980) '"Women's language" or "powerless language"?' in McConnell-Ginet S., Barker R. and Furman N. (eds) *Women and Language in Literature and Society*, New York, Praeger, pp. 93-110.

witnesses behave differently from males and thus special kinds of treatment they require.

In this paper, we describe our study of how women (and men) talk in court. The research we report here is part of a 30-month study of language variation in trial courtrooms.[3] It is the thesis of this study that so-called "women's language" is in large part a language of powerlessness; a condition that can apply to men as well as women. That a complex of such features should have been called "women's language" in the first place reflects the generally powerless position of many women in American society, a point recognized but not developed extensively by Lakoff.[4] Careful examination in one institutional setting of the features which were identified as constituting "women's language" has shown clearly that such features are simply not patterned along sex lines. Moreover, the features do not, in a strict sense, constitute a *style* or *register* since there is not perfect co-variation.

This chapter proceeds as follows: first, it examines the phenomenon of "women's language" in the institutional context of a court of law; second, it shows that the features of "women's language" are not restricted to women and therefore suggests renaming the concept "powerless" language due to its close association with persons having low social power and often relatively little previous experience in the courtroom setting; and finally, it calls for a refinement of our studies to distinguish powerless language features from others which may in fact be found primarily in women's speech.

HOW TO HANDLE WOMEN IN COURT — SOME ADVICE FROM LAWYERS

One of the means which we used in our study of courtroom language to identify specific language variables for detailed study was information provided to us in interviews with practicing lawyers. More useful, however, were *trial practice manuals* — books written by experienced lawyers which attempt to discuss systematically successful methods and tactics for conducting trials. Typically, little effort is devoted to teaching and developing trial practice skills in the course of a legal education. Rather it is expected that they will be acquired through personal experimentation, through watching and modeling one's behavior after successful senior lawyers, and through reading the advice contained in such manuals. Those who write trial practice manuals are experienced members of the legal profession who are reporting on both their own experiences and the generally accepted folklore within the profession. In all these situations, the basis for claims about what works or what does not tends to be the general success of those who give advice or serve as models — judged primarily by whether they win their cases most of the time.

One kind of advice which struck us in reading through several of these manuals was that pertaining to the special treatment which should be accorded women. The manuals which discuss special treatment for women tend to offer similar advice regarding female witnesses. Readers are instructed to behave generally the same toward women as men, but to note that, in certain matters or situations, women require some special considerations. Some of this advice includes the following:

1. *Be especially courteous to women.* ("Even when jurors share the cross-examiner's reaction that the female witness on the stand is dishonest or otherwise undeserving individually, at least some of the jurors are likely to think it improper for the attorney to decline to extend the courtesies customarily extended to women."[5]

2. *Avoid making women cry.* ("Jurors, along with others, may be inclined to forgive and forget transgressions under the influence of sympathy provoked by the genuine tears of a female witness." "A crying woman does your case no good."[6]

3. *Women behave differently from men and this can sometimes be used to advantage.* ("Women are contrary witnesses. They hate to say yes. ... A woman's desire to avoid the obvious answer will lead her right into your real objective — contradicting the testimony of previous prosecution witnesses. Women, like children, are prone to exaggeration; they generally have poor memories as to previous fabrications and exaggerations. They also are stubborn. You will have difficulty trying to induce them to qualify their testimony. Rather, it might be easier to induce them to exaggerate and cause their testimony to appear incredible. An intelligent woman will very often be evasive. She will avoid making a direct answer to a damaging question. Keep after her until you get a direct answer — but always be the gentleman."[7]

These comments about women's behavior in court and their likely consequences in the trial process further raised our interest in studying the speech behavior of women in court. Having been told by Lakoff that women do speak differently from men, we interpreted these trial practice authors as saying that at least some of these differences can be consequential in the trial process. Thus, one of the kinds of variation which we sought to examine when we began to observe and tape record courtroom speech was patterns unique to either women or men. We did not know what we would find, so we started out by using Lakoff's discussion of "women's language" as a guide.

Briefly, what Lakoff had proposed was that women's speech varies from men's in several significant ways. Although she provides no firm listing of the major features of what she terms "women's language" (hereafter referred to in this paper as WL), we noted the following features, said to occur in high frequency among women, and used these as a baseline for our investigation of sex-related speech patterns in court.

1. *Hedges.* ("It's sort of hot in here."; "I'd kind of like to go."; "I guess ..."; "It seems like ..."; and so on.)

2. *(Super) polite forms.* ("I'd really appreciate it if ..."; "Would you please open the door, if you don't mind?"; and so on.)

3. *Tag questions.* ("John is here, isn't he?" instead of "Is John here?"; and so on.)

4. *Speaking in italics.* (intonational emphasis equivalent to underlining words in written language; emphatic *so* or *very* and so on.)

5. *Empty adjectives.* (*divine; charming; cute; sweet; adorable; lovely*; and so on.)

6. *Hypercorrect grammar and pronounciation.* (bookish grammar; more formal enunciation.)

7. *Lack of a sense of humor.* (Women said to be poor joke tellers and to frequently "miss the point" in jokes told by men.)

8. *Direct quotations.* (use of direct quotations instead of paraphrases)

9. *Special lexicon.* (in domains like colors where words like *magenta, chartreuse,* and so on are typically used only by women)

10. *Question intonation in declarative contexts.* (For example, in response to the question, "When will dinner be ready?", an

answer like "Around 6 o'clock?", as though seeking approval and asking whether that time will be okay)

WHAT WE FOUND

During the summer of 1974, we recorded over 150 hours of trials in a North Carolina superior criminal court. Although almost all of the lawyers we observed were males, the sex distribution of witnesses was more nearly equal. On looking for the speech patterns described by Lakoff, we quickly discovered some women who spoke in the described manner. The only major discrepancies between Lakoff's description and our findings were in features which the specific context of the courtroom rendered inappropriate, for example, *tag questions* (because witnesses typically answer rather than ask questions) and *joking*, (because there is little humor in a courtroom, we did not have occasion to observe the specifically female patterns of humor to which she referred).

In addition to our early finding that some women approximate the model described by Lakoff, we also were quick to note that there was considerable variation in the degree to which women exhibited these characteristics. Since our observations were limited to about ten weeks of trials during which we were able to observe a variety of cases in terms of offense (ranging from traffic cases, drug possession, robbery, manslaughter, to rape) and length (from a few hours to almost five days), we believe that our observations cover a reasonably good cross-section of the kinds of trials, and hence witnesses, handled by this type of court. Yet, ten weeks is not enough to produce a very large number of witnesses. Even a single witness may spend several hours testifying. In addition, the court spends much time selecting jurors, hearing summation remarks, giving jury instructions, and handling administrative matters. Thus, when looking at patterns of how different women talk in court, we are in a better position to deal with the range of variation we observed than to attempt any precise frequency counts of persons falling into various categories. Thus, we will concentrate our efforts here on describing the range and complement this with some non-statistical impressions regarding frequency.

Our observations show a continuum of use of the features described by Lakoff.[8] We were initially at a loss to explain why some women should speak more or less as Lakoff had described and why others should use only a few of these features. We will deal with our interpretation of these findings later, but first let us examine some points along the continuum from high to low.

A. Mrs. W,[9] a witness in a case involving the death of her neighbor in an automobile accident, is an extreme example of a person speaking WL in her testimony. She used nearly every feature described by Lakoff and certainly all those which are appropriate in the court room context. Her speech contains a high frequency of *intensifiers* ("*very* close friends," "*quite* ill," and so on often with intonation emphasis); *hedges* (frequent use of "you know," "sort of like," "maybe just a little bit," "let's see," and so on); *empty adjectives* ("this *very* kind policeman"); and other similar features. The first example below is typical of her speech and shows the type of intensifiers and hedges she commonly uses.[10] (To understand what her speech *might* be like without these features, example (2) is a rewritten version of her answers with the WL features eliminated.)

(1) L.   State whether or not, Mrs. W., you were acquainted with or knew the late Mrs. E.D.

Mrs. W.   Quite well.

L.   What was the nature of your acquaintance with her?

Mrs. W.   Well, we were, uh, very close friends. Uh, she was even sort of like a mother to me.

(2) L.   State whether or not, Mrs. W., you were acquainted with or knew the late Mrs E.D.

Mrs. W.   Yes, I did.

L.   What was the nature of your acquaintance with her?

Mrs. W.   We were close friends. She was like a mother to me.

Table 1 summarizes the frequency of several features attributed to WL by Lakoff. Calculated as a ratio of WL forms for each answer, this witness's speech contains 1.14 — among the highest incidences we observed.

B. The speech of Mrs. N, a witness in a case involving her father's arrest, shows fewer WL features. Her ratio of features for each answer drops to .84. Her testimony contains instances of both WL and a more assertive speech style.

Frequently, her speech is punctuated with responses like:
"He, see, he thought it was more-or-less me rather than the
police officer." Yet it also contains many more straightforward and assertive passages than are found in A's
speech. In example (3), for instance, Mrs. N. is anything but
passive. She turns questions back on the lawyer and even
interrupts him. Example (4) illustrates the ambivalence of
this speaker's style better. Note how she moves quickly to
qualify — in WL — an otherwise assertive response.

(3)	L.	All right. I ask you if your husband hasn't beaten him up in the last week?
	Mrs. N.	Yes, and do you know why?
	L.	Well, I ...
	Mrs. N.	Another gun episode.
	L.	Another gun episode?
	Mrs. N.	Yessiree.
(4)	L.	You've had a controversy going with him for a long time, haven't you?
	Mrs. N.	Ask why — I mean not because I'm just his daughter.

C. The speech of Dr. H., a pathologist who testifies as an
   expert witness, exhibits fewer features of WL than either of
   the other two women. Her speech contains the lowest incidence of WL features among the female witnesses whose
   speech we analyzed. Dr. H's ratio of WL features is .18 for
   each answer. Her responses tend to be straightforward, with
   little hesitancy, few hedges, a noticeable lack of intensifiers,
   and so on. (See Table 1.) Typical of her speech is example
   (5) in which she explains some of her findings in a patho-
   logical examination.

(5)	L.	And had the heart not been functioning, in other words, had the heart been stopped, there would have been no blood to have come from that region?
	Dr. H.	It may leak down depending on the position of the body after death. But the presence of blood in the alveoli indicates that some active respiratory action had to take place.

Table 1. Frequency Distribution of Women's Language Features[a] in the Speech of Six Witnesses in a Trial Courtroom

	Women			Men		
	A	B	C	D	E	F
Intensifiers[b]	16	0	0	21	2	1
Hedges[c]	19	2	3	2	5	0
Hesitation Forms[d]	52	20	13	26	27	11
W asks L questions[e]	2	0	0	0	0	0
Gestures[f]	2	0	0	0	0	0
Polite Forms[g]	9	0	2	2	0	1
Sir[h]	2	0	6	32	13	11
Quotes[i]	1	5	0	0	0	0
Total (all powerless forms)	103	27	24	85	47	24
# of Answers in Interview	90	32	136	61	73	52
Ratio (# powerless forms for each answer)	1.14	0.84	0.18	1.39	0.64	0.46

Notes: [a]The particular features chosen for inclusion in this table were selected because of their saliency and frequency of occurrence. Not included here are features of WL which either do not occur in court or ones which we have difficulty operationalising and coding. *Based on direct examinations only.* [b]Forms which increase or emphasize the force of assertion such as *very, definitely, very definitely, surely, such a,* and so on. [c]Forms which reduce the form of assertion allowing for exceptions or avoiding rigid commitments such as *sort of, a little kind of,* and so on. [d]Pause fillers such as *uh, um, h,* and "meaningless" particles such as *oh, well, let's see, now, so, you see,* and so on. [e]Use of question intonation in response to lawyer's questions, including rising intonation in normally declarative contexts (for example, "thirty?, thirty-five?") and questions asked by witness of lawyer like "Which way do you go ...?". [f]Spoken indications of direction such as *over there,* and so on. [g]Include *please, thank you,* and so on. Use of *sir* counted separately due to its high frequency. [h]Assumed to be an indication of more polite speech. [i]Not typically allowed in court under restrictions on hearsay which restrict the situations under which a witness may tell what someone else said.
Source: Original data.

What all of this shows is the fact that some women speak in the way Lakoff described, employing many features of WL, while others are far away on the continuum of possible and appropriate styles for the courtroom. Before discussing the reasons which may lie behind this variation in the language used by women in court, we first examine an equally interesting finding which emerged from our investigation of male speech in court.

We also found men who exhibit WL characteristics in their courtroom testimony. To illustrate this, we examine the speech of three male witnesses which varies along a continuum of high to low incidence of WL features.

D. Mr. W. exhibits many but not all of Lakoff's WL features.[11] Some of those which he does employ, like intensifiers, for example, occur in especially high frequency — among the highest observed among all speakers, whether male or female. His ratio of WL features for each answer is 1.39, actually higher than individual A. Example (6), while an extreme instance of Mr. W.'s use of WL features, does illustrate the degree to which features attributed to women are in fact present in high frequency in the speech of some men.

(6) L.   And you saw, you observed that?

Mr. W.   Well, after I heard — I can't really, I can't definitely state whether the brakes or the lights came first, but I rotated my head slightly to the right, and looked directly behind Mr. Z., and I saw reflections of lights, and uh, very, very, very instantaneously after that, I heard a very, very loud explosion — from my standpoint of view it would have been an implosion because everything was forced outward, like this, like a grenade thrown into a room. And, uh, it was, it was terrifically loud.

E. Mr. N., more toward the low frequency end of the continuum of male speakers, shows some WL features. His ratio of features for each answer is .64, comparable to individual B. Example (7) shows an instance of passages from the testimony of this speaker in which there are few WL features. Example (8), by comparison, shows the same hedging in a way characteristic of WL. His speech falls between the highest and lowest incidences of WL features we observed among males.

(7) L.   After you looked back and saw the back of the ambulance, what did you do?

Mr. N.   After I realized that my patient and my attendant were thrown from the vehicle, uh, which I assumed, I radioed in for help to the dispatcher, tell her that we had been in an accident and, uh, my patient and attendant were thrown from the vehicle and I didn't know the extent of their injury at the time, to hurry up and send help.

(8) L.   Did you form any conclusion about what her problem was at the time you were there?

Mr. N.   I felt that she had, uh, might have had a sort of heart attack.

F. Officer G. among the males lowest in WL features, virtually lacks all features tabulated in Table 1 except for hesitancy and using *sir*. His ratio of WL forms for each answer is .46. Example (9) shows how this speaker handles the lack of certainty in a more authoritative manner than by beginning his answer with "I guess ...". His no-nonsense, straight-forward manner is illustrated well by example (10), in which a technical answer is given in a style comparable to that of individual C.

(9) L.   Approximately how many times have you testified in court?

Off. G.   It would only have to be a guess, but it's three or four, five, six hundred times. Probably more.

(10) L.   You say that you found blood of group O?

Off. G.   The blood in the vial, in the layman's terms, is positive, Rh positive. Technically referred to as a capital r, sub o, little r.

Taken together these findings suggest that the so-called "women's language" is neither characteristic of all women nor limited only to women. A similar continuum of WL features (high to low) is found among speakers of both sexes. These findings suggest that the sex of a speaker is insufficient to explain all of this variation.

Once we had realized that WL features were distributed in such a manner, we began to examine the data for other factors which might be associated with a high or low incidence of the features in question. First, we noted that we were able to find *more* women toward the high end of the continuum. Next, we noted that all the women who were aberrant (that is, who used relatively few WL features) had something in common — an unusually high social status. Like Dr. H., they were typically well-educated, professional women of middle-class background. A corresponding pattern was noted among the aberrant men (that is, those high in WL features).

Like Mr. W., they tended to be men who held either subordinate, lower-status jobs or were unemployed. Housewives were high in WL features while middle-class males were low in these features. In addition to social status in the society at large, another factor associated with low incidence of WL is previous courtroom experience. Both individuals C and F testify frequently in court as expert witnesses, that is, as witnesses who testify on the basis of their professional expertise. However, it should be noted that not all persons who speak with few WL features have had extensive courtroom experience. The point we wish to emphasize is that a powerful position may derive from either social standing in the larger society and/or status accorded by the court. We carefully observed these patterns and found them to hold generally.[12] From some individuals whom we had observed in the courtroom, we analyzed their speech in detail in order to tabulate the frequency of the WL features as shown in Table 1. A little more about the background of the persons we have described will illustrate the sort of pattern we observed.

A is a married woman, about 55 years old, who is a housewife.
B is married, but younger, about 35 years old. From her testimony, there is no information that she works outside her home.
C is a pathologist in a local hospital. She is 35-40 years old. There is no indication from content of her responses or from the way she was addressed (always *Dr.*) of her marital status. She has testified in court as a pathologist on many occasions.
D is an ambulance attendant, rather inexperienced in his job, at which he has worked for less than 6 months. Age around 30. Marital status unknown.
E is D's supervisor. He drives the ambulance, supervises emergency treatment and gives instructions to D. He has worked at his job longer than D and has had more experience. Age about 30-35; marital status unknown.
F is an experienced member of the local police force. He has testified in court frequently. Age 35-40; marital status unknown.

"WOMEN'S LANGUAGE" OR "POWERLESS LANGUAGE"?

In the previous section, we have presented data which indicate that the variation in WL features may be related more to social power-lessness than to sex. We have presented both observational data and some statistics to show that this style is not simply or even primarily a sex-related pattern. We did, however, find it related to sex in that more women tend to be high in WL features while more men tend to be low in these same features. The speech patterns of three men and three women were examined. For each sex, the individuals varied from social statuses with relatively low power to more power (for women: housewife to doctor; for men: subordinate job to one with a high degree of independence of action). Experience may also be an important factor, for those whom we observed speaking with few WL features seemed more comfortable in the courtroom and with the content of their testimony. Associated with increasing shifts in social power and experience were corresponding decreases in frequency of WL features. These six cases were selected for detailed analysis because they were representative of the sorts of women and men who served as witnesses in the trials we observed in 1974. Based on this evidence, we would suggest that the phenomenon described by Lakoff would be better termed *powerless language,* a term which is more descriptive of the particular features involved, of the social status of those who speak in this manner, and one which does not link it unnecessarily to the sex of a speaker.

Further, we would suggest that the tendency for more women to speak powerless language and for men to speak less of it is due, at least in part, to the greater tendency of women to occupy relatively powerless social positions. What we have observed is a reflection in their speech behavior of their social status. Similarly, for men, a greater tendency to use the more powerful variant (which we will term *powerful language*) may be linked to the fact that men much more often tend to occupy relatively powerful positions in society.

NOTES

1. Robin Lakoff, *Language and Woman's Place* (New York: Harper & Row, 1975).

2. Naomi Quinn, "Anthropological Studies of Women's Status," *Annual Review of Anthropology* 6 (1977): 181-225.

3. The research reported here was supported by a National Science Foundation Law and Social Science Program Grant (No. GS-42742), William M. O'Barr, principal investigator. The authors wish to thank especially these other members of

the research team for their advice and assistance: John Conley, Marilyn Endriss, Bonnie Erickson, Bruce Johnson, Debbie Mercer, Michael Porter, Lawrence Rosen, William Schmidheiser, and Laurens Walker. In addition, the cooperation of the Durham County, North Carolina, Superior Court is gratefully acknowledged.

   4. Lakoff, *Language and Woman's Place*, pp. 7-8.

   5. Robert E. Keeton, *Trial Tactics and Methods* (Boston: Little, Brown, 1973), p. 149.

   6. Keeton, *Trial Tactics*, p. 149; F. Lee Bailey and Henry B. Rothblatt, *Successful Techniques for Criminal Trials* (Rochester, N.Y.: Lawyers Co-Operative Publishing Co., 1971), p. 190.

   7. Bailey and Rothblatt, *Successful Techniques*, pp. 190-91.

   8. Actally each feature should be treated as a separate continuum since there is not perfect co-variation. For convenience, we discuss the variation as a single continuum of possibilities. However, it should be kept in mind that a high frequency of occurrence of one particular feature may not necessarily be associated with a high frequency of another.

   9. Names have been changed and indicated by a letter only in order to preserve the anonymity of witnesses. However, the forms of address used in the court are retained.

   10. These examples are taken from both the direct and cross examinations of the witnesses, although Table 1 uses data only from direct examinations. Examples were chosen to point out clearly the differences in style. However, it must be noted that the cross examination is potentially a more powerless situation for the witness.

   11. This speaker did not use some of the intonational features that we had noted among women having high frequencies of WL features in their speech.

   12. We do not wish to make more of this pattern than our data are able to support, but we suggest that our grounds for these claims are at least as good as Lakoff's. Lakoff's basis for her description of features constituting WL are her own speech, speech of her friends and acquaintances, and patterns of use in the mass media.

3.6 Patterns of Power and Authority in Classroom Talk

A.D. EDWARDS

Classroom talk is organised for the controlled transmission of knowledge. In this article I want to consider whether sociological investigation of the resulting discourse has identified a 'basic' structure to the communicative strategies normally employed. Has it detected a 'relatively stable, socially structured series of events' even where the participants themselves may be more *immediately* aware of a 'fluid, transient and fragile situation'?[1] Is such an analysis irredeemably static and normative, or can it meet Bernstein's criterion for an 'exciting' sociological account by *relating* structural features and interactional practices?[2] Although these questions have particular meaning for me in the context of a recent study of 'the language of teaching', my purpose here is not to summarise the findings of that research but to reflect on some of the issues which it raised.[3]

THE STRUCTURE AND STRUCTURING OF INSTRUCTIONAL RELATIONSHIPS

My concern is with the instructional context, and with structural analyses of classroom talk which focus on the very unequal communicative rights created and sustained by the transmission of knowledge. In most classrooms, sharply defined boundaries between 'knowledge' and 'ignorance' mark the pupil's main communicative role as that of a receiver of news. In so far as the teacher's expertise is accepted, he is entitled to do most of the talking, to do a great deal of *telling*, and to evaluate most of what his pupils are permitted to say. The normal relationship of teacher and learner should therefore be 'sufficiently well-defined for us to

Source: Edwards, A.D. (1980) 'Patterns of power and authority in classroom talk' in Woods P. (ed.), *Teacher Strategies: Explorations in the Sociology of the School*, London, Croom Helm, pp. 237-53. © A.D. Edwards

expect clear evidence of this in the text', and the resulting displays of situationally-typical forms of communicative competence have drawn the attention of sociolinguists interested in how talk is managed in settings where there are 'clearly recognised roles, objectives and conventions.[4] In their own analysis of instruction, Sinclair and Coulthard show how the teacher's 'responsibility for the direction of the discourse' was evidenced in his virtual monopoly of the 'acts' labelled as (e.g.) starters, elicitations, directives, informatives and evaluations, and in the virtual restriction of pupils to the 'acts' of bidding (for the right to speak), acknowledging, replying and reacting. Underlying the fast-moving surface of events was a single source of authoritative definitions. There were therefore severe *functional* constraints on what pupils could say because it had to be contained within the limits of what the positional authority of the teacher defined as being relevant and correct. This evidence would suggest that the typical form of teacher-pupil relationships produces a predominance of restricted codes.

In conditions where there is strong classification and framing of school knowledge, this is what Bernstein's theory of educational transmission *would* suggest. Yet in his writing on communicative discontinuities between schools and lower working-class homes, he assumes that classrooms are normally 'predicated upon elaborated codes and their system of social relationships'. [...]

However, the necessary classroom conditions for a predominance of elaborated codes would include some encouragement for the verbal expression of feeling, an emphasis on individual rather than group identity, some involvement of pupils in verbally explicit formulations and enforcements of rules, and frequent opportunities for pupils to 'reconstruct knowledge for themselves rather than to receive it from some authority'.[5] This is not what research shows classrooms to be like. In Flanders' words, they are 'an affectional desert'. Pupils' activities are normally organized according to universalistic criteria of sex, age and ability. In the regulative context, teachers' control is often exercised with verbal mediation or 'explicit rationality', and it is an important part of pupils' situational competence to recognise how proper and improper behaviour are indirectly defined.[6] In the instructional context, typically sharp boundaries between the one who 'knows' and the many who do not certainly generate verbally-elaborated exposition of *un*commonsense knowledge. Pupils have to be prepared to make explicit what the listening teacher knows already, or what any 'competent' pupil should know by that stage of his career in that part of the curriculum. Yet it is also common for the relevant display of knowledge to be very inexplicit, the pupil needing only to touch on the required facts to launch the teacher into filling-out an answer which was itself highly allusive. Such verbal elaborations by the *teacher* help to maintain his semantic control by presenting a full authorised version of what the facts 'really' are. What pupils 'can mean' is located within the teacher's frame of reference. In relation to the knowledge being handed down to them, their existing knowledge is likely to be treated as slight, partial or defective. These are not the conditions for a predominance of elaborated codes, however verbally explicit the teacher's authoritative expositions may be. [...]

Despite the preceding exchange of typifications, the relevance of Bernstein's approach to my own argument is that it relates 'structural features and interactional practices' by showing how social identities and social relationships are signalled and reproduced *in the act of speaking*. The hierarchical relationship of teacher and pupils provides them with a pervasive context for their exchanges, a basic resource for expressing and assigning meaning. But that relationship is itself 'realised' in appropriate ways of speaking — or of course challenged by speaking inappropriately. Any 'causal' connections between 'the structure of social relationships and the structure of communication' are therefore reciprocal.[7] Typical classroom talk constitutes the 'working-out of a power relation' in so far as the respective rights and obligations of teacher and pupils are the basis from which they 'accomplish comprehensible talk and action'.[8] The teacher has authority in so far as pupils address him, and respond to him, as though he is indeed in charge. In orderly classrooms, and in the central business of instruction (the 'lesson proper'), pupils normally listen when required to do so, bid properly for the right to speak themselves, and convey in their contributions to 'discussion' a willingness to set aside their own knowledge as irrelevant unless and until it fits into the teacher's frame of reference. Indeed, 'good discipline' might be defined as a teacher's capacity to construct and maintain this kind of discourse, and his authority is regularly manifested and reconstituted in the routine patterns of classroom talk. For example, as he assesses a pupil's answer, he is announcing, acting on, and confirming a general right to make pronouncements of this kind.[9] To identify a basic structure to classroom talk is not to offer a static or reified description, but to show how the authority of the teacher as guardian and mediator of school knowledge is the basis from which so many features of the discourse are generated, features which themselves serve to reproduce the conditions of their own production.

THE FACT OF PREALLOCATION AND THE 'WORKING-OUT OF A POWER RELATION'

The preceding section rests implicitly on my recent research with John Furlong, which was concerned with how the teacher's authority is routinely expressed and reproduced in the shaping of instructional meanings. Although that account is 'supported' by extensive transcript material, it remains open to the criticism of merely 'exampling' a predetermined theory with selected, heavily interpreted, evidence. I want now to consider a more systematic approach to how teachers' 'ownership' of classroom interaction is achieved and maintained, and to where 'in the text' that ownership is most evidently displayed, managed, and recognised.

Sinclair and Coulthard describe their method of discourse analysis as being applicable to anything recognisable as 'teaching', but as being unable to cope with conditions of 'participant-equality'. 'Ordinary desultory conversation', the least *overtly* rule-governed form of talk, is certainly beyond its range. As practised by ethnomethodologists, however, conversational analysis has given special attention to talk between equals, where no participant has predetermined special rights and where the management of turns and topics is a shared responsibility. But the rules generating orderly talk in such democratic conditions can be adapted (or 'transformed') to more status-marked settings. Social facts like the relative age, prestige or expertise of the speakers will be included in the analysis 'where warrant for the relevance of such characterisations of the data from the data themselves' — that is, where the participants' recognition and confirmation of these facts is *displayed* in the organisation of the talk.[10] What they are likely to display is not a set of features specific to that situation, but an unusual frequency of some of those generally encountered and perhaps their virtual ascription to one participant. For example, any question obliges someone to produce something recognisable as a reply, or as a preparation for a reply, or as a legitimate evasion of a reply. The teacher's power is more pervasive, not only because he asks so *many* questions, but because the asking of questions by someone who 'already knows' allows the questioner to retain the initiative by evaluating the response. Such questioning may generate extended sequences in which the teacher speaks every other turn so as to manage the required answer. The obligation on pupils is not only to answer if they can (or to convey that they would if they could); it is also to wait for an assessment of what they say, and to adapt any further contributions to the cues and clues which they are offered.[11]

Briefly, then, the teacher's 'ownership' of instructional talk is evident in preallocated rights of participation — for example, in the initiation of opening and closing sequences — and of assigning obligated positions to others. In ordinary conversation, turn-taking is 'locally' managed as the interaction proceeds. The possibilities for each next turn — whose, when, and what — are decided during each current turn. In classrooms, the allocation, duration and content of particular turns may be improvised, but the right to make the relevant decisions is the teacher's. Only he can 'direct speaker-ship in any creative way'.[12] He either selects himself as next speaker, or selects a pupil as next speaker, or accepts a pupil's bid for that turn. To adapt a comment of Ned Flanders, the teacher tells pupils when to talk, what to talk about, when to stop talking, and how well they talked. The power-relation is displayed through a general preallocation of turns, and especially of turns involving questioning, informing, and formulating. The teacher's control is exerted largely through his rights to 'invite stories', to tell 'stories', and to announce in so many words what these expositions have 'really' been about. I want now to comment on each of these activities.[13] Of course, that control is always liable to be diminished or repudiated by pupils' refusal to participate 'appropriately', or by their taking over the initiative themselves. But the account which follows is not an idealisation. It is an attempt to identify major components of conventionally orderly classroom talk.

'Invited stories' are invitations to talk in which the speaker is denied the usual conversational rights to tell his own story, in his own words, to determine the sequence of the narrative, and to avoid revealing matters which might discredit himself. They are common in courtrooms, consulting rooms, and police stations, and they are structurally similar in that the talk is organised so as to produce a

single outcome (a damaging admission, a diagnosis, or a con-
fession) and that one participant's expert knowledge or claim to
prior knowledge warrants closing the talk when that outcome has
been achieved.[14] Like lawyers, doctors and policemen, teachers
learn to ask questions — indeed, are often trained to ask questions
— which restrict the scope of the answers so as to get only as much
as is required. Underlying such questions is a claim to prior knowledge which authorises *recipient*-control of the information being
provided:

T: Why do you think the creature (*an ammonite*) used to live
    inside a shell like that?
PN: (numerous bids to speak next)
T: No, put your hands up please. Er, Carl?
P: For protection.
T: What does protection mean? Any idea, Carl?
P: Sir, to stop other things hurting it.
T: Right, stops other things hurting it. Now if it came out of
    its shell, and waggled along the sea bed, what would
    happen to it? Yes?
P: It might get ate.
T: It might get eaten by something else, yeah. Um, why do
    you think this is made out of stone now? [...] Why isn't —
    er, why don't we find the remains of the creature inside
    here?
P: It would have rotted away.
T: It would have rotted away. Why didn't the shell rot away?
P: Sir, because it's too hard.
T: It's too hard, good.

Control is exerted and facilitated by the *presequences* which
teachers often employ to indicate that a question is coming, and to
provide clues as to what an appropriate (and appropriately elaborated) answer might be.[15] It is also evident in the frequency with
which teachers interrupt pupil-turns so as to challenge, modify or
supplement what is being said, or to reallocate the turn altogether.
Such interruptions are clear 'expressions of dominance'.[16] In
ordinary conversation, it is rare for 'errors' to be identified inter-
ruptively, and very rare for the 'correction' to be supplied by a
listener. There is a marked 'preference' — that is, an organisational
predominance — for self-initiated self-correction.[17] But in an

instructional setting, there is likely to be a 'correct' version which is
not open to negotiation, and many errors which cannot be allowed
to stand. There may well be an organisational preference both for
inviting *self*-correction, and for using intonational and other
devices for not marking the error too obtrusively. But if more
subtle indications of inadequacy do not work, then the teacher has
to supply the omission. [...]

The sufficiency of the teacher's own 'stories' is also a matter for
him to decide. Not being 'invited', and not being subjected to the
scrutiny of the already knowledgeable, they involve the usual
narrator's immunity from interruption, and the right to resume the
floor after checking on the listeners' attention or comprehension.
Characteristic of classroom talk are the frequency and length of
the teacher's expositions, and their smooth resumption even after
extended sequences of question-and-answer 'discussion'. Indeed, it
is important not to separate exposition from questioning, since a
great deal of teaching is done through the interpolation of
additional information into the skeleton framework which pupils
provide. This is another obvious display of dominance. The conversational preference for self-correction is likely to be modified in
any interaction involving the not-yet-competent, and other-
correction may then function as 'a vehicle of socialisation ... a
transitional usage whose supersession by self-correction is continuously awaited'.[18] In conditions of transmission teaching, however, pupils are not likely to be socialised into ways of constructing
future knowledge for themselves, and the competence to be
achieved through the teacher's management is often limited to the
immediately relevant facts and skills.

In ordinary conversation, the speakers' common understanding
of what the talk is about is largely displayed implicitly in the
organisation of turns. There will also be occasions, however, when
it becomes necessary to check that understanding by explicitly
announcing or querying what is going on. Where such formulations are a shared responsibility, they are always open to challenge as being inaccurate in themselves or as representing an
unwarranted imposition of one person's views. But where the
commonsense to be achieved is seen as problematic, or as likely to
bring disputes, then formulations may not only be unusually frequent but also the prerogative of one participant. In classrooms,
the teacher has a pervasive responsibility for monitoring what is
said, and for repairing breakdowns of all kinds. He dominates

those occasions when the achievement of orderly discourse becomes a topic in its own right. It is almost always he who says, in so many words, what has happened, is happening, and will happen, and who regularly sums up what has been achieved so far. In a study of 'giving the gist' in radio interviews, Heritage and Watson distinguish between the frequent and decisive formulations of the 'bringers of news', and the relatively infrequent and tentative formulations of those who receive it. When it is the news-bringer who sums up, the receiver is unlikely to do more than signal that the summary has been understood. But when it is the receiver who supplies the summary, often by explicit invitation as a check on attention or understanding, then a confirmation or contradiction of that summary by the informant is likely to follow immediately.[19] In the terms of this study, the teacher is a persistent bringer of news, the transmission of which is rarely seen as a smoothly self-explicating process. Pupils' attention to what is being said, and their competence in comprehending it, cannot be taken for granted. There will be many occasions when it is the *teacher's* business to announce what has been achieved so far, to exhibit meanings which should now be 'shared', or to display some *failure* to understand which has now to be remedied. For all practical purposes, these definitions constitute authorised versions of what has 'really' been learned, even where it may have appeared to pupils until the last moment that something different was going on:

T: Right, do you notice what we've done? We started off saying we're going to look at ideas about the world, how people long ago explained the world. But what else — and this is very important — what else have we also done?

P: Saw how men looked at women.

T: We saw how men looked at women — you're nearly there. What exactly do you mean? Can you say — tell us a bit more, go on.

P: How he doesn't like her, and how he thinks she's weak.

T: Yeah (tentatively) — so we've also looked then — anybody else before I say it, anybody else have any ideas? He's on the right track here. He said we've also looked at how man looked at woman. What else have we looked at here?

P: God.

T: No, not to do with God.

P: How they lived.

T: How they lived! In other words the ideas they had about themselves and how they lived. So from a story long ago we've used that story to work out how people thought about themselves, how they lived, as well as looking at their stories about the world we've used the stories to work out something about them. Let's go on because this is *very* important, because all the time you're in Humanities you'll be doing this. You'll be looking at what people have said about themselves long ago, and trying to work out how they lived, and we call that something that you look for — *evidence.*

The meanings that are made public knowledge are those that the teacher has provided or sponsored. As the transmitter of news, he is 'entitled' to take up pupil contributions as pieces in the jigsaw being built, to deny them 'existence' by ignoring them or translating them into more convenient form, to display them as representing a common understanding, or to formulate a failure to understand which has to be remedied by bringing pupils to (or back to) the appropriate meanings.[20]

In these and other ways, classroom talk can be seen as displaying a power-relation, and the scope and tightness of the teacher's control will be 'evident in the text'. Where that control is relaxed, the greater range of semantic options available to pupils is likely to be evident in more overlapping talk, more pupil-selected and self-selected next speakers, more interruptions by pupils, fewer invited stories, and less tying of formulations to one participant. In short, more of the speech exchange system will be locally managed, and pupils too will be able to 'direct speakership in a creative way'. In some of the 'dialectical' (as opposed to 'didactic') teaching reported by Massialas and Zevin, this seems to be what occurs.[...] [A] 'common' outcome is being collectively managed, with no obvious tying of critical activities to one role:[21]

P1: I think that all violent secret societies sprang up in countries where people were oppressed by their governments.

P2: We could make up a rule for ourselves; if we hear of a violent secret society in a certain place or country, then we can say that there is an oppressive government there also.

P3: Many of the societies we studied fit in very well with our rule.

T: What if I asked you to prove your rule?

P3: Well, I could get examples of secret societies that fit our rule.

T: Well?

P3: For instance, the Serbian Black Hand was very violent, and helped to bring about World War 1 ... The Serbs wanted to unite their people and free themselves from Austrian rule and pressure, so many Serbs joined the Black Hand to hurt the Austrians.

P4: They even used bombs and all kinds of terrorist methods.

P5: The Carbonari in Italy also wanted to free their country from the rule of an oppressive foreign government. I think it was Austrian too. They wanted to have Italy governed by Italians.

P6: Italy for the Italians!

P7: When Israel fought for independence ...

The teacher takes only eight of the ensuing 64 turns, and most of these are questions which do not lead to any evaluation of the response. At the end, he makes no attempt to announce a consensual 'verdict'. The normal presupposition of teacher-knowledge and pupil-ignorance has been at least temporarily relinquished, and the resulting interplay of alternative frames of reference and relevance is evident in the talk.

CONTEXTS OF CLASSROOM TALK

Conversational analysts are not interested in 'doing explanations', and would reject any normative reference to some 'external' reality from which orderly interaction might be derived. It may therefore seem unprincipled to use their methods in the service of an explanatory account of classroom talk. But I have argued that the power of the teacher to define reality is a fact which is both oriented to by teacher and pupils *and* reproduced in the appropriate ways of speaking. Sociolinguistic analysis often seeks to identify what the speakers 'must be assuming' to talk as they do, while ethnomethodologists' own interest in the context-sensitivity of conversational rules often directs their attention to how turn-taking is adapted to the properties of the particular activity in which the participants are engaged.[22] I want to turn now to the 'considerable sociological interest' of showing not only *how* the rules regulating teacher-pupil relationships 'generate distinctive texts', but also *why* those rules rather than others. 'What we observe are the productions of texts. What we infer at the interactional level are the ground rules generating those texts; what we infer at the structural level are the forms of social relationship which regulate the selection and structure of meanings and the mode of their contextual realisation.'[23] What are the salient structural features which the rules regulating classroom talk both reflect and reproduce?

Much of the organisation of classroom talk can be accounted for by teachers' attempts to maintain orderly interaction in conditions where 'good discipline' not only demands the suppression of noticeable 'noise', but also that a large number of often unwilling learners are contained for long periods of time in a single communication system. In a sense it *is* as 'simple' as described by one teacher: 'There's a lot of 'em, and if you don't keep them under control they'll run all over you.' Although the rules governing turn-taking in ordinary conversation are in principle independent of the number of possible talkers, the difficulties of getting a turn where that number is large are likely to lead rapidly to 'schism' — to the forming and reforming of less crowded conversational groups. Yet teachers spend much of their time trying to maintain a single verbal encounter, in which whatever is being said is supposed to have the attention of all. The large pool of potential speakers is therefore a constant threat to securing one speaker at a time with few gaps and little overlapping talk. Independently of the content of the talk, and often despite the teacher's intention of 'opening up discussion', there are strong organisational pressures towards retaining recipient control over pupil contributions so as to allocate, reallocate and terminate turns. Those features of classroom talk outlined in the previous section are ways of coping with teachers' perceived need to treat a crowd as one. Some of them involve techniques explicitly taught during teacher training, or passed on as tips by more experienced colleagues. But it seems more realistic to regard them as common responses to common problems. Such 'coping strategies' are rightly seen by Andy Hargreaves as 'linking structural questions to interactionist concerns'. They are constructive and adaptive — 'creatively articulated solutions to recurring daily problems'. In so far as they seem to work, they become taken for granted as legitimate and even unavoidable constituents of 'teaching'.[24]

The 'structural feature' most relevant to this present article is the existence of a predetermined body of knowledge to be transmitted. What the teacher 'knows' has the external and constraining properties which Durkheim attributed to social facts. For all practical purposes, it is neither supposition nor whim but accredited knowledge which is there to be passed on. The presupposition on which teacher and pupils make commonsense of their interaction in the instructional context is that 'learning' is the result of 'teaching'. As in the therapeutic discourse described by Labov and Fanshel, there is 'an underlying web of rights and obligations' derived from the relative 'strength' and 'weakness' of the participants.[25] An assumption of pupil ignorance provides an interpretative basis for much that goes on. Where that assumption is qualified, as in the 'dialectical' teaching referred to earlier, then quite different forms of discourse may be generated. But where it is the preallocated rights of the expert which are displayed, then the talk only makes sense as 'the working out of a power relation ... the recognisable attempt of one party to grade the talk of the other'.[26] Teachers' questions are essentially tests of pupils' ability and willingness to move towards the 'official' frame of reference, and what pupils say 'has meaning' in the context of some body of school knowledge which excludes or transforms what is 'irrelevant'. The achievement of the teacher's sense of things, or a sufficient approximation to it, warrants closing that phase of the interaction; pupils may not like the destination, but the talk will display some recognition of arrival.

The question which remains to be considered is how such an analysis of interactional practices can be related to macro-structural features. [...] The kinds of classroom discourse outlined in this chapter do not fit traditional notions of communicative 'discontinuity' between working-class homes and the demands of the school. It is usually argued that such children find the predominant modes of classroom communication too open as well as too verbally explicit. If, as Bernstein suggests, an orientation to context-independent meanings is 'the fundamental level at which educational and familial roles correspond', then the strategic skills are partly a matter of knowing when and how to 'speak out', of having knowledge and knowing how to display it in talk, of being sensitive to words as the *primary* carriers of meaning. But there is also evidence that middle-class children are more likely to be able

to cope with situations where 'a clear-cut task is central, information exchange or knowledge testing is primary, and there is high
role differentiation'.[27] They seem more accustomed to having their
knowledge tested, more concerned with getting their answers right,
most constrained by what they perceive as being relevant to the
adult listener, and more experienced in known-answer question
drills which prepare them to ignore verbally the fact that the
questioner already knows. If middle-class children have had more
experience of adults in an active 'tutorial' role, and of being drawn
into adult ways of thinking by means of clues and assessments,
then they are more likely to have learned thoroughly the ground
rules for generating appropriate performances of the kind I have
described.[28]

I want to make a final and inevitably programmatic point.
Analysis of classroom discourse makes it possible to show at the
'local' level how 'social structures are both constituted by human
agency and yet at the same time are the very medium of this con-
stitution',[29] and perhaps to show that middle-class children have
greater access to 'privileged' forms of discourse. It is much more
difficult to demonstrate, rather than merely assert, the larger processes of 'structuration' evident in classrooms. Conversational
analysis may help to do this by its refusal to get lost in surface
descriptions of specific speech systems. Classrooms are not unique
in the preallocation of turns, the frequency of invited stories, or the
monopolising of formulations. These are characteristics of hierarchical relationships. They are all ways of displaying and recognising power. As Mardle and Walker argue, it is a perennial
problem for interactionist theory how far the accumulated experience of 'situations of that kind' are 'limiting and structuring
features of any present encounter'.[30] In learning the ground-rules
of classroom discourse, pupils are also learning how to work out a
power-relation. To reapply Bernstein's comment, the predominant
uses of language in classrooms to 'focus and filter' children's
experience are 'a microcosm of the macroscopic orderings of
society'; they both reflect and help to reproduce a particular form
of social order.[31] Where teacher knowledge and pupil ignorance
are clearly categorised and persistently announced, then classroom
encounters provide innumerable and generalisable lessons in how
to work within a received frame of reference. Basic rules for
'experiencing, interpreting and telling about the world' are learned
in many contexts. Those learned and acted on in classrooms may

be critical because the practices they generate are repeated so often and questioned so rarely.

NOTES

1. Walker and Adelman (1975), pp. 25-6.
2. Bernstein (1977), p. 11.
3. Edwards and Furlong (1978). This present paper contains residues of many prolonged discussions with Viv Furlong and with David Hargreaves. An earlier version of it was heavily but constructively criticised by Douglas Barnes, Dianne Phillips and Rod Watson. I am grateful for what I learned from them, even where I did not follow their guidance.
4. Sinclair and Coulthard (1975), p. 7; Coulthard (1977), p. 101. That classroom research is *basic* sociolinguistic research is argued in Dell Hymes' introduction to Cazden *et al.* (1972).
5. Cazden and Bartlett (1973). In this review of the experimental language programme developed by Bernstein's Research Unit, Cazden and Bartlett describe in the way I have outlined what a 'full programme to stimulate elaborated codes' might be like. They see it as requiring extensive changes in typical pupil roles. Whether pupils in such 'open' classrooms would enjoy real autonomy is questioned by Andy Hargreaves (1977), and by Bernstein himself in his analysis of implicit forms of control in progressive education.
6. In Bernstein's own terms, there seems to be a predominance of imperatives, and of positional appeals in a restricted code. See, for example, Cooper (1976), and the analysis of deviance imputations in Hargreaves *et al.* (1975).
7. Bernstein (1977), pp. 11 and 30. Hymes (1977) argues strongly for such a 'socially-constituted linguistics'.
8. Silverman and Jones (1976). Though there are some obvious surface similarities between teaching and the interviewing described in this book, its 'deeper' relevance lies in its account of how a form of talk which is 'the antithesis of dialogue' is produced and maintained.
9. This argument is elaborated in Edwards and Furlong (1978), pp. 150-5. An emphasis on 'the structuring activities that assemble the social structures of education' can also be found in Mehan (1978).
10. Schegloff and Sacks (1974), p. 291. The organisation of orderly conversation is examined in detail in Sacks *et al.* (1974).
11. Such extended sequences of question and answer are analysed by Mehan (1978) and by Hammersley (1977).
12. McHoul (1978), p. 188.
13. The following contrastive analysis is heavily indebted to the work of Paul Drew and Rod Watson, who have compared conversational turn-taking with the organisation of talk in courtroom cross-examinations and in police interrogations. I am grateful to both for the opportunity to read work not yet published, and for drawing my attention to similarities with classroom 'interrogations'.
14. Atkinson and Drew (1979), ch. 2; Watson (1979). Both emphasise that the participants may have very different *interests* in that outcome. The relevance of prior knowledge, or claims to knowledge, to the organisation of talk is also examined in Smith (1978).
15 Teachers' use of preformulations in managing pupil contributions is described by French and MacLure (1979).
16. West and Zimmerman (1977). Adults' special rights in conversation with

children are discussed by Speier (1976).

  17. Schegloff *et al.* (1977). In this context, 'errors' refer to any 'trouble' or 'breakdown' which participants address as being in need of 'repair'.

  18. Schegloff *et al.* (1977), p. 381.

  19. Heritage and Watson (1979).

  20. The monitoring functions of teacher talk are well described by Stubbs (1976).

  21. Massialas and Zevin (1967), pp. 42-7. Such exploratory talk in the absence of a teacher is illustrated and analysed in Barnes and Todd (1977).

  22. See, for example, Labov and Fanshel (1977). Ethnomethodological interest in what I have called status-marked settings is evident in the work of Drew, Watson, Smith and Speier.

  23. Bernstein's introduction to Adlam (1977), p. ix.

  24. A. Hargreaves (1978), p. 77. Grace (1978, pp. 38-42) describes the emergence of such strategies to cope with the demand for 'measurable results in a short space of time' in the crowded conditions of nineteenth-century schools, and their persistence as adaptations to the somewhat different problems presented by modern classrooms. The pressing problems of avoiding 'noise' are discussed in Pollard (1980) and Denscombe (1980).

  25. Labov and Fanshel (1977).

  26. Silverman and Jones (1976), p. 22.

  27. Ervin-Tripp and Mitchell-Kernan (1977), p. 4.

  28. This argument is developed in Edwards (1978).

  29. Giddens (1976), p. 122.

  30. Mardle and Walker (1980).

  31. Bernstein (1973), p. 198. A similar point is made by Halliday (1975, pp. 80-1) — that 'all the deepest and most pervasive patterns of the culture' are learned through the 'micro-semantic exchanges' of family, peer group and school life. Meanings are decoded in ways relevant not only to the immediate situation, but also to the 'wider context of culture'.

REFERENCES

Adlam, D. (1977), *Code in Context* (Routledge and Kegan Paul, London).
Atkinson, J. and Drew, P. (1979). *Order in Court: The Organisation of Verbal Interaction in Judicial Settings* (Macmillan, London).
Barnes, D. and Todd, F. (1977). *Communication and Learning in Small Groups* (Routledge and Kegan Paul, London).
Bernstein, B. (1973). *Class, Codes and Control Volume 1* (Routledge and Kegan Paul, London).
Bernstein, B. (1977). *Class Codes and Control Volume 3*, 2nd edn. (Routledge and Kegan Paul, London).
Cazden, C. and Bartlett, E. (1973). Review of D. and G. Gahagan, 'Talk Reform', *Language in Society*, 2, pp. 147-51.
Cazden, C., John, V. and Hymes, D. (1972). *The Functions of Language in the Classroom* (Teachers' College Press).
Cooper, B. (1976). *Bernstein's Codes: A Classroom Study*, University of Sussex Education Area, Occasional Paper No. 6.
Coulthard, M. (1977). *An Introduction to Discourse Analysis* (Longmans, London).
Denscombe, M. (1980) '"Keeping 'Em Quiet"; the significance of noise for the practical activity of teaching' in Woods, P. (ed.).

Edwards, A. (1978). 'Social Class and the Acquisition of Meaning', paper given in the Sociolinguistics Programme of the 9th World Congress of Sociology (Uppsala).

Edwards, A. and Furlong, V. (1978). *The Language of Teaching* (Heinemann, London).

Ervin-Tripp, S. and Mitchell-Kernan, C. (1977). *Child Discourse* (Academic Press, London).

French, P. and MacLure, M. (1979) 'Getting the Right Answer and Getting the Answer Right', *Research in Education*, 22, Nov.

Giddens, A. (1976). *New Rules of Sociological Method* (Hutchinson, London).

Grace, G. (1978). *Teachers, Ideology and Control: A Study in Urban Education* (Routledge and Kegan Paul, London).

Halliday, M. (1975). *Learning How to Mean* (Arnold, London).

Halliday, M. (1978). *Language as Social Semiotic: The Social Interpretation of Language and Meaning* (Arnold, London).

Hammersley, M. (1977). 'School Learning: the cultural resources required to answer a teacher's question', in P. Wood and M. Hammersley (eds.), *School Experience* (Croom Helm, London).

Hargreaves, A. (1977). 'Progressivism and Pupil Autonomy', *Sociological Review*, 25, pp. 585-621.

Hargreaves, A. (1978). 'The Significance of Classroom Coping Strategies', in L. Barton and R. Meighan (eds.), *Sociological Interpretations of Schooling and Classroom: A Reappraisal* (Nafferton Press, Driffield).

Hargreaves, D., Hestor, S. and Mellor, F. (1975). *Deviance in Classrooms* (Routledge and Kegan Paul, London).

Heritage, J. and Watson, R. (1979). 'Formulations as Conversational Objects', in G. Psathas (ed.), *Studies in Language Analysis: Ethnomethodological Approaches* (Irvington Press).

Hextall, I. and Sarup, M. (1976). 'School Knowledge, Evaluation and Alienation', in M. Young and G. Whitty (eds.), *Society, State and Schooling* (Falmer Press).

Hymes, D. (1977). *Foundations in Sociolinguistics* (Tavistock, London).

Labov, W. and Fanshel, D. (1977). *Therapeutic Discourse: Psychotherapy as Conversation* (Academic Press, London).

Mardle, G. and Walker, M. (1980) 'Strategies and Structure: some critical notes on teacher socialisation' in Woods, P. (ed.).

McHoul, A. (1978). 'The Organisation of Turns at Formal Talk in the Classroom', *Language in Society*, 7, pp. 183-213.

Massialas, B. and Zevin, J. (1967). *Creative Encounters in the Classroom: Teaching and Learning Through Discovery* (Wiley, New York).

Mehan, H. (1978). 'Structuring School Structure', *Harvard Educational Review* 48, pp. 32-64.

Pollard, A. (1980) 'Teacher Interests and Changing Situations of Survival Threat in Primary School Classrooms' in Woods, P. (ed.).

Sacks, H., Schegloff, E. and Jefferson, G. (1974). 'A Simplest Systematics for the Organisation of Turn-Taking in Conversation', *Language*, 50, pp. 696-735.

Schegloff, E. and Sacks, H. (1974). 'Opening Up Closings', *Semiotica*, 8, pp. 289-327.

Schegloff, E., Jefferson, G. and Sacks, H. (1977). 'The Preference for Self-Correction in the Organisation of Repair in Conversation', *Language*, 53, pp. 361-82.

Silverman, D. and Jones, J. (1976). *Organisational Work: The Language of Grading and the Grading of Language* (Collier-Macmillan, London).

Sinclair, J. and Coulthard, M. (1975). *Towards an Analysis of Discourse: the English of Teachers and Pupils.* (Oxford University Press, Oxford).

Smith, D. (1978). ' "K is mentally Ill": The Anatomy of a Factual Account',

Sociology, 12.1, pp. 23-53.

Speier, M. (1976). 'The Child as Conversationalist', in M. Hammersley and P. Woods (eds.), *The Process of Schooling* (Routledge and Kegan Paul, London).

Stubbs, M. (1976). 'Keeping in Touch: Some Functions of Teacher Talk', in M. Stubbs and S. Delamont (eds.), *Explorations in Classroom Observation* (Wiley, New York).

Walker, R. and Adelman, C. (1975). *A Guide to Classroom Observation* (Methuen, London).

Watson, R. (1979). 'Some Features of the Elicitation of Confessions in Murder Interrogations', unpublished paper (Manchester University Department of Sociology).

West, C. and Zimmerman, D. (1977). 'Woman's Place in Everyday Talk: Reflections on Parent-Child Interaction', *Social Problems*, 24, pp. 521-9.

Woods, P. (1980) (ed.), *Teacher Strategies: Explorations in the Sociology of the School*, London, Croom Helm.

SECTION 4
LEARNING COMMUNICATION SKILLS

INTRODUCTION

There are a number of common themes which run through this seemingly diverse collection of articles. Chief amongst these is that learning to communicate is not just a matter of learning to talk. Indeed, learning to communicate begins before spoken language is acquired and continues long after. It involves non-verbal as well as verbal aspects and demands sensitivity to social situations and a shared understanding of the world.

The article by Bruner makes the point that action and communication precede the development of language and that these are systematically analysed by the infant in ways which have their parallel in language structure: people perform actions on things; some events happen only once, whilst others are recurrent; some things are specific instances of general categories etc. etc. It is on this framework for interpreting and interacting with the world that language is superimposed. Bruner argues that language has its roots in the pragmatics of communication: 'learning a language consists of learning how to realise one's intentions by the appropriate use of grammar'. (p. 254.)

The article by Brice Heath similarly argues that exposure to the written word runs alongside and may, in some communities, *precede* speech development. It thus forms part of the child's wider learning of the culture. As Brice Heath puts it, 'ways of taking from books are as much part of learned behaviour as are ways of eating, sitting, playing games, and building houses' (p. 258). Her article describes in detail how literacy plays a different role in three neighbouring communities of differing social class and racial background. Brice Heath found no evidence of a clear-cut division between oral and literate traditions in these communities. Rather, children in the different communities learn to interact with print in different ways, some of which may be more appropriate to the demands of subsequent classroom learning than others. Does this approach run the risk of presenting yet another 'deficit' model? There is no doubt that the so-called 'mainstream' values are those which are currently reflected and rewarded in the educational system. However, as Brice Heath recognises, there is scope for incorporating some of the skills fostered in other communities such as story-telling, mimicry, and the ability to synthesise and draw analogies.

The article by Corder on the learning of second languages picks up two points made by Bruner — firstly, that the motivation to speak has to be the desire to communicate something and, secondly, that feedback in normal interaction is to the *content* and not the form of an utterance. He argues that second-language learners need to take risks with a language in order to learn the limits of their own communicative effectiveness. In so doing, they will draw on all the resources available to them, which include a knowledge of their own first language, and this may lead for a time (a long time, if it proves communicatively effective!) to a form of language which does not correspond precisely to either the first or the second language but includes the simpler common features of both. 'It is one of the strategies of learning to find out just how far down the scale it is going to be necessary to go before starting to build up again' (p. 293). Corder argues that this skill of reverting to an earlier, simpler register is one which speakers of a language never lose. It may be drawn on in other contexts, such as speaking to children ('baby talk') or to speakers of other languages ('foreigner talk'), where the primary goal is to get the message across.

The article by Mackey broadens out the focus from the individual language learner to a consideration of the 'complex psychological, linguistic and social interrelationships' (p. 311) which underlie bilingualism. The description of an individual's bilingualism is not only a matter of relative competence in the two (or more) languages. It also needs to take account of the various dimensions of *use* of the languages, ranging from internal thought processes to arenas of contact in the home, community and wider society. The developing bilingual learns to respond to all these varied situations in the appropriate language (or combination of languages). At one level this is simply an extension of what the monolingual is learning to do with different varieties of a single language. It is, however, immensely more complex, since each of a bilingual's languages will have its own range of varieties, which each add something different to the message communicated.

The final two articles deal with communication skills which go beyond the verbal formulation of messages — such things as sending positive non-verbal signals, having the confidence to 'disclose' oneself honestly, and so on. This level of learning to communicate is not accomplished effortlessly by all individuals. Argyle argues that 'perhaps 10 per cent of the world's population have quite serious difficulties with common social situations or relationships' (p. 322). The author presents an overview of the types of support which social skills training can provide to such individuals, whilst recognising the limitations of the approach. The article by Whitaker moves the focus away from individual competence to the manner in which groups operate. By recounting the experience of a particular group she explores issues such as the way in which a dominant member may be managed by the group and how consensus may be reached. She stresses throughout 'the importance of listening to what is being communicated in behaviour as well as what is communicated in words' (p. 332).

Barbara Mayor

4.1 From Communicating to Talking

JEROME BRUNER,
with the assistance of *Rita Watson*

If we are to consider the transition from prelinguistic communication to language, particularly with a concern for possible continuities, we had better begin by taking as close a look as we can at
the so-called "original endowment" of human beings. Might that
endowment affect the acquisition and early use of language? I do
not mean simply the prelinguistic precursors of grammar or an
"innate capacity" for language. The question must be a more
general one. What predisposes a living being to use language and
be changed by its use? Suppose we grant that there is some innate
capacity to master language as a symbolic system, as Noam
Chomsky urged, or even to be predisposed toward particular linguistic distinctions, as Derek Bickerton has recently proposed?
Why is language used? After all, chimpanzees have some of the
same capacities and they don't use them.

The awkward dilemma that plagues questions about the original
nature and later growth of human faculties inheres in the unique
nature of human competence. For human competence is both
biological in origin and cultural in the means by which it finds
expression. While the *capacity* for intelligent action has deep
biological roots and a discernible evolutionary history, the *exercise*
of that capacity depends upon man appropriating to himself modes
of acting and thinking that exist not in his genes but in his culture.
There is obviously something in "mind" or in "human nature" that
mediates between the genes and the culture that makes it possible
for the latter to be a prosthetic device for the realization of the
former.

When we ask then about the endowment of human beings, the
question we put must be twofold. We must ask not only about
capacities, but also about how humans are aided in expressing
them in the medium of culture. The two questions, of course, are

Source: Bruner, J. (1983) 'From communicating to talking' in '*Child's Talk:
Learning to Use Language*', Oxford, OUP, 1983, pp. 23-42.

inseparable, since human intellectual capacity necessarily evolved to fit man for using the very prosthetic devices that a culture develops and accumulates for the enablement of its members.

There is some point in studying early human capacities and their development in seemingly cultureless laboratories, as if they were simply expressions of man's biological dispositions and endowment. But we must also bear in mind that the realization of this endowment depends on the tool kit of the culture, whatever we choose to do in the laboratory. The main trend of the last quarter century has been to look increasingly at the contexts that enable human beings to act as they do; increasingly, we can see the futility of considering human nature as a set of autonomous dispositions.

I can easily outline what seems to me, at least, to be "infant endowment" in the so-called cognitive sphere. But to do so relevantly I must focus on those aspects that fit and perhaps even compel human beings to operate in the culture. For I think that it is the requirement of *using* culture as a necessary form of coping that forces man to master language. Language is the means for interpreting and regulating the culture. The interpreting and negotiating start the moment the infant enters the human scene. It is at this stage of interpretation and negotiation that language acquisition is acted out. So I shall look at "endowment" from the point of view of how it equips the infant to come on stage in order to acquire the means for taking his place in culture.

INITIAL COGNITIVE ENDOWMENT

Let me begin with some more or less "firm" conclusions about perception, skill, and problem solving in the prelinguistic infant and consider how they might conceivably predispose the child to acquire "culture" through language.

The first of these conclusions is that much of the cognitive processing going on in infancy appears to operate in support of goal-directed activity. From the start, the human infant is *active* in seeking out regularities in the world about him. The child is active in a uniquely human way, converting experience into species-typical means-end structures. Let me begin with the unlikely example of nonnutritive sucking.

The human infant, like mammals generally, is equipped with a variety of biological processes that ensure initial feeding, initial attachment to a caretaker, initial sensory contact with the world — all quite well buffered to prevent the infant from overreacting. Nonnutritive sucking, an example of one of these buffering mechanisms, has the effect of relaxing large muscle groups, stilling movements of the gut, reducing the number of eye movements in response to excessively patterned visual fields, and in general assuring the maintenance of a moderate level of arousal in the face of even a demanding environment. That much is probably "hard-wired."

But such sucking soon comes under the child's own control. Infants as young as five to six weeks are quite capable, we found, of sucking on a pacifier nipple in order to bring a visual display from blur into focus — increasing their rate of sucking well above baseline when the picture's focus is made contingent on speed of sucking. Sucking and looking, moreover, are coordinated to assure a good view. When babies suck to produce clarity, they suck as they look, and when they stop they soon learn to look away. The same infants, when their sucking in a later session produces blur, suck while looking away from the blurred picture their sucking is producing and desist from sucking while looking at the picture. (We should note, by the way, that infants do not like blurred pictures.)

The Czech pediatrician Hanus Papousek has reported the same capacity for coordination of action in another domain, head turning. He taught six-to-ten-week-old babies to turn their heads to the right (or the left) in order to activate an attractive set of flashing lights. The infants soon learned the required response and, indeed, could even be taught to turn twice to each side for the desired lights. With mastery, their reactions became quite economical. They turned just enough to bring on the lights. But more interesting still, as the experiment progressed and the light display became familiar, they looked at it only briefly, just enough of a glance to confirm that the lights had gone on as expected (following which there was often a smile) and would then begin visually exploring other features of the situation. Successful prediction seems finally to have been the rewarding feature of the situation. With habituation, performance deteriorated — prediction was no longer interesting.

The point is not that infants are cleverer than was suspected before. Rather, it is that their behaviour from early on is guided by active means-end readiness and by search. To put it another way, more in keeping with our general point, the infant from the start is tuned to the coordinative requirements of action. He seems able to appreciate, so to speak, the structure of action and particularly the manner in which means and ends must be combined in achieving satisfactory outcomes — even such arbitrary means as sucking to produce changes in the visual world. He seems, moreover, to be sensitive to the requirements of prediction and, if Papousek's interpretation of the "smile of predictive pleasure" is to be taken seriously, to get active pleasure from successful prediction. Anyone who has bothered to ponder the pleasure infants derive from achieving repetitive, surefire prediction will appreciate this point.

To say that infants are also "social" is to be banal. They are geared to respond to the human voice, to the human face, to human action and gesture. Their means-end readiness is easily and quickly brought into coordination with the actions of their caretakers. The pioneering work of Daniel Stern and Berry Brazelton and their colleagues underlines how early and readily activated infants are by the adults with whom they interact and how quickly their means-end structuring encompasses the actions of another. The infant's principal "tool" for achieving his ends is another familiar human being. In this respect, human infants seem more socially interactive than any of the Great Apes, perhaps to the same degree that Great Apes are more socially interactive than Old or New World Monkeys, and this may be a function of their prolonged and uniquely dependent form of immaturity, as I have argued elsewhere.

Infants are, in a word, tuned to enter the world of human action. Obvious though the point may seem, we shall see that it has enormous consequences for the matter at hand. This leads directly to the second conclusion about infant "endowment."

It is obvious that an enormous amount of the activity of the child during the first year and a half of life is extraordinarily social and communicative. Social interaction appears to be both self-propelled and self-rewarding. Many students of infant behaviour, like Tom Bower, have found that a social response to the infant is the most powerful reinforcer one can use in ordinary learning experiments. And withholding social response to the child's initiatives is one of the most disruptive things one can do to an infant — e.g., an unresponding face will soon produce tears. Even in the opening weeks of life the infant has the capacity to imitate facial and manual gestures (as Andrew Meltzoff has shown); they respond with distress if their mothers are masked during feeding; and, they show a sensitivity to expression in the mother by turn taking in vocalization when their level of arousal is moderate and by simultaneous expression when it is high.

While the child's attachment to the mother (or caretaker) is initially assured by a variety of innate response patterns, there very quickly develops a reciprocity that the infant comes to anticipate and count on. For example, if during play the mother assumes a sober immobile face, the infant shows fewer smiles and turns his head away from the mother more frequently than when the mother responds socially, as Edward Tronick and his colleagues have shown. The existence of such reciprocity — buttressed by the mother's increasing capacity to differentiate an infant's "reasons" for crying as well as by the infant's capacity to anticipate these consistencies — soon creates a form of mutual attention, a harmony of "intersubjectivity," whose importance we shall take up later.

In any case, a pattern of inborn initial social responses in the infant, elicited by a wide variety of effective signs from the mother — her heartbeat, the visual configuration of her face and particularly her eyes, her characteristic smell, the sound and rhythms of her voice — is soon converted into a very complex joint anticipatory system that converts initial biological attachment between mother and child into something more subtle and more sensitive to individual idiosyncracies and to forms of cultural practice.

The third conclusion is that much of early infant action takes place in constrained, familiar situations and shows a suprisingly high degree of order and "systematicity." Children spend most of their time doing a very limited number of things. Long periods are spent in reaching and taking, banging and looking, etc. Within any one of these restricted domains, there is striking "systematicity." Object play provides an example. A single act (like banging) is applied successively to a wide range of objects. Everything on which the child can get his hands is banged. Or the child tries out on a single object all the motor routines of which he or she is capable — grasping the object, banging it, throwing it to the floor, putting it in his mouth, putting it on top of the head, running it through the entire repertory.

Nobody has done better than Jean Piaget in characterizing this systematicity. The older view that pictured the infant as "random" in his actions and saw growth as consisting of becoming "coordinated" can no longer stand up to the evidence. Given the limits of the child's range of action, what occurs within that range is just as orderly and systematic as is adult behaviour. There may be differences of opinion concerning the "rules" that govern this orderly behaviour, but there can be no quarrel about its systematicity. Whether one adopts a Piagetian view of the matter or one more tuned to other theories, like Heinz Werner's, is, in light of the more general issues, quite irrelevant.

It is not the least surprising, in light of this conclusion, that infants enter the world of language and of culture with a readiness to find or invent systematic ways of dealing wth social requirements and linguistic forms. The child reacts "culturally" with characteristic hypotheses about what is required and enters language with a readiness for order. We shall, of course, have much more to say about this later.

There are two important implications that follow from this. The first is obvious, though I do not recall ever having encountered the point. It is that from the start, the child becomes readily attuned to "making a lot out of a little" by combination. He typically works on varying a small set of elements to create a larger range of possibilities. Observations of early play behaviour and of the infant's communicative efforts certainly confirm this "push" to generativeness, to combinatorial and variational efforts. Indeed, Ruth Weir's classic study of the child's spontaneous speech while alone in his crib after bedtime speaks volumes on this combinatorial readiness, as does Melissa Bowerman's on children's spontaneous speech errors.

The second implication is more social. The acquisition of prelinguistic and linguistic communication takes place, in the main, in the highly constrained settings to which we are referring. The child and his caretaker readily combine elements in these situations to extract meanings, assign interpretations, and infer intentions. A decade ago there was considerable debate among developmental linguists on whether in writing "grammars" of child speech one should use a method of "rich interpretation" — taking into account not only the child's actual speech but also the ongoing actions and other elements of the context in which speech was occurring. Today we take it for granted that one must do so. For it is precisely the combining of all elements in constrained situations (speech and nonspeech alike) that provides the road to communicative effectiveness. It is for this reason that I shall place such heavy emphasis on the role of "formats" in the child's entry into language.

A fourth conclusion about the nature of infant cognitive endowment is that its systematic character is surprisingly abstract. Infants during their first year appear to have rules for dealing with space, time, and even causation. A moving object that is transformed in appearance while it is moving behind a screen produces surprise when it reappears in a new guise. Objects that seem to be propelled in ways that *we* see as unnatural (e.g., without being touched by an approaching object) also produce surprise reactions in a three-month-old as well. Objects explored by touch alone are later recognized by vision alone. The infant's perceptual world, far from being a blooming, buzzing confusion, is rather orderly and organized by what seem like highly abstract rules.

Again, it was Piaget who most compellingly brought this "abstractness" to our attention in describing the logical structure of the child's search for invariance in his world — the search for what remains unchanged under the changing surface of appearance. And again, it is not important whether the "logic" that he attributed to this systematic action is correct or not. What is plain is that, whether Piagetian logical rules characterize early "operational behaviour" or whether it can be better described by some more general logical system, we know that cognitively and communicatively there is from the start a capacity to "follow" abstract rules.

It is *not* the case that language, when it is encountered and then used, is the first instance of abstract rule following. It is not, for example, in language alone that the child makes such distinctions as those between specific and nonspecific, between states and processes, between "punctual" acts and recurrent ones, between causative and noncausative actions. These abstract distinctions, picked up with amazing speed in language acquisition, have analogues in the child's way of ordering his world of experience. Language will serve to specify, amplify, and expand distinctions that the child has already about the world. But these abstract distinctions are already present, even without language.

These four cognitive "endowments" — means-end readiness, transactionality, systematicity, and abstractness — provide foundation processes that aid the child's language acquisition. None of them "generates" language, for language involves a set of phonological, syntactic, semantic, and illocutionary rules and maxims that constitute a problem space of their own. But linguistic or communicative hypotheses depend upon these capacities as enabling conditions. Language does not "grow out of" prior protophonological, protosyntactic, protosemantic, or protopragmatic knowledge. It requires a unique sensitivity to a patterned sound system, to grammatical constraints, to referential requirements, to communicative intentions, etc. Such sensitivity grows in the process of fulfilling certain general, nonlinguistic functions — predicting the environment, interacting transactionally, getting to goals with the aid of another, and the like. These functions are first fulfilled primitively if abstractly by prelinguistic communicative means. Such primitive procedures, I will argue, must reach requisite levels of functioning before *any* Language Acquisition Device (whether innate or acquired) can begin to generate "linguistic hypotheses."

ENTRY INTO LANGUAGE

We can turn now to the development of language *per se*. Learning a native language is an accomplishment within the grasp of any toddler, yet discovering how children do it has eluded generations of philosophers and linguists. Saint Augustine believed it was simple. Allegedly recollecting his own childhood, he said, "When they named any thing, and as they spoke turned towards it, I saw and remembered that they called what one would point out by the name they uttered. ... And thus by constantly hearing words, as they occurred in various sentences, I collected gradually for what they stood; and having broken in my mouth to these signs, I thereby gave utterance to my will." But a look at children as they actually acquire language shows Saint Augustine to be far, far off target. Alas, he had a powerful effect both on his followers and on those who set out to refute him.

Developmental linguistics is now going through rough times that can be traced back to Saint Augustine as well as to the reactions against him. Let me recount a little history. Saint Augustine's view, perhaps because there was so little systematic research on language acquisition to refute it, prevailed for a long time. It was even put into modern dress. Its most recent "new look" was in the form of behaviourist "learning theory." In this view's terms, nothing particularly linguistic needed to be said about language. Language, like any other behaviour, could be "explained" as just another set of responses. Its principles and its research paradigms were not derived from the phenomena of language but from "general behaviour." Learning tasks, for example, were chosen to construct theories of learning so as to ensure that the learner had no predispositions toward or knowledge of the material to be learned. All was as if *ab initio*, transfer of response from one stimulus to another was assured by the similarity between stimuli. Language learning was assumed to be much like, say, nonsense syllable learning, except that it might be aided by imitation, the learner imitating the performance of the "model" and then being reinforced for correct performance. Its emphasis was on "words" rather than on grammar. Consequently, it missed out almost entirely in dealing with the combinatorial and generative effect of having a syntax that made possible the routine construction of sentences never before heard and that did not exist in adult speech to be imitated. A good example is the Pivot-Open class, P(0), construction of infant speech in which a common word or phrase is combined productively with other words as in *all-gone mummy, all-gone apple,* and even *all-gone bye-bye* (when mother and aunt finally end a prolonged farewell).

It is one of the mysteries of Kuhnian scientific paradigms that this empiricist approach to language acquisition persisted in psychology (if not in philosophy, where it was overturned by Frege and Wittgenstein) from its first enunciation by Saint Augustine to its most recent one in B.F. Skinner's *Verbal Behaviour.* It would be fair to say that the persistence of the mindless behaviouristic version of Augustinianism finally led to a readiness, even a reckless readiness, to be rid of it. For it was not only an inadequate account, but one that damped inquiry by its domination of "common sense." It set the stage for the Chomskyan revolution.

It was to Noam Chomsky's credit that he boldly proclaimed the old enterprise bankrupt. In its place he offered a challenging, if counterintuitive hypothesis based on nativism. He proposed that the acquisition of the *structure* of language depended upon a Language Acquisition Device (LAD) that had at its base a universal grammar or a "linguistic deep structure" that humans know innately and without learning. LAD was programmed to recognize in the surface structure of any natural language encountered its deep structure or universal grammar by virtue of the kinship between innate universal grammar and the grammar of any and all natural languages. LAD abstracted the grammatical realization rules of the local language and thus enabled the aspirant speaker potentially to generate all the well-formed utterances possible in the language and none that were ill-informed. The universal grammatical categories that programmed LAD were in the innate structure of the mind. No prior nonlinguistic knowledge of the world was necessary, and no privileged communication with another speaker was required. Syntax was independent of knowledge of the world, of semantic meaning, and of communicative function. All the child needed was exposure to language, however fragmentary and uncontextualized his samples of it might be. Or more correctly, the acquisition of syntax could be conceived of as progressing with the assistance of whatever *minimum* world knowledge or privileged communication proved necessary. The only constraints on rate of linguistic development were psychological limitations on *performance*: the child's limited but growing attention and memory span, etc. Linguistic *competence* was there from the start, ready to express itself when performance constraints were extended by the growth of requisite skills.

It was an extreme view. But in a stroke it freed a generation of psycholinguists from the dogma of association-cum-imitation-cum-reinforcement. It turned attention to the problem of rule learning, even if it concentrated only on syntactic rules. By declaring learning theory dead as an explanation of language acquisition (one of the more premature obituaries of our times), it opened the way for a new account.

George Miller put it well. We now had *two* theories of language acquisition: one of them, empiricist associationism, was impossible; the other, nativism, was miraculous. But the void between the impossible and the miraculous was soon to be filled in, albeit untidily and partially.

To begin with, children in fact had and *needed* to have a working knowledge of the world before they acquired language. Such knowledge gave them semantic targets, so to speak, that "corresponded" in some fashion to the distinctions they acquired in their language. A knowledge of the world, appropriately organized in terms of a system of concepts, might give the child hints as to where distinctions could be expected to occur in the language, might even alert him to the distinctions. There were new efforts to develop a generative semantics out of which syntactical hypotheses could presumably be derived by the child. In an extreme form, generative semantics could argue that the concepts in terms of which the world was organized are the same as those that organize language. But even so, the *linguistic* distinctions still had to be mastered. These were not about the *world* but about morphology or syntax or whatever else characterized the linguistic *code*.

The issue of whether rules of *grammar* can somehow be inferred or generalized from the structure of our knowledge of the world is a very dark one. The strong form of the claim insists that syntax can be derived directly from nonlinguistic categories of knowledge in some way. Perhaps the best claim can be made for a case grammar. It is based on the reasonable claim that the concepts of action are innate and primitive. The aspiring language learner already knows the socalled arguments of action: who performed the action, on what object, toward whom, where, by what instrument, and so on. In Charles Fillmore's phrase, "meanings are relativized to scenes," and this involves an "assignment of perspective." Particular phrases impose a perspective on the scene and sentence decisions are perspective decisions. If, for example, the agent of action is perspectively forefronted by some grammatical means such as being inserted as head word, the placement of the nominal that represents agency must be the "deep subject" of the sentence. This leaves many questions unanswered about how the child gets to the point of being able to put together sentences that assign his intended action perspectives to scenes.

The evidence for the semantic account was nonetheless interesting. Roger Brown pointed out, for example, that at the two-word stage of language acquisition more than three-quarters of the child's utterances embody only a half dozen semantic relations that are, at base, case or caselike relations — Agent–Action, Action–Object, Agent–Object, Possession, etc. Do these semantic relations generate the grammar of the language? Case notions of this kind, Fillmore tells us, "comprise a set of universal, presumably innate, concepts which identify certain types of judgments human beings are capable of making about the events that are going on around them ... who did it, who it happened to, and what got changed." The basic structures are alleged to be these arguments of action, and different languages go about realizing them in different ways: by function words, by inflectional morphemes as in the case endings of Latin, by syntactic devices like passivization, and so on. Grammatical forms might then be the surface structures of language, depending for their acquisition on a prior understanding of deep semantic, indeed even protosemantic, concepts about action.

Patricia Greenfield then attempted to show that the earliest *one-word* utterances, richly interpreted in context, could also be explained as realizations of caselike concepts. And more recently Katherine Nelson has enriched the argument that children acquire language already equipped with concepts related to action: "The functional core model (FCM) essentially proposed that the child came to language with a store of familiar concepts of people and objects that were organized around the child's experience with these things. Because the child's experience was active, the dynamic aspects would be the most potent part of what the child came to know about the things experienced. It could be expected that the child would organize knowledge around what he could do with things and what they could do. In other words, knowledge of the world would be functionally organized from the child's point of view." To this earlier view she has now added a temporal dimension — the child's mastery of "scripts for event structures," a sequential structure of "causally and temporarily linked acts with the actors and objects specified in the most general way." These scripts provide the child with a set of syntagmatic formats that permit him to organize his concepts sequentially into sentencelike forms such as those reported by Roger Brown. The capacity to do this rests upon a basic form of representation that the child uses from the start and gradually elaborates. In effect, it is what guides the formation of utterances beyond the one-word stage.

The role of world knowledge in generating or supporting language acquisition is now undergoing intensive study. But still another element has now been added — the pragmatic. It is the newest incursion into the gap between "impossible" and "miraculous" theories of language acquisition. In this view, the central idea is communicative intent: we communicate with some end in mind, some function to be fulfilled. We request or indicate or promise or threaten. Such functionalism had earlier been a strong thread in linguistics, but had been elbowed aside by a prevailing structuralism that, after Ferdinand de Saussure's monumental work, became the dominant mode.

New developments revived functionalism. The first was in the philosophy of language spearheaded by Ludwig Wittgenstein's use-based theory of meaning, formulated in his *Philosophical*

Investigations, and then by the introduction of speech acts in Austin's *How to Do Things with Words.* Austin's argument (as already noted) was that an utterance cannot be analyzed out of the context of its use and its use must include the intention of the speaker and interpretation of that intention by the addressee in the light of communication conventions. A speaker may make a request by many alternative linguistic means, so long as he honours the conventions of his linguistic community. It may take an interrogative construction ('What time is it?'), or it may take the declarative form ('I wonder what time it is').

Roger Brown notes an interesting case with respect to this issue: in the protocols of Adam, he found that Adam's mother used the interrogative in two quite different ways, one as a request for action, the other as a request for information: "Why don't you ... (e.g. play with your ball now)?" and "Why are you playing with your ball?" Although Adam answered informational *why* questions with *Because*, there was no instance of his ever confusing an action and an information-seeking *why* question. He evidently recognized the differing intent of the two forms of utterance quite adequately from the start. He must have been learning speech acts rather than simply the *why* interrogative form.

This raises several questions about acquisition. It puts pragmatics into the middle of things. Is intent being decoded by the child? It would seem so. But linguistics usually defines its domain as "going from sound to sense." But what is "sense?" Do we in fact go from sound to intention, as John Searle proposed? A second question has to do with shared or conventional presuppositions. If children are acquiring notions about how to interpret the intentions encoded in utterances, they must be taking into account not only the structure of the utterance, but also the nature of the conditions that prevail just at the time the utterance is made. Speech acts have at least three kinds of conditions affecting their appropriateness or "felicity"; a preparatory condition (laying appropriate ground for the utterance); an essential condition (meeting the logical conditions for performing a speech act, like, for example, being uninformed as a condition for asking for information related to a matter); and sincerity conditions (wishing to have the information that one asks for). They must also meet affiliative conditions: honouring the affiliation or relation between speaker and hearer, as in requesting rather than demanding when the interlocutor is not under obligation.

Paradoxically, the learning of speech acts may be easier and less mysterious than the learning either of syntax or semantics. For the child's syntactic errors are rarely followed by corrective feedback, and semantic feedback is often lax. But speech acts, on the contrary, get not only immediate feedback, but also correction. Not surprising, then, that prelinguistic communicative acts precede lexico-grammatical speech in their appearance. Not surprising, then, that such primitive "speech act" patterns may serve as a kind of matrix in which lexico-grammatical achievements can be substituted for earlier gestural or vocal procedures.

In this view, entry into language is an entry into discourse that requires both members of a dialogue pair to interpret a communication and its intent. Learning a language, then, consists of learning not only the *grammar* of a particular language but also learning how to realize one's intentions by the appropriate use of that grammar.

The pragmatician's stress on intent requires a far more active role on the part of the adult in aiding the child's language acquisition than that of just being a "model." It requires that the adult be a consenting partner, willing to negotiate with the child. The negotiation has to do, probably, least with syntax, somewhat more with the semantic scope of the child's lexicon, and a very great deal with helping make intentions clear and making their expression fit the conditions and requirements of the "speech community," i.e., the culture.

And the research of the last several years — much of it summarized in Catherine Snow and Charles Ferguson's *Talking to Children* — does indeed indicate that parents play a far more active role in language acquisition than simply modeling the language and providing, so to speak, input for a Language Acquisition Device. The current phrase for it is "fine tuning." Parents speak at the level where their children can comprehend them and move ahead with remarkable sensitivity to their child's progress. The dilemma, as Roger Brown puts it, is how do you teach children to talk by talking baby talk with them at a level that they already understand? And the answer has got to be that the important thing is to keep communicating with them, for by so doing one allows them to learn how to extend the speech that they have into new contexts, how to meet the conditions on speech acts, how to maintain topics across turns, how to know what's worth talking about — how indeed to regulate language use.

So we can now recognize two ways of filling the gap between an impossible empiricist position and a miraculous nativist one. The child must master the conceptual structure of the world that language will map — the social world as well as the physical. He must also master the conventions for making his intentions clear by language.

SUPPORT FOR LANGUAGE ACQUISITION

The development of language, then, involves two people negotiating. Language is not encountered willy-nilly by the child; it is shaped to make communicative interaction effective — fine-tuned. If there is a Language Acquisition Device, the input to it is not a shower of spoken language but a highly interactive affair shaped, as we have already noted, by some sort of an adult Language Acquisition Support System.

After all, it is well known from a generation of research on another "innate" system, sexual behavior, that much experiential priming is necessary before innate sexual responses can be evoked by "appropriate" environmental events. Isolated animals are seriously retarded. By the same token, the recognition and the production of grammatical universals may similarly depend upon prior social and conceptual experience. Continuities between prelinguistic communication and later speech of the kind I alluded to earlier may, moreover, need an "arranged" input of adult speech if the child is to use his growing grasp of conceptual distinctions and communicative functions as guides to language use. I propose that this "arranging" of early speech interaction requires routinized and familiar settings, formats, for the child to comprehend what is going on, given his limited capacity for processing information. These routines constitute what I intend by a Language Acquisition Support System.

There are at least four ways in which such a Language Acquisition Support System helps assure continuity from prelinguistic to linguistic communication. Because there is such concentration on familiar and routine transactional formats, it becomes feasible for the adult partner to highlight those features of the world that are already salient to the child and that have a basic or simple grammatical form. Slobin has suggested, for example, that there are certain prototypical ways in which the child experiences the world:

e.g., a "prototypical transitive event" in which "an animate agent is seen willfully ... to bring about a physical and perceptible change of state or location in a patient by means of direct body contact." Events of this kind, we shall see, are a very frequent feature of mother-child formats, and it is of no small interest that in a variety of languages, as Slobin notes, they "are encoded in consistent grammatical form by age two." Slobin offers the interesting hypothesis "that [these] prototypical situations are encoded in the most basic grammatical forms available in a language." We shall encounter formats built around games and tasks involving both these prototypical means-end structures and canonical linguistic forms that seem almost designed to aid the child in spotting the referential correspondence between such utterances and such events.

Or to take another example, Bickerton has proposed that children are "bioprogrammed" to notice certain distinctions in real world events and to pick up (or even to invent) corresponding linguistic distinctions in order to communicate about them. His candidates are the distinctions (a) between specific and non-specific events, (b) between state and process, (c) between "punctual" and continuous events, and (d) between causative and noncausative actions. And insofar as the "fine tuning" of adult interaction with a child concentrates on these distinctions — both in reality and in speech — the child is aided in moving from their conceptual expression to an appreciation of their appropriate linguistic representation. Again, they will be found to be frequent in the formats of the children we shall look at in detail.

A second way in which the adult helps the child through formating is by encouraging and modeling lexical and phrasal substitutes for familiar gestural and vocal means for effecting various communicative functions. This is a feature of the child's gradual mastery of the request mode that we will be exploring in a later chapter.

H.P. Grice takes it as a hallmark of mature language that the speaker not only has an intention to communicate, but that he also has *conventionalized* or "nonnatural" means for expressing his intention. The speaker, in his view, presupposes that his interlocutor will accept his means of communication and will infer his intention from them. The interlocutor presupposes the same thing about the speaker. Grice, concerned with adults, assumes all this to be quite conscious, if implicit.

An infant cannot at the prelinguistic outset be said to be participating in a conscious Gricean cycle when signaling conventionally in his games with his mother. That much self-consciousness seems unlikely. But what we find is that the mother acts as if he did. The child in turn soon comes to operate with some junior version of the Gricean cycle, awaiting his mother's "uptake" of his signaling.

In Katherine Nelson's terms, the young child soon acquires a small library of scripts and communicative procedures to go with them. They provide steady frameworks in which he learns effectively, by dint of interpretable feedback, how to make his communicative intentions plain. When he becomes "conscious" enough to be said to be operating in a Gricean cycle is, I think, a silly question.

What is striking is how early the child develops means to signal his focus of attention and his requests for assistance — to signal them by conventionalized means in the limited world of familiar formats. He has obviously picked up the gist of "non-natural" or conventionalized signaling of his intentions before ever he has mastered the formal elements of lexico-grammatical speech. [It is] the functional framing of communication which starts the child on his way to language proper.

Thirdly, it is characteristic of play formats particularly that they are made of stipulative or constitutive "events" that are created by language and then recreated on demand by language. Later these formats take on the character of "pretend" situations. They are a rich source of opportunity for language learning and language use.

Finally, once the mother and child are launched into routinized formats, various psychological and linguistic processes are brought into play that generalize from one format to another. Naming, for example, appears first in indicating formats and then transfers to requesting formats. Indeed, the very notion of finding linguistic parallels for conceptual distinctions generalizes from one format to another. So too do such "abstract" ideas as segmentation, interchangeable roles, substitutive means — both in action and in speech.

These are the mundane procedures and events that constitute a Language Acquisition Support System, along with the elements of fine tuning that comprise "baby talk" exchanges.

4.2 What No Bedtime Story Means: Narrative Skills at Home and School

SHIRLEY BRICE HEATH

In the preface to *S/Z*, Roland Barthes' work on ways in which readers read, Richard Howard writes: "We require an education in literature ... in order to discover that *what we have assumed —* with the complicity of our teachers — *was nature is in fact culture, that what was given is no more than a way of taking*" (emphasis not in the original; Howard 1974: ix).[1] This statement reminds us that the *culture* children learn as they grow up is, in fact, "ways of taking" meaning from the environment around them. The means of making sense from books and relating their contents to know-ledge about the real world is but one "way of taking" that is often interpreted as "natural" rather than learned. The quote also reminds us that teachers (and researchers alike) have not recog-nized that ways of taking from books are as much a part of learned behavior as are ways of eating, sitting, playing games, and building houses.

As school-oriented parents and their children interact in the pre-school years, adults give their children, through modeling and specific instruction, ways of taking from books which seem natural in school and in numerous institutional settings such as banks, post offices, businesses, or government offices. These *mainstream* ways exist in societies around the world that rely on formal educational systems to prepare children for participation in settings involving literacy. In some communities these ways of schools and insti-tutions are very similar to the ways learned at home; in other communities the ways of school are merely an overlay on the home-taught ways and may be in conflict with them.[2]

Yet little is actually known about what goes on in story-reading and other literacy-related interactions between adults and pre-

Source: *Language in Society* II, 49-76. © 1982 Cambridge University Press.

schoolers in communities around the world. Specifically, though there are numerous diary accounts and experimental studies of the preschool reading experiences of mainstream middle-class children, we know little about the specific literacy features of the environment upon which the school expects to draw. Just how does what is frequently termed "the literate tradition" envelope the child in knowledge about interrelationships between oral and written language, between knowing something and knowing ways of labelling and displaying it? We have even less information about the variety of ways children from *non-mainstream* homes learn about reading, writing, and using oral language to display knowledge in their preschool environment. The general view has been that whatever it is that mainstream school-oriented homes have, these other homes do not have it; thus these children are not from the literate tradition and are not likely to succeed in school.

A key concept for the empirical study of ways of taking meaning from written sources across communities is that of *literacy events*: occasions in which written language is integral to the nature of participants' interactions and their interpretive processes and strategies. Familiar literacy events for mainstream preschoolers are bedtime stories, reading cereal boxes, stop signs, and television ads, and interpreting instructions for commercial games and toys. In such literacy events, participants follow socially established rules for verbalizing what they know from and about the written material. Each community has rules for socially interacting and sharing knowledge in literacy events.

This paper briefly summarizes the ways of taking from printed stories families teach their preschoolers in a cluster of mainstream school-oriented neighborhoods of a city in the Southeastern region of the United States. We then describe two quite different ways of taking used in the homes of two English-speaking communities in the same region that do not follow the school-expected patterns of bookreading and reinforcement of these patterns in oral storytelling. Two assumptions underlie this paper and are treated in detail in the ethnography of these communities (Heath forthcoming b): (1) Each community's ways of taking from the printed word and using this knowledge are interdependent with the ways children learn to talk in their social interactions with caregivers. (2) There is little or no validity to the time-honored dichotomy of "the literate tradition" and "the oral tradition." This paper suggests a frame of reference for both the community patterns and the paths of development children in different communities follow in their literacy orientations.

MAINSTREAM SCHOOL-ORIENTED BOOKREADING

Children growing up in mainstream communities are expected to develop habits and values which attest to their membership in a "literate society." Children learn certain customs, beliefs, and skills in early enculturation experiences with written materials: the bedtime story is a major literacy event which helps set patterns of behavior that recur repeatedly through the life of mainstream children and adults.

In both popular and scholarly literature, the "bedtime story" is widely accepted as a given — a natural way for parents to interact with their child at bedtime. Commercial publishing houses, television advertising, and children's magazines make much of this familiar ritual, and many of their sales pitches are based on the assumption that in spite of the intrusion of television into many patterns of interaction between parents and children, this ritual remains. Few parents are fully conscious of what bedtime story-reading means as preparation for the kinds of learning and displays of knowledge expected in school. Ninio and Bruner (1978), in their longitudinal study of one mainstream middle-class mother–infant dyad in joint picture-book reading, strongly suggest a universal role of bookreading in the achievement of labelling by children.

In a series of "reading cycles," mother and child alternate turns in a dialogue: the mother directs the child's attention to the book and/or asks what-questions and/or labels items on the page. The items to which the what-questions are directed and labels given are two-dimensional representations of three-dimensional objects, so that the child has to resolve the conflict between perceiving these as two-dimensional objects and as representations of a three-dimensional visual setting. The child does so "by assigning a privileged, autonomous status to pictures as visual objects" (1978: 5). The arbitrariness of the picture, its decontextualization, and its existence as something which cannot be grasped and manipulated like its "real" counterparts is learned through the routines of structured interactional dialogue in which mother and child take turns playing a labelling game. In a "scaffolding" dialogue (cf.

Cazden 1979), the mother points and asks "What is x?" and the child vocalizes and/or gives a nonverbal signal of attention. The mother then provides verbal feedback and a label. Before the age of two, the child is socialized into the "initiation-reply-evaluation sequences" repeatedly described as the central structural feature of classroom lessons (e.g., Sinclair and Coulthard 1975; Griffin and Humphry 1978; Mehan 1979). Teachers ask their students questions which have answers prespecified in the mind of the teacher. Students respond, and teachers provide feedback, usually in the form of an evaluation. Training in ways of responding to this pattern begins very early in the labelling activities of mainstream parents and children.

Maintown Ways

This patterning of "incipient literacy" (Scollon and Scollon 1979) is similar in many ways to that of the families of fifteen primary-level school teachers in Maintown, a cluster of middle-class neighborhoods in a city of the Piedmont Carolinas. These families (all of whom identify themselves as "typical," "middle-class," or "mainstream,") had preschool children, and the mother in each family was either teaching in local public schools at the time of the study (early 1970s), or had taught in the academic year preceding participation in the study. Through a research dyad approach, using teacher-mothers as researchers with the ethnographer, the teacher-mothers audio-recorded their children's interactions in their primary network — mothers, fathers, grandparents, maids, siblings, and frequent visitors to the home. Children were expected to learn the following rules in literacy events in these nuclear households:

(1) As early as six months of age, children *give attention to books and information derived from books.* Their rooms contain bookcases and are decorated with murals, bedspreads, mobiles, and stuffed animals which represent characters found in books. Even when these characters have their origin in television programs, adults also provide books which either repeat or extend the characters' activities on television.

(2) Children, from the age of six months, *acknowledge questions about books.* Adults expand nonverbal responses and vocalizations from infants into fully formed gram-

matical sentences. When children begin to verbalize about
the contents of books, adults extend their questions from
simple requests for labels (What's that? Who's that?) to ask
about the attributes of these items (What does the doggie
say? What colour is the ball?).

(3) From the time they start to talk, children *respond to conversational allusions to the content of books; they act as
question-answerers who have a knowledge of books.* For
example, a fuzzy black dog on the street is likened by an
adult to Blackie in a child's book: "Look, there's a Blackie.
Do you think *he's* looking for a boy?" Adults strive to
maintain with children a running commentary on any event
or object which can be book-related, thus modelling for
them the extension of familiar items and events from books
to new situational contexts.

(4) Beyond two years of age, children *use their knowledge of
what books do to legitimate their departures from "truth."*
Adults encourage and reward "book talk," even when it is
not directly relevant to an ongoing conversation. Children
are allowed to suspend reality, to tell stories which are not
true, to ascribe fiction-like features to everyday objects.

(5) Preschool children *accept book and book-related activities
as entertainment.* When preschoolers are "captive
audiences" (e.g., waiting in a doctor's office, putting a toy
together, or preparing for bed), adults reach for books. If
there are no books present, they talk about other objects as
though they were pictures in books. For example, adults
point to items, and ask children to name, describe, and
compare them to familiar objects in their environment.
Adults often ask children to state their likes or dislikes,
their view of events, and so forth, at the end of the captive
audience period. These affective questions often take place
while the next activity is already underway (e.g., moving
toward the doctor's office, putting the new toy away, or
being tucked into bed), and adults do not insist on answers.

(6) Preschoolers *announce their own factual and fictive narratives* unless they are given in response to direct adult elicitation. Adults judge as most acceptable those narratives
which open by orienting the listener to setting and main
character. Narratives which are fictional are usually marked
by formulaic openings, a particular prosody, or the borrow-

ing of episodes in story books.

(7) When children are about three years old, adults discourage the highly interactive participative role in bookreading children have hitherto played and children *listen and wait as an audience.* No longer does either adult or child repeatedly break into the story with questions and comments. Instead, children must listen, store what they hear, and on cue from the adult, answer a question. Thus, children begin to formulate "practice" questions as they wait for the break and the expected formulaic-type questions from the adult. It is at this stage children often choose to "read" to adults rather than to be read to.

A pervasive pattern of all these features is the authority which books and book-related activities have in the lives of both the preschoolers and members of their primary network. Any initiation of a literacy event by a preschooler makes an interruption, an untruth, a diverting of attention from the matter at hand (whether it be an uneaten plate of food, a messy room, or an avoidance of going to bed) acceptable. Adults jump at openings their children give them for pursuing talk about books and reading.

In this study, writing was found to be somewhat less acceptable as an "anytime activity," since adults have rigid rules about times, places, and materials for writing. The only restrictions on bookreading concern taking good care of books: they should not be wet, torn, drawn on, or lost. In their talk to children about books, and in their explanations of why they buy children's books, adults link school success to "learning to love books," "learning what books can do for you," and "learning to entertain yourself and to work independently." Many of the adults also openly expressed a fascination with children's books "nowadays." They generally judged them as more diverse, wide-ranging, challenging, and exciting than books they had as children.

The Mainstream Pattern

A close look at the way bedtime story routines in Maintown taught children how to take meaning from books raises a heavy sense of the familiar in all of us who have acquired mainstream habits and values. Throughout a lifetime, any school-successful individual moves through the same processes described above thousands of times. Reading for comprehension involves an internal replaying of the same types of questions adults ask children of bedtime stories. We seek *what-explanations*, asking what the topic is, establishing it as predictable and recognizing it in new situational contexts by classifying and categorizing it in our mind with other phenomena. The what-explanation is replayed in learning to pick out topic sentences, write outlines, and answer standardized tests which ask for the correct titles to stories, and so on. In learning to read in school, children move through a sequence of skills designed to teach what-explanations. There is a tight linear order of instruction which recapitulates the bedtime story pattern of breaking down the story into small bits of information and teaching children to handle sets of related skills in isolated sequential hierarchies.

In each individual reading episode in the primary years of schooling, children must move through what-explanations before they can provide *reason-explanations* or *affective commentaries*. Questions about why a particular event occurred or why a specific action was right or wrong come at the end of primary-level reading lessons, just as they come at the end of bedtime stories. Throughout the primary grade levels, what-explanations predominate, reason-explanations come with increasing frequency in the upper grades, and affective comments most often come in the extra-credit portions of the reading workbook or at the end of the list of suggested activities in text books across grade levels. This sequence characterizes the total school career. High school freshmen who are judged poor in compositional and reading skills spend most of their time on what-explanations and practice in advanced versions of bedtime story questions and answers. They are given little or no chance to use reason-giving explanations or assessments of the actions of stories. Reason-explanations result in configurational rather than hierarchical skills, are not predictable, and thus do not present content with a high degree of redundancy. Reason-giving explanations tend to rely on detailed knowledge of a specific domain. This detail is often unpredictable to teachers, and is not as highly valued as is knowledge which covers a particular area of knowledge with less detail but offers opportunity for extending the knowledge to larger and related concerns. For example, a primary-level student whose father owns a turkey farm may respond with reason-explanations to a story about a turkey. His knowledge is intensive and covers details perhaps not known to the teacher and not judged as relevant to the story. The knowledge is unpredictable and questions about it do not continue to repeat the common core of content knowledge of the story. Thus such configured knowledge is encouraged only for the "extras" of reading — an extra-credit oral report or a creative picture and story about turkeys. This kind of knowledge is allowed to be used once the hierarchical what-explanations have been mastered and displayed in a particular situation and, in the course of one's academic career, only when one has shown full mastery of the hierarchical skills and subsets of related skills which underlie what-explanations. Thus, reliable and successful participation in the ways of taking from books that teachers view as natural must, in the usual school way of doing things, precede other ways of taking from books. [...]

Close analyses of how mainstream school-oriented children come to learn to take from books at home suggest that such children learn not only how to take meaning from books, but also how to talk about it. In doing the latter, they repeatedly practice routines which parallel those of classroom interaction. By the time they enter school, they have had continuous experience as information-givers; they have learned how to perform in those interactions which surround literate sources throughout school. They have had years of practice in interaction situations that are the heart of reading — both learning to read and reading to learn in school. They have developed habits of performing which enable them to run through the hierarchy of preferred knowledge about a literate source and the appropriate sequence of skills to be displayed in showing knowledge of a subject. They have developed ways of decontextualizing and surrounding with explanatory prose the knowledge gained from selective attention to objects.

They have learned to listen, waiting for the appropriate cue which signals it is their turn to show off this knowledge. They have learned the rules for getting certain services from parents (or teachers) in the reading interaction (Merritt 1979). In nursery school, they continue to practice these interaction patterns in a group rather than in a dyadic situation. There they learn additional signals and behaviors necessary for getting a turn in a group, and responding to a central reader and to a set of centrally defined reading tasks. In short, most of their waking hours during the preschool years have enculturated them into: (1) all those habits associated with what-explanations, (2) selective attention to items of the written text, *and* (3) appropriate interactional styles for orally displaying all the know-how of their literate orientation to the environment. This learning has been finely tuned and its habits are highly interdependent. Patterns of behaviors learned in one setting or at one stage reappear again and again as these children learn to use oral and written language in literacy events and to bring their knowledge to bear in school-acceptable ways.

ALTERNATIVE PATTERNS OF LITERACY EVENTS

But what corresponds to the mainstream pattern of learning in communities that do not have this finely tuned, consistent, repetitive, and continuous pattern of training? Are there ways of behaving which achieve other social and cognitive aims in other sociocultural groups?

The data below are summarized from an ethnography of two communities — Roadville and Trackton — located only a few miles from Maintown's neighborhoods in the Piedmont Carolinas. Roadville is a white working-class community of families steeped for four generations in the life of the textile mill. Trackton is a working-class black community whose older generations have been brought up on the land, either farming their own land or working for other landowners. However, in the past decade, they have found work in the textile mills. Children of both communities are unsuccessful in school; yet both communities place a high value on success in school, believing earnestly in the personal and vocational rewards school can bring and urging their children "to get ahead" by doing well in school. Both Roadville and Trackton are literate communities in the sense that the residents of each are able to read printed and written materials in their daily lives, and on occasion they produce written messages as part of the total pattern of communication in the community. In both communities, children go to school with certain expectancies of print and, in Trackton especially, children have a keen sense that reading is something one does to learn something one needs to know (Heath 1980). In both groups, residents turn from spoken to written uses of language and vice versa as the occasion demands, and the two modes of expression seem to supplement and reinforce each other. Nonetheless there are radical differences between the two communities in the ways in which children and adults interact in the preschool years; each of the two communities also differs from Maintown. Roadville and Trackton view children's learning of language from two radically different perspectives: in Trackton, children "learn to talk," in Roadville, adults "teach them how to talk."

Roadville

In Roadville, babies are brought home from the hospital to rooms decorated with colorful, mechanical, musical, and literacy-based stimuli. The walls are decorated with pictures based on nursery rhymes, and from an early age, children are held and promoted to "see" the wall decorations. Adults recite nursery rhymes as they twirl the mobile made of nursery-rhyme characters. The items of the child's environment promote exploration of colors, shapes, and textures: a stuffed ball with sections of fabrics of different colors and textures is in the crib; stuffed animals vary in texture, size, and shape. Neighbors, friends from church, and relatives come to visit and talk to the baby, and about him to those who will listen. The baby is fictionalized in the talk to him: "But this baby wants to go to sleep, doesn't he? Yes, see those little eyes gettin' heavy." As the child grows older, adults pounce on word-like sounds and turn them into "words," repeating the "words," and expanding them into well-formed sentences. Before they can talk, children are introduced to visitors and prompted to provide all the expected politeness formulas, such as "Bye-bye," "Thank you," and so forth. As soon as they can talk, children are reminded about these formulas, and book or television characters known to be "polite" are involved as reinforcement.

In each Roadville home, preschoolers first have cloth books, featuring a single object on each page. They later acquire books which provide sounds, smells, and different textures or opportunities for practising small motor skills (closing zippers, buttoning buttons, etc.). A typical collection for a two-year-old consisted of a dozen or so books — eight featured either the alphabet or numbers, others were books of nursery rhymes, simplified Bible stories, or "real-life" stories about boys and girls (usually taking care of their pets or exploring a particular feature of their environment). Books based on Sesame Street characters were favorite gifts for three- and four-year-olds.

Reading and reading-related activities occur most frequently before naps or at bedtime in the evening. Occasionally an adult or older child will read to a fussy child while the mother prepares dinner or changes a bed. On weekends, fathers sometimes read with their children for brief periods of time, but they generally prefer to play games or play with children's toys in their interactions.

[...] Bookreading time focuses on letters of the alphabet, numbers, names of basic items pictured in books, and simplified retellings of stories in the words of the adult. If the content or story plot seems too complicated for the child, the adult tells the story in short, simple sentences, frequently laced with requests that the child give what-explanations.

In Roadville's literacy events, the rules of cooperative discourse around print are repeatedly practiced, coached, and rewarded in the preschool years. Adults in Roadville believe that instilling in children the proper use of words and understanding of the meaning of the written word are important for both their educational and religious success. Adults repeat aspects of the learning of literacy events they have known as children. In the words of one Roadville parent: "It was then that I began to learn ... when my daddy kept insisting I *read* it, *say* it right. It was then that I *did* right, in his view."

The path of development for such performance can be described in three overlapping stages. In the first, children are introduced to discrete bits and pieces of books — separate items, letters of the alphabet, shapes, colors, and commonly represented items in books for children (apple, baby, ball, etc.). The latter are usually decontextualized, not pictured in their ordinary contexts, and they are represented in two-dimensional flat line drawings. During this stage, children must participate as predictable information-givers and respond to questions that ask for specific and discrete bits of information about the written matter. In these literacy events, specific features of the two-dimensional items in books which are different from their "real" counterparts are not pointed out. A ball in a book is flat; a duck in a book is yellow and fluffy; trucks, cars, dogs, and trees talk in books. No mention is made of the fact that such features do not fit these objects in reality. Children are not encouraged to move their understanding of books into other situational contexts or to apply it in their general knowledge of the world about them.

In the second stage, adults demand an acceptance of the power of print to entertain, inform, and instruct. When [children can] no longer participate by contributing their knowledge at any point in the literacy event, they learn to recognize bookreading as a performance. The adult exhibits the book to [the child; the child is] to be entertained, to learn from the information conveyed in the material, and to remember the book's content for the sequential followup questioning, as opposed to ongoing cooperative participatory questions.

In the third stage, [children are] introduced to preschool workbooks which provide story information and are asked questions or provided exercises and games based on the content of the stories or pictures. Follow-the-number coloring books and preschool "push-out and paste" workbooks on shapes, colors, and letters of the alphabet reinforce repeatedly that the written word can be taken apart into small pieces and one item linked to another by following rules. [Children are given] practice in the linear, sequential nature of books: begin at the beginning, stay in the lines for coloring, draw straight lines to link one item to another, write your answers on lines, keep your letters straight, match the cutout letter to diagrams of letter shapes.

The differences between Roadville and Maintown are substantial. Roadville adults do not extend either the content or the habits of literacy events beyond bookreading. They do not, upon seeing an item or event in the real world, remind children of a similar event in a book and launch a running commentary on similarities and differences. When a game is played or a chore done, adults do not use literate sources. Mothers cook without written recipes most of the time; if they use a recipe from a written source, they do so usually only after confirmation and alteration by friends who have tried the recipe. Directions to games are read, but not carefully followed, and they are not talked about in a series of questions and answers which try to establish their meaning. Instead, in the putting together of toys or the playing of games, the abilities or preferences of one party prevail. For example, if an adult knows how to put a toy together, he does so; he does not talk about the process, refer to the written material and "translate" for the child, or try to sequence steps so the child can do it.[3] [...]

Adults at tasks do not provide a running verbal commentary on what they are doing. They do not draw the attention of the child to specific features of the sequences of skills or the attributes of items. They do not ask questions of the child, except questions which are directive or scolding in nature. [...] Explanations which move beyond the listing of names of items and their features are rarely offered by adults. Children do not ask questions of the type "But I

don't understand. What is that?" They appear willing to keep trying, and if there is ambiguity in a set of commands, they ask a
question such as "You want me to do this?" (demonstrating their
current efforts), or they try to find a way of diverting attention
from the task at hand. [...]

Roadville parents provide their children with books; they read
to them and ask questions about the books' contents. They choose
books which emphasize nursery rhymes, alphabet learning,
animals, and simplified Bible stories, and they require their children to repeat from these books and to answer formulaic questions
about their contents. Roadville adults also ask questions about oral
stories which have a point relevant to some marked behavior of a
child. They use proverbs and summary statements to remind their
children of stories and to call on them for simple comparisons of
the stories' contents to their own situations. Roadville parents
coach children in their telling of a story, forcing them to tell about
an incident as it has been pre-composed or pre-scripted in the
head of the adult. Thus, in Roadville, children come to know a
story as either an accounting from a book, or a factual account of a
real event in which some type of marked behavior occurred and
there is a lesson to be learned. Any fictionalized account of a real
event is viewed as a *lie*; reality is better than fiction. Roadville's
church and community life admit no story other than that which
meets the definition internal to the group. Thus children cannot
decontextualize their knowledge or fictionalize events known to
them and shift them about into other frames.

When these children go to school they perform well in the initial
stages of each of the three early grades. They often know portions
of the alphabet, some colors and numbers, can recognize their
names, and tell someone their address and their parents' names.
They will sit still and listen to a story, and they know how to
answer questions asking for what-explanations. They do well in
reading work-book exercises which ask for identification of
specific portions of words, items from the story, or the linking of
two items, letters, or parts of words on the same page. When the
teacher reaches the end of story-reading or the reading circle and
asks questions such as "What did you like about the story?", relatively few Roadville children answer. If asked questions such as
"What would you have done if you had been Billy [a story's main
character]?", Roadville children most frequently say "I don't
know" or shrug their shoulders.

Near the end of each year, and increasingly as they move through the early primary grades, Roadville children can handle successfully the initial stages of lessons. But when they move ahead to extra-credit items or to activities considered more advanced and requiring more independence, they are stumped. They turn frequently to teachers asking "Do you want me to do this? What do I do here?" If asked to write a creative story or tell it into a tape recorder, they retell stories from books; they do not create their own. They rarely provide emotional or personal commentary on their accounting of real events or book stories. They are rarely able to take knowledge learned in one context and shift it to another; they do not compare two items or events and point out similarities and differences. They find it difficult either to hold one feature of an event constant and shift all others or to hold all features constant but one. For example, they are puzzled by questions such as "What would have happened if Billy had not told the policeman what happened?" They do not know how to move events or items out of a given frame. To a question such as "What habits of the Hopi Indians might they be able to take with them when they move to a city?", they provide lists of features of life of the Hopi on the reservation. They do not take these items, consider their appropriateness in an urban setting, and evaluate the hypothetical outcome. In general, they find this type of question impossible to answer, and they do not know how to ask teachers to help them take apart the questions to figure out the answers. Thus their initial successes in reading, being good students, following orders, and adhering to school norms of participating in lessons begin to fall away rapidly about the time they enter the fourth grade. As the importance and frequency of questions and reading habits with which they are familiar decline in the higher grades, they have no way of keeping up or of seeking help in learning what it is they do not even know they don't know.

Trackton

Babies in Trackton come home from the hospital to an environment which is almost entirely human. There are no cribs, car beds, or car seats, and only an occasional high chair or infant seat. Infants are held during their waking hours, occasionally while they sleep, and they usually sleep in the bed with parents until they are about two years of age. They are held, their faces fondled, their cheeks pinched, and they eat and sleep in the midst of human talk and noise from the television, stereo, and radio. Encapsuled in an almost totally human world, they are in the midst of constant human communication, verbal and nonverbal. They literally feel the body signals of shifts in emotion of those who hold them almost continuously; they are talked about and kept in the midst of talk about topics that range over any subject. As children make cooing or babbling sounds, adults refer to this as "noise," and no attempt is made to interpret these sounds as words or communicative attempts on the part of the baby. Adults believe they should not have to depend on their babies to tell them what they need or when they are uncomfortable; adults know, children only "come to know."

When a child can crawl and move about on his own, he plays with the household objects deemed safe for him — pot lids, spoons, plastic food containers. Only at Christmastime are there special toys for very young children; these are usually trucks, balls, doll babies, or plastic cars, but rarely blocks, puzzles, or books. As children become completely mobile, they demand ride toys or electronic and mechanical toys they see on television. They never request nor do they receive manipulative toys, such as puzzles, blocks, take-apart toys or literacy-based items, such as books or letter games.

Adults read newspapers, mail, calendars, circulars (political and civic-events related), school materials sent home to parents, brochures advertising new cars, television sets, or other products, and the Bible and other church-related materials. There are no reading materials especially for children (with the exception of children's Sunday School materials), and adults do not sit and read to children. Since children are usually left to sleep whenever and wherever they fall asleep, there is no bedtime or naptime as such. At night, they are put to bed when adults go to bed or whenever the person holding them gets tired. Thus, going to bed is not framed in any special routine. Sometimes in a play activity during the day, an older sibling will read to a younger child, but the latter soon loses interest and squirms away to play. Older children often try to "play school" with younger children, reading to them from books and trying to ask questions about what they have read. Adults look on these efforts with amusement and do not try to convince the small child to sit still and listen.

Signs from very young children of attention to the nonverbal behaviors of others are rewarded by extra fondling, laughter, and cuddling from adults. For example, when an infant shows signs of recognizing a family member's voice on the phone by bouncing up and down in the arms of the adult who is talking on the phone, adults comment on this to others present and kiss and nudge the child. Yet when children utter sounds or combinations of sounds which could be interpreted as words, adults pay no attention. Often by the time they are twelve months old, children approximate words or phrases of adults' speech; adults respond by laughing or giving special attention to the child and crediting him with "sounding like" the person being imitated. When children learn to walk and imitate the walk of members of the community, they are rewarded by comments on their activities: "He walks just like Toby when he's tuckered out."

Children between the ages of twelve and twenty-four months often imitate the tune or "general Gestalt" (Peters 1977) of complete utterances they hear around them. They pick up and repeat chunks (usually the ends) of phrasal and clausal utterances of speakers around them. They seem to remember fragments of speech and repeat these without active production. In this first stage of language learning, the repetition stage, they imitate the intonation contours and general shaping of the utterances they repeat. Lem 1; 2 in the following example illustrates this pattern.

Mother:	[talking to neighbor on porch while Lem plays with a truck on the porch nearby] But they won't call back, won't happen=
Lem:	=call back
Neighbor:	Sam's going over there Saturday, he'll pick up a form=
Lem:	=pick up on, pick up on [Lem here appears to have heard *form* as *on*]

The adults pay no attention to Lem's "talk," and their talk, in fact, often overlaps his repetitions.

In the second stage, repetition with variation, Trackton children manipulate pieces of conversation they pick up. They incorporate chunks of language from others into their ongoing dialogue, applying productive rules, inserting new nouns and verbs for those used in the adults' chunks. They also play with rhyming patterns and varying intonation contours.

Mother: She went to the doctor again.
Lem (2; 2): [in a sing-song fashion] went to de doctor, doctor,
             tractor, dis my tractor, doctor on a tractor, went to
             de doctor.

Lem creates a monologue, incorporating the conversation about him into his own talk as he plays. Adults pay no attention to his chatter unless it gets so noisy as to interfere with their talk.

In the third stage, participation, children begin to enter the ongoing conversations about them. They do so by attracting the adult's attention with a tug on the arm or pant leg, and they help make themselves understood by providing nonverbal reinforcements to help recreate a scene they want the listener to remember. For example, if adults are talking, and a child interrupts with seemingly unintelligible utterances, the child will make gestures, extra sounds, or act out some outstanding features of the scene he is trying to get the adult to remember. Children try to create a context, a scene, for the understanding of their utterance.

This third stage illustrates a pattern in the child's response to their environment and their ways of letting others know their knowledge of the environment. Once they are in the third stage, their communicative efforts are accepted by community members, and adults respond directly to the child, instead of talking to others about the child's activities as they have done in the past. Children continue to practice for conversational participation by playing, when alone, both parts of dialogues, imitating gestures as well as intonation patterns of adults. By 2;6 all children in the community can imitate the walk and talk of others in the community, or frequent visitors such as the man who comes around to read the gas meters. They can feign anger, sadness, fussing, remorse, silliness, or any of a wide range of expressive behaviors. They often use the same chunks of language for varying effects, depending on nonverbal support to give the language different meanings or cast it in a different key (Hymes 1974). Girls between three and four years of age take part in extraordinarily complex stepping and clapping patterns and simple repetitions of hand clap games played by older girls. From the time they are old enough to stand alone, they are encouraged in their participation by siblings and older children in the community. These games require anticipation and recognition of cues for upcoming behaviors, and the young girls learn to watch for these cues and to come in with the appropriate words and movements at the right time.

Preschool children are not asked for what-explanations of their environment. Instead, they are asked a preponderance of analogical questions which call for non-specific comparisons of one item, event, or person with another: "What's that like?" Other types of questions ask for specific information known to the child but not the adults: "Where'd you get that from?" "What do you want?" "How come you did that?" (Heath 1982). Adults explain their use of these types of questions by expressing their sense of children: they are "comers," coming into their learning by experiencing what knowing about things means. As one parent of a two-year-old boy put it: "Ain't no use me tellin' 'im: learn this, learn that, what's this, what's that? He just gotta learn, gotta know; he sees one thing one place one time, he know how it go, see sump'n like it again, maybe it be the same, maybe it won't." Children are expected to learn how to know when the form belies the meaning, and to know contexts of items and to use their understanding of these contexts to draw parallels between items and events. Parents do not believe they have a tutoring role in this learning; they provide the experiences on which the child draws and reward signs of their successfully coming to know.

Trackton children's early stories illustrate how they respond to adult views of them as "comers." The children learn to tell stories by drawing heavily on their abilities to render a context, to set a stage, and to call on the audience's power to join in the imaginative creation of story. Between the ages of two and four years, the children, in a monologue-like fashion, tell stories about things in their lives, events they see and hear, and situations in which they have been involved. They produce these spontaneously during play with other children or in the presence of adults. Sometimes they make an effort to attract the attention of listeners before they begin the story, but often they do not. Lem, playing off the edge of the porch, when he was about two and a half years of age, heard a bell in the distance. He stopped, looked at Nellie and Benjy, his older siblings, who were nearby and said:

Way
Far
Now
It a church bell
Ringin'

Dey singin'
Ringin'
You hear it?
I hear it
Far
Now.

Lem had been taken to church the previous Sunday and had been much impressed by the church bell. He had sat on his mother's lap and joined in the singing, rocking to and fro on her lap, and clapping his hands. His story, which is like a poem in its imagery and line-like prosody, is in response to the current stimulus of a distant bell. As he tells the story, he sways back and forth.

This story, somewhat longer than those usually reported from other social groups for children as young as Lem,[4] has some features which have come to characterize fully-developed narratives or stories. It recapitulates in its verbal outline the sequence of events being recalled by the storyteller. At church, the bell rang while the people sang. In the line "It a church bell," Lem provides his story's topic, and a brief summary of what is to come. This line serves a function similar to the formulae often used by older children to open a story: "This is a story about (a church bell)." Lem gives only the slightest hint of story setting or orientation to the listener; where and when the story took place are capsuled in "Way, Far." Preschoolers in Trackton almost never hear "Once upon a time there was a ——" stories, and they rarely provide definitive orientations for their stories. They seem to assume listeners "know" the situation in which the narrative takes place. Similarly, preschoolers in Trackton do not close off their stories with formulaic endings. Lem poetically balances his opening and closing in an inclusio, beginning "Way, Far, Now." and ending "Far, Now." The effect is one of closure, but there is no clearcut announcement of closure. Throughout the presentation of action and result of action in their stories, Trackton preschoolers invite the audience to respond or evaluate the story's actions. Lem asks "You hear it?" which may refer either to the current stimulus or to yesterday's bell, since Lem does not productively use past tense endings for any verbs at this stage in his language development.

Preschool storytellers have several ways of inviting audience evaluation and interest. They may themselves express an emotional response to the story's actions; they may have another character or narrator in the story do so often using alliterative language play; or they may detail actions and results through direct discourse or sound effects and gestures. All these methods of calling attention to the story and its telling distinguish the speech event as a story, an occasion for audience and storyteller to interact pleasantly, and not simply to hear an ordinary recounting of events or actions.

Trackton children must be aggressive in inserting their stories into an ongoing stream of discourse. Storytelling is highly competitive. Everyone in a conversation may want to tell a story, so only the most aggressive wins out. The content ranges widely, and there is "truth" only in the universals of human experience. Fact is often hard to find, though it is usually the seed of the story. Trackton stories often have no point — no obvious beginning or ending; they go on as long as the audience enjoys and tolerates the storyteller's entertainment.

Trackton adults do not separate out the elements of the environment around their children to tune their attentions selectively. They do not simplify their language, focus on single-word utterances by young children, label items or features of objects in either books or the environment at large. Instead, children are continuously contextualized, presented with almost continuous communication. From this ongoing, multiple-channeled stream of stimuli, they must themselves select, practice, and determine rules of production and structuring. For language, they do so by first repeating, catching chunks of sounds, intonation contours, and practicing these without specific reinforcement or evaluation. But practice material and models are continuously available. Next the children seem to begin to sort out the productive rules for speech and practice what they hear about them with variation. Finally, they work their way into conversations, hooking their meanings for listeners into a familiar context by recreating scenes through gestures, special sound effects, etc. These characteristics continue in their story-poems and their participation in jump-rope rhymes. Because adults do not select out, name, and describe features of the environment for the young, children must perceive situations, determine how units of the situations are related to each other, recognize these relations in other situations, and reason through what it will take to show their correlation of one situation with another. The children can answer questions such as "What's that like?" ["It's like Doug's car"] but they can rarely name the specific feature or features which make two items or events alike. For example, in the case of saying a car seen on the street is "like Doug's car," a child may be basing the analogy on the fact that this car has a flat tire and Doug's also had one last week. But the child does not name (and is not asked to name) what is alike between the two cars.

Children seem to develop connections between situations or items not by specification of labels and features in the situations, but by configuration links. Recognition of similar general shapes or patterns of links seen in one situation and connected to another, seem to be the means by which children set scenes in their non-verbal representations of individuals, and later in their verbal chunking, then segmentation and production of rules for putting together isolated units. They do not decontextualize; instead they heavily contextualize nonverbal and verbal language. They fictionalize their "true stories," but they do so by asking the audience to identify with the story through making parallels from their own experiences. When adults read, they often do so in a group. One person, reading aloud, for example, from a brochure on a new car decodes the text, displays illustrations and photographs, and listeners relate the text's meaning to their experiences asking questions and expressing opinions. Finally, the group as a whole synthesizes the written text and the negotiated oral discourse to construct a meaning for the brochure (Heath forthcoming a).

When Trackton children go to school, they face unfamiliar types of questions which ask for what-explanations. They are asked as individuals to identify items by name, and to label features such as shape, color, size, number. The stimuli to which they are to give these responses are two-dimensional flat representations which are often highly stylized and bear little resemblance to the "real" items. Trackton children generally score in the lowest percentile range on the Metropolitan Reading Readiness tests. They do not sit at their desks and complete reading workbook pages; neither do they tolerate questions about reading materials which are structured along the usual lesson format. Their contributions are in the form of "I had a duck at my house one time." "Why'd he do that?" or they imitate the sound effects teachers may produce in stories they read to the children. By the end of the first three primary grades, their general language arts scores have been consistently low, except for those few who have begun to adapt to and adopt some of the behaviors they have had to learn in school. But the majority not only fail to learn the content of lessons, they also do not adopt the social interactional rules for school literacy events. Print in isolation bears little authority in their world. The kinds of questions asked of reading books are unfamiliar. The children's abilities to metaphorically link two events or situations and to recreate scenes are not tapped in the school; in fact, *these abilities often cause difficulties*, because they enable children to see parallels teachers did not intend, and indeed, may not recognize until the children point them out (Heath 1978).

By the end of the lessons or by the time in their total school career when reason-explanations and affective statements call for the creative comparison of two or more situations, it is too late for many Trackton children. They have not picked up along the way the composition and comprehension skills they need to translate their analogical skills into a channel teachers can accept. They seem not to know how to take meaning from reading; they do not observe the rules of linearity in writing, and their expression of themselves on paper is very limited. Orally taped stories are often much better, but these rarely count as much as written compositions. Thus, Trackton children continue to collect very low or failing grades, and many decide by the end of the sixth grade to stop trying and turn their attention to the heavy peer socialization which usually begins in these years.

FROM COMMUNITY TO CLASSROOM

A recent review of trends in research on learning pointed out that "learning to read through using and learning from language has been less systematically studied than the decoding process" (Glaser 1979: 7). Put another way, how children learn to use language to read to learn has been less systematically studied than decoding skills. Learning how to take meaning from writing before one learns to read involves repeated practice in using and learning from language through appropriate participation in literacy events such as exhibitor/questioner and spectator/respondent dyads (Scollon and Scollon 1979) or group negotiation of the meaning of a written text. Children have to learn to select, hold, and retrieve content from books and other written or printed texts in accordance with their community's rules or "ways of taking," and the children's learning follows community paths of language socialization. In each society, certain kinds of childhood participation in literacy events may precede others, as the developmental sequence builds toward the whole complex of home and community behaviors characteristic of the society. The ways of taking employed in the school may in turn build directly on the preschool development, may require substantial adaptation on the part of the children, or may even run directly counter to aspects of the community's pattern. [...]

In the early reading stages, and in later requirements for reading to learn at more advanced stages, children from the three communities respond differently, because they have learned different methods and degrees of taking from books. In comparison to Maintown children, the habits Roadville children learned in book-reading and toy-related episodes have not continued for them through other activities and types of reinforcement in their environment. They have had less exposure to both the content of books and ways of learning from books than have mainstream children. Thus their need in schools is not necessarily for an intensification of presentation of labels, a slowing down of the sequence of introducing what-explanations in connection with bookreading. Instead they need *extension of these habits to other domains* and to opportunities for practicing habits such as producing running commentaries, creating exhibitor/questioner and spectator/respondent roles. Perhaps most important, Roadville children need to have articulated for them *distinctions in discourse strategies and structures*. Narratives of real events have certain strategies and structures; imaginary tales, flights of fantasy, and affective expressions have others. Their community's view of narrative discourse style is very narrow and demands a passive role in both creation of and response to the account of events. Moreover, these children have *to be reintroduced to a participant frame of reference to a book*. Though initially they were participants in bookreading, they have been trained into passive roles since the age of three years, and they must learn once again to be active information-givers, taking from books and linking that knowledge to other aspects of their environment.

Trackton students present an additional set of alternatives for procedures in the early primary grades. Since they usually have few of the expected "natural" skills of taking meaning from books, they must not only learn these, but also *retain their analogical practices* for use in some of the later stages of learning to read. They must *learn to adapt the creativity in language, metaphor, fictionalization, recreation of scenes and exploration of functions and settings of items they bring to school.* These children already use narrative skills highly rewarded in the upper primary grades. They distinguish a fictionalized story from a real-life narrative. They know that telling a story can be in many ways related to play; it suspends reality, and frames an old event in a new context; it calls on audience participation to recognize the setting and participants. They must now *learn as individuals to recount factual events in a straightforward way* and *recognize appropriate occasions for reason-explanations and affective expressions.* Trackton children seem to have skipped learning to label, list features, and give what-explanations. Thus they need to *have the mainstream or school habits presented in familiar activities with explanations related to their own habits of taking meaning* from the environment. Such "simple," "natural" things as distinctions between two-dimensional and three-dimensional objects may need to be explained to help Trackton children learn the stylization and decontextualization which characterizes books.

To lay out in more specific detail how Roadville and Trackton's ways of knowing can be used along with those of mainstreamers goes beyond the scope of this paper. However, it must be admitted that a range of alternatives to ways of learning and displaying knowledge characterizes all highly school-successful adults in the advanced stages of their careers. Knowing more about how these alternatives are learned at early ages in different sociocultural conditions can help the school to provide opportunities for *all* students to avail themselves of these alternatives early in their school careers. [...]

NOTES

1. First presented at the Terman Conference on Teaching at Stanford University, 1980, this paper has benefitted from cooperation with M. Cochran-Smith of the University of Pennsylvania. She shares an appreciation of the relevance of Roland Barthes' work for studies of the socialization of young children into literacy; her research (1981) on the story-reading practices of a mainstream school-oriented nursery school provides a much needed detailed account of early school orientation to literacy.

2. Terms such as *mainstream* or *middle-class* cultures or social groups are frequently used in both popular and scholarly writings without careful definition. Moreover, numerous studies of behavioral phenomena (for example, mother-child interactions in language learning) either do not specify that the subjects being described are drawn from mainstream groups or do not recognize the importance of

this limitation. As a result, findings from this group are often regarded as universal. For a discussion of this problem, see Chanan and Gilchrist 1974, Payne and Bennett 1977. In general, the literature characterizes this group as school-oriented, aspiring toward upward mobility through formal institutions, and providing enculturation which positively values routines of promptness, linearity (in habits ranging from furniture arrangement to entrance into a movie theatre), and evaluative and judgmental responses to behaviors which deviate from their norms.

In the United States, mainstream families tend to locate in neighborhoods and suburbs around cities. Their social interactions center not in their immediate neighborhoods, but around voluntary associations across the city. Thus a cluster of mainstream families (and not a community — which usually implies a specific geographic territory as the locus of a majority of social interactions) is the unit of comparison used here with the Trackton and Roadville communities.

3. Behind this discussion are findings from cross-cultural psychologists who have studied the links between verbalization of task and demonstration of skills in a hierarchical sequence, e.g., Childs and Greenfield 1980; see Goody 1979 on the use of questions in learning tasks unrelated to a familiarity with books.

4. Cf. Umiker-Sebeok's (1979) descriptions of stories of mainstream middle-class children, ages 3-5 and Sutton-Smith 1981.

REFERENCES

Basso, K. (1974). The ethnography of writing. In R. Bauman & J. Sherzer (eds.), *Explorations in the ethnography of speaking.* Cambridge University Press.
Cazden, C.B. (1979). Peekaboo as an instructional model: Discourse development at home and at school. *Papers and Reports in Child Language Development* **17**: 1-29.
Chanan, G., & Gilchrist, L. (1974). *What school is for.* New York: Praeger.
Childs, C.P. & Greenfield, P.M. (1980). Informal modes of learning and teaching. In N. Warren (ed.), *Advances in cross-cultural psychology*, vol. 2 London: Academic Press.
Cochran-Smith, M. (1981). The making of a reader. Ph.D. dissertation. University of Pennsylvania.
Cohen, R. (1968). The relation between socio-conceptual styles and orientation to school requirements. *Sociology of Education* **41**: 201-20.
——. (1969). Conceptual styles, culture conflict, and nonverbal tests of intelligence. *American Anthropologist* **71** (5): 828-56.
——. (1971) The influence of conceptual rule-sets on measures of learning ability. In C.L. Brace, G. Gamble, & J. Bond (eds.), *Race and intelligence.* (Anthropological Studies, No. 8, American Anthropological Association). 41-57.
Glaser, R. (1979). Trends and research questions in psychological research on learning and schooling. *Educational Researcher* **8** (10): 6-13.
Goody, E. (1979). Towards a theory of questions. In E.N. Goody (ed.), *Questions and politeness: Strategies in social interaction.* Cambridge University Press.
Griffin, P., & Humphrey, F. (1978). Task and talk. In *The study of children's functional language and education in the early years.* Final report to the Carnegie Corporation of New York. Arlington. Va.: Center for Applied Languages.
Heath, S. (1978). *Teacher talk: Language in the classroom.* (Language in Education 9.) Arlington, Va.: Center for Applied Linguistics.
——. (1980). The functions and uses of literacy. *Journal of Communication* **30** (1): 123-33.

———. (1982). Questioning at home and at school: A comparative study. In G. Spindler (ed.), *Doing ethnography: Educational anthropology in action.* New York: Holt, Rinehart & Winston.

———. (forthcoming a). Protean shapes: Ever-shifting oral and literate traditions. To appear in D. Tannen (ed.), *Spoken and written language: Exploring orality and literacy.* Norwood, N.J.: Ablex.

———. (forthcoming b). *Ways with words: Ethnography of communication in communities and classrooms.*

Howard, R. (1974). A note on S/Z. In R. Barthes, *Introduction to S/Z.* Trans. Richard Miller. New York: Hill and Wang.

Hymes, D.H. (1973). On the origins and foundations of inequality among speakers. In E. Haugen & M. Bloomfield (eds.), *Language as a human problem.* New York: W.W. Norton & Co.

———. (1974). Models of the interaction of language and social life. In J.J. Gumperz & D. Hymes (eds.), *Directions in sociolinguistics,* New York: Holt, Rinehart & Winston.

Kagan, J., Sigel, I., & Moss, H. (1963). Psychological significance of styles of conceptualization. In J. Wright & J. Kagan (eds.), *Basic cognitive processes in children.* (Monographs of the society for research in child development.) **28** (2): 73-112.

Mehan, H. (1979). *Learning lessons.* Cambridge, Mass.: Harvard University Press.

Merritt, M. (1979). Service-like events during individual work time and their contribution to the nature of the rules for communication. NIE Report EP 78-0436.

Ninio, A., & Bruner, J. (1978). The achievement and antecedents of labelling. *Journal of Child Language* **5**: 1-15.

Payne, C., & Bennett, C. (1977). "Middle class aura" in public schools. *The Teacher Educator* **13** (1) 16-26.

Peters, A. (1977). Language learning strategies. *Language* **53**: 560-73.

Scollon, R., & Scollon, S. (1979). The literate two-year old: The fictionalization of self. *Working Papers in Sociolinguistics.* Austin, TX: Southwest Regional Laboratory.

Sinclair, J.M., & Coulthard, R.M. (1975). *Toward an analysis of discourse.* New York: Oxford University Press.

Sutton-Smith, B. (1981). *The folkstories of children.* Philadelphia: University of Pennsylvania Press.

Umiker-Sebeok, J.D. (1979). Preschool children's intraconversational narratives. *Journal of Child Language* **6** (1): 91-110.

Witkin, H., Faterson, F., Goodenough, R., & Birnbaum, J. (1966). Cognitive patterning in mildly retarded boys. *Child Development* **37** (2): 301-16.

4.3 Language-learner Language

S.P. CORDER

It is not so long ago that people ceased to think of dialect speakers as some sort of second-class citizens because the language they spoke was considered to be no more than a distorted, incorrect, or defective form of their mother tongue. It is only more recently that people have come to think of pidgins and creoles as languages in their own right and not some "inferior, haphazard, broken, bastardised version of older, longer-established languages," as Loreto Todd (1974) puts it. It is even more recently still that some people have been prepared to consider the ['inter-language'] of the second language learner as other than a defective, distorted, or incorrect form of the language they are learning. And yet to do so is now coming to be seen as a necessary preliminary step toward investigating objectively the whole phenomenon of second language learning and second language use. Only by treating language learners' language as a phenomenon to be studied in its own right can we hope to develop an understanding of the processes of second language acquisition, just as it is only by treating child language as a phenomenon to be studied in its own right that we can hope to understand something about the processes of first language acquisition and the use that infants make of language. [...]

It is now well established that mothers or other adults, when interacting with infants and young children acquiring their mother tongue, simplify their language in various ways which correspond to the age or linguistic development of the child (Snow and Ferguson, 1977). This simplification is not so much in terms of the range of structures employed but rather in terms of the range of speech functions and topics, the length of utterances, the tempo, pitch, and other prosodic features as well as the amount of partial or total repetition, rephrasing, and redundancy in their speech. This means that, in general, *mother talk* is an adaptation of the

---

Source: Corder, S.P. (1978) 'Language-learner language' in Richards J.C. (ed.), '*Understanding Second and Foreign Language Teaching*', Rowley (Mass.), Newbury House, pp. 71-92.

adult's normal language behavior which has the effect of facili-
tating the child's perceptual processes and interpretation of utterances. Mother talk is perceptually simpler and more explicitly
related to situational context.

When we turn to the way native speakers modify their speech
when interacting with second or 'interlanguage' speakers, we frequently find similar, though not quite identical, adaptations. There
is rarely any simplification of the structure employed. Normally the
utterances are fully grammatical, but the rhetoric is adapted to
assist the learner in processing the signal and the range of speech
functions is limited and closely related to context (Hatch, 1978). If
we observe a sensitive teacher interacting with his pupils or other
interlanguage speakers in authentic communicative activity we can
observe the same thing happening. The data available to the
learner can be, and normally are, controlled, but not in the way
specified in a linguistic syllabus. The data available to the language
learner we can refer to as *teacher talk*. [...]

COMMUNICATIVE STRATEGIES

If those who interact with interlanguage speakers adopt a strategy
of rhetorical simplification to maximize the probability of successful communication, what strategies does the learner adopt to
achieve the same end? Let us start by adopting the common
sensical assumption that in a free learning situation it is through
attempting to communicate that a learner acquires his grammar,
that necessity is the mother of invention in a very true sense. He
develops his interlanguage system in response to his experienced
communicative needs (Schumann, 1974). The logical implications
of this are twofold: if he experiences no needs he won't learn at all;
if he finds that he can manage with whatever knowledge he has, he
won't go on learning. His interlanguage grammar will *fossilize* at
the point in its development where his needs are satisfied. As
Valdman (1978) has pointed out, learning in a classroom situation
is the exact converse. There are fewer, if any, communicative
demands of an authentic sort on the learner in most classrooms; he
experiences no needs and, therefore, what we can regard as the
immediate motivations for interlanguage development do not exist
and have to be replaced artificially either by long-term motivations
or basically irrelevant incentives. At the present time we do not

know very much about the relationship between different kinds of communicative needs or types of discourse and the levels of complexity in the interlanguage grammar that are required to meet them. But that there is such a relationship is certain and is felt by anyone who cares to observe his own reactions when confronted by the need to engage in different types of discourse in his interlanguage.

The question is: what strategies do we employ when we find ourselves in such a situation? Again common sense supplies at least a framework for discussion. We can adopt the basically conservative risk-avoiding strategy of *message adjustment*, either refusing further interaction or trying to sidestep certain topics, saying less than we would wish to, or otherwise opting out in various degrees. Or we can adopt a risk-taking strategy, the risk being that we shall fail to some degree in achieving our communicative ends. Basically this strategy is aimed at increasing by one means or another our linguistic resources, either by skillful manipulation of what we already know: paraphrase, circumlocution or principled guessing, word-coinage, borrowing from whatever resources we have available, notably our mother tongue, but often from other languages we know, greater recourse to paralinguistic behavior (gesture, etc.), and only in extreme cases switching to another language or seeking our interlocutor's help by asking for a translation, or picking up clues from his language. These I shall call *resource-expansion* strategies.

The study of communicative strategies of learners was initiated by Varadi (1973), who was interested in explaining the origin of certain types of errors produced by interlanguage speakers. It is fairly clear that it is the risk-taking strategies which are most likely to result in unacceptable utterances. But this merely highlights the principle that it is by taking risks that we develop our interlanguage, that we learn. The pedagogical moral of this is obvious: the encouragement of the learner to take risks even at the expense of committing errors and, by implication, a willingness on the part of the teacher, beyond what is usually found in most classrooms, to accept error as a sign of a motivation for learning, or indeed a strategy of learning, and not something to be deprecated, let alone penalized. As Holley and King (1975) say:

A case can be made for permitting and even encouraging foreign language students to produce sentences that are ungrammatical in terms of full native competence. This would allow the learner to progress like a child by forming a series of increasingly complete hypotheses about the language.

One might note here that it is well established that the feedback the infant receives from his adult interlocutors is almost always related to the *content* of his utterances and not to their *form*, that is, their adequacy or otherwise as attempts at communication.

The theoretical interest, then, in studying the interlanguage speaker's communicative strategies lies in their relation to learning. I have already enunciated the principle that learning derives, in a free learning situation, from the attempt to communicate. How do these strategies lead to learning, that is, development of the interlanguage grammar? The risk-avoiding strategies (too often encouraged in the classroom because they do not produce errors), can scarcely lead to learning. If we are never prepared to operate beyond our self-assessed capacities then we never enlarge our knowledge. The risk-taking strategies, on the other hand, may all yield in principle, learning outcomes. If a guess is accepted by our interlocutor, then the form is incorporated into our repertoire as part of the target language. A translation or borrowing that succeeds is similarly incorporated. Those that fail provide information about the limits of the target language. Analogizing errors (overgeneralization of a learned rule) may be evidence of guessing which proved unsuccessful. But we learn something about the scope of a rule by doing such guessing. Principled guessing and hypothesis testing are one and the same thing.

There is one type of guessing strategy which is of particular theoretical interest: that of borrowing from the mother tongue. I have already noted that the utterances of language leaners may frequently show features which resemble those of the mother tongue. Where there is a similarity between the mother tongue and the target language in respect to these features they will, of course, pass unnoticed by the native speaker, since they do not produce errors and are communicatively successful. We are, therefore, in some difficulties in deciding on any particular occasion whether these features are the result is a restructuring process or the result of creative learning (Tarone, 1976). Where there is a difference, of course, the result is error. We cannot immediately distinguish those erroneous mother tongue features which are a result of restructuring from those which are borrowings resulting from a guessing strategy of communication, but which do not derive from (are not generated by) the current state of the speaker's interlanguage grammar. We must, therefore, make an important distinction between transfer features in utterances, which may be the result of either a restructuring process or a creative learning process, and borrowed features, which are the result of a communicative strategy. I have already pointed out that successful borrowing may lead to learning–incorporation into the learner's interlanguage system. In the end the only way we can distinguish between the two is the systematic nature of transfer features and the non-occurrence of borrowings.

The theoretical import of this distinction between transfer as a learning process (restructuring) and borrowing as a strategy of communication is that the mere presence of mother tongue-like features in learners' utterances does not logically entail (as is usually believed) that the learner's interlanguage must be following a restructuring principle. It is a matter of some interest to discover what principles the learner is following in his guessing and borrowing strategies. It has been suggested that we all have certain notions about the language-specific characteristics of our mother tongue (Kellerman, 1977) which inhibit our borrowing these features when attempting to communicate, because we believe it will be unsuccessful or lead to error. It has also been suggested that we all have notions about the degree of difference between other commonly studied languages in our culture and our own mother tongue — what we may call perceptions of language distance — and that these perceptions or beliefs may determine whether we adopt a basically restructuring or recreating strategy of learning. If we believe that another language is only distantly related structurally to our own (e.g., Chinese-English) we may opt for a recreative strategy, starting from scratch, on the grounds that the path to the target will be shorter, while if we believe that the target is closely related, (e.g., Danish-English) we may prefer a restructuring strategy as being more economical.

I have spoken about strategies that are available to learners both in order to learn — to develop their interlanguage — and in order to communicate, and how these may be related. What is implicit in what I have said is that these represent options, not, of course, normally conscious options, but a set of alternatives nonetheless. The moment we introduce the notion of alternatives we must necessarily abandon the idea that we are all programmed to learn in the same way, and it becomes relevant to enquire into the circumstances that incline us to adopt one or another strategy. In discussing, for example, the notion of language distance as a factor in causing learners to adopt one rather than another strategy of learning, we may ask where does the concept of language distance come from? Or, in the case of borrowing, where does the concept of language-specific or unique features come from? We can suppose that there are several possibilities — the learner's experience of learning the language, the stereotyped attitudes of the community, or the beliefs of his teachers. When it comes to selecting a risk-avoiding strategy of communication as against a risk-taking strategy, this may be determined by the nature of the interaction the speaker is engaged in — whether he is more concerned at the moment in maintaining contact with his interlocutor than with passing on some piece of information he has available, i.e., whether the *interpersonal* function of language prevails over the *ideational* function on a particular occasion (Halliday, 1973). It may also have to do with personality factors: is he a risk-taker or not? What seems certain is that we can discern in the speech of individuals distinct personal preferences for certain communicative strategies. We may also suppose that age, social background, linguistic sophistication, attitudes toward the culture related to the language, and so on may all play a part in determining the strategies of learning and communication adopted by interlanguage speakers. These affective and social factors which influence learning are poorly understood, but may all be expected to account for the variability we may find both in terms of sequence and speed of movement which overlays the basic pattern of interlanguage development which I referred to earlier (cf. Schumann, 1975).

VARIABILITY

I have drawn attention to the variability of interlanguage as one of the stumbling blocks in conceptualizing it as a language in the same way as we conceptualize pidgins, creoles, and child language as languages. I suggested that we could locate any individual or group of interlanguage speakers along some sort of continuum of approximation toward the target language. But there is another sort of variability which we must deal with, not just the variability found within interlanguage because of its dynamic nature, but variability found in the performance of any one particular inter-language speaker.

A distressing experience that most teachers suffer is to find that their pupils sometimes appear to go backwards and to forget what they have learned. At one moment they seem to have acquired some form and at the next to have lost it. They are apparently inconsistent in their behavior. How can it be that having achieved some piece of learning they can promptly forget it, reverting to earlier forms derived from a previous stage of their interlanguage grammar? Inconsistency is another name for variability. It was this inconsistency in learners' behavior which was used as the principal argument against the validity of the concept of interlanguage as a coherent and regular language system underlying learners' speech. These arguments, however, overlooked the well-established fact that we are all variable in our use of our mother tongue. This variability is not random, but patterned and related to the social context of speech activity. It is principled variation (cf. Labov. 1970). We range over some area of variation which we call a verbal repertoire. This variability has been shown to correlate with the amount of attention we are giving to how we are speaking in contrast to our attention to the content of our speech. Is there any reason, we may ask, why a learner should not attempt to exploit his admittedly more restricted repertoire for the same social ends? In fact, quite young children show variability in their speech in pre-cisely the same way as adults. Systematic variability in speech is learned early and is all-pervasive.

It is now clear that, at least at the phonological level, language learners also vary their speech in a similar way (Dickerson, 1975). They utilize the more advanced level of their interlanguage development in formal spoken and written communication and regress to earlier levels in their casual and informal spoken lan-guage. They vary their speech by moving up and down the continuum of their own development. This is one reason why, if we wish to obtain an adequate account of the current state of a learner's interlanguage, we must not confine ourselves to data elicited from one type of performance, e.g., tests and written exer-cises, but must sample his performance over a range of different types of discourse.

The difference between native speakers and learners is that native speakers have a far larger room for maneuver; they can vary their performance in at least two dimensions, i.e., across a *lectal* continuum of equal complexity, and by using certain *simplified registers* — baby talk, foreigner talk, headlines, telegraphese, etc. The interlanguage speaker has only one effective option: to move up and down the scale of complexity represented by his own interlanguage development. His informal style will be simpler, representing an earlier stage of his development, than his more formal spoken or written style. Variability of this sort is not a sign of forgetting or backsliding but is an exploitation of his restricted resources to convey social meanings, e.g., attitudes toward his interlocutor, and should thus be no cause of concern to the teacher.

SIMPLIFIED REGISTERS AND THE LEARNER'S STARTING POINT

I have just said that native speakers of a language can vary their performance by moving up and down a scale of complexity and mentioned what have been called simplified registers (Ferguson, 1971). It appears that all of us have available, for certain types of discourse, codes which are linguistically simpler than the fully complex code with which we operate most of the time. These simplified registers are stereotyped in language communities and can be plotted according to the degree of their structural complexity along a development-like continuum. Thus, the language of instructions, telegraphese, and headlinese show only a moderate degree of structural simplification, e.g., omission of articles and omission of the copula, while baby talk and foreigner talk show a much greater degree of simplification, e.g., omission of all morphological marking, fixed word order, reduced vocabulary, etc. There are probably many other intermediate stages of simplification between these two which regularly occur, but which have not become institutionalized and thus received recognition and a name. There is still a great field of research into the variability of performance which involves movement up and down a scale of complexity in native speaker's speech.

What is clear is that from a very early age all of us regularly exploit this range of variability. Jakobson (1968) reports on quite young children using baby talk to their younger brothers and sisters; children regularly use foreigner talk to represent or make fun of undifferentiated foreigners speaking their language, sometimes without ever having met a foreigner. All of us then have access to registers or codes which are linguistically extremely simple. When we come to analyze these codes linguistically we find that they have striking formal resemblances to pidgin languages and to the earliest stages in the interlanguage continuum and of child language acquisition. This can scarcely be accidental.

It is commonly assumed that we learn these simplified registers of our mother tongue by hearing them spoken around us, as we might pick up other dialect forms of our language in early youth. An alternative and equally if not more plausible hypothesis is that these registers are remembered stages in our own linguistic development to which we can revert or regress on socially approved occasions. In other words, we do not kick away the ladder of our own linguistic development, but keep it available for climbing up and down, all our lives.

As I have said, whether we learn these simplified registers or not, we do have available in our repertoire a range of linguistic systems of varying degrees of complexity and, furthermore, the further down the scale of simplicity we go the more similar these systems appear to be in different languages. It has been suggested that they may represent something we can call an approximation to some basic universal linguistic system or *natural semantax*. As Elizabeth Traugott (1973) speculates in relation to the development of pidgins:

Does it not involve the acquisition of lexical items so typical of adult innovation, combined with a return to earlier processes especially syntactic ones, that have in the speaker's native language been partially or wholly suppressed? This would make sense if we wish to relate pidgin simplification to the general ability we all have to simplify in various ways when talking to foreigners, babies — and, I may add, stupid people. Even small children seem to do this ... and do so largely by reverting to structures similar to their own earlier ones.

Ervin-Tripp (1974) has also observed that children acquiring a second language "regress to a processing strategy still available to them for use under certain conditions." The effect is that they regularly produce utterances which show no specific structural resemblance either to their mother tongue or the target language. [...]

We do not, in learning a second language perhaps start from scratch, but neither do we start from the fully complex code of our mother tongue. Our starting point may be some simple register of our mother tongue, some basic linguistic system, some natural semantactic system from which all language development starts, mother tongue, pidgin, creole, or interlanguage which, as Bickerton (1974) has suggested, may be innate, not in a Chomskyan sense of being language specific, but in the sense that it is the product of the innate cognitive and perceptual processes of the human mind. One could, however, add this qualification: just how far down the scale of simplification one moves before starting to build up again (recomplexify) will depend upon the relatedness of the mother tongue to the target language; this is our old friend, the notion of perceived language distance. In other words, economy of effort suggests that we do not necessarily always have to strip down to bare essentials, but only so far as to reach a point at which the two languages begin to diverge structurally. In the case of such closely related languages as Danish this may not be very far down, but in the case of Chinese and English it may involve a good deal of simplification. It is one of the strategies of learning to find out just how far down the scale it is going to be necessary to go before starting to build up again.

REFERENCES

Bailey, C.J.N. *Variation and Linguistic Theory*. Washington: Center for Applied Linguistics, 1973.

Bailey, N., S.D. Krashen, and C. Madden. "Is there a 'Natural Sequence' in Adult Second Language Learning?" *Language Learning 24*. 2, 1974, 235-243.

Bickerton, D. "Creolization, Linguistic Universals, Natural Semantax and the Brain," *Working Papers*, 6, No. 3, 1974, Dept. of Linguistics, University of Hawaii.

—— *Dynamics of a Creole System*. Cambridge: Cambridge University Press, 1975.

Brown, R. *A First Language*. London: Allen and Unwin, 1973.

Corder, S.P. "The Significance of Learners' Errors," *IRAL*, *5*.4. Reprinted in Richards, J.C., ed., *Error Analysis*, 1974.

Dickerson, L.J. "The Learner's Interlanguage as a System of Variable Rules," *TESOL Quarterly*, 9.4, 1975, 401-408.

Dulay, H., and M. Burt. "Errors and Strategies in Child Second Language Acquisition," *TESOL Quarterly*, 8.2, 1974, 129-136.

Ervin-Tripp, S. "Is Second Language Learning like the First?" *TESOL Quarterly*, 8.2, 1974, 111-128.

Ferguson, C.A. "Absence of the Copula and the Notion of Simplicity," in Hymes, D., Ed., *Pidginization and Creolization of Languages*, Cambridge: Cambridge University Press, 1971.

Hatch, E. "Discourse Analysis and Second Language Acquisition," in Hatch, E., ed., *Second Language Acquisition: A Book of Readings.* Rowley, Mass.: Newbury House, 1978.

Halliday, M.A.K. *Explorations in the Function of Language.* London: Edward Arnold, 1973.

Holley, F., and J.K. King. "Imitation and Correction in Foreign Language Learning," in Schumann, J.H., and N. Stenson, eds., *New Frontiers,* 1975.

Jakobson, R. *Child Language, Aphasia and Phonological Universals.* New York: Humanities Press, 1968.

Kellerman, E. "Towards a Characterization of the Strategy of Transfer in Second Language Learning," Utrecht: *Interlanguage Studies Bulletin, 2,* No. 1, 1977, 58-145.

Labov, W. "The Study of Language in its Social Context," *Studium Generale, 23.* Reprinted in Labov, *Sociolinguistic Patterns.* Philadelphia: Univ. of Pennsylvania Press, 1970.

Nemser, W. "Approximative Systems of Foreign Language Learners," *IRAL, 9.*2. Reprinted in Richards, J.C., *Error Analysis,* 1974.

Richards, J.C., ed. *Error Analysis; Perspectives on Second Language Acquisition.* London: Longman, 1974.

Sankoff, G., and S. Laberge. "On the Acquisition of Native Speakers by a Language," KIVUNG, 6.1, 1973.

Schumann, J.H. "Implications of Pidginization and Creolization in the Study of Adult Second Language," in Schumann and Stenson, eds., *New Frontiers,* 1974.

—— "Affective Factors and the Problem of Age in Second Language Acquisition," *Language Learning, 25.*2, 1975, 209-236.

—— and N. Stenson, eds. *New Frontiers in Second Language Learning.* Rowley, Mass.: Newbury House, 1974.

Selinker, L. "Interlanguage," *IRAL, 10.*3. Reprinted in Richards, J.C., *Error Analysis* 1974.

Snow, C., and C.A. Ferguson, eds. *Talking to Children.* Cambridge: Cambridge University Press, 1977.

Tarone, E. "Some Influences on Interlanguage Phonology," *Working Papers in Bilingualism,* No. 8, 1976, 87-111.

Todd, L. *Pidgins and Creoles.* London: Routledge & Kegan Paul, 1974.

Traugott, E. "Some Thoughts on Natural Syntactic Processes," in Bailey, C-J. and R.W. Shuy, eds., *New Ways of Analyzing Variation in English.* Washington: Georgetown University Press, 1973.

Valdman, A. "On the Relevance of Pidginization and Creolization Model for Second Language Learning," Proceedings of the 6th Neuchatel Colloquium, 1978.

Varadi, T. "Strategies of Target Language Learners' Communication: Message Adjustment," paper presented to the 6th Conference of the Romanian-English Linguistic Project, May 1973.

4.4 The Description of Bilingualism*

WILLIAM F. MACKEY

INTRODUCTION

Bilingualism is not a phenomenon of language; it is characteristic of its use. It is not a feature of the code but of the message. It does not belong to the domain of "langue" but of "parole".[1]

If language is the property of the group, bilingualism is the property of the individual. An individual's use of two languages supposes the existence of two different language communities; it does not suppose the existence of a bilingual community. The bilingual community can only be regarded as a dependent collection of individuals who have reasons for being bilingual. A self-sufficient bilingual community has no reason to remain bilingual, since a closed community in which everyone is fluent in two languages could get along just as well with one language. As long as there are different monolingual communities, however, there is likelihood of contact between them; this contact results in bilingualism.

The concept of bilingualism has become broader and broader since the beginning of the century. It was long regarded as the equal mastery of two languages; and this is the definition still found in certain glossaries of linguistics, e.g., "Qualité d'un sujet ou d'une population qui se sert couramment de deux langues, sans aptitude marquée pour l'une plutôt que pour l'autre".[2] Bloomfield

---

* This framework of description is based on the conclusions of my article on the definition of bilingualism in the *Journal of the Canadian Language Association* in 1956 (see note 6 below). During the 1960 International Seminar on Bilingualism in Education (held in Aberystwyth in August), I had an opportunity of discussing this with students of bilingualism in different parts of the world who encouraged me to elaborate this into a general framework for the description of bilingualism. I am grateful to the members of this seminar for their encouragement, criticism, and helpful suggestions. I also thank the Canadian National Commission for UNESCO for making it possible for me to attend this seminar.

Source: Mackey, W.F. (1970) 'The description of bilingualism' in Fishman, J. (ed.), *Readings in the Sociology of Language*, The Hague, Mouton, pp. 554-71

considered bilingualism as "the native-like control of two languages".[3] This was broadened by Haugen to the ability to produce "complete meaningful utterances in the other language".[4] And it has now been suggested that the concept be further extended to include simply "passive-knowledge" of the written language or any "contact with possible models in a second language and the ability to use these in the environment of the native language".[5] This broadening of the concept of bilingualism is due to realization that the point at which a speaker of a second language becomes bilingual is either arbitrary or impossible to determine. It seems obvious, therefore, that if we are to study the phenomenon of bilingualism we are forced to consider it as something entirely relative.[6] We must moreover include the use not only of two languages, but of any number of languages.[7] We shall therefore consider bilingualism as the alternative use of two or more languages by the same individual.

What does this involve? Since bilingualism is a relative concept, it involves the question of DEGREE. How well does the individual know the languages he uses? In other words, how bilingual is he? Second, it involves the question of FUNCTION. What does he use his languages for? What role have his languages played in his total pattern of behavior? Third, it includes the question of ALTERNATION. To what extent does he alternate between his languages? How does he change from one language to the other, and under what conditions? Fourth, it includes the question of INTERFERENCE. How well does the bilingual keep his languages apart? To what extent does he fuse them together? How does one of his languages influence his use of the other? Bilingualism is a behavioral pattern of mutually modifying linguistic practices varying in degree, function, alternation, and interference. It is in terms of these four inherent characteristics that bilingualism may be described.[8]

DEGREE

The first and most obvious thing to do in describing a person's bilingualism is to determine how bilingual he is. To find this out it is necessary to test his skill in the use of each of his languages, which we shall label A and B. This includes separate tests for comprehension and expression in both the oral and written forms of each language, for the bilingual may not have an equal mastery of all four basic skills in both languages. He may indeed be able to understand both languages equally well; but he may be unable to speak both of them with equal facility. Since the language skills of the bilingual may include differences in comprehension and expression in both the spoken and written forms, it is necessary to test each of these skills separately if we are to get a picture of the extent of his bilingualism. If, however, we are only interested in determining his bilingualism rather than in describing it, other forms of tests are possible: word-detection tests, word-association and picture vocabulary tests, for example, have been used for this purpose.[9]

The bilingual's mastery of a skill, however, may not be the same at all linguistic levels. He may have a vast vocabulary but a poor pronunciation, or a good pronunciation but imperfect grammar. In each skill, therefore, it is necessary to discover the bilingual's mastery of the phonology (or graphics), the grammar, the vocabulary, the semantics, and the stylistics of each language. What has to be described is proficiency in two sets of related variables, skills and levels.

It is easy to see how the relation between skills and levels may vary from bilingual to bilingual. At the phonological-graphic level, for example, we have the case of the Croatian who understands spoken Serbian but is unable to read the Cyrillic script in which it is written. At the grammatical level, it is common to find bilinguals whose skill in the use of the grammatical structures of both languages cannot match their knowledge of the vocabularies. At the lexical level it is not unusual to find bilinguals whose reading vocabulary in Language B is more extensive than it is in Language A, and far beyond their speaking vocabulary in either language. At the semantic level a bilingual may be able to express his meaning in some areas better in one language than he can in the other. A bilingual technician who normally speaks Language A at home and speaks Language B indifferently at work may nevertheless be able to convey his meaning much better in Language B whenever he is talking about his specialty. Finally, a bilingual's familiarity with the stylistic range of each language is very likely to vary with the subject of discourse.

To get an accurate description of the degree of bilingualism it is necessary to fill in the above framework with the results of tests. Types and models of language tests are now being developed.[10] On these models it is possible to design the necessary tests for each of the languages used by the bilingual in the dialects which he uses.

FUNCTION

The degree of proficiency in each language depends on its function, that is, on the uses to which the bilingual puts the language and the conditions under which he has used it. These may be external or internal.

External Functions

The external functions of bilingualism are determined by the number of areas of contact and by the variation of each in duration, frequency, and pressure. The areas of contact include all media through which the languages were acquired and used — the language-usage of the home, the community, the school, and the mass media of radio, television, and the printed word. The amount of influence of each of these on the language habits of the bilingual depends on the duration, frequency, and pressure of the contact. These may apply to two types of activity — either comprehension alone, or expression as well. [...]

Home Languages   The language or languages of the home may differ from all or any of the other areas of contact. Within the home the language of the family may differ from that of its domestics and tutors. Some families encourage bilingualism by engaging a domestic worker or governess who speaks another language to the children. Others send their children as domestic workers into foreign families for the purpose of enabling them to master the second language. This is a common practice in a number of bilingual countries. Another practice is the temporary exchange of children between families speaking different languages. There are even agencies for this purpose.[11] Some families who speak a language other than that of the community insist on keeping it as the language of the home.

Within the family itself the main language of one member may be different from that of the other members. This language may be used and understood by the other members; or it may simply be understood and never used, as is the practice of certain Canadian Indian families where the children address their parent in English and receive replies in the native Indian language of the parents.

In families where one of the parents knows a second language, this language may be used as one of two home languages. Studies of the effects of such a practice have been made by Ronjat,[12] Pavlovitch,[13] and Leopold[14] to test the theory that two languages can be acquired for the same effort as one. Each experiment used Grammont's formula "une personne: une langue",[15] whereby the same person always spoke the same language to the child, the mother limiting herself to one of the languages and the father to the other.

Community Languages   These include the languages spoken in the bilingual's neighbourhood, his ethnic group, his church group, his occupation group and his recreation group.

1. *Neighbourhood.* A child is surrounded by the language of the neighbourhood into which he is born, and this often takes the place of the home as the most important influence on his speech. A corrective to this has been the periods of foreign residence which bilinguals have long found necessary in order to maintain one of their languages.

2. *Ethnic group.* The extent to which the bilingual is active in the social life of his ethnic group is a measure of the possibility of maintaining his other language. This may be the most important factor in a community with no other possible contact with the language.

3. *Church group.* Although church groups are often connected with ethnic groups, it is possible for the bilingual to associate with one and ignore the other. Although he may attend none of the activities of his ethnic group, he may yet bring his children to the foreign church or Sunday school, where sermons and instructions are given in a language which is not that of the community.

4. *Occupation group.* The bilingual's occupation may oblige him to work with a group using a language different from that which he uses at home. Or, if he lives in a bilingual city like Montreal, the language of his place of work may be different from that of the neighbourhood in which he lives. Or, if he is engaged in one of the service occupations, he may have to use both his languages when serving the public.

5. *Recreation group.* A bilingual may use one of his languages with a group of people with whom he takes part in sports, in music,

or in other pastimes. Or he may attend a club in which the language spoken is not that of his home or his neighbourhood. Or the foreign children in a unilingual school may be in the habit of playing together, thus maintaining the use of their native language.

School Languages   A person's language contact in school may be with a language taught as a subject or with a language used as a medium of instruction. Both may be found in three instructional media: single, dual, and private.

1. *Single medium.* Some parents will go to a lot of trouble and expense to send their children to a school in which the instruction is given in another language — schools in foreign countries, foreign ethnic communities, or bilingual areas.[16]

In bilingual areas, the language of single medium schools must be determined by the application of some sort of language policy. This may be based on one of the four following principles: nationality, territoriality, religious affiliation, ethnic origin.

According to the principle of nationality, a child must always take his schooling in the language of the country, regardless of his ethnic origin, religious affiliation, or of the language which he speaks at home. This is the policy of most of the public school systems in the United States.

According to the principle of territoriality, the child gets his schooling in the language of the community in which he happens to be living. This is the practice in Switzerland, for example.

The principle of religious affiliation may be applied in countries where linguistic divisions coincide to a great extent with religious ones. A sectarian school system may take these language divisions into account. In Quebec, for example, there are French Catholic schools, English Protestant schools, and English Catholic schools. The French Protestants in some areas may not be numerous enough to warrant a separate school system, in which case a French Protestant family might send their children to an English Protestant school rather than to a French Catholic one.

The principle of ethnic origin takes into account the home language of the child. In countries where bilingual communities are closely intermingled the policy may be to have the child do his schooling in the language which he normally speaks at home. This is the policy, for example, in many parts of South Africa.

2. *Dual media.* The bilingual may have attended schools in

which two languages were used as media of instruction. Dual media schools may be of different types. In their use of two languages they may adopt a policy of parallelism or one of divergence.

Parallel media schools are based on the policy that both languages be put on an equal footing and used for the same purposes and under the same circumstances. The parallelism may be built into the syllabus or into the time-table. If it is part of the syllabus, the same course, lesson, or teaching point will be given in both languages. This has been the practice in certain parts of Belgium. If the parallelism is built into the time-table, the school makes exclusive use of one of the languages during a certain unit of time — day, week, or month — at the end of which it switches to the other language for an equal period, so that there is a continual alternation from one language to the other. This is the practice of certain military and technical schools in Canada.

Another type of dual media school is governed by a policy of divergence, the use of the two languages for different purposes. Some subjects may be taught in one language, and some in the other. This is the practice in certain parts of Wales. In describing the influences of such practices on a person's bilingualism it is important to determine which subjects are taught in which language. If one of the languages is used for religion, history, and literature, the influence is likely to be different than it would if this language were used to teach arithmetic, geography, and biology instead.[17]

3. *Private tuition.* Schooling may be a matter of private instruction, individually or in small groups. This may be in a language other than that of the community. The second language may be used as a medium of instruction or simply taught as a subject.

Some people may prefer to perfect their knowledge of the second language by engaging a private tutor in the belief that they thus have a longer period of direct contact with the language than they would otherwise have.

Finally, there is the bilingual who tries to improve his knowledge of the second language through self-instruction. This may involve the use of books and sound recordings (see below).

Mass Media   Radio, television, the cinema, recordings, newspapers, books, and magazines are powerful media in the maintenance of bilingualism. Access to these media may be the main factor in maintaining one of the languages of a bilingual, especially if his other language is the only one spoken in the area. Regular attendance at foreign film programmes and the daily reading of foreign books and magazines may be the only factors in maintaining a person's comprehension of a foreign language which he once knew. Reading is often the only contact that a person may have with his second language. It is also the most available.

Correspondence   Regular correspondence is another way by which the bilingual may maintain his skill in the use of another language. He may, for business reasons, have to correspond regularly in a language other than the one he uses at home or at work. Or it may be family reasons that give him an occasion to write or read letters in one of his languages. The fact that immigrants to the New World have been able to correspond regularly with friends and relatives in Europe is not to be neglected as a factor in the maintenance of their native languages.

Variables
Contacts with each of the above areas may vary in duration, frequency, and pressure. They may also vary in the use of each language for comprehension only, or for both comprehension and expression.

Duration   The amount of influence of any area of contact on the bilingualism of the individual depends on the duration of the contact. A 40-year-old bilingual who has spent all his life in a foreign neighbourhood is likely to know the language better than one who has been there for only a few years. A language taught as a school subject is likely to give fewer contact hours than is one which is used as a medium of instruction.

Frequency   The duration of contact is not significant, however, unless we know its frequency. A person who has spoken to his parents in a different language for the past twenty years may have seen them on an average of only a few hours a month, or he may have spoken with them on an average of a few hours a day. Frequency for the spoken language may be measured in average contact-hours per week or month; for the written language it may be measured in average number of words.

Pressure   In each of the areas of contact, there may be a number of pressures which influence the bilingual in the use of one language rather than the other. These may be economic, administrative, cultural, political, military, historical, religious, or demographic.

1. *Economic.* For speakers of a minority language in an ethnic community, the knowledge of the majority language may be an economic necessity. Foreign parents may even insist on making the majority language that of the home, in an effort to prevent their children from becoming economically underprivileged. Contrariwise, economic pressure may favour the home language, especially if the mastery of it has become associated with some ultimate monetary advantage.

2. *Administrative.* Administrative workers in some areas are required to master a second language. A bilingual country may require that its civil servants be fluent in the official languages of the country. Some countries may require that foreign service personnel be capable of using the language of the country in which they serve. A few governments have been in the practice of granting an annual bonus to the civil servant for each foreign language he succeeds in mastering or maintaining; this is the case in some branches of the German Civil Service.

3. *Cultural.* In some countries, it may be essential, for cultural reasons, for any educated person to be fluent in one or more foreign languages. Greek and Latin were long the cultural languages of the educated European. Today it is more likely to be French, English, or German. The quantity and quality of printed matter available in these languages constitute a cultural force which an educated person cannot afford to ignore.

4. *Political.* The use of certain languages may be maintained by the pressure of political circumstances. This may be due to the geographical contiguity of two countries or to the fact that they are on especially friendly terms. Or the pressure may be due to the influence of the political prestige of a great world power. Political dominance may result in the imposition of foreign languages, as is the case for certain colonial languages. After many years of such dominance the foreign colonial language may become the dominant one, develop a regional standard, and be used as the official language of the country.

5. *Military.* A bilingual who enters the armed forces of his

country may be placed in situations which require him to hear or speak his second language more often than he otherwise would. People serving in a foreign army must learn something of the language which the army uses. The fact that two countries make a military treaty may result in large-scale language learning such as that witnessed in Allied countries during the Second World War. Military occupation has also resulted in second language learning, either by the populace, by the military, or by both.

6. *Historical.* Which languages the bilingual learns and the extent to which he must learn them may have been determined by past historical events. If the language of a minority has been protected by treaty, it may mean that the minority can require its children to be educated in their own language. The exact position of the languages may be determined by the past relations between two countries. The important position of English in India is attributable to the historical role of Great Britain in that country.

7. *Religious.* A bilingual may become fluent in a language for purely religious reasons. A person entering a religious order may have to learn Latin, Greek, Coptic, Sanskrit, Arabic, or Old Church Slavonic, depending on the religion, rite, or sect of the particular order into which he enters. Some languages, also for religious reasons, may be required in the schools which the bilingual may have attended; Latin and Hebrew are examples of such languages.

8. *Demographic.* The number of persons with whom the bilingual has the likelihood of coming into contact is a factor in the maintenance of his languages. A language spoken by some five hundred million people will exert a greater pressure than one used by only a few thousand. But number is not the only fact; distribution may be equally important. Chinese, for example, may have a greater number of native speakers than does English; but the latter has a greater distribution, used, as it is, as an official and administrative language in all quarters of the globe.

Internal Functions

Bilingualism is not only related to external factors; it is also connected with internal ones. These include non-communicative uses, like internal speech, and the expression of intrinsic aptitudes, which influence the bilingual's ability to resist or profit by the situations with which he comes in contact.

Uses   A person's bilingualism is reflected in the internal uses of each of his languages, such as counting, reckoning, praying, cursing, dreaming, diary writing and note taking. Some bilinguals may use one and the same language for all sorts of inner expression. This language has often been identified as the dominant language of the bilingual. But such is by no means always the case. Other bilinguals use different languages for different sorts of internal expression. Some count in one language and pray in another; others have been known to count in two languages but to be able to reckon only in one. It would be possible to determine these through a well-designed questionnaire.

Aptitude   In describing bilingualism it is important to determine all those factors which are likely to influence the bilingual's aptitude in the use of his languages or which in turn may be influenced by it. These may be listed as follows: sex; age; intelligence; memory; language attitude; motivation.

1. *Sex.* If sex is a factor in language development, as past research into the problem seems to indicate, it is also a factor in bilingualism (see note 9).

2. *Age.* Persons who become bilingual in childhood may have characteristics of proficiency and usage different from those who become bilingual as adults. Studies of cases where two languages were learned simultaneously in childhood have given us some indication of the process (see notes 12, 13, 14). Although Leopold's study reveals an effort on the part of the child to weld two phoneme systems into one, it does not indicate any lasting effect on either language (see note 14). But it does show a great deal of forgetting on the part of the child. Indeed, the child's reputed ability to remember is matched by his ability to forget. For him, bilingualism may simply mean a transition period from one native language to another. Children can transfer from one mother-tongue to another in a matter of months. This has been demonstrated by Tits in his experiment with a six-year-old Spanish girl who was suddenly placed in a completely French environment and, after only 93 days, seems to have lost her Spanish completely; in less than a year, she had a knowledge of French equal to that of the neighbourhood children.[18]

The child's adaptability has been related to the physiology of the human brain. Penfield and other neurologists have put forth theories to explain the child's linguistic flexibility.[19] Before the age of nine, the child's brain seems particularly well suited to language learning, but after this age the speech areas become "progressively stiff" and the capacity to learn languages begins to decrease. Some experienced teachers and psychologists, however, have claimed that there is no decline in language-learning capacity up to the age of twenty-one.[20]

3. *Intelligence.* We are here concerned more with the relation of intelligence to bilingualism than with the influence of bilingualism on intelligence.[21] A number of testable mental traits such as figure-grouping ability, number, space and pattern perception, and others have already been tested on groups of bilinguals (see note 9).

Although it seems safe to include intelligence as a factor in bilingualism, we have as yet been unable to discover its relative importance. Experimental research into the problem has mostly been limited to selected samples of persons of the same intellectual level and has often been based on the assumption that the ability to speak is simply a motor-skill which can be measured by tests of imitation and reading aloud. One would expect intelligence to play some sort of role, nevertheless, in such a skill as comprehension, where a bilingual's reasoning ability and general knowledge should help him guess meanings from context.

4. *Memory.* If memory is a factor in imitation, it is also a factor in bilingualism; for the auditory memory span for sounds immediately after hearing them is related to the ability to learn languages. An analogy may be taken from the learning of sound-codes like those used in telegraphy. It has been demonstrated that the span of auditory comprehension is the main difference between the beginner in telegraphy and the expert; whereas the beginner can handle only one word at a time, the expert can deal with ten, keeping them all in his memory before interpreting them.[22] As his degree of proficiency increases, the bilingual keeps more and more words in his memory before deciding on the meaning of an utterance. There is conflicting evidence, however, on the exact role of rote memory in language learning.

5. *Attitude.* The attitude of a bilingual towards his languages and towards the people who speak them will influence his behaviour within the different areas of contact in which each language is used. It may in turn be influenced by his hearer's attitude towards him as a foreign speaker. In certain situations he may avoid using one of his languages because he is ashamed of his

accent. In other situations he may prefer to use his second language because his first language may be that of an unpopular country or community. It has been said that some speakers of minority languages even harbour an attitude of disrespect toward their first language and an admiration for their second.

Because of such influences as these, the attitude of the speaker may be regarded as an important factor in the description of his bilingualism. The attitudes of bilinguals towards their languages have been tested directly by questionnaire and indirectly by having the bilinguals list traits of speakers whose recorded accent reveals their ethnic origin.[23]

6. *Motivation.* It seems obvious that the motivation for acquiring the first language is more compelling than the motivation for learning a second. For once the vital purposes of communication have been achieved, the reasons for repeating the effort in another language are less urgent. In the case of simultaneous childhood bilingualism, however, the need for learning both languages may be made equally compelling. Not so for the person who becomes bilingual as an adult. Yet a need or desire of the adult to master a second language may be strong enough to enable him to devote the necessary time and energy to the process of becoming bilingual.

ALTERNATION

The function of each language in total behaviour and the degree to which the bilingual and his hearers have mastered both languages determine the amount of alternation which takes place from one language to the other.

The readiness with which a bilingual changes from one language to the other depends on his fluency in each language and on its external and internal functions. There seems to be a difference in alternation, for example, between bilinguals brought up on Grammont's "une personne: une langue" formula and bilinguals conditioned at an early age to speak two different languages to the same person.[24]

Under what conditions does alternation from one language to another take place? What are the factors involved? The three main factors seem to be topic, person, and tension. Each of these may vary both the rate of alternation and the proportion of each language used in a given situation — oral or written. [...] If we examine the alternation in the speech or writings of bilinguals we notice that it may vary in both rate and proportion. The switch may occur only once, or it may take place every few sentences, within sentences, or within clauses. The rate may be measured by establishing a ratio between the number of units in the stretch of text examined and the number of switches which take place.

Alternation in the speech or writings of a bilingual will also vary in proportion. For example, a French-English bilingual when speaking English may, in a given situation, switch from time to time to French. But the amount of French used may be less than 5 per cent of the entire text. On the other hand, his interlocutor, who switches less often, but for longer stretches, may use as much as 50 per cent French in his replies.

Rate and proportion of alternation may vary greatly in the same individual according to the topic about which he is speaking, the person he is speaking to, and the tension of the situation in which he speaks. A German-English bilingual speaking in English to a close friend who he knows understands German may permit himself to lapse into German from time to time in order to be able to express himself with greater ease. On the other hand, when speaking to a person with whom he is less well acquainted he may avoid the use of German switches except when forced to speak about topics which his English does not adequately cover. Or his control of English may break down and he may switch frequently to German only when speaking in a state of tension due to excitement, anger, or fatigue.

INTERFERENCE

The foregoing charcteristics of degree, function, and alternation determine the interference of one language with another in the speech of bilinguals. Interference is the use of features belonging to one language while speaking or writing another.

The description of interference must be distinguished from the analysis of language borrowing. The former is a feature of "parole"; the latter of "langue". The one is individual and contingent; the other is collective and systematic. In language borrowing we have to do with integration;[25] features of one language are used as if they were part of the other. These foreign features are used by monolingual speakers who may know nothing of the language from which such features originated. The loans, however, may be integrated into only one of the dialects of the language and not the others. If loan-words are integrated into the French of Switzerland, for example, they do not necessarily become part of the French of Belgium. And the loan-words of Belgium are not necessarily those of Canada; and in Canada, the loans current in Acadian are not necessarily those of the French of Quebec. Indeed, the integration of borrowed features may be limited to the language of a village community. A good example, of this may be found by studying the varieties of German spoken in the multi-lingual Banat, where German ethnic groups are scattered among non-German language groups speaking Hungarian, Serbian, and Rumanian. If we look at the use of the article among the Banat Germans we find that it may vary from village to village. One German village may use *die Butter*, while another village may use *der Butter*; one village may use *das Auto*, while another may use *der Auto*. In some cases, the borrowed feature may be integrated into the language of a section of a village. No matter how small the area concerned, a borrowed feature may be distinguished by its integration into the speech of the community.

In contradistinction to the consistency in use of borrowed features in the speech of the community is the vacillation in the use of foreign features by its bilingual individuals. In the speech of bilinguals the pattern and amount of interference is not the same at all times and under all circumstances. The interference may vary with the medium, the style, the register, and the context which the bilingual happens to be using.

The medium used may be spoken or written. Bilinguals seem to resist interference when writing to a friend more than they do when speaking to him.

Interference also varies with the style of discourse used — descriptive, narrative, conversational, etc. The type and amount of interference noted in the recounting of an anecdote may differ considerably from that noted in the give-and-take of everyday conversation.

Interference may also vary according to the social role of the speaker in any given case. This is what the Edinburgh School has called REGISTER.[26] A bilingual may make sure that all his words are French if he is broadcasting a French speech over the radio; but at the same time he may be quite unconscious of many cases of syntactic interference which have crept into his speech. If, however, he is telling the contents of the speech to his drinking partner, he may be far less particular about interlarding his account with non-French words; yet the proportion of syntactic interference may be considerably less.

Within each register, there are a number of possible contexts, each of which may affect the type and amount of interference. The bilingual may be speaking to the above drinking partner in the presence of his superiors or in the company of his colleagues.

In each of these contexts the interference may vary from situation to situation. A French-Canadian business man just back from a sales conference in Atlantic City will tell his friends about it with more English interference immediately upon his return than will be noticed when he recounts the same events three months later.

In the last analysis, interference varies from text to text. It is the text, therefore, within a context of situation used at a specific register in a certain style and medium of a given dialect, that is the appropriate sample for the description of interference. [...]

CONCLUSION

Bilingualism cannot be described within the science of linguistics; we must go beyond. Linguistics has been interested in bilingualism only in so far as it could be used as an explanation for changes in a language, since language, not the individual, is the proper concern of this science. Psychology has regarded bilingualism as an influence on mental processes. Sociology has treated bilingualism as an element in culture conflict. Pedagogy has been concerned with bilingualism in connection with school organization and media of instruction. For each of these disciplines bilingualism is incidental; it is treated as a special case or as an exception to the norm. Each discipline, pursuing its own particular interests in its own special way, will add from time to time to the growing literature on bilingualism. But it seems to add little to our understanding of bilingualism as such, with its complex psychological, linguistic, and social interrelationships.

What is needed, to begin with, is a perspective in which these interrelationships may be considered. What I have attempted in this study is to give an idea of the sort of perspective that is needed. In order to imagine it, it was necessary to consider bilingualism as an individual rather than a group phenomenon. This made possible a better and more detailed analysis of all that it entails; and the object of our analysis appeared as a complex of interrelated characteristics varying in degree, function, alternation, and interference. By providing a framework of analysis for each of these, we hope to have contributed to a more accurate description.

NOTES

1. It is important not to confuse bilingualism — the use of two or more languages by the individual — with the more general concept of language contact, which deals with the direct or indirect influence of one language on another resulting in changes in "langue" which become the permanent property of monolinguals and enter into the historical development of the language. Such foreign influences may indeed be due to past periods of mass bilingualism, as in the case of the Scandinavian element in English. But bilingualism is not the only cause of foreign influence; the presence of words like *coffee* and *sugar* in English does not argue a period of English-Arabic bilingualism. Language contact includes the study of linguistic borrowing.

2. J. Marouzeau, *Lexique de la terminologie linguistique* (Paris, Geuthner, 1951).

3. L. Bloomfield, *Language* (New York, Holt, 1933), p. 56.

4. E. Haugen, *The Norwegian Language in America: a study in bilingual behaviour*, 2 vols. (Philadelphia, University of Pennsylvania Press, 1953). Vol. 1 (The Bilingual Community), p. 7.

5. A.R. Diebold, Jr., "Incipient Bilingualism", *Lang.*, 37 (1961), p. 111.

6. W.F. Mackey, "Toward a Redefinition of Bilingualism", *Journal of the Canadian Language Association* 2 (1956), p. 8.

7. W.F. Mackey, "Bilingualism", *Encyclopaedia Britannica* (1959 ed.).

8. We must not confuse "bilingual description" with the "description of bilingualism". "Bilingual description" is a term which has been used to denote the contrastive analysis of two languages for the purpose of discovering the differences between them. This is also known as "differential description". Differential description is a prerequisite to the analysis of one of the most important characteristics of bilingualism — interference.

9. E. Peal and W.E. Lambert, "The Relation of Bilingualism to Intelligence", *Psychological Monographs*, 1962, 76.

10. For a study of test making, see R. Lado, *Language Testing* (London, Longmans, 1961).

11. Examples of this are the Canadian "visites interprovinciales", a description of which may be found in "French or English — with Pleasure!" in *Citizen* 7.5 (1961), pp. 1-7.

12. J. Ronjat, *Le développement du langage observé chez un enfant bilingue* (Paris, Champion, 1913).

13. M. Pavlovitch, *Le langage enfantin: l'acquisition du serbe et du français par un enfant serbe* (Paris, 1920).

14. W.F. Leopold, *Speech Development of a Bilingual Child.* 4 vols. (Chicago and Evanston, Northwestern University Press, 1939-1949).

15. M. Grammont, "Observation sur le langage des enfants", *Mélanges Meillet* (Paris, 1902).

16. W.F. Mackey, "Bilingualism and Education", *Pédagogie-Orientation*, 6 (1952), pp. 135-147.

17. W.F. Mackey and J.A. Noonan, "An Experiment in Bilingual Education", *English Language Teaching*, 6 (1952), pp. 125-132.

18. D. Tits, *Le mécanisme de l'acquisition d'une langue se substituant à la langue maternelle chez une enfant espagnole âgée de six ans* (Bruxelles, Veldeman, 1948), p. 36.

19. W. Penfield and L. Roberts, *Speech and Brain-Mechanisms* (Princeton, Princeton University Press, 1959).

20. M. West, "Bilingualism", *English Language Teaching*, 12 (1958), pp. 94-97.

21. N.T. Darcy, "A Review of the Literature on the Effects of Bilingualism upon the Measurement of Intelligence", *Journal of Genetic Psychology*, 82 (1953), pp. 21-57.

22. D.W. Taylor, "Learning Telegraphic Code", *Psychological Bulletin*, 40 (1943), pp. 461-487.

23. W.E. Lambert et al., "Evaluation Reactions to Spoken Language", *Journal of Abnormal and Social Psychology*, 60 (1958), pp. 44-51.

24. M.E. Smith, "A Study of the Speech of Eight Bilingual Children of the Same Family", *Child Development*, 6 (1935), pp. 19-25.

25. E. Haugen, *Bilingualism in the Americas: a bibliography and research guide* (University of Alabama, American Dialect Society 1956), p. 40. (See review by W.F. Mackey in *JCLA* 4, pp. 94-99)

26. I wish to thank M.A.K. Halliday and J.C. Catford for introducing me to this term and to the important variable it represents in language description.

4.5 Some New Developments in Social Skills Training*

MICHAEL ARGYLE

Social skills training (SST) has become very widely used (*a*) in clinical settings, (*b*) in many areas of occupational training — for teachers, doctors and others, including training to work in other cultures, and (*c*) for the general public, e.g. training in assertiveness and dating skills (Argyle, 1981*a*, *b*). And every kind of psychologist is administering it — occupational, clinical, educational, prison, and social. While this is generating jobs it is also starting to meet an immense human need.

THE NEED FOR SST — THE EXTENT OF SOCIAL INADEQUACY

Clinical Settings

From 25 to 30 per cent of neurotic out-patients have serious social inadequacy; many studies have documented the social failings of different kinds of patients and offenders. What do they do wrong? They often have inadequate non-verbal communication, are poor conversationalists, are cold, unrewarding, unassertive, can't see another's point of view, find many situations difficult, can't make friends or maintain relationships (Bryant *et al.*, 1976; Trower *et al.*, 1978).

People at Work

Studies of supervisors have found a ratio of 5:1 or more in the absenteeism, labour turnover and frequency of complaints among their subordinates (Fleishman & Harris, 1962). Our studies of

---

* The Myers lecture, given at the Annual Conference of the British Psychological Society, University of Warwick, 1984.

Source: Argyle, M. (1984) 'Some new developments in social skills training', *Bulletin of The British Psychological Society* 37, 405-410. © 1984 The British Psychological Society.

sales staff have found ratios of 5:1 in amounts sold by different people at the same counter. Those who go to work abroad as salesmen, or for organizations like the Peace Corps, have a failure rate of 60 per cent or more in some parts of the Far East and Middle East, i.e. they come home before their one- or two-year term is completed (Argyle, 1982).

Everyday Life

About 40 per cent of students say that they are 'shy' (Zimbardo, 1977); 55 per cent are often lonely (Brennan, 1982); in the adult population of this country 24 per cent sometimes feel lonely, 4 per cent feel lonely every day (MORI, 1984). We found that 9 per cent of Oxford students could not cope with common situations like going to parties or going out with the opposite sex (Bryant & Trower, 1974).

THE ASSESSMENT AND ENHANCEMENT OF SOCIAL COMPETENCE

By social competence is meant the ability to meet professional goals, e.g. in teaching, selling or interviewing, or the ability to meet personal goals, e.g. making friends and influencing people. The best way of assessing it is in terms of results — amount sold, patients cured, productivity of group, popularity. However, those being compared may be in somewhat different situations, e.g. selling different goods. Role-played tests have been found to be of rather poor validity, though it is important to see the client in action. Use is now being made of reactions to videotaped vignettes, for police (Bull & Horncastle, 1983). Self-ratings are useful, and we have used lists of situations which trainees rate for degree of difficulty or discomfort. These methods can be followed by interviews to find out more about the nature of the inadequacy. In SST in clinical settings it is usual to agree targets for training, e.g. stop quarrelling, make a friend (Spence & Shepherd, 1983).

In order to carry out SST it is necessary to know what skills to teach. The traditional logic has been to compare groups of effective and ineffective performers, discover how their social behaviour differs, and teach the good skills to others. However, as we shall see, the differences may be quite subtle; and there may be reverse causation. It is necessary to survey where the main problems lie; a current example is the development of training for the police to deal with ethnic minority groups, where the difficulties wait to be listed.

There have been many follow-up studies of SST of all kinds. Shepherd (1983) recently reviewed 52 such studies. It was concluded that SST was better than no treatment, that it was most successful if the full package was included (see below), but that it was not much better than desensitization, though it was better for the socially inadequate. Many kinds of SST in occupational settings and for adults have been found to be quite successful.

However, these studies were all of fairly traditional forms of SST. In this article I want to show how SST can be extended on the basis of recent findings in social psychology.

TRADITIONAL METHODS OF SST

The most widely practised method at present is an elaborated version of role playing. There are three or four phases:

1. Explanation and modelling, live or from video.
2. Role playing with other trainees or stooges, for 7-15 minutes.
3. Comments from trainer and playback of videotape.
(4. Repeat performance.)

This is typically carried out in groups of six, for one to one-and-a-half hours, once or twice a week. The full package includes all the above features, and the groups may be supplemented by individual sessions.

A serious problem is how to achieve generalization to real-life situations. For those not inside institutions 'homework' is often used: trainees are asked to repeat the exercises (e.g. to make someone else talk more, or less) between sessions in real-life settings and to report back. For those in hospital or prison, other staff can continue the training between the formal sessions. And there can be 'training for generalization', e.g. teaching general principles and overlearning (Goldstein, 1979).

However, for some professional skills, like those of managers and police, role-played sessions are too far removed from reality, so there has been a growth of on-the-job training. Managers are sometimes trained for leadership with group tasks like building towers of bricks, but I feel that this is absurdly distant from the real thing.

Clinical SST has to some extent been absorbed into behaviour modification, with reinforcement schedules for smiling, asking questions, etc. I believe that, while this is a good start, there is a great deal more to social competence.

DEVELOPMENTS IN SOCIAL PSCYHOLOGY WHICH HAVE IMPLICATIONS FOR SST

Non-verbal Communication (NVC)

This is incorporated in some kinds of SST, but there have been important new developments. It is found that patients with social difficulties smile, look and gesture less than others (Trower, 1980). In order to make friends it is necessary to send positive non-verbal signals. The face and the voice are the most important channels for signalling emotions and attitudes to others (Argyle, 1975). In distressed marriages husband-to-wife NVC is ineffective, since the husbands are bad at sending positive signals via tone of voice (Noller, 1984). Training for intercultural communication needs to take account of the different gestures, distances, etc., in other cultures. American police are now trained to stand further away when stopping blacks on the street (Garratt *et al.*, 1981). Training to send facial expression can be done by modelling photographs, and by using mirrors or video. Tones of voice can be trained by means of an audiotape recorder, counting 1-5 in different emotions, and copying model performances. On the other hand effective social skill does not always consist of communicating one's true feelings.

Perception of NVC

In order to respond effectively to others it is necessary to perceive them correctly, including their emotions and attitudes. More socially skilled individuals are more accurate decoders (Rosenthal, 1979), while anxious persons overestimate signs of rejection. Sensitivity can be measured by tests in which photographs, films or audiotapes are presented. It is now realized that these should be of spontaneous, not posed expressions, which are different (Buck, in press). There are problems over detecting deception on the part of others; the face is particularly well controlled and can be misleading. While women are somewhat more accurate decoders than men, they also attend more to faces and perceive what others intend them to, while men attend to the 'leakier' channels of voice and body (Hall, 1978). Training can be given in decoding by studying photographs (e.g. Ekman & Friesen, 1975) and tapes.

In addition there can be training in metaperception or meta-cognition, i.e. judging the thoughts or emotions of others. The socially unskilled are often very bad at this. Training can consist of role-reversal exercises, or in simple interviewing, to discover another's ideas and point of view. James Gray at Oxford is using role-reversal to help disruptive school children to appreciate the teacher's view of the classroom situation.

Rewardingness

Being rewarding to others is one of the main ways of influencing them during social interaction, perhaps via operant verbal conditioning, and is also one of the main sources of popularity. Many clinical patients are extremely unrewarding. This can be increased by regular methods of SST — modelling, coaching and the rest.

Rewardingness is very important for friendship. The rewards which are needed include showing affection (which involves appropriate NVC), being helpful, sympathetic, interested, cheerful, and fun to be with. One of the main problems in disturbed marriages is the lack of rewards, and the high level of negative messages, such as criticism, which tend to be reciprocated (Gottman, 1979). 'Behavioral marital therapy' is based on increasing the level of rewards, for example by finding what rewards the other most, by weekly 'love days', and the use of 'contingency contracting' — for example one partner agrees to take the other dancing once a week if the other agrees to go to football matches.

Self-presentation and Self-disclosure

The sending of information about the self is done mainly by clothes, hair, accent, etc., and is an important part of social behaviour. It can go wrong in various ways, especially by projecting an image which is just inappropriate. The training is simple, and may consist of advice on clothes, or voice training. Self-disclosure is normally gradual and reciprocated; the most common failure is not disclosing enough. One application is to loneliness: recent research has found that some lonely people spend as much time with friends as non-lonely people do; the difference is in their lower level of self-disclosure (Williams & Solano, 1983). They also lack other social skills, e.g. are less rewarding (Jones *et al.*, 1982). Loneliness is reduced much more by contact with women than with men — because women are disclosed to more and disclose more themselves (Wheeler *et al.*, 1983).

Conversational Skills

Some socially unskilled people cannot sustain a conversation at all. Some have special ways of killing conversation, for example giving a short answer to a polite question, and not reciprocating or leading the conversation forward. One approach to these skills is by formulating maxims. Grice (1975) suggested maxims such as 'Be relevant to what has been said before', 'be responsive to previous speaker', 'make your contribution no less and no more informative than is required'. Other maxims which can be suggested are 'Hand over the conversation', 'be polite', and 'be friendly'.

Some progress has been made with the development of 'behavior grammars' which specify the correct (i.e. acceptable) ordering of utterances within conversations. The social skill model suggests a basic four-stage sequence, including corrective action following feedback. For example: question — inadequate answer — modified question — useful answer. Elaboration of this model includes cases where both parties are taking corrective action simultaneously in order to attain their goals (Clarke & Argyle, 1982).

Specialized conversation sequences occur, and need to be learnt, for example for teaching, sales, and management–union negotiation (Argyle *et al.*, 1981). Conversations can be regarded as competitive games, in which each person makes tactical moves which are responsive to what has gone before, and which could lead to a possible successful outcome for the actor (Clarke, 1983). Politeness is also important — to avoid damaging others' self-esteem or constraining their autonomy (Brown & Levinson, 1978). Women have been found to be more polite, and powerful people less so (Baxter, unpub.). Humour is another conversational skill — it can avert conflict, soften criticism, by discharging tension and redefining the situation as less serious or threatening.

Handling Difficult Social Situations

Some situations are commonly found difficult, such as making complaints, dealing with conflict, difficult superiors or public performances. Situations can be looked at on the analogy of games. In order to cope with them effectively the necessary goals, rules and other properties must be understood, and special skills learnt.

The *rules* are behaviours which it is widely agreed should or should not be performed. They are functional in relation to situational goals, as in the case of the rule of the road. We have found rules, some of which are fairly general, e.g. 'should be friendly', others which are specific to particular kinds of situation, e.g. 'should keep to cheerful topics of conversation' (Argyle *et al.*, 1979). The *goals* are central to situations, as are the relations between them — how far they interfere with or help one another. Clients for SST sometimes do not understand what the goals of situations are (Graham *et al.*, 1980). The *physical environment* is the aspect of situations which can be changed most easily. The governor of a prison stopped the inmates from fighting by finding the situations in which the fighting occurred — they were at the corners of corridors and he changed them — by rounding off the brickwork to avert collisions. A number of forms of crime can be prevented by environmental modification, including shoplifting, vandalism and car theft (Clarke & Mayhew, 1980).

SST can be situationally focused, if a group of clients find the same situations difficult. The method is to work through the key features of a situation, and then to learn the special skills. This is done in inter-cultural learning: the Culture Assimilator is based on the main situations in the other culture which cause problems, e.g. shopping, dealing with women (Fielder *et al.*, 1971). Situational methods are used in psychiatry, for example for obesity and alcoholism, by finding the situations in which overeating occurs, and finding ways of coping with them. Special skills may also be needed, e.g. of refusing drinks.

Long-term Relationships

Most social behaviour takes place with friends, kin, workmates, etc., and many difficulties arise in connection with these relationships. They are important since happiness, health, mental health and even length of life are greatly improved by strong supportive relationships. Relationships either buffer the effects of stress or have direct positive effects (Argyle & Henderson, 1984*a*).

We have already seen that husbands in unhappy marriages are poor senders of NVC, that the level of rewardingness is low in failing friendships and marriages, and that there are certain unfavourable sequences of interaction, such as negative reciprocity.

Recent research has found that there are certain *activities* which are characteristic of each relationship. In marriage these include: being in bed together, watching TV, doing domestic jobs together, informal meals, intimate conversation, and having arguments (Argyle & Furnham, 1982). There are also characteristic sources of satisfaction and conflict for each kind of relationship. Both are very high for marriage, and the balance of rewards over costs is greater in voluntary relationships like friendship and marriage than in less voluntary ones like work relationships (Argyle & Furnham, 1983). Generally accepted *informal rules* develop for each relationship to contain the main conflicts. So for neighbours these are about noise, fences and pets, while for marriage there are rules about faithfulness, creating a harmonious home atmosphere, engaging in sexual activity and being tolerant of the other's friends (Argyle, Henderson & Furnham, 1985). Collapse of friendship is attributed to the breaking of friendship rules, particularly those about rewardingness, and 'third-party' rules like keeping confidences, standing up for the other in their absence, and not being jealous (Argyle & Henderson, 1984*b*).

It is necessary to have a correct *understanding* of the basic properties of relationships. For example a high level of conflict is normal in marriage, and is perfectly compatible with a high level of satisfaction, as we have seen. Friendship is not just about receiving rewards from others — as children, and disturbed adolescents without friends think (La Gaipa & Wood, 1981). Friendship involves loyalty, commitment and concern for the other. Parent–child relations may go through a bad spell when the children are adolescents, who may rebel and run away from home. When this is over, however, the parent–child bond usually persists undiminished until the death of the parents. The basis of bonding varies between relationships. For close kin there appears to be a permanent relationship, probably established in the young family. For other relationships joint activities, instrumental to rewards, are important, as in male friendship, while talk and the sharing of cognitive worlds are more important for female friendships (Argyle & Henderson, 1984*a*).

Men and women typically have different needs for SST. We have seen a number of areas in which women are usually more socially competent than men — they are better at sending and receiving NVC and are more rewarding and polite, they disclose more and form closer friendships, are better at reducing the loneliness of others. However, it is mostly women who seek assertiveness training, and their problems are more general than this. Many studies have shown how women like to form close friendships with equals but are less able or willing to cope with hierarchical, structured groups engaged in joint tasks, and rarely emerge as the leaders of such groups (Shaver & Buhrmeister, 1983).

IMPLICATIONS FOR TRAINING METHODS

The research developments just described have clear implications for the practice of SST.

The Use of Role Playing and Modelling

This basic method is very valuable. However it is necessary to discover first where the social behaviour problems lie. It is also necessary to find out the most effective skills for handling them; these may not be at all obvious, as in the case of loneliness. And detailed analysis may be needed of the social performance of trainees to find out precisely what they are doing wrong.

The Use of On-the-job Training

Homework is very successful for many skills; the main problem is persuading people to do it. However, for police, managers, and some other professions it is not possible to simulate the problems at all realistically in the laboratory. Trainers such as 'tutor constables', who can provide 'street supervision' are needed.

Special Training Methods

Some of the research described has led to suggestions for specific forms of training, apart from role playing. Examples are (a) NVC training, using mirrors and audio- and video-recorders to train face and voice; (b) role-reversal, to improve ability to see others' point of view; (c) situational analysis, for dealing with the specific situations which were found difficult; (d) self-presentation — helping to change appearance, accent, etc.; (e) conversational analysis — to correct errors by detailed analysis of conversational style.

The Use of Educational Methods

Lecture and discussion methods were abandoned long ago as methods of SST when they were found to be ineffective, and because it is obvious that motor skills can't be learnt in this way. However some recent research should make us think again. The Culture Assimilator, a kind of tutor text, is quite successful, perhaps because there is a lot of new information to learn. Our research on rules suggests another area where straightforward instruction is indicated. Much trouble with relationships arises because of misunderstanding the nature of friendship, marriage, etc. Conversational skills involve some understanding of the principles of conversational structure. In all these cases direct teaching may be the best method.

CONCLUSIONS

I do not want to claim too much for SST, though it is clearly one way of tackling a very wide range of individual and social problems. It is of limited value for one major social problem — conflict between social groups. Even here it can make some contribution, since the skills of the 'mediating person' who is acceptable to both sides can be very important here (Bochner, 1982), and intergroup conflict is partly due to failures of communication.

However, perhaps 10 per cent of the world's population have quite serious difficulty with common social situations or relationships. This could be entirely avoided or removed if appropriate SST was available. The problem of who is going to do all this I leave to another occasion.

I apologize for the omission of many figures and tables. Most of them can be found in Argyle (1983) and Argyle & Henderson (1984a).

REFERENCES

Argyle, M. (1975). *Bodily Communication.* London: Methuen.
Argyle, M. (ed.) (1981a). *Social Skills and Health.* London: Methuen.
Argyle, M. (ed.) (1981b). *Social Skills and Work:* London: Methuen.
Argyle, M. (1982). Inter-cultural communication. In S. Bochner (ed.), *Cultures in Contact.* Oxford: Pergamon.
Argyle, M. (1983). *The Psychology of Interpersonal Behaviour,* 4th ed. London: Penguin.
Argyle, M. & Furnham, A. (1982). The ecology of relationships: Choice of situation as a function of relationship. *British Journal of Social Psychology,* **21**, 259-262.

Argyle, M. & Furnham, A. (1983). Sources of satisfaction and conflict in long-term relationships. *Journal of Marriage and the Family*, **45**, 481-493.

Argyle, M., Furnham, A. & Graham, J.A. (1981). *Social Situations*. Cambridge: Cambridge University Press.

Argyle, M., Graham, J.A., Campbell, A. & White, P. (1979). The rules of different situations. *New Zealand Psychologist*, **8**, 13-22.

Argyle, M. & Henderson, M. (1984*a*). *The Anatomy of Relationships*. London: Heinemann.

Argyle, M. & Henderson, M. (1984*b*). The rules of friendship. *Journal of Personal and Social Relationships*, **1**, 211-237.

Argyle, M., Henderson, M. & Furnham, A. (1985). The rules of social relationships. *British Journal of Social Psychology* (in press).

Baxter, L. (unpub.) An investigation of compliance-gaining as politeness. Lewis and Clark College, Portland.

Bochner, S. (ed.) (1982). *Cultures in Contact.* Oxford: Pergamon.

Brennan, T. (1982). Loneliness at adolescence. In L.A. Peplau & D. Perlman (eds), *Loneliness*. New York: Wiley.

Brown, P. & Levinson, S. (1978). Universals in language: Politeness phenomena. In E.N. Goody (ed.), *Questions and Politeness: Strategies in Social Interaction* (Cambridge Papers in Anthropology, 8). Cambridge: Cambridge University Press.

Bryant, B. & Trower, P. (1974). Social difficulty in a student population. *British Journal of Educational Psychology*, **44**, 13-24.

Bryant, B., Trower, P., Yardley, K., Urbieta, H. & Letemendia, F. (1976). A survey of social inadequacy among psychiatric outpatients. *Psychological Medicine*, **6**, 101-112.

Buck, R. (in press). *The Communication of Emotion.* New York: Guilford.

Bull, R. & Horncastle, P. (1983). *An Evaluaton of the Metropolitan Police Recruit Training Programme.* London: The Police Foundation.

Clarke, D.D. (1983). *Language and Action: A Generative Account of Interaction Sequences.* Oxford: Pergamon.

Clarke, D. & Argyle, M. (1982). Conversation sequences. In C. Fraser & K. Scherer (eds), *Advances in the Social Psychology of Language.* Cambridge: Cambridge University Press.

Clarke, R.V.G. & Mayhew, P. (eds) (1980). *Designing Out Crime.* London: HMSO.

Ekman, P. & Friesen, W.V. (1975). *Unmasking the Face.* Englewood Cliffs, NJ: Prentice-Hall.

Feilder, F.E. Mitchell, R. & Triandis, H.C. (1971). The cultural assimilator: An approach to cross-cultural training. *Journal of Applied Psychology*, **55**, 95-102.

Fleishman, E.A. & Harris, E.F. (1962). Patterns of leadership behavior related to employee grievances and turnover. *Journal of Occupational Psychology*, **53**, 65-72.

Garratt, G.A., Baxter, J.C. & Rozelle, R.M. (1981). Training university police in Black-American non-verbal behaviors: An application to police–community relations. *Journal of Social Psychology*, **113**, 217-229.

Goldstein, A. (1979). Social skills training. In A. Goldstein *et al.* (eds), *In Response to Aggression.* New York: Pergamon.

Gottman, J.M. (1979). *Marital Interaction.* New York: Academic Press.

Graham, J.A., Argyle, M. & Furnham, A. (1980). The goals and goal structure of social situations. *European Journal of Social Psychology*, **10**, 345-366.

Grice, H.P. (1975). Logic and conversation. In P. Cole & J. Morgan (eds), *Syntax and Semiotics*, vol. 3: *Speech Acts.* New York and London: Academic Press.

Hall, J.A. (1978). Gender effects in decoding nonverbal cues. *Psychological Bulletin*, **85**, 845-857.

Jones, W.H., Hobbs, S.A. & Hockenbury, D. (1982). Loneliness and social skill deficits. *Journal of Personality and Social Psychology*, **42**, 682-689.

La Gaipa, J.J. & Wood, H.D. (1981). Friendship in disturbed adolescents. In S. Duck & R. Gilmour (eds), *Personal Relationships*, vol 3: *Personal Relationships in Disorder*. London: Academic Press.

MORI (1984). *Neighbours and Loneliness*. London: Market Opinion and Research International.

Noller, P. (1984). *Nonverbal Communication and Marital Interaction*. Oxford: Pergamon.

Rosenthal, R. (ed.) (1979). *Skill in Nonverbal Communication: Individual Differences*. Cambridge, MA: Oelgeschlager, Gunn & Hain.

Shaver, P. & Buhrmeister, D. (1983). Loneliness, sex-role orientation and group life: A social needs perspective. In P.B. Paulus (ed.), *Basic Group Processes*. New York: Springer-Verlag.

Shepherd, G. (1983). Social skills training with adults. In S. Spence & G. Shepherd, *Developments in Social Skills Training*. London: Academic Press.

Spence, S. & Shepherd, G. (1983). *Developments in Social Skills Training*. London: Academic Press.

Trower, P. (1980). Situational analysis of the components and processes of socially skilled and unskilled patients. *Journal of Consulting and Clinical Psychology*, **48**, 327-339.

Trower, P., Bryant, B. & Argyle, M. (1978). *Social Skills and Mental Health*, London: Methuen.

Wheeler, L. Reis, A. & Nezlek, J. (1983). Loneliness, social interaction, and social roles. *Journal of Personality and Social Psychology*, **45**, 943-953.

Williams, J.G. & Solano, C.H. (1983). The social reality of feeling lonely. *Personality and Social Behavior Bulletin*, **9**, 237-242.

Zimbardo, P. (1977). *Shyness*. New York: Addison-Wesley.

4.6 A Case Study of a T-group

DOROTHY STOCK WHITAKER

The T-group in question consisted of five men and four women, ranging in age from the late twenties to about sixty, and representing a variety of occupations — business managers, teachers, a social worker, a youth worker and a personnel officer. All were participating in a general Human Relations Laboratory (Seminar); all had come because they hoped to gain a further knowledge of groups and of their own behaviour in groups which might prove helpful to them in their work.

The first several sessions of the group took on their special flavour from the participation of two of the business managers. The trainer opened the session by saying that the T-group was an opportunity for the members to learn more about groups and their own functioning in groups by constituting a group themselves and observing their own interaction and development. After a brief silence, James, an older business man, began to describe the situation in his factory. The session focused on his affairs, with the others asking questions about the details of his business. While James dominated this discussion, Alex's behaviour was also quite conspicuous. He interjected brief comments and questions in an aggressive, insistent and sometimes rude way. The others were polite and matter-of-fact in their reactions to Alex, showing no sign that his behaviour might be annoying. Such a beginning is not unusual in a T-group. Although the trainer has suggested that a profitable form of discussion will be to examine what goes on among the members in the immediate 'here and now' situation, the members adopt the more familiar pattern of talking shop about one person's back-home problems.

James appeared eager to hold the floor and be the centre of attention; the others seemed no less eager to encourage him to do so. About midway through this session the trainer asked the group

Source: Whitaker, D.S. (1965) 'Case study of a T-group' in Whitaker, G. (ed.), *T-group Training in Group Dynamics in Management Education*, ATM Occasional Papers 2, Oxford, Basil Blackwell, pp. 14-22.

how it was that everyone seemed willing to allow James to dominate the situation. This comment was an attempt to focus the group's attention on the events of the immediate situation, but no one responded. One way to look at this is to assume that if the members did adhere to the trainer's implicit instruction to examine the events of the immediate interactive situation, then individuals would have to express feelings, allow their behaviour to be discussed by others and perhaps expose themselves to embarrassment or criticism. In a new group, in which the members do not yet know one another and have had no opportunity to establish mutual trust, it is not surprising that the members would avoid such a potentially uncomfortable situation and resort instead to the more familiar and 'safer' focusing on an outside problem.

During the second session the character of the group changed a little. While James seemed just as willing as before to go on talking about his problems at the factory, the others were less encouraging. James subsided somewhat and the group discussion became more general, focusing in a rather intellectual way on the issue of leadership and influence. It seemed as if the members were beginning, in an indirect and still safe and impersonal way, to discuss the issue which had been the main feature of their own interaction up to this point, namely the domination of the group by one member.

During this discussion Alex was aggressive and rude at first, but later seemed to shift his behaviour, becoming more subdued and courteous. One might consider that initially he felt sufficiently uncomfortable in this new situation that he had to fight against it and against the people in the group. As the group's discussion proceeded and nothing disturbing occurred, perhaps Alex was able to relax his vigilant 'I'll fight you before you fight me' attitude. The group seemed less tense as Alex's behaviour shifted.

After discussing the problem of dominance, influence and leadership in a general way for some time, the group began to speculate as to whether James had been the leader in their own group and from whence he had derived his influence. James joined in by telling the others what he felt his own motivation to have been. There was some recognition that if James had dominated the group, this had occurred at least in part because the others had allowed and even encouraged him to do so. Some of the members seemed intrigued by the recognition that if a dominant member exists in a group, this problem does not lie only within the

dominant member, but it is a problem in interpersonal management for the group as a whole. This episode marked the first time
that the members had been ready to look at their own interaction.
One can hypothesize that because no unfavourable consequences
occurred — no one felt excessively uncomfortable and no one
behaved hurtfully towards the person (James) who was the centre
of attention — this episode contributed to the members' later
readiness to discuss their own feelings about the events in the
group. During this session some of the members appeared to learn
something new about the commonly experienced problem of the
dominant member in a group. Presumably their learning had more
impact and was more meaningful because it occurred as a
reflected-upon experience, rather than, for example, something
that was told to them in a lecture.

As the early sessions went on, various members of the group
again returned to back-home problems, but now in a different way.
Rather than describe the details of the way in which a factory or a
social work agency was organized, the members began to reflect on
what seemed to them their own typical behaviour with the people
they interacted with on their jobs. For example, Carl said he felt
unable to influence the people he worked with in the way that he
would like. Marie said that she was habitually so reluctant to give
orders to others that she would often rather do the work herself.
Not only did she find herself overworked, but became resentful
towards her subordinates, who might not even know that she had
work for them to do. As the group felt more and more free to
share these feelings and problems with one another, they also
began, intermittently, to focus on events within the group.

One of the first such episodes involved looking retrospectively
at the behaviour which Alex and James had displayed earlier. They
compared Alex's current courteous and co-operative behaviour
with his aggressive, rude behaviour at the beginning and for the
first time revealed that they had been annoyed with him. Several
said that Alex's earlier behaviour had made them dislike him.
There was some discussion as to whether this behaviour was characteristic of Alex when he entered new situations. In talking about
James, some had seen James' references to his back-home situation as boasting (since he had emphasized his accomplishments in
building up his business). One person suggested that James might
be so concerned about potential lack of acceptance from others
that he had to describe at length his accomplishments in his job.

The two men reacted quite differently to what the others said about them. Alex accepted the possibility that what he regarded as determined, but not aggressive or rude behaviour, should have been seen as rudeness by others. James, on the other hand, could not accept the view that his behaviour was boastful, or even that he could have been seen by others as boasting. He insisted that he had only been trying to help the group and that the others were simply wrong.

One of the features of a T-group is the opportunity to share information about the impact of various members' behaviour. Some persons seem ready to accept such information and to gain some new understanding of their impact on others; this was true of Alex. Others, such as James, are not prepared to make use of this new information and see it as irrelevant, or simply wrong.

During this period another member of the group, Gladys, had slowly been emerging as a problem person. Gladys talked a great deal, often in a way which seemed to the others irrelevant or hard-to-follow. She did not respond to polite hints to let others have their say and when asked to clarify her meaning, became nervous and even harder to understand. On one occasion she missed a T-group session, after having become upset earlier in the day during another Lab activity. The other members were worried about her and were relieved after she returned to the group.

At about the eighth session, the group was confronted with a special problem. A new participant had arrived at the Seminar, nearly a week late, and this group was asked to consider accepting him as a new member. It was understood that the decision was up to the group. Nearly half the group felt very strongly that this person should not be admitted because he would set the group back, interfere with their free discussion, etc. The others had no special objection to allowing him into the group. As far as numbers were concerned, the group was split down the middle. However, in terms of intensity, feelings were far stronger on the negative side. The discussion lasted for nearly an hour. Finally, those who had been ready to admit the new person seemed to recognize and respect the intensity of the negative feelings of a few persons. Without changing their own opinion, they began to feel that such strong feelings should carry weight. A consensus developed that the new person should not join, but be placed in a different T-group. In reflecting on their decision, the members recognized that numbers had not been important, for if a majority vote had been accepted as grounds for making the decision, the outcome would have been different. Instead there was some recognition of how a decision by consensus may occur in a group; of the appropriateness of taking into account the intensity of the feelings on the two sides of a question; and of assessing the consequences of a decision in level of discomfort for specific members. This was an example of the members' learning something about group functioning by experiencing it themselves and then reflecting upon their experience.

For the rest of this session the group fell into a prolonged period of flight. That is, there were long periods of silence, no topic or issue could be sustained and there was a sense that only trivial matters were brought up. The group was immobilized and the feeling was one of gross tension and frustration. After the session ended, three members of the group asked to discuss something with the trainer. About twenty minutes were spent in discussing the issue which proved to have been interfering with the group's progress.

They said that Gladys was a tremendous problem to the group. They felt that she was interfering with the progress of the group with her prolonged and difficult-to-understand contributions. At the same time they felt that any efforts on their part to change this would be shattering to Gladys. They appealed to the trainer to deal with this problem. It developed that they had accumulated so much anger towards this member that they were afraid that if they told her how they felt, they would come out with their anger in some destructive way. When they mentioned various ideas they had had for 'helping' Gladys by providing feedback, it became clear that these were indeed potentially hurtful and were motivated much more by revenge than by any desire to help. After some discussion of their feelings and of the probable consequences of the actions about which they had been speculating, there was a spontaneous recognition of the revengeful character of their feelings. It was left that while the trainer could not solve this problem for them, she could offer support in helping to explore the problem in the group. The trainer told these three members that a specific plan need not be made, but that she was confident that the group could find some way to deal appropriately with the problem.

During the next session the group did indeed deal effectively and appropriately with their problem member. It was, in fact, a good example of the sensitivity and skill a group can display in dealing with a difficult situation or a person who might easily be hurt, provided that covert needs to behave destructively — in this case revengefully — are recognized so that they can be dealt with. The approach which the group adopted — without prior plan — was to tell Gladys that they were having trouble understanding her communications and were distressed by this because they were convinced that she had important and valuable things to say. They said they felt deprived and wondered what they could do to help matters. In the discussion which followed, Gladys expressed some of her own feelings. She said that she herself recognized her difficulties in communicating with others and tried frantically to correct for it. The more she tried to correct, the more confusing she felt her comments became. She was able to explain this in very clear, direct terms to the group. They pointed out to her that she had been very clear in *this* communication and were able to show her how pleased they were. Gladys talked about how this problem showed up in her job and other areas of her life and appealed to the others for help. In her behaviour at this time and also later in the group, she showed that she was able to succeed in her efforts to communicate more clearly, and she was not again a problem for the group. Although her comments were still occasionally hard to follow, both she and the group found ways to prevent such occasions from intensifying into a difficult situation for all concerned.

This is an example of a personal change of considerable importance to the person involved. The question arises as to whether it was likely to persist, or whether it could be maintained only within the T-group. While no information is available, one might suppose that Gladys experienced diminished anxiety in the supportive atmosphere of the group, and thus was able to communicate more clearly. There was no evidence that a fundamental change occurred in her which would make it possible for her to change her behaviour in less supportive situations.

After the group's feelings about Gladys were dealt with the group turned its attention to their feelings about the trainer. They discussed their reactions to having a woman trainer and agreed that most of them had initially felt rather cheated. Feelings about professional women were expressed, which proved to be especially important to Marian. The discussion, rather intellectual in character and centring about Marian and her feelings about her professional job, concentrated on such matters as whether it was possible to be competent though female, aggressive though female, competent without being aggressive, and so forth. The discussion was carried primarily by Marian and Clarice.

At another point during this period of the group, there was some focusing of attention on Robert. He said that he felt that he was not able to get close to people and not ever able to yield to impulsivity. At first the group did not take seriously what Robert said, since he had been seen up to then as a constructive member of the group, without problems. Robert pointed out that this was exactly his problem — he typically was efficient and constructive, but quite bland and because he was so careful in his relationships with others, they never knew how he really felt and he never felt close to them. The others could offer him little help except to suggest that the group might be a place for him to 'practise' expressing himself more freely. Robert himself suggested that his cautiousness and apparent need to protect himself might be related to expectations that he would be rejected by others. At this point, all Robert's comments about himself were controlled and deliberative and intellectual in character — in other words, expressed in the same style which he complained of as being typical of himself.

Nevertheless the fact that he had been able to share these feelings with the group suggested that at least in this setting his expectations of rejection were not so strong as usual. In subsequent sessions, Robert did express himself more freely, even going so far as to interrupt others a few times. At the close of the sessions he said he felt that he would be able to behave a little differently with his work colleagues, and perhaps even with his family.

This appeared to be an example of a personal change which occurred on two levels; his behaviour shifted towards being more freely expressive and his underlying fear that he would be rejected if he revealed himself diminished. Here, too, the question arises as to whether Robert might be able to maintain this change in other situations. He felt that he could, but this of course is no guarantee. Again, information is lacking, but it seems reasonable to suppose that the change might persist if Robert experienced in the T-group enough 'disconfirmation' of his fears to enable him to test out the consequences in other situations as well, and if he continued to have the positive experience that more frankness on his part did not lead others to reject him. If this happened — and this would depend not only on Robert, but on his back-home interpersonal environment — then one might see a permanent personal change gradually become established. Such a change could rightfully be regarded as therapeutic in character. It is important to realize, however, that consolidated therapeutic change cannot occur *in* a T-group since the group does not go on long enough to permit the occurrence of the many and varied experiences which constitute the 'working-through' process. Sometimes though, as in the case of Robert, critical experiences occur which might later lead to therapeutic change, if the back-home conditions support the necessary working-through experiences.

Soon after this, some discussion was devoted to James, who had been so important during the early phases of this group. James' continuing introduction of anecdotes about his factory presented a problem to the group, for by now most of the members valued concentration on interpersonal feelings. During one session the members made a concerted effort to talk to James about how they felt about his behaviour and to get him to talk about himself and his job in personal rather than technical terms.

These efforts failed, since James showed by his behaviour that he was really unable to talk about himself or his work situation in any other way. The situation was complicated by the fact that James provided the group with rather mixed signals. On the one hand he indicated that he wanted the group to continue listening to his accounts of events which concerned him, but on the other hand he also indicated that he wanted the group to maintain a 'hands off' policy by not explicitly discussing his feelings about these events. This created confusion and ambivalence in the others, particularly on the part of Marian, who seemed quite unable to stop her efforts, yet at the same time recognized James' underlying unwillingness to proceed. After some time a general awareness grew that the members were indeed receiving a double message from James, and there was an implicit agreement to stop trying to change him and to accept him as he wished to be accepted. This episode was useful to some of the members in the group, who saw the importance of listening to what is being communicated in behaviour as well as what is communicated in words. For some, the idea that two contradictory messages could be communicated by the same person at the same time was a new one; their ability to listen and to be sensitive to the behaviour of others increased.

Towards the end of this same session Clarice said that she would like to have some of the group's time in order to discuss some problems which were important to her. The group agreed that the next session, which was to be that evening, would be devoted to Clarice. At the beginning of the session that evening, Marian and Alex appeared only long enough to say that they had decided not to attend the session. After they left, a number of the members expressed strong feelings of anger and disappointment at this breach of an implicit group standard. Someone noticed that Clarice, who ought to feel most offended, was in fact the most tolerant and forebearing. This led Clarice to reflect that she never felt anger, and did not in fact experience it now towards Marian and Alex. She said that she felt hurt, but not angry. She seemed to recognize for the first time that this might not be appropriate, and to wonder what happened to her angry feelings, which she now recognized must be present at some level. Someone suggested that Clarice might find it easier to blame herself than to blame others. This seemed right to Clarice, and she subsided into a thoughtful silence. (Later, outside the group, Clarice told the trainer that this episode had led her to think about herself in a new way and especially to realize that she made a martyr of herself in her job. She said that previously she felt too old to change, but now somehow felt more hopeful.) After much discussion of their feelings towards Alex and Marian, the members agreed that they could not deal with this issue further until the next session, when Alex and Marian would be present.

The next session, which was also the final session, saw the group confronted with two difficult problems; one was that of healing the breach which had occurred as a result of the absence of two members; the other was that of closing the whole rather intensive and eventful shared experience of the T-group. They began by asking Alex and Marian how they felt about having been absent. Alex was rather contrite, but Marian was defiant, saying she felt she had done nothing wrong, was not sorry, and would do it again. The members who had been present the previous evening described their reactions of resentment and hurt. Marian continued to say that she did not regard their feelings as important and some members expressed a feeling of despair at not being able to deal with the situation more adequately. They found they could accept Alex, but that they still felt resentful towards Marian. During the ensuing discussion, Marian shifted her position dramatically. She said she had come to the meeting determined not to be touched by anyone or anything, but now she found herself responding in spite of herself and recognized that she did indeed have feelings about her behaviour and about the group's reaction to her. She went on to discuss her feeling that women who become 'emotional', sacrifice competence and rationality. Others told her that she appeared far more competent to them when she was honestly revealing feelings than when she had been trying to conceal them. This seemed to strike Marian as something new and important; one can be strong through recognizing and expressing emotionality rather than through suppressing it. Though this same issue had been discussed earlier in the group, in the context of the professional woman, with Marian as the central figure, the first discussion had been sterile and intellectual, while the second was an affect-infused experience.

At this point, the group felt able to accept Marian again, as well as Alex, and in the remaining time turned their attention to the fact that the group was soon to close. Various members shared their feelings about what had happened in the group, what they felt to have gained and the difference they thought it might make when they returned to their jobs and to their usual lives. Most felt that the experience had been worth while, but most agreed that it would be hard to communicate exactly what it had been like to others and it might be some time before they understood exactly what gains they had derived.

From the trainer's point of view, this group had been unique, as are all groups, but at the same time not atypical of T-groups in general. The interaction among the members had generated experiences which, when examined, could provide them with the opportunity for new learnings about the manner in which groups operate. In this case, these included dealing with a dominant and troublesome member, understanding the meaning of decision-making by consensus, appreciating the need to 'listen' to an individual's behaviour as well as to his words, understanding the importance of implicit standards in a group and the consequences of breaching such standards, and getting a feeling for how far an individual can and cannot be pushed to conform to a group standard. One could not say that everyone learned these things, but only that the opportunity to learn such things was present and that some people indicated afterwards that they were looking at group events and the behaviour of others in a somewhat different and fuller way than previously.

As for individual change: some individuals showed no evidence of change — in some cases this may have been because they were already functioning quite well and in other cases because they feared and resisted change. A few persons seemed to enter the group at a particularly crucial point in their lives, when they were experiencing some dissatisfaction or conflict about their characteristic behaviour. These persons seemed able to make use of the experiences which came their way in the group to test out new ways of behaving and especially to test the consequences of changing their behaviour. Depending upon further experiences which could only occur subsequently to the closing of the T-group, some of these changes might be reinforced and become established aspects of the individual's life style. The group as a whole also developed; in what started as a group of strangers, appropriately cautious about revealing personal information or feelings, a prevailing feeling of trust and mutual confidence came to prevail. Troublesome and delicate situations were dealt with appropriately and the group learned when to probe and when to desist from probing. It was under these group conditions that each individual made the group experience into something which was appropriate for him at that time.

SECTION 5

LANGUAGE IN CLASSROOM LEARNING

INTRODUCTION

A good deal of the research concerned with language in education has addressed children's linguistic abilities, the ways of developing these abilities, the psychological and other correlates of language 'problems' and so on. In this approach 'language' has often tended to be treated as though it were yet another school subject, albeit an important one. It is only recently that attention has been focused on the language of the classroom, as opposed to that which children should learn or that which teachers might use to instruct them better.

As the three articles in this section show, it is now well realised that the classroom is an environment in which language is used interactively to construct meanings. The approach taken has more in common with analysis of conversation and discourse than with the more traditional approaches to developing children's language. Classroom language is patently an important topic of study in itself; research into it is of broader interest since it views language in the round and in use and examines its essential role in cognition as well as in social interaction.

The reading from Edwards and Furlong stresses the interactive nature of classroom learning and draws attention to its similarities with conversation. The participants in a conversation have to have regard for the differences in perspective which result from differences in background knowledge, different associations of terminology and so on, and they must work together to arrive at shared meanings. However, as the reading shows, the analogy with ordinary conversation cannot be taken too far, for the participants in classroom conversations are not equal. Indeed teachers are not only experts in subject matter but also expert at controlling and directing children's use of language so that the teacher's meanings prevail. If Edwards and Furlong hint that this is not always desirable, that it brings its own problems especially by encouraging transmission of knowledge by the teacher rather than learning by the pupil, nevertheless they do not fundamentally question that teachers have to guide children towards the teacher's meanings.

Although they favour resource-based learning, in which pupils participate rather than are simply instructed, nevertheless this is a means whereby pupils can best accumulate academic knowledge, i.e. teachers' meanings, so that they can be led further in the subject.

Mercer and Edwards are also concerned with classroom dialogue and examine examples of classroom questioning. Their examination of what they term the ground-rules of classroom questioning shows that there are, for example, implicit conventions whereby teachers delimit the kind of answers which can be given to their questions. This particular example is held to be typical of the kind of implicit knowledge which it is crucial should be shared for mutual intelligibility and hence learning. However, this is not to say that education is always successful and that learning takes place. When it does not, it is argued that lack of mutual understanding of what is expected and what is implied contributes greatly to failure.

The reading by Phillips which concludes this section includes a useful review of the background to the acceptance of the importance of talk in school. Unlike the other articles which are mainly concerned with teacher/pupil interaction, Phillips focuses upon group talk. This, with judicious direction, can provide opportunities for developing the necessary ability to use spoken language in a range of contexts. However, it is also noted that our knowledge of older children's talk is slight in comparison with what we know of early language development. Thus, not only changes in teaching approach but also increased understanding of the area are needed.

Tony Pugh

5.1 Teaching and Learning as the Creation of Meanings

A.D. EDWARDS and V.J. FURLONG

1 CLASSROOM KNOWLEDGE AND THE RECIPROCITY OF PERSPECTIVES

When we engage in some form of social interaction, like a conversation, we assume that the situation we face means the same to us as to the person (or persons) we are talking to. We assume that we both draw on the same body of commonsense knowledge to interpret what the other says and does. Yet, because we are all individuals with different biographies and possibly separate interests, we may well have different perspectives on the situation at hand. But if we are to maintain social interaction, we will either have to gloss over or suspend these differences, or else establish new meanings we both can accept.[1] What the Humanities teachers [referred to in an earlier chapter] were doing in the first weeks of the autumn term was explicitly establishing a common sense of classroom organization. This organizational talk was itself dependent on another body of knowledge — about classroom relationships — which teachers assumed they already held in common with their pupils. Their organizational talk subsumed within it, and was dependent for its comprehensibility on, this common relationship knowledge. After the first few weeks a reciprocity of perspectives about classroom organization was assumed too, and as long as that assumption was maintained, explicit references to procedure largely disappeared from the transcripts. That too could become part of the background knowledge participants were assumed to fill in appropriately when they engaged in curriculum talk.

Despite the fact that teachers and pupils assume a reciprocity of perspectives when talking about organizational and disciplinary

---

Source: Edited version of Chapter 6 of Edwards, A.D. and Furlong, V.J. (1978) *The Language of Teaching*, London, Heinemann Educational, pp. 103-20.

work, they both assume that filling in the right meanings is a problem when it comes to the material to be learned. In this chapter we will show that teachers assume that pupils will not know what material means until they have been taught — until, for example, they have had a lead lesson, or been told what to look out for in the booklets. Pupils are likely to assume this too, and until they have been taught they suspend anything they already know about the subject matter. They must accept that they are 'ignorant' until they have taken over the teacher's system of meanings.[2]

In any piece of social interaction, it may become apparent that the participants do not have a reciprocity of perspectives. In the course of conversation, they may become aware that each means something different by a key term. If the difference is too obtrusive, it becomes a stumbling-block to the conversation; they must give their attention to it, and either establish a working definition or else change the subject. In talk between equals, neither has the right to insist on *his* definition or the obligation to wait for a ruling. But in most classrooms, academic meanings are the province of the teacher. The pupil will normally suspend any knowledge he has about the subject until he has found out the teacher's frame of reference, and moved (or appeared to move) into it. For the academic curriculum to proceed, a reciprocity of meanings has to be established. But in the unequal relationship between most teachers and pupils, the movement is nearly always in one direction; the pupil has to step into the teacher's sytem of meanings and leave them relatively undisturbed.[3] Being taught usually means suspending your own interpretations of the subject matter and searching out what the teacher means. Thus the very process of learning demonstrates and maintains the authority relationship, because the pupil is nearly always attempting to move into the teacher's world of meanings. The pupil's suspension of his own interpretation may be so complete that if he cannot understand what the material means to the teacher, then it becomes literally meaningless for himself.

The following extract illustrates this point. A boy was stuck on the question, 'Why do you think the Abraham Moss Centre is called a community centre?', and called the teacher over to help him.

6.1   T: Well, Abraham Moss is a community centre, isn't it? Now

why do people come here?
P: To work.
T: What else? Not only — I mean, you come to work, yeah, but there are other things as well.
P: Help.
T: To get help, yes. OK. What else?
P: ((Silence.))
T: Name some other parts of the Centre.
P: ((Mumbles.))
T: Pardon?
P: The gym.

Here the pupil is having difficulty answering questions about the very place in which he has spent a large part of his life for some months past. He must have extensive knowledge about the Centre. But in this context, he sets this knowledge aside and tries to search out the particular meanings which the teacher is after. The suspension of his own knowledge is so complete that he gives only monosyllabic replies — which he hopes, perhaps, can be slotted into whatever the teacher has in mind — and eventually falls into silence. As so often when there is something to be learned, teacher and pupil do not assume a reciprocity of perspectives. They do not assume that the material or the question means the same to them, and that the pupil will therefore be able to fill in the 'right' background meanings. The same meaning has to be *achieved*, and in most teaching this involves moving towards whatever the teacher will accept and validate.

It is possible, however, to look at this pupil's difficulty in a different way. Rather than setting aside his existing knowledge, he is perhaps being faced with a new situation. His silence might be because he has never before had to think about *why* people come to the Centre; this has not been a problem for him. This would frequently be the case with more technical subjects, when pupils are confronting new knowledge on matters which are initially meaningless to them. But even when they are on more familiar ground, a persistent boundary between classroom knowledge and everyday knowledge may lead them to search out meanings in line with what the teacher wants rather than to look to themselves and their own past experience, which might throw some light on the topic.[4] As we will argue in more detail later, the novelty of the task confronting them may not be that the content is new, but that it has to be formulated in unusual ways or with unusual explicitness. As in the example already cited, they may also be required to consider as a problem something that they had previously taken for granted. In either case, they will have to work, in order to generate the same framework of meanings as the teacher has.

The ways in which pupils move into the teacher's system of meanings can be illustrated by looking in detail at the following example. A boy had got stuck on the question, 'Work out using the scale how wide the island is to the nearest mile', and had called the teacher over to him for help. The question involved looking at a map reproduced in the booklet, referring to a scale marked out in miles and kilometres, and then measuring the island.

6.2   T: You know what a scale is?
    P: Sir, yeah.
    T: Right. ((Points to the scale.)) What's that letter there?
    P: One.
    T: That letter?
    P: Two.
    T: Have you measured the distance between them?
    P: Sir, yeah.
    T: And how far is it?
    P: Sir, one centimetre.
    T: No. What's the distance between one and two on the scale?
    P: Sir, in miles?
    T: Yeah.
    P: Sir, a mile.
    T: No. What's the distance on the ruler?
    P: Twenty millimetres.
    T: What's that — convert twenty millimetres into centimetres.
    P: Ten centimetres.
    T: *Two* centimetres. Look, turn that ((*the ruler*)) round. It's *two* centimetres, right. So one mile equals how far?
    P: Er, two centimetres.
    T: Can you work out the distance?
    P: Yes, sir.
    T: What's the scale again?
    P: Er, two centimetres to every mile.
    T: Right, one mile equals ...?
    P: Two centimetres.

> T: And then you can work it out?
> P: Yeah.
> T: Get it right. Do it slow and get it right. ((Teacher moves off.))

Here we can suggest that while the pupil may have come across the notion of a scale before, he recognizes that he does not know how to work out this particular question. He does not know what it is supposed to mean. At the end of the sequence we assume, as does the teacher, that the pupil has a new perspective on what the question wants. By following the teacher through a series of operations, he has come to see it in a new light; he now understands what is involved, because he apparently sees it in the way the teacher does. In this process of moving to the teacher's meaning, he offers possible answers of his own but is willing to abandon these if they are not confirmed. His first answer to the question about the distance between the two points — 'Sir, one centimetre' — would have been settled on as *the* answer if it had been confirmed. But it is wrong, and he has to try again. To narrow the area of search, the teacher asks a different question which implicitly provides a clue.

> T: No. What's the distance between one and two on the scale?
> P: Sir, in miles?

The pupil seems to recognize that he is not 'with' the teacher, and so makes suggestions which force the teacher to do more of the work. Further tentative answers are offered, which again are not confirmed.[5] In the end, the teacher has to *tell* him, but he does not tell him the answer. Rather, he leads him to the edge of it. Through the interaction, by suggesting possible meanings and then abandoning these as they are seen to be wrong, the pupil has come to see the question more in the way it was intended in the booklet — he has entered into the teacher's framework of meanings.

What we want to suggest is that this process of moving pupils towards the teacher's meanings, and maintaining them there, is at the heart of most teaching. Even in the more open environment being developed at Abraham Moss, pupils still have to suspend their own meanings and generate new ones in line with those implied by the teacher. This is not to say that some teaching technologies are not more efficient, and more flexible, than others. But essentially the same process is taking place. It involves pupils in producing tentative suggestions which may then be abandoned or locked in in the light of further clues from the teacher.

To present this view so bluntly is to risk diminishing the quality of much of the teaching we observed. [...] It also risks making that process look altogether too easy. We therefore turn at this point to consider some of the major problems involved.

2 FROM DIFFICULTIES TO PROBLEMS

As experts teachers have specialist meanings for the material that they teach, and learning involves the pupils' generating the same specialist interpretative frames. By interacting with teachers and with the written content of the curriculum pupils have to learn to interpret different aspects of their environment as physics, maths, music, or in this case Humanities.[6] But if pupils are to learn, if they are to take over and use these specialist meanings, they cannot be simply transmitted. Pupils have to build up or generate the same meanings from the evidence provided in the textbook or from what the teacher says. As we saw in the last example, if the pupil finds his proposed interpretation wrong, if it does not fit the facts as defined by the teacher, he abandons it and attempts to generate a new framework.

This process of generating specialist meanings from evidence provided by the teacher is at the heart of most academic learning, but for most of the time it is hidden from view. Ethnomethodology has shown that whenever any of us want to understand something new we usually begin with an assumption that some sort of understanding is possible. We then propose tentative theories which we will abandon or change as necessary while at the same time we continue to reinterpret the facts. Some we will come to see in a new light and we will emphasize certain aspects of them, while others we will perhaps consider less important and we will push them to the back of our minds. Eventually, by this documentary process we achieve some sort of fit between our theory and the facts as we perceive them.[7]

Unfortunately, this generative process usually goes on inside our heads — we do not always talk it out. The same is true in the classroom. Pupils have to work to generate some sort of understanding of what the teacher means (though the process is simpler than in everyday life because the teacher unilaterally defines what the facts are), yet here too most of the interpretive process is hidden from view. It does not usually get into words. Barnes has demonstrated that in certain circumstances pupils can be encouraged to engage in exploratory talk amongst themselves and talk through these interpretive processes.[8] Unfortunately, because we only recorded the teachers we do not know if this sort of exploratory talk occurred in Abraham Moss classrooms. This interpretive work will also come to the surface when pupils have a problem. Pupils and teachers will then have to put into words what usually goes on behind the scenes. Concentrating on how teachers and pupils recognize and deal with problems has therefore become a major source of interest for us for it clearly demonstrates the process by which pupils generate meanings; we can see how a reciprocity of academic meanings is achieved. In other words we can see how people learn.

How much of what teachers say is being understood, or is already understood, by their pupils? How much pupil knowledge is already within the appropriate frame of reference, and how much new knowledge is being taken? In normal class teaching, finding the answers to these questions is a haphazard business. A few pupils answer questions; and this can give the impression that everyone understands. It is not until the teacher looks at the pupils' written work that he discovers how much of his cherished exposition went over the heads of many of his class. To overcome this difficulty, teachers employ a number of evidential procedures to find out if the class is following them. They may ask questions, or simply monitor pupils' looks and glances to see how much attention they are paying. But this is often doubtful evidence. As John Holt suggests, pupils are highly skilled at hiding the fact that they do not understand.

In resource-based learning, the evidential procedures can be more intensive. Largely released from the role of teller, the teacher has far more time for problem-solving. Indeed, this becomes his major function. He deals with a barrage of questions — some procedural, some to do with equipment and resources, and others to do with the substantive content of the lesson. Most of these contacts are initiated by pupils, though in his quieter moments the teacher himself initiates contacts with pupils whom he has not seen for a while or who do not seem to be working well. The demands on his time make it necessary to assume that if there is no pressing evidence of problems, then the children are working satisfactorily and understanding what they are doing. This assumption was put into words in an early lesson with first-year pupils. The group were asked if they had any problems in 'getting on'. Only four children put up their hands. After a pause, the teacher said, 'Now does that mean that everybody else except Peter, Paul, Abdul, and Shirley can carry on? ((Pause.)) Right.' He was asking them if *not* putting up their hands meant what he took it to mean, and he took their silence as evidence that they could indeed 'carry on'.

This notion of evidence is important in understanding how the teacher diagnoses the problems of pupils who do come up to him. His first task is to find out where the pupil is, what his precise difficulties are. He has to build up some conception of a problem, and this process of formulation, of making a problem from the pupil's less specific difficulty, is an integral part of providing a solution. We have argued that pupils frequently suspend any meanings which classroom topics may have had for them in the past, and search out the way the teacher sees it. The initial statement of the difficulties being encountered may be very non-specific. For example, this pupil was working on a question about the concept of community:

6.3   P: Sir, about the people.
      T: What about the people?
      P: They all work together?
      T: Of course, a group of people all living and working together in the same area — so a community is what, then?

The teacher quickly builds up some notion of what problem the pupil has. The pupil's first utterance is highly ambiguous, even to the teacher, and he is asked to expand it. When he does so, the teacher assumes that he now understands what the difficulty is, and he elaborates, 'They all work together?' into 'a group of people living and working in the same area'.[9] This elaboration of the pupil's statement has introduced two new features of a community: that it involves *living* as well as working together, and that it involves people doing these things in the *same area*. So we can assume that the teacher has engaged in a documentary process by fitting the pupil's initial ambiguous utterance into some category of normal difficulties about what communities are. Since he gets no counter-evidence from the pupil that he is wrong in his assumption that this is where the problem lies, he goes on to integrate the pupil's expanded utterance into this new 'telling'. In a sense he has defined and solved his own problem.

In this section, the teacher seems to be acting as a kind of detective. He integrates his evidence of the pupil's difficulty into some form of normal problem, but, of course, as each case is unique he is creating or at least extending his notion of what a normal problem is at the same time. In this lesson the teacher had already established an idea that normal problems related to the concept of community. The course material was directed to developing an understanding of it, and one of the set questions was explicitly concerned with it. In the course of the lesson, a number of other pupils appeared to have similar difficulties. The teacher therefore quickly recognized their problems. In medical parlance, it was the most available diagnosis of trouble because there was a lot of it about.

The context (in this case the study of communities) therefore determined how the teacher heard the pupil's query and how he constructed a problem from it; it provided him with a theme around which to document the pupil's initial rather confused statement. In the early lessons with new pupils, queries were often heard as indicating that they did not understand how work was to be organized. An ambiguous question like 'Sir, what do we do there?' was likely to be heard not as a question about the content of the lesson but as a question about how to use the booklets. On this occasion, the teacher's reply was, 'There, you read through it again and find out what happened when the earth was made.' As pupils became more accustomed to working independently teachers were more likely to assume that they knew about working procedures, and the 'same' question would be heard as an indication of some semantic difficulty. [...]

3 GENERATING MEANINGS

We turn now to look at a piece of interaction which illustrates how the pupil moves into the teacher's frame of reference by generating his own meanings from the clues provided by the teacher. [...] The following conversation was initiated by a pupil in trouble. He was stuck on the questions, 'Which side of the island ... has most trees? Why?'

6.7 P: Sir, I don't understand. I've done the answer to that one, but then it says. 'Why?'
    T: Right, why's are always difficult, the difficult one. Which side of the island, east or west, has most trees?
    P: The east.

This answer is correct, and we might guess that the pupil has found it out simply by looking at the map in his booklet, which showed trees growing on the eastern side. If he knows east from west, he can answer the question simply by looking. But the next question is not so easy. There are a few hints in the text about the importance of strong winds, but the pupil will have to draw on some knowledge from outside the curriculum. What the teacher does next is to provide some clues as to the kind of knowledge which might be involved. He is 'mapping' the problem itself, defining the area of search. Thus he says, 'Well, go on, what sort of things would decide where things grow?' This is a re-elaboration of the question 'Why?' which specifies that what needs to be considered in constructing an answer is information about soil conditions, climate, etc. There are many possible answers which the pupil could have provided from his commonsense knowledge, but he waits until he gets more guidance from the teacher about the *sort* of answer which is required. The teacher's elaboration of the written question shows him what information is likely to be relevant, and he then finds no difficulty in making suggestions.[10]

    T: Well, what sort of things would decide where things grow?
    P: Well, there's moisture and good soil.
    T: Moisture, good soil. What else?
    P: A bit of rain, sun.
    T: Well, rain would be part of moisture. Sun.
    P: Sun.
    T: There's one important thing you've left out.
    P: Growth.
    T: That's connected with the things you've just mentioned. But there's one important thing that you've left out.
    P: ((Silence.))

> T: One important thing you've left out. ((He makes a movement with his hand to indicate a tree blowing in the wind.))
>
> P: ((Silence.)) Sir, I don't know. ((Silence again.)) Sir, whether it's been planted .
>
> T: Yeah, but you talked about that. It's really the sort of — um, if it's sheltered, if it's windy.

Once the pupil has been told to search around in his general knowledge for ideas about plant growth, he finds it easy to come up with some suggestions. But the teacher's non-commital responses indicate that something more is needed. When the pupil still fails to come up with the answer, he is told twice that he missed something 'important'. When even the strong visual clue is insufficient, there is a final more specific clue which indicates clearly the frame within which the answer is to be found.

> T: ... It's really the sort of — um, if it's sheltered, if it's windy. Now wind conditions are going to affect that, aren't they? How?
>
> P: 'Cos if it is a strong hurricane it might blow it up, blow it down.
>
> T: And if it is a cold wind, what might it do?
>
> P: Freeze it and, um, it will die.
>
> T: So it won't grow so well, will it?

What the teacher is doing is to supply a context within which the answer is located. He does so by providing a series of increasingly specific clues from which the child can elaborate his own meanings. The pupil draws on part of his general knowledge and integrates it into the framework of this particular problem. By indicating that one important factor affecting growth is wind conditions, the teacher has provided the pupil with a theme around which to document information from the written text and from his own general knowledge. Just as the teacher generates an understanding of the pupil's difficulties by interpreting what he says in terms of some pattern or conception of normal problems, so the pupil has to generate some pattern to fit the information the teacher is trying to communicate. In doing so he has to scan specific areas of his general knowledge as well as information in the booklet in order to try to make the same links between the two as the teacher obviously does.[11] As we saw he puts forward his answers in a tentative way and is ready to abandon them or lock in on them depending on whether or not they are confirmed by the teacher. Thus, when the pupil says the cold will 'freeze it and, um, it will die', the teacher is able to take this as evidence that the pupil does now understand why trees do not grow on the west of Tristan. He hears this reply as evidence that the pupil has made the right links between the strong cold wind and the lack of trees. The pupil has (apparently) entered his system of meanings.

The implication of this analysis is that even where as in this example the search for the answer is closely guided, teachers can never actually *transmit* knowledge, for they are still dependent on the pupil undertaking his own interpretive work and making the necessary links for himself. Only by engaging in this essentially creative process can he enter the teacher's system of meanings. Only in this way can he learn.

4 CUMULATIVE CURRICULUM KNOWLEDGE

Before we go on to look at resource-based learning in terms of this model two further points need to be made. We have suggested that behind this curriculum talk which we have been analysing lies a reciprocity of perspectives about, amongst other things, how teachers and pupils should behave and how classroom work is organized. This reciprocity of perspectives needs to be established and maintained as a prerequisite to curriculum talk. But it is also apparent that through the process of teaching, a reciprocity of perspectives is being established about academic meanings as well. Once the pupils have moved into the teacher's way of looking at a particular topic, this too can become part of the unspoken back-cloth of meaning to which they refer in order to understand what is being said. For example, one question in the booklet about Tristan de Cunha read, 'What colour is the sand on the beaches?' In discussing this question with a pupil, the teacher says:

6.8 T: What colour will the sand be?
       P: Black.
       T: Why?
       P: Sir, the volcanic ash.

The idea of volcanic ash had not been made explicit during this particular topic, but pupils had been told that the island was a volcano and they had previously learned about volcanoes. The written question therefore assumes the cumulative nature of the curriculum, requiring a piece of information which pupils are assumed to have learned earlier. They know what the question means because through earlier exposition they have developed a reciprocity of perspective with the teacher who set this question.[12]

One regular way in which teachers control cumulative subject meanings is by the use of a specialized language. Of course, as was pointed out earlier, not all the esoteric terms used by teachers are strictly needed in the sense that they do not all involve intellectual work.[13] Yet to the extent that a term makes some discrimination which is either not available to all, or is vaguer or more 'polluted' with everyday meanings in ordinary language — then the teacher cannot afford to tolerate apparent differences in meanings between himself and the pupils. He has to insist on *his* definition. Thus a reciprocity of meanings has to be established around each key term. The advantage of this definitional work for the teacher is that once a specialist meaning has been established he can talk with more precision to his pupils, because he knows that the term will summon up the same meanings in their minds as it does in his own.

Such terms also help to maintain the boundaries of different subjects, reminding the pupils *which* meanings it is appropriate to employ in this context. However, this process is easier to spot in some subjects than others. Physics teachers and chemists simply insist on the use of appropriate terms as part and parcel of their teaching. Of course, one of the difficulties of a subject such as Humanities is that there is no universal agreement about the meaning of many specialist terms. Nevertheless, they are still coined by teachers and help in maintaining a reciprocity of meanings. In the following example the teacher is introducing a term where there is general agreement about its meaning. A pupil had returned from the library room where he had gone to look up the term 'semi-detached'.

6.9 P: Sir, I know what it means now. Sir, two or more houses together, built together.

      T: Two or more?

      P: Yes.

      T: No. Semi-detached is two built together, if it's more what

> do they call them — when you've got a long row of houses
> built together? That's called terraced housing.
> P: Terraced?
> T: When you've got two, two together, that's a semi — a semi-
>   detached.
> P: ((To friend.)) Doreen and our Nicky's is a semi-detached
>   then, isn't it?
> Friend: Yes.

The pupil has been introduced to a new term and is actually able to
reorganize some of his existing knowledge in the light of it
('Doreen and our Nicky's house ...'). In the future the teacher will
be able to use this term and know that it means the same to him as
to the pupil.

One of the major areas of study in the section of a curriculum
package called MACOS on the pre-literate Netsilik Eskimos was
beliefs — the way in which they explained their world to themselves. Within the course, the notion of beliefs and explanations
had particular functionalist overtones; they were seen as being
used by people to help them get through life. In the following
example it is apparent that the pupil too subscribes to this quite
unusual notion of what beliefs are for. The question had read,
'How is it an advantage for the Netsilik to believe the seals allow
themselves to be caught?'

> 6.10 T: Go on then, what do you think?
> P: Sir, if they don't catch them they don't think they've done it
>   wrong.
> T: Mmm. What other ideas can you think of? It is quite a hard
>   question, that, I think. ((Pause.)) Think about the time of
>   the year and the difficulties of getting food. ((Pause.))
> P: Sir, sir, it would make them try harder ...
> T: What will?
> P: It will make them try harder.
> T: Believing that seals allow themselves to be caught?
> P: Yes.
> T: Maybe it will, yes, maybe. There's another reason I can
>   think of, though, which I think is more important. Is it easy
>   or difficult to get seals at this time of the year?
> P: That time? Difficult.
> T: Yes. Now then, supposing that they go for days sometimes,

they might go for days not managing to catch the seals. Now because they believe that seals allow themselves to be caught, it means that even if they go for days, they're going to think eventually they're bound to catch a seal because the seal will come to them and be caught. Right, so it's like a belief that keeps them going through a very difficult time.

Even though the girl did not get the answer quite right her attempt illustrates that she did understand the idea of beliefs correctly. Her suggestion that the Eskimos' belief would 'make them try harder' shows that she was at least on the same wavelength as the teacher. She had entered into this course's world of specialist meanings.

We can now see that the words exchanged in curriculum talk not only depend on a background of organizational and relationship knowledge, but increasingly involve cumulative academic knowledge as well. By participating in a dialogue with their teachers, and by confronting the written curriculum, the pupils enter into a world of meanings some of which are specific to their own particular course of study and others related to the specialist subject as a whole. As in the case of organizational and relationship talk, these new academic meanings will soon disappear from the classroom transcripts. When they have been established they can be referred to in increasingly truncated ways, but once again they do not disappear from the interaction, they form an increasingly detailed background of meanings which teachers and pupils have to draw on together if they are to move on to the next topic of the curriculum.

NOTES

1. Cicourel, A. *et al.* (1974), *Language Use and School Performance*, Academic Press. Cicourel notes: 'The basic issue here is that the participants must assume they are oriented to the "same" environment of objects despite cultural differences ... If participants cannot make this assumption ... then their interaction will become difficult at best' (p. 303).
2. The idea of a situationally embedded ignorance is not a new one and of course it is not always accepted by the pupils. Keddie (1971), 'Classroom Knowledge' in M.F.D. Young (ed.), *Knowledge and Control*, Collier-Macmillan, showed how some middle-class children more readily accepted that they were 'ignorant' than working-class children.
3. Cooper, B. (1976), *Bernstein's Codes: A Classroom Study*, p. 15, University of Sussex Education Area: Occasional Paper no. 6.
4. Barnes, D. (1976), *From Communication to Curriculum*, Penguin Books.

Barnes has recently pointed out how little opportunity there is in most classrooms for pupils to relate their own out-of-school knowledge to the curriculum.

5. There are parallels here with experiments described by Garfinkel, H. (1967), *Studies in Ethnomethodology*, Social Problems, 11, pp. 225-50, where students were put in deliberately unusual situations. Like these pupils, Garfinkel's students would propose tentative interpretations of their situation and abandon them or lock in on them as the meaning of what was going on, depending on whether or not they were confirmed by what happened later.

6. For a discussion of teachers' control over what is to count as legitimate school knowledge, see Whitty, G. and Young, M. (1976), *Explorations in the Politics of School Knowledge*, Nafferton Books.

7. Garfinkel, M. (1967), op. cit. defines the documentary method as follows: 'The method consists of treating an actual appearance as a "document of", as "pointing to", as "standing on behalf of" a presupposed underlying pattern. Not only is the underlying pattern derived from its individual documentary evidences, but the individual documentary evidences in their turn are interpreted on the basis of "what is known" about the underlying pattern. Each is used to elaborate the other' (p. 78).

8. Barnes, D. (1976), op. cit.

9. Turner, R. (1972) 'Some Formal Properties of Therapy Talk' in Sudnow, D. (ed.), *Studies in Interaction*, Free Press. There is a parallel here with Turner's description of group therapy sessions where the lay member is expected to offer a layman's version of his trouble and the expert transforms it into the language of the expertise involved (pp. 385-6).

10. This is a very explicit example of what goes on all the time in normal conversations. Cicourel, A. (1973), *Cognitive Sociology*, Penguin Books, describes how 'Routine conversation depends upon speakers and hearers waiting for later utterances to decide what was uttered before'. This 'enables the speaker and hearer to maintain a sense of social structure despite deliberate or presumed vagueness' (p. 54).

11. Cicourel, A. (1974), op. cit., explains how the ability to make such links is part of normal social competence. 'The hallmark of normal social competence is the reflexive linking of selectively attended information to what is stored in memory so that the emergent context can be handled routinely ... The child must learn to fill in information from existing wholes or fragments and then retrospectively or prospectively to link the information to past and possible future objects of events' (p. 305).

12. As Cicourel, A. (1974), op. cit., notes, 'The child must possess the ability to go beyond the information given and recognize that general appearances, utterances and gestures imply additional meanings' (p. 304).

13. Barnes, D. *et al.* (1969), *Language, the Learner, and the School*, Penguin Books.

5.2 Ground-rules for Mutual Understanding: a Social Psychological Approach to Classroom Knowledge

NEIL MERCER and DEREK EDWARDS

EDUCATIONAL GROUND RULES

When teachers, examiners or testers ask questions or pose problems for children to answer, there are always particular rules of interpretation which define the sort of answer which is appropriate, and these rules of interpretation ('ground-rules' as we will call them) are generally implicit rather than overtly stated. Let us examine some contrasting examples:

1. It takes three men six hours to dig a certain sized hole. How long would it take two men working at the same rate?
2. John runs faster than George. Nigel runs slower than George. Who is the fastest?
3. Who was the more successful king of England, George IV or George V?

Superficially, these are straightforward questions, all involving verbal reasoning about the characteristics and activities of certain people. But of course, question 3 is rather different from the others. It concerns real historical persons and demands reference to facts, considerations, events not specified in the question. Questions 1 and 2 are abstract and hypothetical, one essentially a matter of arithmetic and the other a matter of logic. John, George, Nigel and the men digging the hole are in no sense real — they are merely arbitrary but convenient tokens with which to pose abstract

Source: Edited version of Chapter 2 of Mercer, N. (1981, ed.), *Language in School and Community*, London, Edward Arnold, pp. 30-46.

problems which would remain essentially the same if rewritten in terms of the comparative lengths of three rivers, or the times taken by several taps to fill a tank with water. However, none of this is explicit in the questions themselves.

'Ground-rules' define not correct answers, but appropriate ones. The distinction can be clarified in terms of our three questions. Consider question 1. An inappropriate answer would involve a misinterpretation of the abstract nature of the question. For example, it could be argued that, despite working at the same rate, some people work more efficiently than others, such that a change of personnel will have a complex effect on total time expended, and besides, a reduction or increase in expended time will lead to complications due to fatigue, number of tea breaks, etc. Moreover, if the same hole were re-dug the ground would be easier to work; if it were dug somewhere else, the ground would be different. No matter how ingenious such an answer might become, it is simply *inappropriate.* Similarly with question 2 — one is not supposed to point out such unquestionable truths as that people do not always run their fastest, so that maybe Nigel was having an off day. By contrast, an *incorrect* answer would be one where the question was interpreted appropriately, but wrongly reasoned or calculated. (For example, if it takes three men six hours that makes two hours each, so two men should take four hours. Clearly, according to this calculation, two men work better than three!) The same applies to question 3 also; an incorrect answer would contain historical errors and poor arguments, while an inappropriate one, given the terms of the question, might begin 'I don't believe in monarchies anyway, so there is no way in which any king can be considered successful ...'.

As Margaret Donaldson (1978) has recently stressed, formal education demands of children the ability to deal with abstract logical problems, and hypothetical states of affairs, and increasingly so as they get older. What is at issue here is not the development of such abilities, of what Piaget for instance calls 'formal operational intelligence', but rather the fact that these and other sorts of classroom expertise are communicated, demonstrated and assessed in ways that depend on *shared* rules of interpretation, ground-rules for *mutual* understanding that largely remain implicit. And of course children differ considerably in terms of how far their own modes of language, communication and argument, and particularly the nature and extent of their accumulated knowledge and experience, are at one with those of the school.

The issue here is not one of inherent intelligence or reasoning ability, but one of mutual understanding. The problem is social-psychological, not psychological, not inherent in the child but in the encounter between child and school. Its cultural nature can be illustrated by a quotation from a paper by Ulric Neisser in which he describes and interprets some cross-cultural research by Michael Cole:

> For some years Michael Cole and his associates ... have been studying cognitive processes in a Liberian people called the Kpelle. They are an articulate people, debate and argument play an important role in their society. Many are entirely illiterate never having gone to school. Like members of traditional societies everywhere, unschooled Kpelle get poor scores on tests and problems that seem easy to people with some formal education. The following example gives some idea of the reason why:
>
> *Experimenter*: Flumo and Yakpalo always drink cane juice (rum) together. Flumo is drinking cane juice. Is Yakpalo drinking cane juice?
>
> *Subject*: Flumo and Yakpalo drink cane juice together, but the time Flumo was drinking the first one Yakpalo was not there on that day.
>
> *Experimenter*: But I told you that Flumo and Yakpalo always drink cane juice together. One day Flumo was drinking cane juice. Was Yakpalo drinking cane juice that day?
>
> *Subject*: The day Flumo was drinking cane juice Yakpalo was not there on that day.
>
> *Experimenter*: What is the reason?
>
> *Subject*: The reason is that Yakpalo went to his farm that day and Flumo remained in town on that day. ...

Such answers are by no means stupid. The difficulty is that they are not answers *to the questions*. The respondents do not accept a ground rule that is virtually automatic with us: 'Base your answer on the terms defined by the questioner'. People who go to school (in Kpelle-land or elsewhere) learn to work within the fixed limitations of this ground rule. ... It is clear that (unschooled) subjects take their particular actual situation into account more fully than schooled people do, when they are presented with formal problems. This may seem to be a poor strategy, from the problem setter's point of view. In general, however, it is an extremely sensible course of action. In the affairs of daily life it matters whom we are talking to, what we are measuring and where we are. ... Intelligent behaviour in real settings often involves actions that satisfy a variety of motives at once — practical and interpersonal ones, for example. ... All this is different in school. We are expected to leave our life situations at the door, as it were, and to solve problems that other people have set.

(Ulric Neisser, 1976, pp. 135-6)

Clearly this example is similar to those we have been discussing. Despite the inclusion of culturally-appropriate activities, such as drinking 'cane-juice', the unschooled Kpelle do not deal with the question in the way the experimenter intends. They treat it as a 'real-world' problem, rather than a purely formal, logical one. Of course, it would have been wrong for the experimenter to assume from the answers that this 'subject' was simply being illogical or stupid. The answers are quite reasonable if one accepts the alternative ground-rule that the questions are to be taken to refer to actual persons, or persons in a fictional story. We are told that the Kpelle are skilled in debate; it is quite possible that they were trying to avoid being tricked into giving the simple logical answer (that Yakpalo was also drinking cane juice) and were demonstrating their ingenuity in thinking up alternative possibilities.

We have tried to illustrate here just one sort of ground-rule, of direct importance to the business of classroom education. Learning in school, as Bruner (1972) and Donaldson (1978) have stressed, is often disembedded from the everyday sorts of occasions in which we reason and use language. What tends to happen is that when faced with logical, disembedded problems (well represented in the Piagetian operational thinking tasks that Donaldson discusses), children unused to the conventions of interpretation, or ground-rules, of such questions will treat them as contextually embedded, real-world ones and answer accordingly. One of us (D.E.) asked his ten-year-old daughter the question about the men digging the hole. She replied, 'It depends how strong they were.' Having been informed that the men are understood to work equally well, she revised her answer to 'Four hours'. Then, appreciating the unlikelihood that two men are more productive than three, asked 'Do they have bulldozers or spades?' The same child had no problem with several three-term series problems (typified by question 2 above).

It is not that such inappropriate answers are simply wrong or unintelligent. This is immediately obvious if we put the problem into a real-world context. Imagine that three men have actually taken six hours to dig a hole outside one's house, and are about to block access to the house by digging another similar one alongside it. But one of the men had gone home ill. We want to calculate the time we are likely to be inconvenienced; but how? The sorts of questions that were previously inappropriate now become very important. Was the sick man's performance impaired when helping to dig the first hole? What about lunch breaks, work schedules, equipment, etc? What if the sick man, or a replacement, returns when the second hole is half dug? What about simply asking the men how long they are likely to take? Indeed, anyone who did otherwise, such as making arithmetical calculations of the sort required in question 1, would probably be considered rather silly.

The cues that distinguish the abstract, logical problems from 'real-world' ones can be subtle; they depend on prior experience with problems of a similar sort. For example, our problem questions (1, 2 and 3 above) can be specified as particular exemplars of more general types of problem according to both context and form. In terms of context, question 1 is likely to appear as part of an exercise in mathematics, along with other arithmetical questions, as part of a maths lesson, in a maths textbook or otherwise, perhaps, presented by the mathematics teacher. In terms of its form, the question is recognizably one of a general type in which certain participants in a process (men digging holes, taps filling water tanks, etc.) are accorded a certain measured characteristic (time taken, temperature achieved, or whatever), and one is required to calculate a value of that characteristic for a different number or nature of participants. Similarly, question 2 is of a sort which occurs in certain IQ tests, having the form of logical syllogism known as a three-term series such that, given two related premises, a particular conclusion can be reached as a logical deduction. Question 3 will normally occur in the context of a history lesson or examination, and refers to actual historical persons who will undoubtedly have been dealt with ('done') in class or in a set text. Put this way, the questions may appear rather more abstruse than before we started to analyse them! But of course, recognizing that the problems are of one sort or another would not normally be a conscious and explicit business. Indeed, the discovery and identification of different sorts of educational problems, of the cues by which they are distinguished and acted on, and of the criteria by which children's responses are assessed, requires empirical research of the sort we are as yet only beginning to undertake.

The cues which distinguish the abstract from the 'real-world' problems can be disguised so as to fool even sophisticated and well educated adults into confusing the one with the other. Even forewarned as you are, try the following puzzle:

> Three old ladies have just enough money to club together to purchase a second-hand television set at £45. So, each contributing £15, they take the £45 to the shop and give it to the salesman, who passes it on to the shop manager. The manager informs the salesman that the set has been reduced to £40, and gives him back £5 to return to the old ladies. The less than honest salesman decides to pocket £2 and gives the old ladies £1 each. Thus, the old ladies are delighted to have paid a net amount of only £14 each. But thrice £14 is £42, which, added to the salesman's £2, accounts for only £44. What has happened to the other £1?[1]

We have to stress that we have been considering here just one albeit general and important sort of ground-rule: one concerning the appropriateness of different sorts of answers to questions whose terms of reference are merely arbitrary tokens of the concrete expression of essentially abstract logical or arithmetical puzzles. The point we want to make is that the whole business of education is based on similar sorts of ground-rules, on *implicit* knowledge and rules of interpretation, such that the extent to which these are truly shared by teacher and learner is always crucial. Education is about the establishment and assessment of *shared* understandings; it is social-psychological, not simply a matter of the psychology (knowledge, motivation, intelligence, stage of cognitive development etc.) of individual children, or indeed of their inherent linguistic or sociolinguistic competence.

Let us take a step backwards, away from particular sorts of ground-rules in the classroom, and consider for a moment the role that ground-rules have in terms of our general understanding of education as the transmission of human knowledge. We have here a contentious notion already, that education is 'the transmission of human knowledge'. This implies that knowledge is something like material possessions that are handed down from generation to generation; the learners are more or less passive recipients. The more recently dominant Piagetian model is that of education as the fostering of mental growth, or cognitive development, such that education needs to be tailored to the particular requirements of the child's own stage of development. Clearly there is some value in both of these views, and the issues are not merely philosophical — they have had a direct and fundamental bearing on how teachers teach, especially in our primary schools.

Our interest in the ground-rules of mutual intelligibility has led us to emphasize a rather different point of view than these. It is that human cognition is itself essentially socio-cultural rather than psychological. It is a product of communication as well as something to be communicated, and the major means of communication is language. We refer to 'human' cognition in order to stress the role of language. It is not merely language itself which is the special hallmark of the human species, but the intimate role it has in the nature of human knowledge and thought. The communications of animals serve the purpose of directing and managing actions, inter-actions and social-emotional relationships in the here-and-now. Animals take with them to the grave, as Bruner, Vygotsky and others have remarked, whatever skills and knowledge they have acquired in life which cannot be overtly demonstrated in action. Human cognition, its principles of operation as well as its contents, transcends personal experience and is a function of generations of human culture, established and changed through acts of communi-cation, and acquired by children through acts of communication. This process is, in the broadest sense, what we call 'education'.

We believe that this inherently social nature of human cognition has been underestimated in the traditions of developmental and cognitive psychology which underline our practices of formal edu-cation. The dominant paradigms, both traditional and 'prog-ressive', have separated the roles of teacher and learner, and placed the onus on the learner. So learners are seen as the passive recipients of what is taught, or else their learning is a function of their inherent cleverness (as measured by IQ tests and the like), or else they are active processors of knowledge, in the Piagetian sense, such that what is learned is essentially a function of their own developing cognitive structures. Our view, if we may state it provocatively, is that knowledge does not meaningfully exist until it is shared. Human cognition is inherently 'intersubjective', designed to be communicable and acquired through acts of communication, represented in communicable symbolic forms (language, pictures, diagrams, etc.). Knowing and learning are not psychological but social-psychological processes. Knowledge and reasoning, cognitive skills such as reading, writing and remembering, can only be demonstrated, recognized, taught, assessed, as all of these terms imply, through acts of communication. And the essence of these communications is that meanings are shared. The single goal of education, one that links teaching, learning and assessment, is the establishment of intersubjectivity — that is, the establishment not merely of cognitive skills in the learner, but of skills recognized and validated by the teacher and examiner — a mutuality of cognitions.

All communications, and by implication the nature of knowledge itself, rely on implicit rules of interpretation. No act of communication is totally explicit (Rommetveit, 1974; see also D. Edwards, 1979) — it is meaningful in terms of who says it to whom, in what context, in reference to some domain of things or ideas, and most especially on the basis of some assumptions about the listener's prior knowledge and processes of interpretation. Overt messages, things actually 'said', are only a small part of the total communication. They are like the tips of icebergs in which the great hidden mass beneath is essential to the nature of what is openly visible above the waterline. The process of education, in the broadest sense in which we have defined it, is essentially like all acts of communication. It occurs most tangibly in the exchange of overt messages where mutual intelligibility is heavily dependent on the nature and extent of implicit knowledge and processes of interpretation. It is these implicit bases of mutual interpretation that we are calling ground rules.

One of the points at which education fails is when incorrect assumptions are made concerning shared knowledge, meanings and processes of interpretation. Moreover, these ground-rules generally remain in the realm of implicit assumption. They define not the correct answer but what sort of answer is appropriate, what sort of written composition is required, what sorts of experience, behaviours, speech etc. are appropriate, what levels of explicitness, and much more. For example, when teachers ask for information, what do they want? Do they not know the answer? Do they want to discover whether or not the child knows the answer? Do they know this already, but want the child to demonstrate how explicitly he can convey the answer in formal language? When children answer inappropriately or not at all, to what is this attributed? To the teacher's own lack of explicitness, to a failed mutuality of meaning, or to some deficiency inherent in the child?

To the extent that the success of classroom communications (which includes most of teaching, learning and assessment) depends on implicit bases of interpretation, it is no use taking a purely behavioural view any more than a view that stresses the individual psychology and competence of the child. Much of what is happening does not directly meet the eye or ear. The sorts of problems we are discussing here are not to be found, at least directly, in any mere record of what was said and done. We have to make inferences, on the basis of what is said and done, about the rules of interpretation that appear to be operating.

The ground-rules approach leads us to make different sorts of inferences from those suggested by other approaches. It leads us to distinguish between incorrect or deficient performances by children, indicative of characteristics of the children themselves, and cases where there is a lack of mutual understanding. And this is just the sort of distinction which needs to be made when we are dealing with children whose cultural, family and linguistic backgrounds do not mesh ideally with those of the teacher or researcher.

UNDERSTANDING MISUNDERSTANDINGS

At this point we can re-address the question of why basic mis-understandings about school work between teachers and pupils arise and persist. On the basis of our discussion, at least two reasons can be offered. First, teachers may assume that the ground-rules of classroom work are self-evident, requiring no special explanation. It is recognized that children will need to be taught how to perform certain specific skills, but not that some children, at least, will need to have the underlying principles of schooling itself explained to them. Difficulties for both teachers and learners often stem from the teacher's limited appreciation of the special nature of language in school, of the relation between school language and children's out-of-school experience, and of the justification for promoting certain kinds of language activities (e.g. exactly what children are meant to be learning by engaging in classroom discussions, in writing up practical reports, in summarizing texts, etc.).

Secondly, children themselves may be uncertain or mistaken about what they are expected to do and why, but not reveal this to the teacher. On entering school, motivated pupils quickly realize that teachers' approval is not gained by revealing that they don't already know things that their teachers expect them to. They learn that, in school, the thing to do is to offer what seems to be required by the game, modifying their actions against such feedback as the teacher provides. David Crystal gives this brief real-life example:

> One six-year-old was recorded reading aloud to his toys at home in a flat, stilted, word-for-word manner, though his mother had often heard him read fluently to her. When asked why he was doing it, he replied that in school that was the correct way to read, for whenever he completed a sentence read thus, the teacher's comment was 'Very good!'
>
> (1976, p. 89)

A simple willingness to play the teacher's game, therefore, may contribute to a situation whereby the process of teaching and learning is being undertaken on the basis of erroneous assumptions of common understanding by both teachers and children.

TEACHER-TALK

One implication of our view of the educational process is that misunderstandings, or failures by children to comprehend concepts and principles inherent in educational activities, cannot be understood merely in terms of individual or social group characteristics of the children themselves. There is some fairly convincing evidence that patterns of communication between parents and children vary both between and within social classes, in such ways as seem likely to affect children's initial appreciation of the nature of classroom communications (e.g. Wootton, 1974; Wells, 1978a, 1978b; see also Stubbs, 1976 Chapter 7; and Mercer, 1979). We are persuaded that some children's language and other experience out of school does prepare them less well for educational achievement than is the case for others; but to try to explain this relative underachievement purely in terms of the children's own intellectual and linguistic abilities and backgrounds is, quite simply, to ignore the interactional nature of the phenomenon. An equally relevant object of our concern must be the communicative behaviour, perceptions and assumptions of the person who controls and largely defines the curriculum in action — the teacher.

If the ground-rules of educational activities are such that pupils must work towards a certain set of task definitions and criteria for success, then a prerequisite of their successful performance must be that the teacher makes explicit these conditions, and ensures that pupils' understanding of them is adequate. There are good reasons for believing that such preparation on the part of teachers is often lacking. Barry Cooper (1976), for example, has attempted to stand Bernstein's theory of codes on its head by claiming that school is often difficult for working-class pupils to understand because *teachers* habitually use the kind of inexplicit language (known as 'restricted speech variants') normally attributed to the *children*. He gives the following examples to illustrate his argument:

> ... a lack of emphasis on understanding in terms of giving reasons is shown in the following example. Mr C., during physics with 1A, was pouring what he called 'distilled' water into a beaker. The following exchange occurred: Anne: that can't be distilled water — it's got germs in it. Mr C. (condescendingly): It's not biologically sterile, it's distilled. That's not the same.
> The teacher used his greater knowledge to cut the child down to size — reminding her of her status as an 'ignorant learner'. He did not go on to explain what he meant and why, therefore, Anne's point was 'incorrect'.
>
> (p. 37)

The next example is from a chemistry lesson in which 1 BQ were being taught about elements, mixtures and compounds by Mr G. The teacher performed various experiments and demonstrations. The pupils were gathered around the front bench watching and filling in the results of the teacher's experiments in a table they had drawn up on his instructions. Several pupils, realizing that they need not pay much attention, just copied from his table on the board — in which he put the results. Jill and Sheila, for example, were discussing haircuts. The teacher eventually arrived at the making of the compound hydrogen chloride (a gas). He then, as part of his demonstration, put a lighted splint into it. It should have quietly 'extinguished', but in fact it 'popped'. The latter occurred because of the presence of uncombined hydrogen — left over from the compounding process. The teacher proceeded to tell the pupils that the splint should have extinguished and that they should write this fact down — not what actually occurred. He did not explain the reason for the 'wrong' result to them, but only to me afterwards. The pupils accepted his command to write down what they had not seen without question.

(p. 36)

Cooper argues that the teachers he observed too often failed to take account of the psychological and social circumstances of the children in their class when presenting information; they often failed to make explicit underlying principles in the curriculum material, and they tacitly encouraged the passive acceptance of 'god-given' knowledge by their pupils. In accord with the present writers, Cooper believes that 'explanations of failure need to take account of classroom communication patterns and not merely individual pupil characteristics.' (p. 37).

PUPIL-TALK

A further implication of our discussion is that any evaluation of a pupil's performance in school has to take particular account of the circumstances in which that performance is elicited. If someone is being evaluated against a certain set of criteria, then their performance is only useful for that purpose if they understand what those criteria are, in the sense that they know what they are being expected to do. Judgements about the quality of children's language are often made without proper consideration of the peculiar language demands of school, and sometimes by people of whom one might least expect it. Douglas Barnes is a researcher who has done much useful and adventurous work, largely aimed at helping teachers identify and encourage the kinds of language use which assist learning in school. In *Communication and Learning in Small Groups*, Barnes and Todd (1977) analyse a set of classroom discussions in secondary schools, and try to distinguish discussion which serves useful educational purposes from that which does not. The discussions are made up of groups of children who are classmates, talking about contemporary issues like 'gang violence'. One of the criteria, used by Barnes and Todd to evaluate discussion is the extent to which the discussants *make their meanings explicit.* Thus, under the heading *Unsuccessful Cognitive Strategies* (pp. 74, 75), they criticize the behaviour of a group (Group 9) who drew extensively on their out-of-school experience to discuss why they thought boys fought in gangs. Barnes and Todd state that 'failure to make meanings explicit ... limits the success of a discussion' (p. 75), and to consider that the children in Group 9 have failed to use the discussion to advance their understanding.

What Barnes and Todd's analysis does not admit is that failure to make some meanings explicit may not limit a discussion's success at all *from the point of view of its members* — they may all have enough out-of-school experience in common to know what each individual member means. It does, however, limit the discussion's success *from the point of view of the observer* — whether a researcher or teacher — who really wants a *demonstration* of learning from the participants. Barnes and Todd expected the children in Group 9 to recognize the discussion as a school task, and follow the appropriate ground-rules. The children, however, whether through ignorance, lack of interest, or misunderstanding, treated it more as an 'ordinary' discussion.
[...]

NOTES

1. We are, unfortunately, unable to give proper credit to the author of this puzzle. The confusion arises because the puzzle presents a real-world situation, in which prices change as transactions take place in real time, and during which specific people and sums of money appear and reappear, but asks for a mathematical analysis. One way of unravelling this confusion is to point out that the figure £44 actually has no reality whatsoever, since it is formed by adding the salesman's £2 to the sum of £42 of which it is already part.

REFERENCES

Barnes, D. and Todd, F. 1977: *Communication and Learning in Small Groups.* London: Routledge & Kegan Paul.
Bruner, J.S. 1972: *The Relevance of Education.* London: George Allen & Unwin.
Cooper, B. 1976: Bernstein's codes: a classroom study, *University of Sussex Education Area Occasional Paper 6.*
Crystal, D. 1976: *Child Language, Learning and Linguistics.* London: Edward Arnold.
Donaldson, M. 1978: *Children's Minds.* London: Fontana.
Edwards, D. 1979: Communication Skills. In N. Mercer and D. Edwards, *Communication and Context* (Block 4, PE232 Language Development). Milton Keynes: Open University Press.
Mercer, N. 1979: Language and social experience. In N. Mercer and D. Edwards, *Communication and Context* (Block 4, PE232 Language Development). Milton Keynes: Open University Press.
Neisser, U. 1976: General, academic and artificial intelligence. In L.B. Resnick, *The Nature of Intelligence.* New York: Erlbaum.
Powell, H. 1976: Unpublished B.Ed. dissertation, North East London Polytechnic.
Rommetveit, R. 1974: *On Message Structure.* Chichester: John Wiley & Sons.
Stubbs, M. 1976: *Language, Schools and Classrooms.* London: Methuen.
Wells, G. 1978a: Language use and educational success; an empirical response to Joan Tough's *The Development of Meaning* (1977). *Research in Education* 18, 9-34.
Wells, G. 1978b: *Language Development in Pre-school Children* (Part 2). SSRC End of Grant Report HR2024.
Wootton, A. 1974: Talk in the homes of young children. *Sociology* 8 (2), 289-95.

5.3 Beyond Lip-service: Discourse Development After the Age of Nine

TERRY PHILLIPS

CHANGING VIEWS OF PUPIL TALK

During the seventies a highly significant change in attitude to children's talk occurred, a change which moved talk from something to be forbidden to something to be encouraged at all costs. As part of that change, many teachers had moved away from the dominant position at the front of the classroom, which research had shown them inhibited children's talk (Barnes, 1969), and had set up situations in which the children could talk to each other freely. By the middle of the decade they were in general agreement with the sociolinguists who suggested that the children's own language should be valued in school (Halliday, 1974; Stubbs, 1976b). As the decade finished most teachers were ready to acknowledge that children's talk was "a good thing!' but they were not quite sure where the talking was going. In the eighties that uncertainty has become more noticeable. It is not that those who teach today are any less sensitive to the need to promote children's confidence in using talk, rather the contrary. They have, however, moved beyond the belief that it is sufficient simply to ensure that there is plenty of talk going on, and are looking for ways of promoting children's spoken language development within that framework. They want to know how they might move off the sidelines to intervene constructively in that developmental process. They are looking once again for a teaching role.

A fairly major problem for the junior/middle teacher, or the secondary teacher, who is searching for guidelines on children's spoken language development after they have passed the age of 9 is the fact that almost none exist. There are guidelines on how to

Source: Edited version, Phillips, T. in Wells, G. and Nicholls, J. (1985, eds), *Language and Learning: an Interactional Perspective*, Lewes, Falmer, pp. 59–82.

set up discussions, sets of topics to be talked about, and lists of materials which will start children talking. But, with a couple of important exceptions (Wilkinson *et al.*, 1974; Barnes and Todd, 1977), there is nothing which systematically investigates what older children are capable of when talking and listening. Because most of the serious research has focused on the development of communication in neonates, pre-school, and infant/first school age children, it is to this that they must turn first.

Research into early language development, which is of necessity spoken language development, shows that adults have a very positive role to play as facilitators. [...] The research shows how sensitive adults, who are ready to listen to children carefully, to respond with interest and to be flexible in their conversational behaviour take an active and irreplaceable role in the developmental process by which young children learn to use talk for the range of functions identified by Halliday (1969 and 1975).

By turning to the extensive literature on early language development, teachers of older children will gain some valuable insights into the role they might take in their classrooms when the circumstances permit. Unfortunately, however, the nature of schooling for children in the later primary years and in secondary schools is somewhat different from that in the early years of schooling. When children first enter school they are still learning how to learn and how to cooperate with others and to a large extent that, rather than any particular piece of factual information, is what their teachers help them learn. By the time children have moved to their next school most of them are ready to be introduced to organized bodies of knowledge in various areas of the curriculum. Whether the curriculum is integrated or classified into discrete subjects, children will have to assimilate a certain number of facts and concepts before they can make progress in understanding. When later they move to a secondary school, where the curriculum is often highly classified and therefore more difficult for certain children to relate to in any case (*cf.* Bernstein, 1971), the bodies of knowledge have become even more complex and remote from children's out-of-school interests. As a consequence of the unavoidable intrusion of more and more material, teachers are limited in the time they have available to allow the children's own conversational initiatives to develop, and in the scope they have for deviating from the topics that appear on the syllabus. They will, of course, be able to create some opportunities for free-ranging discussions, but this will never be as easy as it was for their colleagues during the early years.

CLASS DISCUSSION AS THE CONTEXT FOR DEVELOPMENT?

Society as a whole expects schools to provide children in the middle years with an introduction to organized knowledge and some understanding of the central concepts involved. Part of society also expects children to develop enquiring minds. It might be argued that given constraints upon time the most appropriate route to all three would be through well structured class discussion in which teachers first present information and then get children to explore it with them systematically. Although there would have to be a 'transmission' segment to the class discussion (*cf.* Barnes and Schemilt, 1974), this would not adversely affect either children's thinking or their language because it would be followed by a period of 'interpretation' in which the teacher uses 'open' questions to stimulate thinking and promote more complex verbal responses. This is an argument for teacher-led language development which appears at first sight to be attractive because it gives teachers a way of intervening to promote a wider variety of language functions without jeopardizing 'content'. But what probability of success does it have? For the answer we must turn once again to research into early language development.

As children are learning to use talk, they are also learning about their roles as speakers (Halliday, 1978). Adults know more than children by virtue of having lived longer so children inevitably find themselves more often cast in the role of informed than of informant. This, of itself, is no bad thing. There is often no way in which a child can find out except by getting the information from an adult. A difficulty arises, however, when this particular form of asymmetry, the asymmetry of knowledge, continues to occur over a long period and in combination with *discourse* asymmetry. It is, for instance, common practice for an adult to decide what a child means when that child uses an unfamiliar or an ambiguous word. [...]

All children, even those who were subjected to 'good practice' in their early years, will have learned that adults are potentially authority figures with the ultimate right to sanction meanings and the ultimate right to decide when negotiation over it has come to an end (*cf.* Speier, 1971 and 1976). Even children with favourable backgrounds will, from time to time, experience a combination of not knowing and not being in a position to make their own decisions. Whilst the children are able to engage with an adult in free-ranging one-to-one conversations this residual perception is potentially modifiable; but once they enter the context of a junior/ middle or a secondary classroom, in which the adults are obliged to place fairly heavy constraints upon the children's linguistic freedom as they work in class groups, perceptions will harden. When children hear teachers using linguistic strategies such as asking 'closed' questions (Barnes, 1969; Hammersley, 1977), insisting on specialized linguistic registers (Barnes, 1969 and 1976) and making evaluative follow-up moves to every answer a child gives (Sinclair and Coulthard, 1975), earlier messages about the asymmetry of their own conversational rights are confirmed. Only if it were possible to provide unlimited time for discussion and to do away with all prescribed syllabuses would it be possible to reverse this trend. But the taking of such action would imply a different view of education from the one currently held by the majority of education systems in the western world. In the absence of such dramatic action, teachers will have to find other ways of promoting children's talk development. Useful as it is for various teaching purposes, whole-class discussion is not a solution for it is subject to too many constraints to make it suitable for sustained negotiation of meaning.

CHILDREN'S PERCEPTIONS OF TALK WITH THEIR PEERS

What now? If spontaneous spoken language development through free-ranging one-to-one adult-child conversation is not possible on a large scale once the acquisition of organized knowledge increases in importance, and if whole-class discussion is not suitable as a setting for encouraging language development, where and how are the teachers of the eighties to find a useful language teaching role? It seems strange to suggest that the place might be in peer-group talk, because it would seem that the one place where, by definition, teachers cannot intervene to promote language development is in *peer* groups. And yet there is, in children's pre- and first-school peer-group conversation, evidence of the language of reasoned thinking which is so essential to children if they are to benefit from later schooling.

Before the age of 6 children can formulate simple hypotheses, for example, *Heather*: 'if we had a real one and your daddy had a real one it would be good.' (5-9 years). (McTear, 1981, p. 127), and children as young as 3½ will ask for clarification if there is a meaning they don't fully understand (Garvey, 1975). Four year olds will offer alternative suggestions if they do not agree with what their peers have said, for example,

> *Tessa*: I'll be doing the cooking ... (4) ... no we're going to play schools ... do you remember
> *Jacq*: yes but let's not play it today
> *Tessa*: alright we've stopped

(Shields, 1980, p. 5)

and, between the ages of 3 and 5, children will seek out information using indirect requests (Dore, 1979). In other words, through their peer-group conversations, young children learn to challenge, to question, and to make suggestions of a hypothetical nature. Perhaps it is even more important though that they perceive peer-group discourse as an opportunity to use language in these ways; that it is normal to do so and the status of the interlocutors makes deference to their knowledge unnecessary, even inappropriate. Hence they learn to collaborate in order to make meaning, using their language in the range of ways that has just been described. It is not that they could not use their language in every one of these ways when in conversation with an adult; it is simply that they *do not* because they expect adults to be knowledgeable and thus less open to challenges, questions, and suggestions. Their perceptions of the linguistic options open to them in peer-group interaction are different from their perceptions of the options which are offered by conversation with an adult.

When children enter the later primary stage of schooling they come equipped with a set of perceptions about what they can do with their talk in different types of interaction and with a set of skills to accomplish each type. Then, provided that they don't radically alter their basic perceptions as they get older, they should become better at using their talk in each type of situation. However, we have seen that children's perception of the asymmetry inherent in adult-child talk is likely to be actualized in their school experience. It would probably, therefore repay the time spent if we were to analyze some peer-group conversations to see whether such talk is very different from teacher-led class discussion. [...]

THE LINGUISTIC CHARACTERISTICS OF DISCOURSE MODES

I have suggested earlier that, whereas teachers of young children can promote language development very effectively by presenting the children with an interesting environment and then acting as sympathetic listeners when the children want to talk about it, teachers of older children must do this and more. The responsibility they have for teaching a specified syllabus reduces the scope for negotiation when following (or initiating) a topic for classroom conversation and it is often the case that, in closing down the range of options available as topics for discussion, teachers also reduce children's opportunities to experiment with a range of ways of talking. This means ultimately that the children will not be able to discover for themselves, as they were able to when they were younger, which strategies are most appropriate for a particular educational discourse. They will operate effectively only in non-negotiative situations, that is, in situations where a teacher takes a strong leadership role. Unfortunately this is an asymmetrical interaction in which it becomes more important to 'get it right', in terms of complying with the teacher's discourse rules, than it does to engage in higher order cognitive activity (Stubbs, 1976a; Edwards and Furlong, 1978). It may be possible for teachers of older children to remedy the situation by removing themselves from classroom interaction as much as possible, letting the children carry out discussion in small groups. But what, apart from greater freedom to range over topics, does a small group discussion offer to the children? In particular, how does it help their language development? And finally, are there any lessons to be learned from examining peer-group talk which might help teachers to intervene to some beneficial purpose, and not merely recreate the educationally negative interactional and linguistic behaviour which Barnes (1969) was the first to identify?

The first stage, in answer to those questions is to identify the different kinds of talk that happen in peer groups and then to decide what these tell us about the group members' perception of what they are doing through their talk. To this end I will outline the characteristics of five modes which I found in the talk of 10 to 12 year olds, referring to each mode in turn by the categorical label I have assigned to it. The reasons for particular labels will be made partially clear in the description of the markers and other linguistic features which comprise it, but a full explanation will have to wait until a discussion of the cognitive implications of the modes.

The first mode I have called the *Hypothetical* mode. When working in this mode, children use prefaces such as 'what about' 'how about' and 'say', and the word 'if' is used either in the same utterance or in another utterance soon afterwards. By employing phrases like these the speakers propose a period of speculative discourse in which the group as a whole contributes a number of notions to a 'think-tank' pool. As other speakers respond by using similar marking devices, or by using modalities such as 'could' and 'might', a conversation develops in which the speakers work together in a hypothetical manner. In these conversations the children are content to allow their suggestions to lie on the table as one of a number of alternatives, and they do not seek approbation for them. The following is an example from my data:

B: *how about* things like stop watering ... stop water your garden an' things like that ... that'll save water.

D: *what about* clay pipes ... what about clay pipes ... you know ... if you done them fairly [interrupted]

They also seem content to leave several propositions only partially clarified, even though they possess vocabularies which are more than adequate for their current purposes. A child who in one place speaks of 'vacuum', 'filter' and 'surroundings', elsewhere used imprecise modifying words such as 'fairly' and 'sort of'. In this way, they leave the finer details of the proposition vaguely defined as a way of marking their intentions. They are indicating that they are more interested in working in a hypothetical manner than they are in presenting a well-defined hypothesis which they will defend to the last:

C: well um ... well you could ... um dig *a sort of tunnel* ... *sort of thing*

D: yeah you could dig a trench couldn't you

E: *how about* digging ... getting the water through a big pipe-line ... through the sea ... and cleaning it as it goes through

B: yeah you could have *a sort of filter thing*

The label which I have given to the second mode is *Experiential*.
Like the previous mode, this one is marked with clearly identifiable
prefaces. Children use utterances which begin with 'I remember' or
with a similar structure which indicates that they are recalling a
personal experience; or they begin with the word 'once' as a way of
setting the information that follows into a time and space distanced
from the here and now. As they did with 'if' in the hypothetical
mode, speakers often use 'once' to follow 'I remember'. When they
do this they increase its marking strength. From time to time children will check that their listeners share the same background
knowledge but they do it in a way which suggests they already
know the answer. Their purpose is to show the others that they are
continuing in the same mode. When children hear the words 'you
know Mr X' or the equivalent, they know that they are not really
being asked to supply information, but simply to nod or make a
perfunctory noise so that the speaker can continue with an utterance in the experiential mode. The most powerful way a child will
indicate an intention to take part in a conversation in the experiential mode, however, will be by using a well formulated anecdote.
Such anecdotes usually contain some of the marking devices
mentioned already, but they can also include dramatic re-
enactments of the speech of one of the characters featured in them,
a substantial amount of very precisely defined detail, and a coda.
The three utterances below, which follow each other in the conversation from which they are extracted, show all these features:

J: *I remember* once when we were on holiday ... and my
     uncle and I ... and me dad and I ... we were all walking out
     this fish shop and down on the floor was a five pound note
     ... me uncle picked it up ... he says 'I'm going to keep that'
     ... so he kept it and spent it

K: *it reminds me of when* I found ... um ... er ... a medal in
     the top shelf of my cupboard with toys in and I don't
     remember putting it there so I thought ... went upstairs in
     me bedroom an' thought ... an' I remembered me dad
     dropped it in there ... with all the mess in there he dropped
     it in and it went right through the hole and I found it when I
     was clearing it out ... and I said 'Oh I'll get told off he
     might clear it out again' so I threw it back

L   *once* I found a golden ring ... I think it was nine carat gold I
     don't know ... and I took it home to my mum an' dad and

> she said 'Where'd you get that from' and I said 'I found it'
> and she said, 'Thank you for finding my ring'

When members of a group respond to one anecdote with another, or when they respond by using any of the other markers described, they acknowledge that the focus of the discourse should be personal experience and the mode in which it should be discussed the experiential.

The next mode, the *Argumentational,* is signalled in children's utterances by the use of introductory phrases such as 'yes but' and 'yes well'. When children use one of these prefaces they show that they have registered the previous speaker's point of view but wish to adopt an alternative one. At one linguistic level, the two phrases 'yes but' and 'yes well' carry different pieces of information; the first is that the speaker is simply proceeding to an alternative point, the second that the speaker is rejecting the other person's point (*cf.,* Halliday and Hasan, 1976, p. 254). As mode markers however, both signal that the speaker wishes to engage in disputation. Children also mark their intention to 'argue' by using an assertive tag at the end of an utterance. For example, when they say 'will it' or 'don't they' after a proposition they have just put, they are being slightly more provocative than is possible when using only a preface. This may explain why such tags are less common than prefaces.

As with other modes, once several speakers have recognized the general intention to take part in an 'argument', the mode is properly developed. It might be expected that, when an argument or disputation is taking place in a classroom context, there would be some evidence of the language of logical argument using words such as 'because', 'if ... then', 'on the other hand'. Although there are indeed a few instances of 'cos', most other such features are conspicuous by their absence. Instead, the short extract below is typical:

> *G:* I tried that ... me an' Ia ... me an' Ian tried that at school with ordinary soap an' that didn't work out
> *C:* *yeah well* that isn't ordinary soap in there *is it* ... it's a kind of special soap
> *M:* *yeah but* we're doing different soap [froths up water] ... see them ... see them holes well that's the tip of the skin ... where there's the skin ... you can just see the skin there

The fourth mode, *Operational*, is a little different from the previous three. When children are working in this mode they use deictics — or pointing words — extensively, and often refer to objects by using pronouns. Its main features can occur at any point in an utterance. For reasons which will become clear later, these features are considerably less significant as markers than the others that have been described and there is consequently no good reason why speakers should employ them in a foregrounded position at the beginning of an utterance. The high density of words like 'this', 'that', 'these', 'those', 'it', and 'them' can make the meaning of the talk impenetrable if heard out of context. The frequent use of imperatives which are not addressed to any named person have a similar effect. To counter this, children often give running commentaries — statements about something which is happening in the presence of the group and is therefore already apparent to all its members. And finally, from time to time, someone will issue an injunction that a practical activity should be temporarily suspended. Such injunctions very rarely cause anything more than a hiccough in an activity, however, suggesting that children recognize them as conventionalized markers rather than as serious instructions to stop what they are doing. The following is a typical example:

A: push it down ... now take that off ... *hang on a minute* [looks puzzled]
C: that's ridiculous ... it's easy to light up with just a touch ... look [leans forward to touch]
E: *'ang on a minute* ... first of all y' just want to clip that er ... there ... *'ang on a sec* ... that shouldn't work for a moment

Conversation marked for the final mode is rare in my data. Where it occurs it is interpolated within stretches of talk that are predominantly in another mode. This is the mode which I have called *Expositional.*

D: no well you see he spent it on getting presents 'cos it was the last week we were down at ... Perranporth I think it was
E: where was that wall ... you know ... where you said
J: *along our street*
K what street
J Wingate Road

K   at the top

J   yeah

D   might not have been your mum's ring ... she might have been pretending

In this example K. has decided to ask a 'wh-' question, which he has addressed to a particular speaker, (J), whom he has identified with the word 'you'. In Western European culture, a person may not ignore a question which begins with 'where', 'what', 'who', 'which', or 'when' without appearing to be uncooperative, so J. supplies the requested information. The interesting thing about 'wh-' questions is that they set up a different form of discourse from the others I have described in that they specify the content of the following utterance. On a small number of occasions children will precede a 'wh-' question with a nomination, making it even more difficult for the addressee to avoid answering: ' C: "Gail why do roads sort of block up" G: "there's a trillion cars parked on the side of the road."' The children studied appeared reluctant to use language in the expositional mode for more than the briefest stretches of time, perhaps recognizing strong similarities between it and the discourse mode most often used when a teacher is present — cf., Sinclair and Coulthard (1975) who identify 'elicitations' and 'nominations' in classroom talk.

It would be foolish to suggest that the particular language items used by these children to create each mode are the only ones which they could so use. There is, of course, no one-to-one corres- pondence between specific words and a speaker's intention. What there does appear to be, however, is a range of items which members of a particular speech community accept as significant indicators of that intention. When listeners hear a speaker use an item from that set, they recognize it as a tentative proposal for operating in a certain mode and they often respond in a manner which acknowledges the proposal. Amongst these 10 to 12 year olds there is a readiness to make responses compatible with pre- vious utterances (although not necessarily *immediately* preceding ones) as in the following example:

B: *what about* a bucket shaped roof ... a bucket shaped roof ... the rain falls in it and then it goes into your systems an' that

E: you have sort of an automatic [interrupted]

> P: you have to clean the water
> R: yer don't
> P: you do
> A: yer do
> C: feel it
> E: *what about if* you have sort of an automatic fing what senses
>   dirt. um if water i ... s [drawn out] clean or dirty and you
>   have two different um ...

A consequence of this collaborative behaviour is that there are many times during the discussions when the children produce conversation which has a distinctive and cohesive style. Because of what seems to be a highly developed ability to communicate indirectly their preference for a particular way of conversing, 10 to 12 year olds working in peer groups are able to organize their conversation cohesively without it ever becoming necessary for any individual to take charge, either by *dictating* an agenda or by *prescribing* the language and the discourse strategies to be used. Through no fault of their own, teachers are rarely able to adopt the same strategies; nor indeed does it automatically follow that they should attempt to do so, for we have not yet answered the question, 'what are the implications for teacher intervention?'

DISCOURSE STYLES AND MENTAL PROCESSES

The children studied successfully constructed in any one conversation a series of sequences in particular styles and, when I examined the various sequences, I found that the style of each was closely related to a different sort of mental activity. Each style offered the children *some* opportunity to develop thinking but, not all provided a framework within which educationally valued higher order cognitive activity was facilitated. That is why it is salutory for teachers to compare their intuitive assumptions about classroom talk and children's thinking with the evidence of what is actually taking place. To do so may help one to decide when and how to intervene.

In many later primary and secondary classrooms teachers are happy to allow children to talk whilst they are working on a practical activity and some expect the children to indulge in what they call 'social chit-chat'. They do not take exception to this because they hold with the popular view that, in general, if children are talking whilst engaged in practical work the learning process is being facilitated. Second only to teacher-led class talk, talking whilst doing something practical is the most common form of school talk, judging by the fact that this is what many teachers have in mind when they report that there is peer-group talk in their lessons. In the light of this it is worth looking again at the style which predominated in the conversation of two groups of children who were trying to repair an electric circuit. The style was operational, and lest it be said that practical activity *must* lead to an operational style, I would like to re-iterate the view which informs my whole argument, namely that children negotiate together to arrive at a way of talking and are therefore not constrained to produce any one style more than any other. When they do choose to work in an operational style, however, this has an immediate effect upon the nature of their cognitive activity.

In the operational mode speakers make a large number of references to objects which they are at that moment manipulating or on which they intend someone else in the group to carry out some action. They do not use the name of the object but refer to it in ways which turn listeners' attention towards it, quite literally. Neither do they name people who are to be responsible for the action. Interpersonally this is a sensible strategy as it avoids the problems which arise from the assumption of too much power by individuals. However, what it also leads to is a kind of 'decision-making in action.' The videotapes show that several children move forward in response, one reaches the object of attention first, and the others withdraw. In effect, what language in the operational mode does is to turn the children's attention outwards to the context and to encourage action rather than thoughtful discussion. Only if a request to turn away from the action and 'think' is made successfully will this change. In my tapes, however, there is no evidence of this happening. The nearest that anyone comes to sharing their thoughts with their peers is when they make a commentary on what is happening. This does not mean that individuals in the group are not thinking about the problems, possibilities, and probable outcomes of certain actions; it does mean, though, that they are not sharing any of their thoughts. It seems highly likely, therefore, that the operational mode discourages long-term planning and reflective thought.

Although to my knowledge there has been no serious study of

the styles of spoken language which are most common in post-infant classrooms, informal observations by myself and others with regular access to classes of older children suggest that, after the operational, the next most used peer-group style is the argumentational. If children are asked to get into groups to discuss an issue and reach a decision, one of the possibilities is that their language will develop this style. Hoping to encourage children to think for themselves, a teacher may choose an issue which derives from the syllabus and ask them to come up with a set of views on it. This is one obvious way of removing the teacher from the centre-stage of class discussion and is therefore favoured by those who are aware of some of the less desirable effects of teacher intervention. But when an argumentational style is adopted what are the cognitive outcomes and how closely do they approximate to those that teachers are looking for?

Contrary to many people's expectations, children engaged in an educational argument seem to be oriented in favour of co-operativeness. The fact that they attempt to avoid taking on a dominant role indicates this, and hence makes me a little wary of using the terminology of conflict employed by otherwise highly insightful commentators on small group talk (cf., Barnes and Todd, 1977). This co-operative orientation is reflected in the choice of prefaces, which serve tactfully to put to one side a previous speaker's suggestion without making it obvious. Speakers give a verbal nod in the direction of the previous speaker and then present their own opinion. The willingness to co-operate does not hide the fact that speakers are preoccupied with their own views, however, because we not only see them dismissing other opinions, but we also notice that they confine the use of words like 'cos' to attempts to justify their own position, and refrain from using them to explain why they have rejected the proferred alternatives. When this is combined with the propensity for reinforcing their own statements with tags like 'will it' and 'don't they', we have a discourse style which asserts rather than argues. It follows that the argumentational discourse practised by 10 to 12 year olds does support thoughtful activity, especially when the children feel they must defend an opinion, but it does not lead to a public consideration of the reasoning processes by which speakers select one suggestion rather than any of the alternatives. The children do not seem to be aware that they could delay a decision to 'reject' a proposition until they have considered its pros and cons and reasoned them through in open discussion.

There is very little expositional discourse in the talk of 10 to 12 year olds as they work in peer groups, and consequently I will not devote much space to it here. It is significant only because it is the style of discourse used most often by teachers and pupils in whole class discussions (Sinclair and Coulthard, 1975; Coulthard and Montgomery, 1981; Barnes, 1976). It is the least negotiable form of discourse, irrespective of the authority or status of the people who use it, because a question addressed to a named individual demands of that individual two things. First, that he/she should take the next discourse turn (in other forms of discourse people are not obliged to speak unless they feel they have something to say), and secondly, that the subject matter of the response should be exactly and precisely the one defined by the questioner. The question-answer sequence organizes talk in two-part exchanges, focusing attention on what has just been said instead of encouraging listeners to scan across larger stretches of the discourse. In that respect it actually *dis*courages the non-questioned from engaging in reflective thought and from making explicit their considered reasoning.

What, then, of the remaining styles, the hypothetical and the experiential? How do they differ from the other three, and what is the significance of these differences for the development of thinking? The major difference is in the way the language that is used directs participants' attention. Both oblige group members to review the conversation itself; to treat the text as a shared field and to treat remarks made at any point as remaining present for contemplation during an extended period of time. When children ask 'what about if ...' or 'how about ...' they are signalling that they do not require an immediate response with a definitive answer; that they are seeking other ideas to lie on the table with their own. When they use 'could', 'might' etc. they are encouraging each other to consider a possibility, and to look at that possibility alongside all the others that have been brought up earlier in the conversation. And when they begin with 'I remember ...' or recount an anecdote starting 'once when ...' or enquire 'you know so and so ...', they are saying to each other something like 'please treat the words that follow as something to be shared and savoured and contemplated' (*cf.*, Applebee, 1978). At those points where hypothetical or experiential style talk is developed and sustained, a framework is provided which encourages children to turn away from the immediate and to reflect, hypothesize, evaluate, and order. They are encouraged, in fact, to become actively involved in their own learning.

TEACHING, TALKING AND LEARNING

Teachers of older children sometimes feel guilty because they are not able successfully to adopt the more enlightened practices of their first school colleagues. Although they realize that extensive use of class discussion can have a negative effect upon the children's language if they employ mainly closed questions, they find it difficult to teach without using them. They are aware that they talk twice as much as all the children put together (Bellack *et al.*, 1966), but they also know that you can't hold a discussion with twenty or more children without exercising some leadership. Perhaps that is why, in the seventies, many teachers responded to the call to give talk greater recognition by 'permitting' children to chatter whilst they worked, and by encouraging them to discuss things in small groups. Ironically, however, the increase in the quantity of talk in school turned attention away from a consideration of the overall *quality* of the talk, especially its appropriateness for particular educational purposes. It was almost as if such teachers believed that talk *per se* would promote the range of cognitive processes demanded of children as they moved towards and through secondary schooling.

In the eighties there has been a reaction and many more teachers have reverted totally to class teaching because, as they put it, 'at least you know where you're going' and 'it's the simplest way to teach the basics'. The frustrations of trying to cope with the nearly impossible have become too much for them and, rather than merely pay lip service to the idea of children learning through undifferentiated group talk, they have opted for the simple alternative. At a time when research has shown that there is a range of writing styles, within which one style is more appropriate for a particular function than another (Britton, 1971; Wilkinson *et al.*, 1979; Bereiter and Scardamalia, 1985) there is a trend towards paring back the range of options for talk. But, as I hope I have shown, there are probably as many styles of talking as there are styles of writing, each one fostering a different kind of cognitive process. So what might teachers do instead of going 'back to the basics'? How might they take children 'forward to fundamentals' in terms of such fundamental life-skills as: (a) being able to argue in a way which is rational and does not confuse the argument with its proponent; (b) being able to reflect upon and evaluate ideas and experiences; and (c) being able to adopt a style of language which is appropriate for the purpose it is intended to serve?

It is always easier to give advice than it is to put it into practice, and I do not pretend that it is a simple matter to implement policies for the development of spoken language in the post first school period. Nevertheless I offer some suggestions in the hope that any discussion which arises from them will prove valuable as a first step.

Secondary English teachers, primary teachers with posts of special responsibility for language and researchers must get together as quickly as possible to establish a clearer picture of older children's talk. There is extensive information available from research into the early years of language development, but very little to help our understanding of what occurs in later years. Until we have that information we shall continue to be nervous, even suspicious, of any talk which deviates from the pattern we know most about — class 'discussion' in other words [...]

The other points I have to make are much less hortatory, and are concerned with action at the classroom level. A curriculum which brings children more and more into contact with organized bodies of knowledge demands that we use the school day efficiently. If we aim to facilitate spoken language development and, with it, cognitive processes, we must be selective about the kinds of conversation we encourage; and we must also structure the talk. I don't mean that we should prescribe rules for this kind of talk or that kind of talk, only that we should take account of what is known about styles of discourse and their relationship to children's thinking, and that we should develop routines which will help the talk, where appropriate, to be an instrument for higher order cognitive activity. In view of what has been said about the mode of talk that accompanies much practical activity, for instance, it would seem worthwhile to organize the activity so that there is a planning stage when discussion takes place away from the materials to be used, then an activity stage, followed by a withdrawal for further discussion in which group members can reconsider their initial ideas and fashion modified ones, then a second activity stage, and a final report back stage. It would not be too difficult to establish such a routine for practical activities right across the curriculum, activities such as solving a mathematical problem, constructing a model or designing a layout, or carrying out a scientific experiment. The biggest advantage of such a procedure would be that it would accustom children to the fact that they can interrupt the flow of operational language at any point to do some thinking. In time it might be possible to draw the children's attention to what has been happening, and then invite them to interrupt, themselves, when they perceive the moment to be right.

To take a second example — in this case the language of argument/discussion — it might be beneficial to frame discussion topics in ways which invite speculation and leave conclusions open, instead of requiring children to reach a decision. The kind of topic which involves selecting what to include and what to exclude from a list would then be a first stage, to be followed by a discussion in which children make explicit the reasons for their selection. At that stage of development they can be encouraged to explain why they are rejecting someone else's suggestion before they give reasons for their own.

If, throughout the middle years, children are encouraged to listen to as many different models of spoken language as possible, at the secondary stage they will be ready to work out, with their teachers, *how* speakers achieve their purposes. Taped interviews, radio and television broadcasts, and film are excellent sources for such studies. In media studies it has been realized for quite a while that it is important to study the visual component of such materials and it could only be beneficial to give prominence also to the study of the spoken text.

It would be possible to continue with a list of 'for instances' for a long time, but I shall conclude by drawing out the main principles upon which they were formulated. Spontaneous spoken language development does not stop the moment a child leaves the first school, but the nature of later schooling means that we cannot rely on there being sufficient opportunity for spontaneous classroom conversation to guarantee that the development which does occur will be adequate for a wide range of educational purposes. Teachers have to be ready to structure opportunities for talk in a way which takes cognizance of the fact that different styles of talk are suited to different forms of mental activity.

It should not be forgotten, however, that real conversation is not a series of isolated exchanges but a cumulative process in which meaning is jointly constructed. (*cf.*, Coulthard and Brazil, 1979; Berry, 1980). It would be a retrograde step, therefore, if structuring were to be equated with teacher prescription of ways of talking. This would be to ignore what we know about children's competence in 'doing it themselves'. To be in the best interests of children the structure will have to be one in which talk is presented as being capable of performing a range of functions. In the later primary years this will probably mean the establishment of classroom routines which make it clear that a particular activity can be talked about in several different ways, each one of which is appropriate to a specific outcome.

Children must move toward becoming autonomous learners and, in order to achieve such autonomy they must first be given opportunities to try out their language in a wide range of contexts. They can then be invited to reflect upon how successful they have been, how they might do it differently next time, and why. The teacher intervention consists of making sure that this post-discussion reflection on the way of talking does take place, so that the children can make their own decisions about possible changes in their linguistic behaviour. During the secondary stage it should then become possible to formalize a description of discourse styles, drawing on what the children have learned earlier by using talk and reflecting informally upon it. At that stage it may be appropriate to discuss with them the connection between styles of discourse and forms of cognitive activity. After all, by the time pupils have arrived at that point in their schooling, we expect them to take on at least some complex modes of thought and cope with them in appropriate language. It is true that, more often, they will be required to do this in writing but it seems likely that, if they are able to do it consciously in talk, it will come more easily to them in writing.

Which brings me to my final point. Teachers expect to help children to see how they can develop their written language and are ready to examine written texts — the children's own writing, stories, poems, newspaper articles, etc. — in order to do so. Spoken language forms a text, too, and with current technology it is possible to capture these texts and study them. If we are to do more than pay lip-service to the need to develop children's spoken language after they leave their first school, we need to make a serious study of their spoken texts. [...]

REFERENCES

Applebee, A.N. (1978) *The Child's Concept of Story: Ages Two to Seventeen.* London, University of Chicago Press.

Barnes, D. (1969) 'Language in the secondary classroom' in Barnes, D., Britton, J., and Rosen, H. *Language, the Learner, and the School,* Harmondsworth, Penguin.

Barnes, D. (1976) *From Communication to Curriculum,* Harmondsworth, Penguin.

Barnes, D. and Schemilt, D. (1974) 'Transmission and interpretation', *Educational Review,* 26, 3, pp. 213-28.

Barnes, D. and Todd, F. (1977) *Communication and Learning in Small Groups,* London, Routledge and Kegan Paul.

Bellack, A., Kleibard, H., Hyman, R., and Smith, F. (1966) *The Language of the Classroom,* New York, Teachers' College Press.

Bereiter, C. and Scardamalia, M. (1985) 'Children's Difficulties in Learning to Compose'. In Wells, G. and Nicholls, J. (eds), *Language and Learning: An Interactional Perspective,* Lewes, East Sussex: Falmer.

Bernstein, B. (1971) *Class, Codes, and Control, 3. Towards a Theory of Educational Transmissions,* London, Routledge and Kegan Paul.

Berry, M. (1980). 'Layers of exchange structure', *Discourse Analysis Monographs,* 7, University of Birmingham, English Language Research.

Britton, J. (1971) 'What's the use — a schematic account of language function', *Educational Review,* 23, 3, pp. 205-19.

Britton, J. *et al.* (1975) *The Development of Writing Abilities 11 to 18,* London, Macmillan.

Coulthard, M. and Brazil, D. (1979) 'Exchange structure', *Discourse Analysis Monographs,* 5, University of Birmingham, English Language Research.

Coulthard, M. and Montgomery, M. (1981) 'Originating a description' in Coulthard, M. and Montgomery, M. (eds) *Studies in Discourse Analysis,* London, Routledge and Kegan Paul.

Dore, J. (1979) 'Conversation and pre-school language development' in Fletcher, P. and Garman, M. (eds.) *Language Acquisition,* Cambridge, Cambridge University Press.

Garvey, C. (1975) 'Requests and responses in children's speech', *Journal of Child Language,* 2, pp. 41-6.

Halliday, M. (1969) 'Relevant models of language', in *Education Review,* 22, 1, pp. 26-37.

Halliday, M. (1974) *Language and Social Man,* London, Longmans.

Halliday, M.A.K. (1975a) *Learning How to Mean,* London, Arnold.

Halliday, M.A.K. (1978) *Language as Social Semiotic,* London, Arnold.

Halliday, M.A.K. and Hasan, R. (1976) *Cohesion in English,* London, Longman.

Hammersley, M. (1977) 'School learning: the cultural resources used by pupils to answer a teacher's questions', in Woods, P. and Hammersley, M. (eds.) *School Experience,* London, Croom Helm.

McTear, M. (1981) 'Towards a model for the linguistic analysis of conversation' in *Belfast Working Papers in Language and Linguistics,* 5, pp. 79-92 Belfast, Ulster Polytechnic.

Shields, M. (1978) 'The child as psychologist: Construing the social world' in Lock, A. (ed.) *Action, Gesture and Symbol: The Emergence of Language,* London, Academic Press.

Sinclair, J. and Coulthard, M. (1975) *Towards an Analysis of Classroom Discourse: The English Used by Teachers and Pupils,* London, Oxford University Press.

Speier, M. (1971) 'Some conversational problems for interactional analysis', in Sudnow, D. (ed.) *Studies in Interaction,* New York, Free Press.

Speier, M. (1976) 'The child as conversationalist: some culture-contact features of conversational interactions between adults and children' in Hammersley, M. and Woods, P. (eds.) *The Process of Schooling: A Sociolinguistic Perspective.* London, Routledge and Kegan Paul.

Stubbs, M. (1976b) *Language, Schools and Classrooms,* London, Metheun.

Wilkinson, A., Barnsley, G., Hanna, P. and Swan, M. (1979). 'Assessing language development' *Language for Learning,* 1, 2, Language in Education Centre, University of Exeter, England, pp. 59-76.

Wilkinson, A., Stratta, L. and Dudley, P. (1974) *The Quality of Listening,* London, Macmillan.

SECTION 6

LITERACY

INTRODUCTION

Much of the recent study of language has focused upon spoken forms, though reading and writing have for a long time been an important part of many people's experience of language, and of its learning. The first three articles in this section are mainly concerned with questions about the current moves towards widepread literacy throughout the world, and towards higher levels of literacy in countries where literacy levels are already high.

Literacy is a term with either broad or conflicting definitions. In the first article in this section Kenneth Goodman rejects the older 'elitist' ideas of what constitutes literacy, which he considers to have been espoused in education, whereby the terms 'literate' and 'well-read' are virtually synonymous. Indeed, he advocates a more 'populist stance' involving a broader and more functional notion of literacy and a large extension in the number of people to whom access to information through literacy should be available. Goodman is well known among researchers into reading for his emphasis on reading as a psycholinguistic process, i.e. involving active participation rather than mere reception on the reader's part. Here he argues that literacy can be more easily developed where its function and usefulness are clear, rather than as a scholastic task.

The promotion of worldwide literacy has been a major concern of UNESCO over many years and the achievements of the pro-grammes of that organisation have been considerable. Until recently UNESCO has tended to stress the economic benefits to a country of encouraging and promoting more widespread literacy. Functional literacy was regarded as essential for developing coun-tries, if they were to develop. The article by Fisher, a member of the staff of UNESCO, provides evidence which may seem to lend strong support to the view that illiteracy correlates with many such undesirable factors as poverty, inadequate diet and poor medical provision. It needs to be said that UNESCO has, in recent years, increasingly recognised that there are other more compelling arguments and motivations for becoming literate than the economic one, and that it has supported campaigns which have stressed other more personal benefits such as increased self-esteem, greater political awareness, reduced susceptibility to manipulation and so on. Nevertheless, an organisation which has had to persuade the governments of poorer countries to spend money on literacy has found itself heavily reliant on the economic argument.

Levine, in the next article, seriously questions the claimed economic advantages of literacy, and discerns very mixed motivations for the stress on functional literacy in basic literacy programmes. Unlike Goodman, who sees functional literacy as enabling, Levine sees it as restrictive. This is because the term 'functional' is used, in the instances Levine criticises most, to refer to job-related reading and writing. Although, as is acknowledged, such emphases have now become less pronounced in UNESCO's programmes, they remain important in thinking about basic literacy, revealing in Levine's view simplifications and misunderstandings with regard to such matters as the nature of literacy for individuals, its relevance for access to information and its role in societies.

The final article in this section reviews research into reading comprehension, an area of reading research which has seemed very promising in recent years. It may seem odd that reading without comprehension should ever have seemed a worthwhile pursuit, but it is necessary to understand that the notion of an active reader is quite recent in much educational research. Pearson shows how psychological and linguistic ideas of text processing from the 1960s influenced the revolution which he considers has occurred since that time. Initially, this was associated with a revived interest in case grammars and benefited from the application of ideas from transformational grammar in the context of the rapidly developing study of memory. In the earlier stages of the comprehension research the emphasis was on the structure of text related to the structure of the reader's recall. More recently, interest in metacognition and in the control systems used by readers has laid more stress on the actual and active interaction between reader and text, taking account of factors such as the reader's existing knowledge, needs, skill and so on. If, as implied above, the work has been stronger on promise than on achievement, this is not to diminish the importance of what has been learned or of the change in attitude to reading comprehension which has come about. Nevertheless, Pearson's article concludes with some useful 'future history' which implies that our understanding of reading comprehension has a long way to go.

Tony Pugh

6.1 On Being Literate in an Age of Information

KENNETH S. GOODMAN

The great German Jewish lyric poet Heinrich Heine, writing in the last century, foresaw a time when literacy would no longer be confined to a refined and elite few. He visualized literate but unappreciative shopkeepers wrapping herrings in the pages of his verses. Yet he saw this expansion of literacy as not only inevitable but desirable, even if his poetry got lost in the flood. What Heine sensed is that written language is not just the possession of teachers and poets, that it has other functions, "goods and services functions" Michael Halliday calls them, which, while less aesthetic, would become universally essential. Heine knew that literacy must be made available to everyone, with no limitations.

In this article, I am going to explore what it means to be literate in an age of information. I am going to argue that the universal literacy corequisite with full participation of citizens in modern information societies produces a qualitative change in both the scope of literacy and the nature of education for literacy.

I will make two essential points. The first is that the expansion of written language to serve the full range of functions for all people in an information age is a manifestation of a basic human characteristic — our ability as individuals and societies to create new language forms as they are needed in the context of their use. Some have argued that the only true literacy is in its most highly constrained use, such as in the formal essay. I will argue that the ultimate achievement of literacy is in the breadth of its functions and use of written language by all people. So I will argue also that the relative literacy of any individual group, society, or nation is dependent on the degree to which literacy is necessary to life and that some of the mundane functions of literacy are the most important because they are most universal.

Source: Goodman, K.S. (1985) 'On being literate in an age of information', *Journal of Reading*, 28 (2), pp. 388-92. Reprinted with permission of K.S. Goodman and The International Reading Association.

My second main point is that education for literacy has been rooted in an absolute, narrow, elitist view of literacy and its uses. It is rooted in a concept of literates as members of a semisecret custodial society whose role is the preservation and selective dissemination of the great thoughts and linguistic products of the past. We've seen our job as teachers as keeping the world's information for society but also *from society*. We have been so awed by what has been achieved through literacy that we missed the even more awesome human achievement of the literacy processes themselves. I will argue that literacy education must abandon this custodial, elitist role, take on a populist stance, and widen its perspective so that it can support the fullest uses of literacy by the widest number of people.

Umberto Eco's philosophical novel *The Name of the Rose* takes place in a major center of 14th century literacy, an Italian abbey with a library which holds most of the books ever written up to that time in Europe, North Africa, and the Middle East. Here monks from all over Europe, many literate in several classic languages, devote their lives to creating beautifully illuminated copies and translations of existing great works. A few create new works — syntheses or commentaries on existing writings or philosophical/religious treatises. But this is a controversial activity. In fact, one major character, an older monk, states what must have been a common belief at the time, and one heard over the ages, that everything that needed to be written had already been written, that all necessary knowledge already existed, and that the role of the literate monks was preservation, and not the creation of knowledge.

It served European society at the time to have a few handsful of monks do all the reading and writing. And even among these literate few, only the abbot, librarian and assistant librarian had complete access to the full collection, some works being considered too dangerous to be made accessible to even this holy brotherhood.

This same literate few also served the secular powers, recording their laws, decrees, and histories and writing letters and orders to be transmitted to their subjects, rivals, and allies.

It is not possible in an information age for society's literacy needs to be performed by only a few. Human experience and human cultures have multiplied the functions of literacy to the point where full participation in society requires that each individual have direct access through written language to information. Full participation in society requires both oral and written language.

Written language is, in one sense, an expanding repository of the world's information, the sum total of its learnings. But in an information age the extent to which people are literate and therefore can directly access, contribute to, and use information will strongly relate to their power and roles in society.

Literacy does not in itself produce power. It is not in itself liberating. It does not in itself change values, aspirations, power relationships, cultures, and world views. Literacy is necessary but not sufficient. It is a concomitant of economic, political, social, and cultural changes.

Literacy is more the result than the cause of the information age. It was not the invention of the printing press which made mass literacy possible; it was the need for mass literacy that made the invention of the printing press necessary.

All this means that the realities of literacy in the world as we approach the 21st century are mixed. In literate societies the forms of language, oral and written, have some overlapping and some different functions. Electronic media, including telephones, radios, television, and computers, constantly enhance the ability of oral language to serve purposes for which written language was created. But these in turn require increased literacy to gain access to them.

There are some other contradictions in today's realities. The world is becoming more literate in every respect as people and cultures cope with the information age. An increasing proportion of the world's population can read and write and they read and write more books, newspapers, letters, signs, and quick copies than ever before. They spend more of their time at work and at leisure reading and writing than ever before.

The rapid expansion of literacy parallels, ironically, increased economic gaps between the most and least favored nations and it also reflects widened gaps between social classes and subpopulations within even the most favored nations.

Tensions are created on existing values, traditions, and cultures by the internal and external pressures to become more literate as part of development into the information age.

In turn, distrust and antiintellectual reaction occur and literacy itself is seen as the enemy, so figuratively or literally, books are purged or burned, teachers killed, schools destroyed.

Developing nations put major resources into literacy campaigns with varying success which seems to relate to the degree to which the conditions of life and distribution of power are also changing. Even with disproportionate spending on education, the resources are often so meager in poor countries that only those successful in becoming literate in the first year or two stay in school.

Developed nations sense the need for greater and greater literacy, so exaggerated alarms are raised about the degree of literacy of school graduates, and school literacy programs are blamed for economic, industrial, and moral failures in society. In fact, schools in industrial nations do have differential success in achieving high levels of literacy with the poor, with immigrants, and with ethnic, racial, and religious minorities. To some extent there are real differences within nations in the degree to which different people need to be literate and the degree to which being literate would make real differences in their lives given other social, political, cultural, and economic realities. Both of these realities limit the effectiveness of literacy education.

In Eco's monastery, the manuscripts were written in several classic languages of literacy such as Hebrew, Greek, Latin, Arabic. Little had been written in any of the emerging vernacular languages: Italian, French, German, English and, in fact, there was general belief that these vernacular languages were not suitable or worthy of literate use. Furthermore, use of classic languages such as Latin made a common body of literature available to a small community of literates who did not share a common vernacular language.

Today, throughout the world a major concern exists for literacy in a new range of vernacular languages. All things being equal, it is much easier to become literate in one's mother tongue than a second language. But literacy in the mother tongue may not have the historical roots and well established functions that exist for English, French, German, Spanish, Russian, Japanese, or Chinese. Vernacular literacy is important to ethnic and personal identity, but academic and economic success and social mobility may require literacy in one or more world languages. The issue of who needs to be literate, for what purposes, in what functions, is a matter of social and political policy and reality and not simply a curricular decision.

PUTTING LITERACY REALITIES INTO PSYCHO-SOCIOLINGUISTIC CONTEXT

These literacy realities need to be put into the context of how and why people learn language. Human beings by nature have a universal need and ability to develop and use language. That's because we can think symbolically and because we need to present our understandings of our experiences and our responses to them to ourselves and others. All language is both personal and social. Language makes it possible to link our minds and thus greatly multiplies the wisdom and problem solving ability of any one person.

As individuals and societies, we never lose our ability to create language. It expands and is changed to serve every new need; experience, or idea. So language is both the means and the product of human progress.

Language is remarkably easy to learn in the context of its use. Children seem to grow so naturally into linguistic competence that we have not fully appreciated what an amazing achievement initial language learning is. If it is useful to do so, children can learn two or more languages as easily as one.

We need to keep this ease of learning language in mind when we consider why schools are not always successful in teaching language, particularly written language.

Why is language so easy to learn outside of school and so hard to learn in school? Why do children already fluent in one or more dialects of one or more languages often have difficulty in learning a new language in school? Why do children who learned oral language easily by themselves, without the help of teachers, often find it hard to become literate with their help?

The answer to both questions is that language is easy to learn when it's functional and hard to learn when it serves no immediate communicative or personal purpose. If Eco's monks had gone out into the countryside to teach Greek or Latin to the peasants or to launch a literacy campaign, neither effort would have succeeded because the conditions of life and culture among those peasants would have made neither functional.

Written language is learned in the same way and with the same ease as oral language when it is functional. In any human society, written language develops when there is need to communicate in ways for which oral language is inadequate, particularly communication over time and space. Individuals also reach a point as they grow up in literate societies where they need written language. As literate societies move toward an information age, the functions of literacy so pervade life that many children show the same growth into literacy that they showed in developing oral language. Many children in literate societies can read and write before starting school — in fact, in some places such preschool literacy development is the expected norm. All children in information age societies have some sense of what written language is for and what it does before they come to school.

Current studies by Ferreiro and Teberosky, Clay, Y. Goodman, Harste, Burke and Woodward, and others indicate a widespread response to print by very young children even in developing countries and among minority populations.

But we have already seen that, even in an information age, literacy is relative to social, economic, cultural, and political factors. Those functions of literacy that are most universal, needed for surviving, like dealing with logos, signs, labels, forms, directories, etc., are the ones to which children will respond most universally. Responses to book-based literacy are much less universal.

Paolo Freire, the great Brazilian educator, became aware of a symbiotic relationship between literacy and life changes. He built the revolution and its goals into his literacy program and in turn built literacy into the revolution so that his pupils could see that the changes they sought made literacy functional and necessary.

EDUCATION FOR LITERACY

How can schools contribute to expansion of literacy for individuals and societies in an information age?

First, governmental policies of universal literacy through schooling are not enough. Literacy development must be socially rooted. It must take into account the values, cultural experiences, life opportunities, and access to functions requiring literacy. So literacy programs must be rooted in the realities of the communities they serve, and they must relate to real opportunities to use literacy in improvement of the quality of life.

Second, school literacy programs must rid themselves of their commitments to the narrow, custodial, elitist view of literacy that has dominated them. The success of the children of the most literate in traditional narrow literacy programs may have much more to do with the characteristics of the learners than any intrinsic merit in the programs.

The new literacy programs must take as their keys relevance and function. They must accept social-cultural, experiential, and motivational differences. They must build on the most universal functional literacy events, working with pupils to meet their immediate literacy needs. They must build a growing sense of personal/social function in their pupils. With due respect for the past, they must focus on literacy processes for the present and future. They must not turn literacy into abstract and meaningless exercises in the manipulation of letters, characters, or words but rather keep it at all times in the context of its use.

In this way literacy can be an extension of natural language learning — the easy kind.

Successful programs for literacy in an information age are expansionist, building out from where the pupils are in their literacy development.

Successful programs are relevant both personally and socially. They are dynamic, keyed to social change and personal/social aspiration. They are holistic in the context of current functions and life experiences.

They are populist and humanistic, tearing away the barriers and constraints on literacy.

Heinrich Heine need not have worried. Practical uses of literacy do not compete with the aesthetic uses, they support them. There are even more people in the world today who would rather read his poetry than wrap herrings in it.

Eco's medieval library is a metaphor for literacy itself. The library is a repository of all the world's information: its great insights, its sublime and profane moments. But all this is the work of people using the process of literacy. The library can be destroyed and all the current information lost as long as the process of literacy and the human minds to use it continue to exist.

In an age of information what's essential for us as educators to understand about literacy is that our main concern must not be the protection and preservation of the purity of the world's information, the product of past literacy, but making the real literacy connection and opening up the literacy processes for everyone to access, create, and use the world's knowledge.

6.2 Illiteracy in Context

E.A. FISHER

When considering the injustice of illiteracy, we should not forget the other injustices that illiterates suffer along with their illiteracy. The illiterate typically lives in a poor developing country where annual income per capita is less than $700, cultural facilities and social services are practically non-existent, living and health conditions are poor, food is scarce and not nutritious, and life-expectancy is short.

The present article attempts to quantify the degree of social, cultural and economic deprivation of countries whose population is highly illiterate (i.e. with an adult illiteracy rate higher than 66 per cent), by comparing them with countries having a largely literate population (i.e. less than 34 per cent illiterate).

Selected social indicators by country covering the fields of demography, education, culture and communication, social welfare, agriculture, consumption and economics will be examined for each group of countries.

The average value and range of values of particular social indicators, relating for the most part to the year 1980, will be used as measures of disparity between the two groups of countries. This approach gives equal weight to each country; an alternative approach would have been to calculate a weighted average using, for example, the size of the population as the weighting factor. A few examples of such weighted averages will also be given to illustrate the effect of weighting.

DEMOGRAPHIC INDICATORS

Table I presents some indicators for these two types of countries highlighting their differences in terms of selected demographic variables. Although most of the analysis that follows relates to the

---

Source: Fisher, E.A. (1982) 'Illiteracy in context', *Prospects*, XII (2), pp. 155-62.

average values of the indicators, the reader can judge from the minimum and maximum values the degree of variability between countries in the same group. Indeed the range of values of one group often overlaps the range of the other group, even though the averages may be quite different.

Population Replacement Indicators

It is fairly widely known that the highest incidences of fertility are associated with the highest levels of illiteracy. This is true both within a given country and between countries. An indicator commonly used to describe fertility is the total fertility rate, i.e. the average number of live children that would be born to a hypothetical female generation.

However, one interesting feature of fertility rates inasmuch as the practice of extended breast-feeding is more prevalent among illiterate than literate women, is that the practice of extended breast-feeding delays subsequent pregnancy. The highest fertility rates can occur among women who are literate, but who have completed the equivalent of only two or three years of primary education: such women have discarded the practice of extended breast-feeding, but have not acceded to the other aspect of the lifestyles associated with women who record the lowest fertility rates.

The average of the total fertility rates of 51 so-called 'literate countries' is 3.7. This corresponds to a crude birth rate per 1,000 population of 27.1; the equivalent figures for the group of 'illiterate countries' are almost double, at 6.5 and 47.7 respectively. Clearly, family sizes in the 'illiterate countries' are quite large, but, as we shall see later, mortality rates are also higher and life expectancy is shorter.

Life Expectancy

Females in the 'literate countries' had an average life expectancy nearly 22 years longer than in the group of 'illiterate countries' (68.3 as compared to 46.5 years); the difference in the case of males — 18.1 years — was not quite so marked (62.2 as compared to 44.1 years), but none the less was still considerable.

These startling disparities in life expectancy of the two groups of countries can be attributed to a variety of causes (some of which we will be examining later), including poor nutrition, bad sanitation and lack of access to medical services.

Table 1. Demographic indicators for countries with low illiteracy rates (less than 34 per cent) and high illiteracy rates (more than 66 per cent)

Indicator	Illiteracy rate (%) (1980)	Number of countries[1]	Average of values	Lowest value	Highest value
Total fertility rate (1975-80)	<34	51	3.7	1.7	7.1
	>66	26	6.5	5.4	7.3
Crude birth rate per 1,000 population (1975-80)	<34	51	27.1	12.4	49.2
	>66	26	47.7	40.0	51.4
Female life expectation at (1975-80)	<34	51	68.3	48.7	78.6
	>66	26	46.5	40.6	57.0
Male life expectation at birth (1975-80)	<34	51	62.2	46.4	73.5
	>66	26	44.1	37.5	54.4
Crude death rate per 1,000 (1975-80)	<34	51	9.0	4.4	17.2
	>66	26	19.8	13.6	25.2
Infant mortality per 1,000 (1970)	<34	29	45	13	97
	>66	10	139	104	200
Child dependency ratio (1980)	<34	51	58.5	30.6	96.7
	>66	26	85.4	68.0	96.8
Urban population as a percentage of total (1980)	<34	51	53.5	4.5	90.3
	>66	26	23.9	2.3	66.8

[1] The number of countries varies according to the availability of the indicator concerned. (Sources of data are indicated at the end of this article.)

Mortality

The crude death rate in 'literate countries' is 9.0 per thousand; in 'illiterate countries' it is more than double, at 19.8 per thousand. Infant mortality in 'illiterate countries' was more than three times higher than in the 'literate countries', and the highest rate (at 200 per 1,000) means that one child in five in that country died before reaching the age of one. The average infant mortality in 'literate countries' was 45 per 1,000 (i.e. the median value was only 40.5). The difference between the crude birth rate and the crude death rate is an indicator of the net increase of the population. In spite of higher mortality rates in the 'illiterate countries', their relatively high birth rate (47.7 per thousand) leaves them with a net increase of 27.9 per thousand as compared with only 18.1 per thousand in the 'literate countries'.

Population Structure

The age-structure of a population is often represented graphically as a population 'pyramid' or numerically in terms of dependency ratios. The concept of dependency is that certain sections of a population are economically dependent on other sections: thus

Table 2. Indicators relating to education for countries with low illiteracy rates (less than 34 per cent) and high illiteracy rates (more than 66 per cent)

Indicator (1979 or latest)	Illiteracy rate (%) (1980)	Number of countries	Average of values	Lowest value	Highest value
Gross enrolment in primary	<34	46	97.7	72	128
education	>66	25	51.3	18	107
Gross enrolment ratio in	<34	46	53.2	9	104
secondary education	>66	25	11.2	2	31
Gross enrolment ratio in	<34	47	13.8	0	56.0
higher education	>66	25	1.5	0	7.1

persons not working (e.g. because they are too young or too old) are supported by the working, or economically active, population. The child dependency ratio is the population aged 0-14 as a proportion of the population aged 15-64. We have already observed that total fertility rates and crude birth rates are higher in the 'illiterate countries', whilst life expectation is lower. Consequently child dependency ratios should be higher in the illiterate countries. This proves to be the case, since the child dependency ratio is nearly 27 percentage points less in 'literate countries' than in the group of 'illiterate countries' (58.5 per cent as compared with 85.4). However, the range of values is quite wide and overlaps to a large degree. Certainly in the 'illiterate countries' the population pyramids are much broader based than in the 'literate countries'.

Clearly the population of the 'illiterate countries' is typically young (more than half are under the age of 17); in the 'literate countries' the majority of the population is 24 or over.

Urbanization

Available statistics on illiteracy rates in urban versus rural areas in individual countries invariably show that illiteracy is much lower in urban centres than in rural areas: it is easier to provide educational facilities in areas where the population density is high. The figures in Table I confirm this situation.

On average the population of the 'literate countries' was 53.5 per cent urban, but the range of values was very extreme, varying from 4.5 per cent to 90.3. The population of the 'illiterate countries' was essentially rural: on average only 23.9 per cent lived in urban areas. We shall see later on that in these 'illiterate countries' there is a much greater economic dependence on agriculture than in the 'literate countries'.

INDICATORS RELATING TO EDUCATION

There is obviously a link between current enrolments in primary education and subsequent levels of literacy of that particular population group, but the literacy rate for the population aged 15 and over reflects the results of enrolments of several successive generations and there can therefore be considerable time-lags before current educational effort is reflected in the adult literacy rate. Thus some countries with relatively high enrolment ratios are still to be found in the group of 'illiterate countries', as can be seen from the highest values recorded in Table 2 above. The gross enrolment ratio is the total enrolment of all ages divided by the population of the specific primary and secondary education. At the third level population data for the age-group 20-24 have been used throughout.

The average of the enrolment ratios of 'literate countries' is consistently higher than that for the 'illiterate countries'. In fact at the first level of education the ratio for literate countries is nearly double (97.7 per cent as compared with 51.3); at the second level of education it is nearly five times as large (53.2 per cent as compared with 11.2); at the third level of education the ratio is more than nine times as large (13.8 per cent as compared with 1.5). These figures indicate a severe shortage of highly qualified manpower in the 'illiterate countries', which will have repercussions on the availability of suitably qualified teachers, engineers, scientists, technicians, managers and professionals.

INDICATORS RELATING TO COMMUNICATIONS

Table 3 opposite presents data for selected indicators of different aspects of communications, whether written, printed, broadcast or implying physical transport of persons or goods.

Mail Traffic and Newspaper Circulation

An illiterate society is perforce an oral society: one could anticipate that mail traffic and newspaper circulation will be much higher in the 'literate countries' than in the 'illiterate countries'. The average of the rates for 'literate countries' of domestic mail traffic is 46.1 items per person per year (in the United States of America it reaches a stunning 416.6 items per person per year);

Table 3. Indicators of communications for countries (around 1979) with low illiteracy rates (less than 34 per cent) and high illiteracy rates (more than 66 per cent)

Indicator	Illiteracy rate (%)	Number of countries	Average of values	Lowest value	Highest value
Domestic mail traffic per	<34	42	46.1	1.0	416.6
inhabitant	>66	22	3.9	0.1	20.1
Newspaper circulation per	<34	48	122	1	569
1,000 inhabitants	>66	23	6.5	0.1	22
Radio receivers per 1,000	<34	51	289	21	2040
inhabitants	>66	26	54	7	177
Television receivers per 1,000	<34	47	145	8	635
inhabitants	>66	17	9.4	0.1	39
Railway passenger kilometres	<34	36	380.3	0.7	2738.9
per capita	>66	12	52.7	4.7	173.6
Motor vehicles per 1,000	<34	47	101.8	2.5	628.2
inhabitants	>66	24	8.1	0.7	27.7

the average of the rates for 'illiterate countries' is only 3.9.

Newspaper circulation per thousand averages out for the 'literate countries' at 122, but is only 6.5 in the 'illiterate countries'. On the one hand literacy is being reinforced in the 'literate countries' by the prevalence of written communications, whilst on the other hand the general lack of written material in the 'illiterate countries' makes it difficult for neo-literates to retain their basic literacy skills.

Radio and Television Receivers

The disparities noted above are not so great for radio receivers per 1,000 inhabitants between the two groups of countries, but between individual countries they are considerable, varying from a low of 7 per thousand (in Ethiopia) to a high of 2,040 (in the United States of America). Television receivers, being much more expensive than radio receivers, are still very much the privilege of inhabitants of the richer countries, which (as we will see later in the analysis by GNP) are in general the more literate countries. Thus the average of the ratios per 1,000 inhabitants is 145 television sets in the 'literate countries' compared to only 9.4 for the 'illiterate countries'.

Railway Passenger Kilometres and Motor Vehicles

The range of values of the number of railway passenger kilometres per capita varies enormously from country to country (0.7 to 2,739 in 'literate countries'): the average of the values is none the less highly in favour of the 'literate countries' (380.3 as compared with 52.7). With regard to the average of the number of motor vehicles per thousand, disparities are much greater (101.8 as compared with 8.1). There is much more extensive travel by railway and motor vehicles in 'literate countries' and much more reliance on animal transport and travel by foot in 'illiterate countries'.

INDICATORS OF NUTRITION AND HEALTH SERVICES

Calorie and Protein Consumption

The average of the values of calorie and protein consumption per capita per day is one-third higher for the 'literate countries' than for the 'illiterate countries': in the 'literate countries' nearly 40 per cent of total protein consumption is derived from animal products, whereas in the 'illiterate countries' only 17.9 per cent comes from animal sources. The highest incidences of malnutrition and starvation occur in areas of the world where illiteracy is highest, and the first priority of many illiterates is not to learn to read and write, but to secure adequate food and water supplies. In fact malnutrition is recognized as an important factor contributing to the inefficiency of education programmes in developing countries, for a hungry child is an inattentive child.

Availability of Doctors

There are enormous disparities between countries in the number of inhabitants per physician: in the Soviet Union there are 350 inhabitants for every physician; in Ethiopia the ratio is 69,340 to 1. The average is 2,898 per physician, for the 'literate countries' and 26,284 per physician in the 'illiterate countries'. If one doctor is responsible for the health of more than 26,000 persons it is no wonder that the mortality rate is so high.

INDICATORS OF FOOD PRODUCTION

Meat and cereal production per thousand inhabitants varies con-

Table 4. Indicators of nutrition and health services for countries with low illiteracy rates (less than 34 per cent) and high illiteracy rates (more than 66 per cent)

Indicator	Illiteracy rate (%) (1980)	Number of countries	Average of values	Lowest value	Highest value
Calorie consumption per day	<34	48	2718	1957	3637
(1972-74) number of calories	>66	26	2086	1728	2592
Proteins per capita per day	<34	48	73.5	40.9	104.6
(1972-74) number of grammes	>66	26	55.2	35.5	69.8
Animal proteins as percentage	<34	48	39.8	12.6	68.6
of total proteins (1972-74)	>66	26	17.9	6.4	44.7
Number of inhabitants per	<34	51	2898	350	21200
physician	>66	26	26284	2480	69340

Table 5. Indicators of food production for countries with low illiteracy rate (less than 34 per cent) and high illiteracy rates (more than 66 per cent)

Indicator	Illiteracy rate (%) (1980)	Number of countries	Average of values	Lowest value	Highest value
Meat production per 1,000	<34	51	39	2	136
inhabitants (in MT), 1977	>66	26	10	5	28
Cereal production per 1,000	<34	49	279	1	1209
inhabitants (in MT), 1977	>66	26	149	32	296
Cereal yield kg/ha (1977)	<34	49	2159	671	5914
	>66	26	859	448	1622

siderably from country to country according to the availability of suitable land and the density of population. Thus small, densely populated countries like Puerto Rico and Hong Kong or an arid country like Saudi Arabia have very low production, and countries with large tracts of arable and pasture land and benign climates (like the United States of America and Argentina) will have the highest production rates. The average of meat production rates per 1,000 inhabitants was 3.9 times higher in the 'literate countries' than in the 'illiterate countries'. Cereal production was twice as high. But cereal yields in kilograms per hectare were two and half times greater (2,159 as compared with 859), in spite of the fact that the extent of urbanization in 'literate countries' was more than double that of 'illiterate countries'.

OTHER INDICATORS

Gross National Product

Although there is a fairly marked positive correlation between literacy and GNP per capita as shown in the averages for the countries in each of the two groups ($2,590 as compared to $622), some countries with very low GNP per capita are highly literate (e.g. Sri Lanka), and vice versa (e.g. Saudi Arabia). It should be noted that although the highest value for GNP per capita in the 'illiterate countries' is $7,370 (in Saudi Arabia), the second highest value is only $1,580 (in Algeria). Furthermore, the disparity between the two groups of countries is considerably greater when calculated as a weighted average ($4,070 for the first group and $600 for the second).

To a certain extent one can argue that the poorer countries (in terms of GNP per capita) are also the illiterate countries because they are poor, and have been unable to afford to develop primary schooling or conduct mass literacy campaigns. But the eradication of illiteracy is not just a question of finance (as is proved by the exceptions noted above). Several countries with relatively low GNP per capita have, in the space of a very few years, made impressive reductions in the number of illiterates — the United Republic of Tanzania, Ethiopia and Nicaragua are some recent examples.

Percentage of GDP Derived from Manufacturing and from Agriculture

In the 'literate countries' the average of the proportion of the gross domestic product (GDP) derived from manufacturing is higher than that derived from agriculture (21 per cent as compared with 15): in the 'illiterate countries' the reverse is true (9 per cent and 36 respectively). Thus 'literate countries' are typically more industry-oriented than agriculture-oriented (which is all the more surprising in view of their relatively high agricultural output, as seen above in the previous section).

Electricity, Energy and Steel Consumption

Electricity, energy and steel consumption per capita is generally much higher in the 'literate countries' than in the 'illiterate countries', the averages being respectively 18 times, 10 times and 6 times those of the 'illiterate countries': once again individual 'literate countries' do not conform to this pattern (as can be seen from the lowest values recorded in Table 6), but on average the disparities are enormous between the two groups of countries.

The current North-South discussions between the 'have' and the 'have-nots' presume a classification of countries according to income per inhabitant. The present article classifies countries according to their level of literacy. To a large degree the groups of countries selected according to these two classifications coincide, but in making the criterion of distinction the question of literacy, one can analyse the disparities between the two groups from an educational rather than an economic viewpoint.

The indicators examined in this article all point in the same direction: the 'have-nots' in terms of literacy are also worse off in terms of life expectancy, infant mortality, educational provision, communications, nutrition, health services, food production and income; their industry is less developed, their agriculture is less productive.

But this is only part of the tragic reality, for within these countries with high illiteracy rates, where nearly everyone is deprived, the illiterate is even worse off than his literate compatriots: his living conditions are worse, and his life is one of drudgery and suffering.

Eliminating illiteracy will not automatically eliminate poverty, deprivation and sorrow, but it could remove a brake to development and progress in other areas by helping, in subtle and indirect

Table 6. Economic and industrial consumption indicators for countries with low illiteracy rates (less than 34 per cent) and high illiteracy rates (more than 66 per cent)

Indicator	Illiteracy rate (%) (1980)	Number of countries	Average of values	Lowest value	Highest value
Gross national product per	<34	50	2590	160	10890
capita (1979)	>66	25	622	110	7370
Percentage of GDP derived	<34	41	21	3	35
from manufacturing	>66	17	9	4	15
Percentage of GDP derived	<34	51	15	1	47
from agriculture	>66	18	36	1	67
Electricity consumption per	<34	49	1750	40	10669
capita (kWh)	>66	26	95	8	488
Energy consumption per capita	<34	49	1939	49	11554
(kg of coal equivalent)	>66	25	184	11	1901
Steel consumption per capita	<34	40	187	2	618
(kg)	>66	15	31	1	207

ways, to trigger off improvements in attitudes and gradually in
living and working conditions. However, illiteracy must not be
viewed as a problem in isolation, and programmes designed to
eradicate illiteracy must take account of the other associated areas
of deprivation and underdevelopment that have been illustrated in
this present article.

SOURCES

Literacy data: UNESCO, Office of Statistics. *Estimates and Projections of Illiteracy*,
    CSR-E-29, Paris, 1978.
Demographic indicators: United Nations, Population Division, *United Nations
    Demographic Indicators by Countries as Assessed in 1978*, New York, 1980;
    United Nations, Statistical Office, *Demographic Yearbook, 1978*, New York,
    1979; WHO, *World Health Statistics 1978*, Vol.1, Geneva, 1978.
Indicators relating to education: UNESCO, Office of Statistics, *Statistical Yearbook,
    1981*, Paris, 1981.
Indicators relating to communications: United Nations *Statistical Yearbook*, New
    York, 1979.
Indicators of nutrition and health services: FAO, Statistics Division, *1977
    Production Yearbook*, Vol. 31, Rome, 1978; WHO, *World Health Statistics
    1977*, Vol.III, Geneva, 1977.
Indicators of food production: FAO Statistics Division, *1977 Production Yearbook*,
    Vol. 31, Rome, 1978.
Economic and industrial consumption indicators: United Nations Statistical Office,
    1978 Statistical Yearbook, New York, 1979; United Nations Statistical Offices,
    1979 Yearbook of World Energy Statistics, New York, 1980; World Bank, *1980
    World Bank Atlas*, Washington, D.C., 1981.

6.3 Functional Literacy: Fond Illusions and False Economies

KENNETH LEVINE

For more than two decades, worldwide efforts at eradicating adult illiteracy have been deeply influenced by and increasingly extended under the rubric of *functional literacy*. A climate now exists, at least in Anglophone societies, in which most literacy programs and organizers are nominally committed to functional literacy as the appropriate objective of instruction, independent of the materials and the teaching arrangements in local operation. As a result of its successful expansion, functional literacy no longer refers to a distinctive perspective or practice. The term is now used to justify everything and anything connected with basic skills education for adults.

Once an idea achieves an unchallenged dominion over an important sphere of human activity, the time has come to subject it and its provenance to a careful scrutiny. Such an inspection will uncover one of the characteristic defects of fashionable ideas — an extreme elasticity of meaning. Although a lack of clarity in theoretical concepts can be defended when, for example, this vagueness stimulates unanticipated but useful connections, there is in the case of functional literacy a systematic and insidious ambiguity that permits incongruent interpretations while simultaneously promoting a comfortable but illusory consensus. An additional hazard is that the term *functional* carries the persuasive force of positive connotations — "purposefully active," "effective," "making a contribution to the whole" — which encourages a variety of hyperbolically optimistic assumptions about the effects of becoming literate for both individuals and societies.

Conspicuously absent in current debates is an analysis that could justify the widespread acceptance of such a woolly and elusive notion. In lieu of a comprehensive and coherent account of

Source: Levine, K. (1982) 'Functional literacy: fond illusions and false economies', *Harvard Educational Review*, 52 (3), pp. 249-66.

the role of literacy and illiteracy in society, we have nothing more than a jumble of ad hoc and largely mistaken assumptions about literacy's economic, social, and political dimensions. These assumptions need to be examined so that what is sound is separated from the faulty and unproven.

The heart of the case to be mounted against current notions of functional literacy is that they obscure the identification of appropriate targets, goals, and standards of achievement in the education of adults by promising, though failing to produce, a quantitatively precise, unitary standard of "survival" literacy. Further, these varying conceptions of functional literacy encourage the idea that relatively low levels of individual achievement — low in relation to the demands of typical literacy-mediated activities — will directly result in a set of universally desired outcomes, such as employment, personal and economic growth, job advancement, and social integration. I will argue, however, that the attainment of functional literacy rarely produces such outcomes, and that the elevation of literacy as a panacea for adults lacking basic skills is disingenuous, particularly with respect to the goal of employment in competitive labor markets.

Although I make no attempt in this paper to provide or examine detailed case studies, the reader will detect an emphasis on the situation in the United States and Great Britain. Nevertheless, the critique and the concluding redefinitions are intended to be applicable to both developing and so-called advanced societies.

FUNCTIONAL LITERACY: A BRIEF HISTORY

The original conjunction of the terms *functional* and *literacy* is hard to date with any certainty. The notion of a level of literacy more sophisticated than the mere capacity to write one's name and to read a simple message, but less than "full fluency," appears to have gained currency in specialist circles during World War II.[1] This intermediate level of attainment was assumed from the outset to be associated with employability and, in a loose and unclarified way, with the social integration and adjustment of its possessors. During the war, the U.S. Army defined illiterates as "persons who were incapable of understanding the kinds of written instructions that are needed for carrying out basic military functions or tasks" (Harman, 1970, p. 227). As in World War I, the draft uncovered extensive illiteracy; in 1942, President Roosevelt reported that 433,000 men graded 1-A (eligible and fit for immediate service) had been deferred because they could not meet the Army's literacy requirement (Cook, 1977, p. 49).

In a 1947 survey the U.S. Bureau of the Census used the term *functional illiterate* to refer to those who had completed fewer than five years of elementary school, on the assumption that this correlated with an inability to comprehend simple written instructions. The Census survey also included a direct question about the respondent's ability to read and write, generating, with the former criteria, a four-cell matrix of literacy/schooling conditions. A total of 20 percent of those with no schooling were counted as literate, whereas 5 percent of those who had completed four years of school were counted as illiterate (Cook, 1977, pp. 50-52).

The Census Bureau was attempting to characterize the literacy levels of large populations with indicators simple enough for respondents and enumerators to use in the field. Unfortunately, its formulation perpetuated the idea of a strict equivalence between amount of schooling and reading and writing attainments. Many of those who subsequently picked up the term *functional literate/illiterate* used it to make inappropriate and potentially misleading distinctions about individual abilities.

The concept of functional literacy first appeared in an authoritative publication that reached an international audience in Gray's (1956) survey of reading and writing for UNESCO. Gray remarked that the concept appeared to have evolved slowly out of a quarter-century of reading research and field experience (p. 21). Although UNESCO's involvement with literacy activities can be traced to that organization's origins, Gray's discussion of functional literacy significantly influenced UNESCO's policies and programs.

At first, UNESCO's literacy activities were played in the context of "fundamental education," which aimed to "help people develop what is best in their own culture" (UNESCO, 1949, p. 16). The core content of fundamental education embraced the skills of thinking, speaking, listening, and calculating, as well as reading and writing. The need for these and associated skills was recognized to exist in both highly industrialized and developing societies (pp. 11; 29).

In the earliest UNESCO documentation, the term "literacy" was not qualified; rather, it signified one of the requirements for the establishment and maintenance of humane and civilized values. Thus "the skills of reading, writing and counting are not ... an end in themselves. Rather they are the essential means to the achievement of a fuller and more creative life" (UNESCO, 1947, p. 115). Commentators like Sir Julian Huxley, Executive Secretary of the Preparatory Commission of UNESCO, attempted, in a somewhat lofty manner, to distinguish what he regarded as the worthy objectives of literacy from those he judged to be less desirable: "Literacy is not enough. ... Certainly for some people literacy has meant merely new ways of filling time, new forms of escape from reality in the shape of cheap newspapers and magazines ... instead of sending them to the stored treasures of art and wisdom or promoting a deeper understanding of nature and human life" (UNESCO, 1947, p. 9).

A postwar current of optimism and internationalism helped to fuel confidence in literacy as an agent of progress. With hindsight, however, it is clear that insufficient attention was devoted to clarifying the basic premises of literacy's efficacy and confronting the major practical difficulties posed by the problems of translating high hopes into successful fieldwork. Aspirations like Huxley's, apparently concerned to establish a taste for the classics of world literature, were not only hopelessly utopian and misguided but also ignored the possibility that literacy programs, based on such views, would promote an undesirable cultural paternalism. One early pamphlet warned:

> There is no place in fundamental education for the view that illiterate people are children who should be disciplined into progress either by force or the cut-and-dried plans of well-intentioned outsiders. The purpose of all fundamental education work is to obtain the active participation of the people themselves in shaping their own future. (UNESCO, 1949, p. 16)

The 1950s saw a wide variety of national initiatives to reduce illiteracy, encouraged by UNESCO but mainly financed by the governments concerned. The prevailing orthodoxy in educational and diplomatic circles held illiteracy to be a kind of cultural pathogen, analogous to smallpox or malaria and, like them, susceptible to complete eradication. The preferred treatment was the general administration of primary schooling, in a more or less standardized form. As the UNESCO survey *World Illiteracy at Mid-Century* declared:

> If all children of school age in any country attended school for a sufficient length of time, there would eventually be no adult illiterates in the population, except those mentally deficient and incapable of learning to read and write. It follows, therefore, that the best means of preventing illiteracy is to provide adequate educations for all children. (1957, p. 165)

The instruction of adults was thought to entail merely an extension of formal schooling to a mature clientele, generally employing the same personnel, techniques, and materials as those used for the instruction of children, since these were the available resources. Arguably, only literacy programs designed specifically for working adults could have created trained and literate labor forces in time to satisfy the requirements of existing plans for national economic development; in actuality, few programs of this kind were implemented.

Consequently, the promotion of schooling was probably in most delegates' minds when, in 1961, the United Nations General Assembly passed a resolution directing UNESCO to study the scale of world illiteracy and to recommend solutions. At this stage there were few, if any, available examples of clearly successful, fully documented and evaluated Third World campaigns to eradicate illiteracy. Some ambitious programs — in Nigeria, for example — had failed to inculcate a rudimentary, permanent literacy in even a modest percentage of their populations (Jeffries, 1967, pp. 50-57). A survey published in 1964, based on the returns from the education ministries of eighty-eight countries, suggested that most of those nations which recognized that they had severe illiteracy problems had major programs already in operation. Unfortunately, it proved easier to be convincing on paper than to perform effectively in the field. To take just one example: Haiti's report stated that they had completed two years of pilot work and were two years into a decade-long plan to reduce their 85 percent illiteracy rate by roughly two-thirds (International Bureau of Education, 1964, p. 68). By 1970, however, shortly before the end of this ten-year plan, the official UNESCO estimate of Haiti's adult illiteracy rate was 78 percent, a decrease of only 7 percent (UNESCO, 1978, p. 94).

In spite of the gap that demonstrably existed between objectives and achievements, UNESCO reacted to the General Assembly's request with a massively ambitious plan for a worldwide frontal assault on illiteracy. Details of *The World Campaign for Universal Literacy*, never published outside the United Nations, were presented, after substantial revisions, to the Secretary-General in 1963. The plans set out a ten-year international drive to make 330 million people literate, at an estimated total cost of two billion dollars (Blaug, 1966, p. 408). This global and unselective strategy represented the culmination of the "humanist" strand in UNESCO thinking about illiteracy. The plan remained consistent with the belief that basic education was a fundamental human right, but implicitly accepted a low level of literacy as the typical attainment. Furthermore, the plans rested on the implausible assumption that the utility of literacy was intrinsic and universal, so that its desirability would be readily recognized even by peasants in subsistence economies lacking access to postal services, writing materials, and vernacular reading matter.

Although the General Assembly passed a resolution in December 1963 supporting the plan, and encouraging in general terms its implementation, the World Campaign was abandoned in 1964. Blaug (1966) suggests the main reason for its abandonment was not the cost but rather accumulating indications that the programs of the 1950s and early 1960s had failed either to enroll sufficient students or to achieve satisfactory standards (p. 408). The rejection of global thinking created the opportunity for the functional conception that supposedly would be congruent with more measured aims and a more calculative approach to literacy instruction.

In Gray's 1956 survey a person was considered functionally literate "when he had acquired the knowledge and skills in reading and writing which enable him to engage in all those activities in which literacy is normally assumed in his culture or group" (p. 24). This definition was intentionally relativistic, allowing for different thresholds of literacy in various societies, while leaving unspecified what standard could apply to wholly preliterate cultures. Gray's formulation did not associate functional literacy training with work or other specific social settings; he merely emphasized that the content of training should reflect the needs and motivations of the groups served, and should aim for a self-sustaining standard — one which permits pupils to make independent use of what they have

FUNCTIONAL LITERACY   423

learned without further help from an instructor (pp. 21-22).

Possibly concerned with the abstract nature of his definition, however, Gray shifted his ground and discussed various quantitative and qualitative criteria relating to the amount and the content of training necessary to reach a self-sustaining standard. He asserted, citing British authorities,[2] that "a person may be considered functionally literate whose attainments in reading and writing are equivalent to those of a person who has successfully completed three years' schooling" (p. 25). Gray did not explain how such a correspondence had been established, and he apparently overlooked the fact that any fixed criterion must be inconsistent with the relativistic definition he had previously formulated. Grade equivalences were nevertheless widely employed as convenient proxies for functional literacy. Completion of secondary school became a "benchmark definition" of functional literacy in the United States, enshrined in legislation like the Adult Education Act of 1966 (Hunter, with Harman, 1979, p. 27); the UNESCO International Committee of experts on literacy proposed a similar criterion in 1962 (UNESCO, 1965).

The intrinsic appeal of the notion of functional literacy transcended the doubts over precisely what range and level of skills it connoted; use of the term probably suggested little more than a general level of attainment which enabled adults to "fit in" and "function" in their social environments. In the complex UNESCO world of delicate diplomatic negotiations, a slightly fuzzy term suggesting mid-range competences could be useful. On the one hand, a standard lower than functionality was morally and pedagogically suspect; research had shown a relapse into illiteracy when only rudimentary levels of literacy were inculcated (Ahmed, 1958; Committee on Plan Projects of the Goverment of India, 1963). On the other hand, the goal of a high-level competence for all could seem unrealistic in a poor country seeking economic aid to fund its literacy programs.

Functionality took on a fundamentally new meaning during the 13th Session of the General Conference of UNESCO in 1964, which substituted a five-year Experimental World Literacy Programme (EWLP) for the original humanist strategy. The EWLP very strongly emphasized the economic and development potential of literacy:

Briefly stated, the essential elements of the new approach to literacy are the following: (a) literacy programmes should be incorporated into and correlated with, economic and social development plans; (b) the eradication of illiteracy should start within the categories of population which are highly motivated and which need literacy for their own and country's benefit; (c) literacy programmes should preferably be linked with economic priorities and carried out in areas undergoing rapid economic expansion; (d) literacy programmes must impart not only reading and writing, but also professional and technical knowledge, thereby leading to a fuller participation of adults in economic and civil life; (e) literacy must be an integral part of the overall educational system of each country; (f) the financial needs of functional literacy should be met out of various resources, public and private, as well as provided for in economic investments; (g) the literacy programmes of this new kind should aid in achieving main economic objectives, i.e. the increase in labour productivity, food production, industrialization, social and professional mobility, creation of new manpower, diversification of the economy, (UNESCO, 1966, p. 97)

The final report of the 1965 Teheran World Conference of Ministers of Education on the Eradication of Illiteracy explicitly reflected the new thinking concerning functionality, though at the same time it harked back to the much older notion that literacy gives people access to their own cultures:

Rather than an end, in itself, (functional) literacy should be regarded as a way of preparing man for a social, civic and economic role that goes far beyond the limits of rudimentary literacy training consisting merely in the teaching of reading and writing. The very process of learning to read and write should be made an opportunity for acquiring information that can immediately be used to improve living standards; reading and writing should lead not only to elementary general knowledge but to training for work, increased productivity, a greater participation in civil life and a better understanding of the surrounding world, and should ultimately open the way to basic human culture. (Quoted in UNESCO, 1976, p. 10)

It is difficult, so long after, to reconstruct the process by which functional literacy became synonymous with literacy for work. After the disappointments and failures of previous efforts, the new thinking regarding literacy — adult, selective, developmental, participative — required a label that suggested the economic benefits that could be expected from investment in literacy. "Functional" carried the appropriate overtones. Although public pronouncements continued to identify functional literacy as only the first step in a staircase of continuing education that led to personal and cultural enrichment in the noblest and widest sense, by the time the pilot schemes of EWLP were in motion its operational meaning had shifted even further from Gray's original definition. A pamphlet published by UNESCO in 1970 directly stated the work-oriented character of the pilot projects: "Functional literacy work should be taken to mean any literacy operation conceived as a component of economic and social development projects. ... The teaching of reading and writing and occupational training cannot be conducted separately or disassociated in time — they are integrated activities" (p. 9).

The literacy content of the eleven pilot projects supported by the EWLP was therefore linked to training in technological skills, varying from weaving to automobile repair, and since the projects were mainly in rural settings, instruction became associated with agricultural development (see UNESCO, 1976, pp. 17-111, for details on the eleven pilot programs). The training for "greater participation in civic life," if it took place at all, seems to have been given little emphasis — *The Practical Guide to Functional Literacy* (UNESCO, 1973) provides no examples of EWLP materials or strategies for such training.

The 1976 UNESCO review of the EWLP acknowledged general disappointment with the results and uncovered shortcomings in project management, numbers of learners recruited, competencies achieved, and dropout and probable relapse-into-illiteracy rates. The EWLP statistics claimed that the entire program reached a million illiterate people at a total cost of approximately $32 million. In those five participating countries with projects that produced analyzable data on success rates, however, fewer than 125,000 people appear to have reached the criterion standards of functional literacy (UNESCO, 1976, pp. 174; 184). Nevertheless, the consensus among the EWLP's evaluating experts was that functional literacy "brings about a change for the better on condition that it is associated with a process of genuine innovation (of a political, social, or technical nature) in which participants are themselves involved. ... The more the content of the course takes into account the workers' cultural environment, the more effective the functional literacy programme" (UNESCO, 1976, p. 160).

Presumably anxious to dispel the major doubts that were generated in many quarters about continued investment in literacy, the experts came up with an elaborately qualified and curiously circular hypothesis about its benefits. Far from triggering the take-off into a spiral of self-sustaining economic growth, literacy's contribution, they now suggested, was contingent upon the prior existence of just that network of institutions, including the media, which is normally regarded as marking the attainment of an advanced stage of societal development:

> For literacy to be effective and lasting it must be sustained by an infrastructure that not only provides literates with abundant reading matter but also maintains their taste for learning and broadening their horizons: information media, stable and mobile libraries, means of producing and disseminating the written word, small museums, cultural clubs, not to mention the schooling of children (who ask questions of their parents). (UNESCO, 1976, p. 192)

The Secretariat of UNESCO, in a paper presented to the international Symposium for Literacy held at Persepolis, Iran, in 1975, was more forthright: "The concept of *functionality*, in the broad sense of the term, comprises not only economic and productivist dimensions (which played too important a role in the operational plans and experimental projects ...), but also political, social and cultural dimensions" (Bataille, 1976, p. 40). By rejecting a narrowly conceived, solely work-oriented literacy, UNESCO thinking had come almost full circle, back to the humanist position associated with the early days of fundamental education.

The vicissitudes and disappointments of UNESCO's EWLP projects did not, however, prevent functionality from being taken up by the "Right to Read" campaigns initiated in 1969 in the United States and 1973 in Britain. The various versions of functionality employed in the United States were reminiscent of Gray's 1956 definition, and in different ways, wrestled with its circularity. The Economic Opportunity Act of 1964 enshrined a con-

ception of functionality into legislation when it referred to adult
basic education for those whose

> inability to read and write the English language constitutes a
> substantial impairment of their ability to get or retain employ-
> ment commensurate with their real ability, so as to help
> eliminate such inability and raise the level of education of such
> individuals with a view to making them less likely to become
> dependent on others, to improving their ability to benefit from
> occupational training and otherwise increasing their oppor-
> tunities for more productive and profitable employment, and
> making them better able to meet their adult responsibilities.
> (quoted in Harman, 1970, pp. 234-235)

The U.S. Office of Education (USOE) defined a literate person
as "one who has acquired the essential knowledge and skills in
reading, writing and computation required for effective functioning in society, and whose attainment in such skills makes it possible
for him to develop new aptitudes and to participate actively in the
life of his times" (Nafziger, Thompson, Hiscox, & Owen, 1975, p.
20). Functional literacy in the context of work becomes, for Sticht,
"a possession of those literary skills needed to successfully perform
some reading task imposed by an external agent between a reader
and a goal the reader wishes to obtain" (quoted in Nafziger et al.,
1975, p. 21).

Much the same view of functional literacy was adopted in
Britain, where the movement took its initiative from voluntary
agencies. The early manifesto of the movement, *A Right to Read,*
quoted with approval the U.S. National Reading Center's
(USNRC) definition: "A person is functionally literate when he
has command of reading skills that permit him to go about his
daily activities successfully on the job, or to move about society
normally with comprehension of the usual printed expressions and
messages he encounters" (British Association of Settlements,
1974, p. 5).

In terms of general approaches to functional literacy, the latter
definitions effectively bring the picture up to date. Taken as a
whole, this conceptual history shows clearly that the core idea of
functional literacy developed in a political and diplomatic arena. It
was appropriated at an early stage in the competition for resources
by those who needed a label for their convictions regarding the

economic potential of, and justification for, adult literacy training. Over time, these convictions were elaborated into an ideology about the foundations of cultural modernity, the contemporary demands of citizenship, and the prerequisites for employment. The central role assigned to literacy by this ideology was derived almost entirely without reference to the existing, although admittedly scanty, linguistic and sociological evidence, and without benefit of a systematic analysis of actual written materials or concrete cultural settings.

THE ECONOMIC APPROACH TO LITERACY AND ITS DEFECTS

In the late 1950s and early 1960s literacy was identified within a multidisciplinary corpus of work on education, the media, and development as playing a catalytic, though not always identical, role in societal processes of urbanization and industrialization (see Deutsch, 1961; Golden, 1957; Hoselitz, 1965; Lerner, 1958; Parsons, 1966; Schultz, 1960, 1963; Strumilin, 1964). Some of these studies, such as Golden's (1957), employed extremely unsophisticated and suspect quantitative techniques to establish historical links between literacy rates and indices of development in particular countries; others, such as Parsons (1966) operated at the highest level of generality. The necessary qualifications were, however, swept aside and the studies were read as general encouragement for Third World investment in schooling and literacy training as a necessary ingredient in the creation of labor forces capable of utilizing advanced agricultural and manufacturing technologies. The literature also contained findings which suggested that literates were more open to change than illiterates (Schuman, Inkeles, & Smith, 1967), and that education and literacy correlated well with support for democratic values and political parties (Lipset, 1959).

Subsequent work by Blaug (1966), explicitly directed at educational planners in poor countries, identified several ways in which adult literacy programs, in contrast to increased school enrollments, were cost-effective means of increasing productivity, stimulating the demand for technical training, and strengthening the appeal of economic incentives. He calculated that the economic benefits of school education would have to be four to five times greater than the benefits of adult literacy to produce identical benefit-cost ratios (Blaug, 1966, p. 395). Blaug, however, did not accept, as some had implied, that literacy could operate as a sufficient condition for the transformation of subsistence economies into modern cash-exchange economies. He was also cautious when discussing the implications of literacy in industrial settings. Although he cited evidence that possession of less than six years of primary schooling appeared to confer little advantage in terms of higher wages, and noted that the link between productivity and literacy was hard to test, Blaug nevertheless reiterated the orthodoxy that "the aim of a functional literacy campaign is to bring the illiterate to a level where they can make profitable use of vocational and technical training, whether in industry or agriculture" (1966, p. 410).

Blaug's approach reflected the increasing influence in the mid-1960s of the "human capital" paradigm in economics. Originally associated with the work of Schultz (1963) and Becker (1975), "human capital" is simply the present value of past investments in the skills of people. This perspective encouraged precisely the kind of "pecuniary calculus" of the costs and benefits of increasing a labor force's skills that Blaug and others had attempted. The concept of "human capital" seemed particularly relevant to advanced industrial economies because it seemed to consolidate two interrelated concerns: first, the demand for noncompulsory education and off-the-job training (workers investing in themselves by foregoing earnings during the period of training); and second, the size of the cumulative, lifetime, wage differentials between jobs requiring specific qualifications and those requiring less stringent or no credentials (employers investing in productive workers). A key assumption is that in fully competitive situations, any form of discrimination — for example, racism or sexism — between job applicants which is not directly justified in terms of cost-minimization and superior productivity will lead over time to lower profits (Arrow, 1972; Becker, 1971).

One important revision of this framework by Arrow (1973) introduced the idea that employers select graduates for key organizational roles not because their academic skills are the basis of productivity, but because a degree is believed to signal diffuse personal abilities, such as persistence. The "screening hypothesis," as Arrow termed it, was later applied to the unskilled sector where the problems of illiteracy and semi-literacy are concentrated. It was argued that employers generally seek schooled and literate employees even for work which requires negligible training because they prefer a disciplined, cooperative, and long-staying worker. Although there are no selection tests that can perfectly predict these characteristics, on commonsense grounds the most relevant indicators are previous work record and, since they relate to an institutional setting entailing production and discipline, the prospective employee's school record. In selection interviews for "lower-grade" jobs, the desire for these work-force characteristics reduces to the requirement that the applicant be able to complete an application form.[3] As recent English research has shown (Blackburn & Mann, 1979, p. 102; Levine, Note 1, p. 80), literacy has become the ultimate criterion of employability for lower-grade work in large organizations.

Here, then, under the auspices of human capital analysis, is one apparently plausible socioeconomic argument for functional literacy training — an argument that serves the interests of individual employees and employers alike. Another, more recent, demonstration of literacy's economic importance in industrial societies is provided by Bormuth (1978), who marshals a large set of indicators to produce a societal cost-benefit analysis of literacy. In essence, his analysis calculates the aggregate contribution of literacy to the U.S. Gross National Product — via such factors as the monetary value of the time expended on reading and writing at work and the value of printed material in circulation — against the total costs of literacy instruction. Bormuth attempts to demonstrate that increasing amounts of information are being exchanged in print, that personal and social investment in literacy is rising, and that the benefits of literacy exceed the costs by a factor of at least five. Significantly, Bormuth does not attempt to show that the marginal return from further investment in literacy will be greater than that from investment in any other medium of communication.

These cost-benefit analyses, however, share a fundamental misconception about the nature of literacy from which many theoretical and practical difficulties have sprung. This misconception is partially articulated by Bormuth (1978), who concludes that, "being the only literate in a society is about as desirable as owning the only telephone in town — the greater the number of literates in a society, the more valuable is the literacy of those who achieve it" (p. 157). Stated more formally, the economists who have advocated personal and public investment in literacy have done so in the belief that: first, literacy is a private "good" sought because it is capable of earning monetary rewards when acquired above the competence threshold represented by functionality; and second, that the higher the proportion of a population achieving functional literacy, the greater is its per capita value.

There are two major flaws in these assumptions. First, literacy is treated as if its societal value could be determined by simply aggregating its monetary value to all the individuals that possess it. I would argue, however, that literacy is individually and collectively more valuable in certain political and cultural environments — for example, where there is a free, uncensored press, public libraries, affordable books, and freedom of information legislation. Second, in order to use the indicators so crucial to economic analyses, literacy has been treated as an entirely objective, utilitarian, and instrumental matter; the crucial subjective dimension of social status has been suppressed. Conspicuous display and status management are as much a part of the motivation for becoming literate as are the possibilities it opens up for income. On the one hand, the possession of advanced or uncommon skills such as being well-read, conversant in foreign languages, and being a published author, provide subjective satisfactions independent of pecuniary advantage. On the other hand, a lack of competence in reading and writing, exemplified by an inability to comprehend printed materials in common use, by misspellings and grammatical errors, earns negative social esteem or stigma. In most industrial societies, this stigma is pervasive and damaging, and many adults desperately seek to master literacy not merely in the hope of employment, or solely for its obvious practical utility, but partly in order to gain or preserve esteem among family and peers.[4]

In terms of the status dimension of literacy, esteem is connected to social exclusivity; that is, wide possession of a particular literacy competence will *devalue* it. It is therefore important to recognize that literacy, and education in general, belongs to what has been called the "positional economy" (Hirsch, 1977, p. 27). This term refers to goods, services and social relationships that are either intrinsically scarce, or whose attractiveness decreases as the number of owners or participants increases. The positional economy is exemplified by the inflation that affects literacy and other educational credentials in the industrial labor market. In the unskilled sector, "lower grade" employees must increasingly demonstrate a literacy competence where once a respectable employment record would have sufficed. At the top end of the labor market, examination certificates and college diplomas remain good investments to the extent that they raise an individual's income relative to what it (hypothetically) would have been if that person had remained unqualified but had been obliged to compete with qualified rivals. In situations where everyone is similarly qualified, certificates cease to improve incomes. To use Hirsch's (1977) analogy, once some people stand on tiptoe in order to get a better view, others will be forced to do the same, everyone ending up in their original, relative positions.

Following this line of argument, a similar inflation has consequences for the value of a particular level of literacy ability outside work. An individual needs a minimum level of mastery in order to "pass" as literate in public and keep intact his or her self-respect; as schools and literacy programs become more effective in equipping their students with these skills, the effective threshold of acceptability will be raised accordingly. There is, quite simply, no finite level of attainment, even within a specific society, which is capable of eliminating the disadvantages of illiteracy or semi-literacy by permitting the less literate to compete on equal terms for employment and enjoy parity of status with the more literate. Certainly, sympathetic and relevant instruction can provide individuals with the competences they need or want. However, as long as there are people credited with special or superior literacy skills, the least competent will remain vulnerable to discrimination. Altering the official benchmark of functionality cannot affect this situation.

MAKING FUNCTIONAL LITERACY OPERATIONAL

Despite a checkered history and unresolved conceptual difficulties, a continuing series of attempts to give functionality some empirical precision testify to a persistent belief in its utility. If, for the sake of convenience, we take Gray's 1956 definition as an authoritative statement of what is meant by "survival" or "functional" literacy, three components need to be measured. First, there is the question of what is to count as survival, or adequate individual functioning within a community. Second, there is the "demand" side of the literacy equation, the range of printed materials encountered by a typical adult in a society or subculture. Third, there is the "supply" side, the minimum set of competences required by the individual to perform the tasks that entail print.

It comes as no surprise that, with the exception of rough grade-equivalents, no empirical criterion for functional literacy is forthcoming in Gray or any other source. Other research programs, such as those concerned with subsistence poverty, have foundered on just such a reef.[5] Functional literacy seems to require a pre-existing notion of functionality. It trades on the prior existence of concealed assumptions about the nature and functions of literacy in society which, in turn, are related to prevalent notions of citizen rights and the good life. The notion of survival, or adequate functioning, which it involves is thus irremediably a political and moral abstraction, placing the concept beyond the reach of any strictly empirical operationalizing procedure.

As far as the demand side is concerned, the problem is to select a single basket of print-mediated activities that adequately reflect the immense variety found in culturally heterogeneous societies. It is one thing to ask, in the abstract, what printed materials a narrowly defined work role requires; it is quite another to justify a selection on behalf of a "prototypical" citizen in an "average" structural location with a "standardized" lifestyle. Many definitions of functional literacy adopt a commonsense approach and choose materials on the basis of convenience and wide availability. The USOE definition, quoted earlier, is linked to a list of everyday reading tasks, but there appears to be no systematic criterion of selection by virtue of which the USOE list would be preferred to the infinite number of rival lists that could be proposed.

Similar material selection problems restrict the possibility of generalizing the results of studies by Harris and Associates (1970; 1971) and Sticht, Caylor, Kern, and Fox (1972), none of which has produced a standard of functional literacy demonstrably applicable across the whole of U.S. society. In the Adult Performance Level Study (APL), carried out on behalf of the USOE (*Adult Functional Competency*, 1975), the range of materials was represented by sixty-five items, probably the most comprehensive coverage attempted to date. What emerged from the study, however, was not a unitary standard of functionality but three levels of competence defined in relation to conveniently measurable variables: income, job status, and educational achievement. Only through crude empiricism and political crassness can this trio of variables be accepted as a satisfactory interpretation of social survival. Part of the problem derives from the fact that print is typically an incidental and auxiliary feature of a great many social situations and settings; there are many substitutes for it and strategies for circumventing it. Although it would be an overstatement to say that the material selection problem is insoluble, an adequate solution does not seem imminent.

When we consider the supply side, the USOE, USNRC, and Sticht definitions all heavily emphasize reading skills in attempting to characterize the minimum level of socially useful literacy competence. The USOE list, for instance, includes items like "reading and comprehending a letter from a debtor or creditor" but does not include writing a similar business letter; the only item that does involve writing is the completion of application forms. The USNRC and Sticht formulations are restricted to reading only.

Such a heavy emphasis on reading at the expense of writing raises far-ranging questions about the political and social interests underlying the adult literacy enterprise as a whole. Although the ability to read is a desirable asset in some situations, the exercise of skills like reading labels and instructions, or filling out forms, has a limited capacity to reduce social deprivation or directly to remedy disadvantages such as unemployment, low pay, or inadequate housing. Though rarely stated explicitly, these are the kinds of dysfunctional conditions that the mastery of basic literacy is supposed to ameliorate. This is the promise made not only by the way definitions of functional literacy are formulated, but also by the propaganda and advertising of involved agencies and groups.

How, in practice, could functional competencies achieve so much? As they have been defined, they are adequate to address only a restricted range of printed materials such as instructions, labels, signs, forms, and form letters — types of communication generally intended to elicit passive behaviors or to encourage conformist responses that reproduce or further institutionalize existing social arrangements. It appears that a functional competence has been defined so that it is merely sufficient to bring its possessor within the reach of bureaucratic modes of communication and authority. A literacy congruent with the USNRC's definition, for example, would undoubtedly be in the interests of the State — employers, social service agencies, and authority generally. Its likely net effect would be to domesticate and further subordinate rather than to increase the autonomy and social standing of the previously illiterate person.

Writing, in all but its most rudimentary forms, is omitted from existing conceptions and operationalizations of functional literacy. Yet it is, on the whole, writing competencies that are capable of initiating change. Writing conveys and records innovation, dissent, and criticism; above all, it can give access to political mechanisms and the political process generally, where many of the possibilities for personal and social transformation lie.

The supply side of functional literacy is commonly made operational by criteria such as school-grade completion or reading age. Both of these measures are essentially proxies for the average length of schooling required to reach various levels of proficiency. One objection to these measures is the extremely low level at which the threshold of functionality has conventionally been set. Gray's initial definition suggests successful completion of only three years of schooling, but he also refers to four- and five-year versions (1956, pp. 25-27). UNESCO's choice of fifth-grade level as the international criterion seems to be related to a study of literacy retention in Tagalog, conducted in 1950 in the Philippines (Hunter, with Harman, 1979, p. 16). Even the highest criteria, however, would leave important written materials beyond the comprehension of the (barely) functionally literate adult. A study of thirty-six different leaflets issued by the Department of Health and Social Security in Britain, designed to explain eligibility for social welfare benefits, found a minimum reading age of 13.5 (using the Dale-Chall readability scale), and an average slightly over 16.5 years (Hampson, Note 2, pp. 8-9). An evaluation of the difficulty of selected news items in British national daily newspapers (using the FORCAST formula) indicates a range of required reading ages between 14 and 16.5 years (British Association of Settlements, 1974, p. 7).[6]

There are a series of more fundamental objections to the use of reading age and grade completion as measures of functional literacy. First, the equivalence between a particular threshold of functional proficiency and a particular grade/reading age attainment, even if it could be validly established, would exist only for a particular school system at a particular juncture in time and would have no universality. Second, there are massive differences between school literacy, which largely consists of academic exercises imposed on pupils as a curricular end in itself, and adult literacy, whose instrumental character naturally derives from its capacity to serve adult needs and projects. The use of grade completion and reading ages in adult contexts begs all the questions about the efficiency and relevance of school training as a route to competence that made the notion of a functional literacy necessary in the first instance. The research programs that set out to create an objective, empirically precise, culture-wide standard of functional literacy have not been successful because the concept of functionality they have employed is ambiguous.

CONSIDERING LITERACY IN ITS SOCIAL CONTEXT

The resilience of the concept of functional literacy suggests that it has been fulfilling however imperfectly, a necessary social role. Its rehabilitation is, nevertheless, no simple matter because its defects are the legacy of a great deal of confused thinking about the problems of literacy and illiteracy. At the heart of existing difficulties lies the fact that the conceptual frameworks within which literacy has been understood have been mainly created by reading experts, psychologists, and school teachers, albeit within a political and diplomatic arena. Each of these groups has been preoccupied with the assessment of the individual's capacity to handle the written word. Very occasionally, questions concerning the social distribution of this capacity have been raised (Postman, 1970), but in such cases literacy is still treated as an individual practice, severed and abstracted from the social transactions and institutional activities in which, in adult life at least, it is normally a constituent. Tests of reading ability, for instance, assume that any text whose difficulty has been calibrated can provide a measure of literacy. The particular character of the information the text contains, and its salience to the testee, are treated as irrelevant to a generalized skill in reading. Once the idea of an autonomous, unified, purely linguistic literacy has taken root — as has happened — it becomes difficult to recognize the social context and its importance. The bulk of existing research on reading has been produced within the setting of the school system of developed states. The complexities of the competing cultural and linguistic traditions that exist in developing societies can be overlooked; it becomes easy to assume that literacy evolves naturally from spoken language forms and is diffused in a standard fashion, via schooling, throughout the communications systems of societies.

I have endeavored to challenge this grossly oversimplified and misleading picture by stressing that literacy is a *social* practice, the history and character of which necessarily reflect the prevailing political and structural realities. The principal task of this final section is to offer conceptions of literacy and functional literacy which encourage an appreciation of the social and institutional dimensions of reading and writing.

What does it mean to insist that the significance of literacy or illiteracy must be seen in relation to their cultural and political contexts? To put it quite simply, if we are interested in the broader national and international ramifications of literacy, we must consider the application and exercise of reading and writing skills to specific bodies and types of information. Literacy cannot be reduced to the question of the fluency with which an individual is capable of reading a newspaper; it is also and equally a matter of the information the newspaper contains. It is relevant and necessary to ask such questions as: How reliable are the news reports the paper carries? Is the paper able to print letters from readers critical of the government in office? We cannot afford to ignore the content and functions of written materials; the information they contain is a strategic social resource. The possession or lack of particular kinds of information constitutes a crucial component in the opportunities — or "life chances" — open to social classes; a channel of information is part of each apparatus of social domination.

In light of these considerations, it is necessary to unite literacy's means and ends. Literacy in general, therefore, becomes the exercised capacity to acquire and exchange information via the written word. Functional literacy is taken to be the possession of, or access to, the competences and information required to accomplish those transactions entailing reading or writing in which an individual wishes — or is compelled — to engage.

Thus, the denotation of *illiterate* is greatly widened — people without access to printed material relevant to their information needs, as well as those lacking rudimentary reading and writing skills, now count as illiterate. Furthermore, as Bormuth points out, this new concept of literacy/illiteracy now has the useful property of applying to the producers as well as the consumers of information (1978, p. 123). Authors become illiterate whenever, whether by design or incapacity, the texts they create mystify, mislead, or pass uncomprehended by interested audiences. Illiteracy now covers not only all instances of straightforward failure to acquire or transmit information in a usable form, but also efforts to appropriate and secrete information while ostensibly passing it into the public domain. The new definition of illiteracy embraces some important and perennial social irritants: the small print of legal contracts, ambiguous or faulty labeling of consumer products, the maze of social service regulations and leaflets, and bureaucratic obfuscation in general.

In the case of functional literacy, the new definition accepts that each individual is an expert arbiter of his or her own literacy and information needs. It does not legislate for minimum norms or fixed societal standards, which at present generate a false sense of security for those who achieve them and an unnecessary burden of failure on those who do not. It attempts to avoid inflicting the cultural tastes and standards derived from highly literate social strata on everyone in a community. It also accepts that for many purposes, *access* to skills and information is a very effective substitute for personal possession. In many countries with low rates of literacy, the one member of a household — or even of a village — who can read and write competently can disseminate vital knowledge and procure substantial advantages for the whole community.

By relating literacy to specific kinds of information and particular information needs, the definitions of illiteracy/literacy are antagonistic to the conception of these terms as having a dichotomous, master status. Few individuals, however polyglot or highly educated, have not occasionally needed to read or write in an unfamiliar language. Similarly, most adult literacy tutors know students who can master texts that address their interests, but encounter persistent difficulty with those that are technically no more difficult, but which the student regards as alien and remote. To imply that everyone is illiterate in relation to some kinds of information is not an empty rhetorical device to destigmatize and salve the feelings of those with severe incapacities. Technological developments like the communications revolutions based on microcomputers and fiber optics make it increasingly necessary to talk about an array or hierarchy of literacies. In fact, a diversity of literacies has long been a familiar aspect of multilingual societies.

The information component of the literacy-information dyad can best be understood by treating it, in a phrase of Berger and

Luckmann's, as "everything that passes for knowledge in society" (1971, p. 26). This is not meant to imply that information is all of a kind; having argued that it is necessary to recognize a multiplicity of literacies, it would be foolish to view information as a monolithic entity. The advantage of such a formulation is that it directs our attention to the sociology of knowledge as a potential source of fruitful insights concerning literacy. The social and political significance of literacy is very largely derived from its role in creating and reproducing — or failing to reproduce — the social distribution of knowledge. If this were not so, if literacy did not have this role, the inability to read would be a shortcoming on a par with tone-deafness, while an ability to write would be as socially inconsequential as a facility for whistling in tune.

NOTES

1. In Cook's 1977 bibliography, the earliest item that refers to functionality is an article by F.S. Chase, a section of which is titled "Attack on Functional Illiteracy Among Negro Adults,' *Elementary School Journal*, 1946, 47, pp. 69-70.

2. Gray cited Ministry of Education (Great Britain) *Reading Ability: Some Suggestions for Helping the Backward*, London: HMSO, 1950; J. Duncan, *Backwardness in Reading and Prevention*, London: Harrap, 1953. Neither source contains anything approaching a justification of the equivalence.

3. "Lower grade" refers to job categories located toward the bottom of any plant-wide hierarchy of categories and is no reflection or judgment on the employees who fill the categories. The term is similar to Etzioni's "lower participant" (1961, p. 51).

4. Adequate research directly bearing on this is lacking. There is, however, evidence that basic education students rarely attribute a new job to increased literacy skills (Greenleigh Associates, 1966; Patten & Clark, 1968).

5. The similarities between functional literacy and the notion of subsistence poverty, with which it has strong affinities, are striking. The tradition of reflection on and inquiry about poverty has attempted to elevate poverty above moral dispute and political prejudice by establishing an allegedly scientific and impartial criterion for judgments about who the poor really are. This criterion was taken to lie in the formulation of the supposedly objective, minimum nutritional requirements for the healthy survival of an individual or household of specified composition. As Rein (1970, p. 60) has pointed out, however, every technical procedure for rigorously measuring human material needs necessarily incorporates abstract ideas such as nutritional values, optimum levels of physical activity and ideally rational purchasing strategies. Any rigor and objectivity that the application of such concepts permits derives from their correspondence with the theoretical systems of biochemistry, physiology, and an idealized home economics. A gulf necessarily exists between this theoretical notion of subsistence, defined, say, by a daily calorie intake, and the actual diet that any human group does or could follow. Some technical experts, faced with this gulf, have attempted to ground their abstractions by collecting new or additional data on actual levels of consumption, real preferences, and prevailing

tastes. However, in order to identify relevant and representative samples of income groups from whom to infer levels, preferences, and tastes, a prior criterion of poverty is needed. The subsistence research program is thus trapped in an infinite regress.

6. Dale-Chall and FORCAST are measures of readability based on the numerical assessment of word difficulty and sentence length expressed as "reading age" — the average competence attained by somebody who has the number of years of schooling appropriate to that age (see Gilliland, 1976).

REFERENCE NOTES

1.   Levine, K. Becoming literate (Final rep. *Adult illiteracy and the socialization of adult illiterates*). Department of Sociology, University of Nottingham, 1980.
2.   Hampson, R. *A study of D.H.S.S. leaflets: The language of bureaucracy.* Unpublished thesis, University of Bristol, 1978.

REFERENCES

Adult functional competency: A summary. Austin: Division of Extension, University of Texas, 1975.

Ahmed, M. *Materials for new literates.* New Delhi: Research Training and Production Centre, 1958.

Arrow, K.J. Models of job discrimination. In A.H. Pascal (Ed.), *Racial discrimination in economic life.* Lexington, Mass.: Heath, 1972.

Arrow, K.J. Higher education as a filter. *Journal of Public Economics*, 1973, **2**, 193-216.

Bataille, L. (Ed.). *A turning point for literacy.* Oxford: Pergamon Press, 1976.

Becker, G.S. *The economics of discrimination* (2nd ed.). Chicago: University of Chicago Press, 1971.

Becker, G.S. *Human capital* (2nd ed.). New York: Columbia University Press, 1975.

Berger, P.L., & Luckmann, T. *The social construction of reality.* Harmondsworth, Eng.: Penguin Books, 1971.

Blackburn, R.M. & Mann, M. *The working class in the labour market.* London: Macmillan, 1979.

Blaug, M. Literacy and economic development. *The School Review*, 1966, **74**, 393-418.

Bormuth, J.R. Value and volume of literacy. *Visible Language*, 1978, **12**, 118-62.

British Association of Settlements. *A right to read.* London: Author, 1974.

Committee on Plan Projects of the Government of India. *Report on social education.* New Delhi: Government Printing Office, 1963.

Cook, W.D. *Adult literacy education in the United States.* Newark, Del.: International Reading Association, 1977.

Deutsch, K.W. Social mobilization and political development. *American Political Science Review*, 1961, **55**, 493-514.

Etzioni, A. *A comparative analysis of complex organizations.* New York: Free Press, 1961.

Gilliland, J. *Readability.* London: Hodder & Stoughton, 1976.

Golden, H.H. Illiteracy and urban industrialization. In *World illiteracy at mid-century.* Paris: UNESCO, 1957.

Gray, W.S. *The teaching of reading and writing.* Paris: UNESCO, 1956.

Greenleigh Associates. *Field test and evaluation of selected adult basic education systems.* New York: Author, 1966.

Harman, D. Illiteracy: An overview. *Harvard Educational Review,* 1970, **40,** 226-243.

Harris, L., and Associates. *Survival literacy study.* (No. 2036). New York: Author, 1970.

Harris, L., and Associates. *The 1971 national reading difficulty index.* New York: Author, 1971.

Hirsch, F. *Social limits to growth.* London: Routledge & Kegan Paul, 1977.

Hoselitz, B.F. Investment in education and its political impact. In J.S. Coleman (Ed.), *Education and political development.* Princeton: Princeton University Press, 1965.

Hunter, C. St. J., with Harman, D. *Adult illiteracy in the United States: A report to the Ford Foundation.* New York: McGraw-Hill, 1979.

International Bureau of Education. *Literacy and education for adults* (27th International Conference on Public Education, Geneva, 1964). Paris: Author and UNESCO, 1964.

Jeffries, C. *Illiteracy: A world problem.* London: Pall Mall Press, 1967.

Lerner, D. *The passing of traditional society.* New York: Free Press, 1958.

Lipset, S.M. Some social requisites of democracy: Economic development and political legitimacy. *American Political Science Review.* 1959, **53,** 3-14.

Nafziger, D., Thompson, R.B., Hiscox, M.D., & Owen, T.R. *Tests of functional adult literacy: An evaluation of currently available instruments.* Portland, Ore.: Northwest Regional Educational Laboratory, 1975.

Parsons, T. *Societies: Evolutionary and comparative perspectives.* Englewood Cliffs, N.J.: Prentice-Hall, 1966.

Patten, T.H., & Clark, C.E., Jr. Literacy training of hard-core unemployed Negroes in Detroit. *Journal of Human Resources,* 1968, **2,** 25-36.

Postman, N. The politics of reading. *Harvard Educational Review,* 1970, **40,** 224-252.

Rein, M. Problems in the definition and measurement of poverty. In P. Townsend (Ed.). *The concept of poverty.* London: Heinemann, 1970.

Schultz, T.W. Capital formation by education. *Journal of Political Economy,* 1960, **68,** 571-583.

Schultz, T.W. *The economic value of education.* New York: Columbia University Press, 1963.

Schuman, H., Inkeles, A., & Smith, D.H. Some social psychological effects and non-effects of illiteracy in a new nation. *Economic Development and Cultural Change,* 1967, **16,** 1-14.

Sticht, T.G., Caylor, J.S., Kern, R.P. & Fox, L.C. Project Realistic: Determination of adult functional literacy levels. *Reading Research Quarterly,* 1972, **7,** 424-465.

Strumilin, S. The economics of education in the U.S.S.R. In *Economic and social aspects of educational planning,* Paris: UNESCO, 1964.

UNESCO. *Fundamental education: Common ground for all peoples.* New York: Macmillan, 1947.

UNESCO. *Fundamental education: A description and programme. Monographs on Fundamental Education No. 1.* Paris: Author, 1949.

UNESCO. *World illiteracy at mid-century.* Paris: Author, 1957.

UNESCO. *World conference of ministers of education on the eradication of illiteracy* (Final Report). Paris: Author, 1965.

UNESCO. *An Asian model of educational development: Perspectives for 1965-80.* Paris: Author, 1966.

UNESCO. *The concept of functional literacy and its application* (Turin Round Table

22-24th April). Mimeo, ED/WS/170. 1970.

UNESCO. *Practical guide to functional literacy: A method of training for development.* Paris: Author, 1973.

UNESCO. *The experimental world literacy programme: A critical assessment.* Paris: Author, 1976.

UNESCO. *Estimates and projections of illiteracy.* Paris: Author, 1978.

6.4 The Comprehension Revolution: a Twenty-year History of Process Related to Reading Comprehension

P. DAVID PEARSON

The purpose of this essay is to characterize the patterns of development in [...] theory and research about basic processes in reading comprehension [...]. I begin by trying to characterize our knowledge and beliefs in the period from 1965-1970. Then I try to answer the question, What have we learned since 1970? Finally, I speculate what the future holds for us in terms of possible advances in our knowledge [...].

THE SCENE IN 1970

In 1970, our knowledge of reading comprehension was fairly well defined by four research strands: readability, the cloze procedure, factor analytic studies, and, the child-bride of the field, psycholinguistics.

Readability research (studying what made texts easy or difficult to understand) by that time had a history of 35 to 40 years stemming back to Gray and Leary (1935) and Lorge (1939) in the thirties, carried on by Flesch (1948) into the forties and George Klare (1963) into the fifties and sixties. Basically what the research told us was that long words and long complex sentences were hard to understand. But we were not sure why. We did not know whether long words and sentences caused, or were merely symptoms of, content that was hard to read for other reasons, such as concept density.

The cloze technique (a procedure in which one deletes every

Source: Edited from Pearson, P.D. (1985) *The Comprehension Revolution: a Twenty-year History of Process and Practice Related to Reading Comprehension* (Reading Education Report No. 57), Urbana, University of Illinois Center for the Study of Reading.

443

5th or 10th or nth word in a test and requires students to guess what fits in the resulting blanks) had been with us for a decade and a half. Taylor (1954), Rankin (1965), and Bormuth (1967, 1969) had used it to great advantage in refining research in comprehension and readability. If nothing else, we knew that we had a good dependent variable for measuring comprehension: It was objective (it did not depend on a test writer's judgment about what questions were important to ask), easy to score, and highly reliable.

It is probably fair to say that Davis (1944) made factor analysis studies (factor analytic studies try to determine whether different tests measure the same or different underlying trait(s)) of reading comprehension respectable. Between 1944 and 1969 several important factor analytic studies of reading comprehension all shared the common purpose of trying to isolate independent components of reading comprehension. All found only a few factors, such as word difficulty and reasoning, to be independent components of reading comprehension.

If readability, cloze, and factor analytic studies represented the conventional wisdom concerning reading comprehension, then psycholinguistics (the interface between psychology and linguistics) was the hope of the future. Simons' (1971) review of reading comprehension reflected this hope. After reviewing and discussing the conventional perspectives on reading comprehension, Simons raised the banner of transformational grammar as the guiding light of the future.

Psycholinguistics had tremendous, immediate, and unprecedented appeal. Part of its appeal stemmed from the impact that Chomsky's (1957) views had on the psychology of language in the decade of the sixties. Based upon studies like those of Miller and Isard (1963), Mehler (1963), Gough (1965), and Slobin (1966), there was a genuine feeling that behavioristic views of language development and processing would have to be replaced by views that were both nativistic (people are born with a genetic capability to learn language) and cognitive (admitting that there is more than a blank black box in the brain) in orientation. Furthermore, these research studies seemed to suggest that the transformational generative grammar created by Chomsky might actually serve as a model of human language processing. Thus, there was a ready-made theory waiting to be applied to reading comprehension. And psycholinguistics commanded academic respectability. There was something invigorating about standing on the shoulders of the new psychology, working within a paradigm for which there was a model that made fairly precise predictions and, thus, had testable hypotheses.

Beginning in the late sixties and extending into the mid-seventies, considerable empirical and theoretical work was completed within the psycholinguistic tradition. The influence of psycholinguistics on reading is nowhere better demonstrated than in the work of Kenneth Goodman (1965) and Frank Smith (1971). For both Goodman and Smith, looking at reading from a psycholinguistic perspective meant looking at reading in its natural state, as an application of a person's general cognitive and linguistic competence. It seems odd even to mention their names in discussing the influence of psycholinguistics on comprehension research because neither Goodman nor Smith distinguishes between reading and reading comprehension. Their failure to make the distinction is deliberate, for they would argue that reading *is* comprehending (or that reading without comprehending is *not* reading). Similarly, a distinction between word identification and comprehension would seem arbitrary to them.

For others, the influence of the psycholinguistic tradition (particularly the use of transformational-generative grammar as a psychological model) on views of reading comprehension was quite direct. The work of Bormuth (1966, 1969), Bormuth, Manning, Carr, and Pearson (1971), Fagan (1971), and Pearson (1974-75) reveals a rather direct use of psycholinguistic notions in studying reading comprehension.

Such was the scene in the early seventies. The conventional modes of research, while still strong, were being challenged by a new interloper from the world of linguistic research — psycholinguistics [...].

WHAT WE HAVE LEARNED SINCE 1970

The force behind the shift from behavioristic to cognitive views of language was a linguist, Noam Chomsky. He exposed the prevailing views on the psychology of language for their gross inadequacies and provided an alternative model (transformational grammar) of language processing. Fittingly, the motive force behind the exodus from a narrow psycholinguistic view based upon transformational grammars was another linguist, Charles Fillmore. In 1968, he published a paper in which he argued for the resurrection of a centuries-old case grammar approach to linguistic explanation. Case grammars are based upon the different relationships between the verb in the sentence and the case (nominative, accusative, recipient, etc.) that the nouns take in relationship to the verb.

Fillmore's case grammar was appealing to psychologists and educators who were experiencing great difficulty with models of comprehension based upon a transformational generative grammar. Those very models that had seemed to be sensible and alluring only five years earlier had not withstood tests of empirical verification. With their emphasis on transformations to realize a variety of surface structures from a single deep structure, transformational models had to stress an analytic view of comprehension. Yet researchers (e.g., Bransford & Franks, 1971) were collecting data that indicated that comprehension consisted of synthesis (integrating ideas) rather than analysis (decomposing ideas). Other researchers (e.g., Sachs, 1967) found that comprehension and recognition memory seemed to be more sensitive to semantic rather than syntactic factors, contrary to the emphasis in a transformational model. Still others, like Pearson (1974-1975), found that the predictions from a derivational theory of complexity (i.e., the theory that comprehension difficulty varies as a function of the number of transformations necessary to travel from the surface structure of a sentence to its deep structure) were exactly the opposite of results obtained in several comprehension studies.

In such a milieu, something like Fillmore's case grammar was quite appealing; it emphasized synthesis rather than analysis and semantic rather than syntactic relations. In addition, case grammar allowed one to begin to examine relations that held between linguistic ideas that crossed sentence boundaries.

The psycholingusitic tradition, based as it was on Chomsky's transformational grammar, had concentrated upon the sentence as the basic unit of analysis. Somewhere in the early to mid-seventies, the proposition (basically, a verb plus the nouns, adjectives, and adverbs that go along with it) replaced the sentence as the basic unit of analysis. Researchers in artificial intelligence began using it in the early seventies (Minsky, 1975; Schank, 1973). Lindsay and Norman (1972) discussed propositions in their revolutionary experimental psychology textbook. Kintsch (1974), Rumelhart

(1975), Frederiksen (1975), Thorndyke (1977), and Stein and Glenn (1977) were all using propositions to parse texts and analyze recall protocols by the mid to late 1970s.

The proposition fits nicely with an emphasis on case grammar. Just as the verb is the center of a proposition [another way of defining a proposition is as a predicate (active or stative verb) and its arguments (nouns, adjectives, adverbs)], so the verb is the central node in a case grammar parsing (parsing is a sort of fancy diagramming) of a sentence. All other form classes revolve around the verb. Also, many of the case relations in a case grammar are really relations among propositions (e.g., cause, condition, time, manner).

As we moved into the late 1970s, no new revolutions occurred; fine tuning better characterizes what took place. The perspective that spawned case grammars and propositions persisted, but the problems researchers addressed changed substantially. In the early 1970s text researchers were still preoccupied with relations within and between sentences, and their research reflected this emphasis on what we have come to call "microstructure." Text researchers in the late 1970s were more concerned about relations that obtain between whole episodes in stories or whole paragraphs or sections in informative text; we have come to call this more holistic emphasis "macrostructure." Accompanying this shift in the study of text was a shift in the study of how human memory is organized, in particular how humans are able to store and retrieve large bodies of information. This latter movement came to be called "schema theory."

Researchers in this period tended to fall into two categories: those who tried to characterize relations among ideas in texts and those who have tried to characterize relations among ideas stored in human memory. Neither group denied the importance or necessity of the other's work; each group simply chose to emphasize one area over the other. Hence, researchers like Rumelhart (1975), Stein and Glenn (1977), and Thorndyke (1977) gave us plausible macrostructures for narrative material in the form of story grammars. Researchers like Meyer (1975) or Halliday and Hasan (1976) tried to provide more general structural accounts that would apply equally well to expositions. Alternatively, the work of Schank (1973), Minsky (1975), Anderson (1977), and Rumelhart (1980; Rumelhart & Ortony, 1977) was more concerned with the structure of knowledge within the human processors (i.e., readers). Still others, such as Kintsch (1974) or Frederiksen (1975) seemed to be trying to provide a balanced emphasis on text and knowledge structure. These differences are more a matter of degree than kind. All of the researchers were concerned with human information processing; they simply tended to emphasize different aspects of the processing. Therefore, researchers focusing on the structure of the text were likely to emphasize something like the number of high level propositions within the story that were recalled. Conversely, those emphasizing the structure of the reader's knowledge were more likely to dwell upon something like non-textual inferences made during recall or how a reader's prior knowledge determines aspects of the text that will be remembered. Put differently, the former group were likely to highlight text structures while the latter group were likely to highlight knowledge structures.

Sometime during the late seventies, a new interloper burst onto the research stage, bearing the cumbersome but intellectually appealing label of metacognition. It seemed a logical extension of the rapidly developing work on both schema theory and text analysis. These latter two traditions emphasized *declarative* knowledge, knowing *that* X or Y or Z is true, but were scant on specifying *procedural* knowledge, knowing *how* to engage a strategy for comprehension or memory (see Gavelek, in press; Paris, in press; or Schwartz, in press). This is precisely the kind of knowledge that metacognitive research has emphasized. The key words associated with metacognition reveal its emphasis: awareness, monitoring, control, and evaluation.

Two parallel strands of research dominated the early work in metacognition. The first, metamemory research, is most typically associated with John Flavell and his associates at Stanford. They have discovered that along with the capacity to remember more information, human beings develop tacit and explicit strategies for remembering. The second line of research, metacomprehension, is more typically associated with Ann Brown and Joe Campione and their colleagues at Illinois, and more recently with Ellen Markman at Stanford and with Scott Paris at Michigan. It emphasizes the strategies that readers use while they are reading as they monitor, evaluate, and repair their comprehension of written text. This line of research has grown so rapidly that it has been reviewed several times within the last few years (Wagoner, 1983; Paris, Lipson, & Wixson, 1983; Baker & Brown, 1984).

Given the tremendous outpouring of research on basic processes in comprehension since the mid-seventies, it is fair to ask what we have learned from it all. The answer, I think, is that we have learned a considerable amount. We view comprehension very differently from the way we did in 1970. Our knowledge is both more extensive and more refined. Here is a sampling of some insights that we have gained.

Prior knowledge (in the form of schemata) influences our comprehension to a much greater degree than earlier research would have suggested. Anderson (1984) has summarized the influences that schemata play in our comprehension in these generalizations (these are close paraphrases of Anderson's assertions):

1. Schemata provide ideational scaffolding for assimilating text information. Schemata have slots that readers expect to be filled with information in a text. Information that fills those slots is easily learned and remembered.

2. Schemata facilitate the selective allocation of attention. Put simply, schemata guide our search for what is important in a text, allowing us to separate the wheat from the chaff.

3. Schemata enable inferential elaboration. No text is ever fully explicit. Schemata allow us to make educated guesses about how certain slots must have been filled.

4. Schemata allow for orderly searches of memory. For example, suppose a person is asked to remember what he did at a recent cocktail party. He can use his cocktail party schema, a specification of what usually happens at cocktail parties, to recall what he ate, what he drank, who he talked to, and so on.

5. Schemata facilitate editing and summarizing. By definition, any schema possesses its own criteria of what is important. These can be used to create summaries of text that focus on important information.

6. Schemata permit inferential reconstruction. If readers have a gap in their memory, they can use a schema, in conjunction with the information recalled, to generate hypotheses about missing information. If they can recall, for example, that the entree was beef, they can infer that the beverage was likely to have been red wine.

So powerful is the influence of prior knowledge on comprehension that Johnston and Pearson (1982; see also, Johnston, 1984) have found that prior knowledge of topic is a better predictor of comprehension than is either an intelligence test score or a reading achievement test score.

Reading is a dynamic, interactive process. To use the language of Collins, Brown, and Larkin (1979), as we read, we are constantly revising our model of what the text means. To view an individual's comprehension of a text as an inadequate reproduction of the original text misses the whole point about the reader's enormous contribution to the comprehension process.

Reading involves the use of many different kinds of knowledge. We have already discussed two of these, declarative and procedural knowledge. Recall that declarative knowledge, knowing *that*, includes our knowledge of the world at large and our knowledge of the world of text (prototypical structures and authorial devices); recall that procedural knowledge, knowing *how*, includes the strategies we use to become aware of, monitor, evaluate, and repair our comprehension. To these, Paris (Paris, in press; Paris, Lipson, & Wixson, 1983) argues convincingly that we should add conditional knowledge, knowing *when* and *why* to call up a particular strategy to aid our comprehension. The point is that we cannot characterize comprehension processes without including all of these kinds of knowledge.

Reading and writing are a lot more similar in process than we had ever thought. Traditionally, in comparing the language arts, we have tended to think of reading and writing as mirror images of one another — that when we read, we more or less *undo* what writers do when they write. Even the attributes we assign to them — productive versus receptive language — reflect this oppositional view. While the research base arguing for the similarity rather than the difference between reading and writing is weak (see Hansen, in press; Tierney, Leys, & Rogers, in press), many theorists have begun to emphasize essential similarities (e.g., Murray, 1982; Tierney & Pearson, 1983; Pearson & Tierney, 1984). Even though strict comparative research is just beginning, one can make the argument for similarity by examining the conclusions permitted from research on the role that schemata play in comprehension. Notice that terms like constructive and reconstructive processes are used to describe what we know about comprehension; these are the very terms writing researchers use to describe the writing process [...].

Pedagogical experiments. Since 1975, a renaissance has taken place in instructional research, and most of the work has been directed toward the development of reading comprehension strategies. While it is beyond the scope of this overview to review that research in depth (see Pearson & Gallagher, 1983, or Tierney & Cunningham, 1984, for complete summaries), the following is a summary of the conclusions that I believe are permitted from this research.

1. Students understand stories better if they are asked questions that focus on integrating story parts than if they are asked questions that do not have a focus (e.g., Beck, Omanson, & McKeown, 1982; Gordon & Pearson, 1983; Singer & Donlan, 1982; Tharp, 1982).

2. Students understand informational texts better if discussions are guided by an attempt to help them see how all the pieces of information in a text fit together than if discussions are guided by a close but piecemeal interrogation of the main points and facts (Gallagher & Pearson, 1983).

3. Vocabulary instruction that focuses on building rich semantic networks of related concepts facilitates transferable growth in both vocabulary and comprehension. It is even better than either a definitional or a context approach (Beck, Perfetti, & McKeown, 1982; Johnson, Toms-Bronowski, & Pittleman, in press; Schachter, 1978).

4. Vocabulary growth is also facilitated by simply reading; however, it is likely that such growth is better characterized as the development of what Isabel Beck (1984) calls an "acquaintanceship" with words rather than "ownership" of concepts (Nagy, Herman, Anderson, & Pearson, 1984).

5. Building background knowledge prior to reading facilitates comprehension of the upcoming story or article, *and* it helps to develop a set within students for learning and evaluating new material in terms of what they already know (Hansen, 1981; Hansen & Pearson, 1983).

6. Teaching the so-called comprehension skills in a model that begins with a fairly heavy reliance on the teacher and builds toward student independence and ownership *and* that includes demonstrations of how to perform the skill is superior to a model that emphasizes practice, assessment, and more practice (Baumann, in press; Gordon & Pearson, 1983; Palincsar &

Brown, 1984; Raphael & Pearson, in press; Raphael & Wonnacutt, in press).

7. Approaches that emphasize students' awareness of their own strategies suggest alternative strategies and help students learn techniques for self-monitoring result in sizable gains in comprehension performance (Palincsar & Brown, 1984; Paris, in press).

8. Approaches that emphasize inferential thinking result in greater growth in inferential thinking (at no loss to and sometimes a gain in literal comprehension) than do approaches that emphasize literal comprehension (Gordon & Pearson, 1983; Hansen, 1981; Hansen & Pearson, 1983).

Of these conclusions, numbers 6 and 7, both of which speak to the promise of explicit instruction in comprehension strategies, deserve special emphasis. In a sense, the studies that support these conclusions justify Durkin's (1978-79) concern about the lack of comprehension instruction in intermediate grade classrooms, for they suggest that student performance improves when teachers take the time and effort to help students learn *how* and *why* and *when* they should perform some of the complex comprehension and problem solving tasks that we require of them in schools [...].

SOME FUTURE HISTORY

The schema theory tradition has provided us with an alternative world view about comprehension processes. But it has emphasized the effect of existing knowledge on comprehension. In the future, researchers will turn their attention to the more difficult question of schema acquisition, or, if you will, the effect of comprehension on knowledge. We will look more carefully at what Bransford, Nitsch, and Franks (1977) identified as the issue of "changing states of schema." And when we do, we will, of course, be returning to a recurrent theme in psychology usually labelled "learning." A vital component of this work on schema acquisition will focus on the issue of vocabulary (it has, in fact, begun — see Nagy & Anderson, in press; and Nagy, Herman, Anderson, & Pearson, 1984), for we will finally recognize that words are but the surface representations of our knowledge.

The text analysis tradition will change its focus also. Now that we can do a decent job of parsing texts to characterize underlying relations among ideas, we will turn to an age-old issue, What makes a text readable? And our search will be guided by principles very different from long sentences and hard words. In their place, we will substitute principles that come under the label of considerateness (see Armbruster & Anderson, 1981, 1982, 1984); these principles will emphasize whether authors provide frameworks for interrelating ideas, analogies that permit cross-topical comparisons, and examples that solidify concept acquisition.

Schema-theoretic and text-analysis traditions will merge so as to become indistinguishable from one another. This event will result from our discovery that the goal of every author is the same as the goal of every reader — to represent knowledge in as coherent a framework as possible.

We will learn much more about basic relationships between reading and writing, more specifically between comprehension and composing strategies. The promise of an exciting integrated view of language processes, expressed so eloquently by many in recent years, will finally reach fruition.

Finally, we will develop the grace and good judgment necessary to overcome our tendency to debate whether reading is a word-based or a meaning-based process so that we can come to understand the intrinsic relationship between growth in comprehension strategies and growth in word identification abilities, particularly in beginning reading [...].

REFERENCES

Anderson, R.C. (1977). The notion of schemata and the educational enterprise. In R.C. Anderson, R.J. Spiro, & W. E. Montague (Eds.), *Schooling and the acquisition of knowledge.* Hillsdale, NJ: Erlbaum.

Anderson, R.C. (1984). Role of the reader's schema in comprehension, learning, and memory, In R.C. Anderson, J. Osborn, & R.J. Tierney (Eds.), *Learning to read in American schools.* Hillsdale, NJ: Erlbaum.

Armbruster, B.B., & Anderson, T.H. (1981). *Content area textbooks* (Reading Education Rep. No. 23). Urbana: University of Illinois, Center for the Study of Reading; (ERIC Document Reproduction Service No. EB203 298).

—— (1982). *Structures for explanations in history textbooks, or so what if Governor Stanford missed the spike and hit the nail?* (Tech. Rep. No. 252). Urbana: University of Illinois, Center for the Teaching of Reading.

—— (1984). *Producing considerate expository text: or easy reading is damned hard writing.* (Reading Education Rep. No. 46). Urbana: University of Illinois, Center for the Teaching of Reading.

Baker, L., & Brown, A.L. (1984). Metacognitive skills of reading. In P.D. Pearson

(Ed.), *Handbook of reading research*. New York: Longmans.

Baumann, J.F. (in press). The effectiveness of a direct instructional paradigm for teaching main idea comprehension. *Reading Research Quarterly.*

Beck. I.L. (1984). Developing comprehension: The impact of the directed reading lesson. In R.C. Anderson, J. Osborn, & R.J. Tierney (Eds.), *Learning to read in American schools*. Hillsdale, NJ: Erlbaum.

Beck, I.L., Omanson, R.C., & McKeown, M.G. (1982). An instructional redesign of reading lessons: Effects on reading comprehension. *Reading Research Quarterly, 17*, 462-481.

Beck, I.L., Perfetti, C.A., & McKeown, M.G. (1982). The effects of long-term vocabular instruction on lexical access and reading comprehension. *Journal of Educational Psychology, 74*, 506-521.

Bormuth, J.R. (1966). Readability: A new approach. *Reading Research Quarterly, 1*, 79-132.

Bormuth, J.R. (1967). *Implications and use of cloze procedure in the evaluation of instructional programs* (Occasional Rep. No. 3). Los Angeles: University of California, Center for the Study of Evaluation of Instructional Programs.

Bormuth, J.R. (1969). An operational definition of comprehension instruction. In K.S. Goodman & J.F. Fleming (Eds.), *Psycholinguistics and the teaching of reading*. Newark, DE: International Reading Association.

Bormuth, J.R., Manning, J.C., Carr, J.W., & Pearson, P.D. (1971). Children's comprehension of between- and within-sentence syntactic structures. *Journal of Educational Psychology, 61*, 349-357.

Bransford, J.D., & Franks, J.J. (1971). The abstraction of linguistic ideas. *Cognitive Psychology, 2*, 331-350.

Bransford, J.D., Nitsch, K.E., & Franks, J.F. (1977). Schooling and the facilitation of knowledge. In R.C. Anderson, R.J. Spiro, & W.E. Montague (Eds.), *Schooling and the acquisition of knowledge*. Hillsdale, NJ: Erlbaum.

Chomsky, N. (1957). *Syntactic structures*. The Hague: Mouton.

Collins, A., Brown, J.S., & Larkin, K.M. (1979). Inference in text understanding. In R.J. Spiro, B.C. Bruce, & W.F. Brewer (Eds.), *Theoretical issues in reading comprehension*. Hillsdale, NJ: Erlbaum.

Davis, F.B. (1944). Fundamental factors of comprehension in reading. *Psychometrika, 9*, 185-197.

Durkin, D. (1978-79). What classroom observations reveal about reading comprehension instruction. *Reading Research Quarterly*, 14, 481-533.

Fagan, W.T. (1971). Transformations and comprehension. *The Reading Teacher, 25*, 169-172.

Fillmore, C. (1968). The case for case. In E. Bach & R.G. Harms (Eds.), *Universals in linguistic theory*. New York: Holt, Rinehart & Winston.

Flesch, R.F. (1948). A new readability yardstick. *Journal of Applied Psychology, 32*, 221-233.

Frederiksen, C.H. (1975). Representing logical and semantic structure of knowledge acquired from discourse. *Cognitive Psychology, 7*, 371-458.

Gallagher, M.C., & Pearson, P.D. (1983). *Fourth grade students' acquisition of new information from text*, National Reading Conference, Austin, TX.

Gavelek, J.R. (in press). The social contexts of literacy and schooling: A developmental perspective. In T.E. Raphael & R. Reynolds (Eds.), *Contexts of school-based literacy*. New York: Longmans.

Goodman, K.S. (1965). A linguistic study of cues and miscues in reading. *Elementary English, 42*, 639-643.

Gordon, C., & Pearson, P.D. (1983, June). *The effects of instruction in metacomprehension and inferencing on children's comprehension abilities* (Tech. Rep. No. 277). Urbana: University of Illinois, Center for the Study of Reading.

Gough, P.B. (1965). Grammatical transformations and speed of understanding.

Journal of Verbal Learning and Verbal Behavior, 4, 107-111.

Gray, W.S., & Leary, B.E. (1935). *What makes a book readable: An initial study.* Chicago: The University of Chicago Press.

Halliday, M.A.K., & Hasan, R. (1976). *Cohesion in English.* London: Longmans.

Hansen, J. (1981). The effects of inference training and practice on young children's reading comprehension. *Reading Research Quarterly, 16,* 391-417.

Hansen, J. (in press) Learners work together. In T.E. Raphael & R. Reynolds (Eds.), *Contexts of school-based literacy.* New York: Longmans.

Hansen, J., & Pearson, P.D. (1983). An instructional study: Improving the inferential comprehension of fourth grade good and poor readers. *Journal of Educational Psychology, 75,* 821-829.

Johnson, D.D., Toms-Bronowski, S., & Pittleman, S. (in press). An investigation of the effectiveness of semantic mapping and semantic feature analysis on vocabulary acquisition and retention. *Reading Research Quarterly.*

Johnston, P. (1984). Prior knowledge and reading comprehension test bias. *Reading Research Quarterly, 19,* 219-239.

Johnston, P., & Pearson, P.D. (1982, June). *Prior knowledge, connectivity, and the assessment of reading comprehension* (Tech. Rep. No. 245). Urbana: University of Illinois, Center for the Study of Reading.

Kintsch, W. (1974). *The representation of meaning in memory.* Hillsdale, NJ: Erlbaum.

Klare, G. (1963). *The measurement of readability.* Ames: Iowa State University Press.

Lindsay, P., & Norman, D. (1972). *Human information processing.* New York: Academic Press.

Lorge, I. (1939). Predicting reading difficulty of selections for children. *Elementary English Review, 16,* 229-233.

Mehler J. (1963). Some effects of grammatical transformations on the recall of English sentences. *Journal of Verbal Learning and Verbal Behavior, 2,* 346-351.

Meyer, B.J.F. (1975). *The organization of prose and its effects on memory.* Amsterdam: North-Holland Publishing.

Miller, G.A., & Isard, S. (1963). Some perceptual consequences of linguistic rules. *Journal of Verbal Learning and Verbal Behavior, 2,* 217-228.

Minsky, M.A. (1975). A framework for representing knowledge. In P. Winston (Ed.), *The psychology of computer vision.* New York: McGraw Hill.

Murray, D.M. (1982). Teaching the other self: The writer's first reader. *College Composition and Communication, 33,* 140-147.

Nagy, W.E., & Anderson, R.C. (in press). How many words are there in printed school English? *Reading Research Quarterly.*

Nagy, W.E., Herman, P.H., Anderson, R.C., & Pearson, P.D. (1984). *Learning words from context* (Tech. Rep. No. 319). Urbana: University of Illinois, Center for the Study of Reading.

Palincsar, A.M., & Brown, A.L. (1984). Reciprocal teaching of comprehension-fostering and comprehension-monitoring activities. *Cognition and Instruction, 1,* 117-175.

Paris, S. (in press). Teaching children to guide their reading and learning. In T.E. Raphael & R. Reynolds (Eds.), *Contexts of school-based literacy.* New York: Longmans.

Paris, S., Lipson, M., & Wixson, K. (1983). Becoming a strategic reader. *Contemporary Educational Psychology, 8,* 293-316.

Pearson, P.D. (1974-75). The effects of grammatical complexity of children's comprehension, recall, and conception of certain semantic relations. *Reading Research Quarterly, 10,* 155-192.

Pearson, P.D., & Gallagher, M.C. (1983). The instruction of reading comprehension. *Contemporary Educational Psychology, 8,* 317-344.

Pearson, P.D., & Tierney, R.J. (1984). On becoming a thoughtful reader: Learning to read like a writer. In A. Purves & O. Niles (Eds.), *Becoming readers in a complex society*. Chicago: National Society for the Study of Education, 144-173.

Rankin, E. (1965). Cloze procedure — a survey of research, *Yearbook of the South West Reading Conference, 14*, 133-148.

Raphael, T.E., & Pearson, P.D. (in press). Increasing students' awareness of sources of information for answering questions. *American Educational Research Journal.*

Raphael, T.E., & Wonnacutt, C.A. (in press). Metacognitive training in question-answering strategies: Implementation in a fourth grade developmental reading program. *Reading Research Quarterly.*

Rumelhart, D.E. (1975). Notes on schema for stories. In D.G. Bobrow & A.M. Collins (Eds.), *Representation and understanding: Studies in cognitive science*. New York: Academic Press.

Rumelhart, D.E. (1980). Schemata: The building blocks of cognition. In R.J. Spiro, B.C. Bruce, & W.F. Brewer (Eds.), *Theoretical issues in reading comprehension*. Hillsdale, NJ: Erlbaum.

Rumelhart, D.E., & Ortony, A. (1977). The representation of knowledge and memory. In R.C. Anderson, R.J. Spiro, & W.E. Montague (Eds.), *Schooling and the acquisition of knowledge*. Hillsdale, NJ: Erlbaum.

Sachs, J.S. (1967). Recognition memory for syntactic and semantic aspects of connected discourse. *Perception and Psychophysics, 2*, 437-442.

Schachter, S. (1978). *An investigation of the effects of vocabulary and schemata orientation upon reading comprehension*. Unpublished doctoral dissertation, University of Minnesota.

Schank, R.C. (1973). Identification of conceptualizations underlying natural language. In R.C. Schank & K.M. Colby (Eds.), *Computer models of thoughts and language*. San Francisco: Freeman.

Schwartz, R.M. (in press). Teachers' classroom learning: Toward the development of expertise in reading instruction. In T.E. Raphael & R. Reynolds (Eds.), *Contexts of school-based literacy*. New York: Longmans.

Simons, H.D. (1971). Reading comprehension: The need for a new perspective. *Reading Research Quarterly, 5*, 338-363.

Singer, H., & Donlan, D. (1982). Active comprehension: Problem solving schema with question generation for comprehension of complex short stories. *Reading Research Quarterly, 17*, 166-186.

Slobin, D.T. (1966). Grammatical transformations and sentence comprehension in childhood and adulthood. *Journal of Verbal Learning and Verbal Behavior, 5*, 219-227.

Smith, F. (1971). *Understanding reading: A psycholinguistic analysis of reading and learning to read*. New York: Holt, Rinehart & Winston.

Stein, N.L., & Glenn, C.G. (1977, March). *A developmental study of children's construction of stories*. Paper presented at the Society for Research in Child Development meetings, New Orleans.

Taylor, W. (1954). *Application of "cloze" and entropy measures to the study of contextual constraint in samples of continuous prose*. Unpublished doctoral dissertation, University of Illinois at Urbana-Champaign.

Tharp, R.C. (1982). The effective instruction of comprehension: Results and description of the Kamehameha Early Education Program. *Reading Research Quarterly, 17*, 503-527.

Thorndyke, P.W. (1977). Cognitive structures in comprehension and memory of narrative discourse. *Cognitive Psychology, 9*, 77-110.

Tierney, R.J., & Cunningham, J. (1984). Research on teaching reading comprehension. In P.D. Pearson (Ed.), *Handbook of reading research*. New York: Longmans.

Tierney, R.J., Leys, M., & Rogers, T. (in press). Comprehension, composition, and collaboration: Analyses of communication influences in two classrooms. In T.E. Raphael & R. Reynolds (Eds.), *Contexts of school-based literacy*. New York: Longmans.

Tierney, R.J. & Pearson, P.D. (1983). Toward a composing model of reading. *Language Arts, 60*, 568-580.

Wagoner, S. (1983). Comprehension monitoring: What it is and what we know about it. *Reading Research Quarterly, 18* (3), 328-341.

INDEX

accents 64-72
   convergence of 66-8
address, rules of 169-73
agnosia 26-7
Ahmed, M. 423
Altmann, S.A. 3, 5-10
American Sign Language (ASL)
   12-14, 19-20
Anderson, R.C. 447, 449, 451-3
apes *see* primates
aphasia 24-6
Applebee, A.N. 385
Argyle, M. 64, 239, 313-22
Armbruster, B.B. 453
Arrow, K.J. 429
Atkins, B.K. 146, 205-17
Augustine, St 248-9
Aull, C.H. 122
Austin, J.L. 253

Baker, L. 448
Baldwin, James 153
Barnes, D. 369, 371-4, 376, 384-5
Barth, E. 109
Barthes, R. 258
Bataille, L. 426
Battison, R. 12
Baumann, J.F. 451
Baxter, L. 318
Beck, I.L. 451
Becker, G.S. 429
Beckman, H.B. 174-203
Bellack, A. 386
Bellin, W. 40, 118-38
Berber house 29-36
Bereiter, C. 386
Berger, P.L. 438-9
Bernstein, B. 218-20, 229-30, 367,
   372
Berry, M. 389
Betts, C. 135
Bickerton, D. 241, 256, 293
bilingualism 295-311
   alternation 110-11, 307-8
   degree 296-8
   functions 298-302, 305-7
   interference 309-10

   variables influencing 302-5
   see also under Wales
Black English Vernacular 85-105,
   111-14
black youth culture 87-92, 97
Blackburn, R.M. 430
Blaug, M. 422, 428-9
Blom, J.P. 74
Bloomfield, L. 295-6
Boal, F.W. 75
Bochner, S. 322
Boissevain, J. 79, 123, 133
Bolinger, D. 145, 153-65
books, read to children 258-82
   mainstream school-oriented 260-6
   others 266-79
   starting school 279-81
Boone, B. 86
Bormuth, J.R. 430, 437, 444-5
Bott, E. 77
Bourdieu, P. 3, 29-36, 86
Bowen, E.G. 122-3, 132
Bower, T. 244
Bowerman, M. 246
brain damage 24-8
Bransford, J.D. 446, 452
Brazelton, B. 244
Brazil, D. 389
Brennan, T. 314
British Sign Language (BSL) 11-22
   classifiers 19-21
   complex signs 18-19
   derivation 12-14
   gestures in 15
   grammar 18-22
   modulation 21-2
   parasitic on English 15-18
   universal nature 11-12
Britton, J. 386
Brown, A.L. 448, 452
Brown, J.S. 450
Brown, P. 318
Brown, R. 251-4
Bruner, J.S. 237, 241-57, 260, 360
Bryant, B. 313-14
Buck, R. 316
Buhrmeister, D. 321

458